MASTERS OF DRAMATIC COMEDY
AND THEIR SOCIAL THEMES

MASTERS OF DRAMATIC COMEDY
AND THEIR SOCIAL THEMES

By HENRY TEN EYCK PERRY

*Edward H. Butler Professor of English Literature in the
University of Buffalo*

KENNIKAT PRESS, INC./PORT WASHINGTON, N. Y.

To

ELIZABETH

Born under a dancing star

MASTERS OF DRAMATIC COMEDY AND THEIR SOCIAL THEMES

Copyright 1939 by the President and Fellows of Harvard College
Reissued 1968 by Kennikat Press by arrangement

Library of Congress Catalog Card No: 68-26236
Manufactured in the United States of America

ESSAY AND GENERAL LITERATURE INDEX REPRINT SERIES

CONTENTS

INTRODUCTION

Laughter and Thoughtful Comedy

THE PRINCIPAL danger of a book on the art of comedy is that it will be taken too seriously by its author, if not by its readers. Comedy is in its essence spontaneous and carefree, gay and volatile. Yet an artist in this field, as well as in any other, must take infinite pains with his work if he wishes it to endure; and a critic may be pardoned if he soberly attempts to analyze what creative artists have accomplished in giving permanent form to one of mankind's most precious and elusive possessions.

Why do we laugh? Many psychologists and philosophers have tried without pronounced success to answer this question. Laughter is such a deep-seated human attribute that it might be described as an "instinct," if that word can be so loosely used. The baby laughs in its cradle before it has learned to speak. Evidently laughter is a necessary part of the mystery of being born into this world, and as such it is closely connected with whatever it is that lies about us in our infancy. If we call divine what we cannot apprehend by the use of our reason, it is entirely logical for us to consider that laughter is a part of our superhuman heritage and should be venerated accordingly. As it has never been possible to discover its ultimate sources, our best attitude may be to accept it without question as a gift of the gods. We shall never know the full meaning of laughter until scientists have arrived at such a complete knowledge of the human organism that they are able to create life; and, Robots to the contrary notwithstanding, that seems a consummation as unlikely of achievement as it is perhaps devoutly not to be wished for. Meanwhile we can enjoy the delights of a sense of humor, critical or otherwise, and we need not worry too much about our inability to understand thoroughly the nature of the physical mechanism by means of which men laugh.

Man has been often called "the laughing animal," and it is notorious that, in spite of the reputation of hyenas and Cheshire Cats, he is the animal who laughs most frequently and most easily. The fact that gorillas and chimpanzees also sometimes indulge in this pastime is just one more argument in favor of the humanness of laughter, because they are the two orders of apes that most resemble mankind in their general characteristics. Laughter seems to be definitely one of the higher powers belonging to animals, and in this respect to be closely akin to the capacity for reasoning, which is based on memory and the ability to coördinate various past experiences by bringing them into a congruous relationship with one another. This ability implies a consciousness of functional harmony, and a pleasure in it, which may be considered the goal of all human activity; interference with it prevents a proper state of adjustment between the individual and his environment. Whether he feels superior to his environment or humble because he is infinitesimal in comparison with it, some sort of conflict between his own personality and the rest of the world occurs, and his disagreeable superiority or his ingratiating humility expresses itself in "an involuntary rhythmic contraction of certain respiratory muscles," which we call laughter.

In other words, laughter is human, because each of us has a finitely limited body and at the same time a yearning for something like absolute perfection which may be called a soul. "In doubt to deem himself a god or beast," man is caught between the upper and the nether millstones: he cannot give himself up to the fleshly lusts of the world without some spark of regret that he is doing violence to the ideals of which he can conceive; and he cannot devote himself exclusively to the realization of noble visions because his bodily functions constantly yoke him to the earth. "The greatest comedy," it has been well said, "is rooted, not in the social order . . . but in the supreme human paradox that man, who lays claim to an immortal spirit, is nevertheless confined in a body and must rely upon the exercise of five imperfect senses for his perception of order, truth and beauty in his earthly pilgrimage." Caught in this dilemma, man half unconsciously realizes the anomalous nature of his position on the terrestrial globe, and he laughs partly from discomfort, partly from exuberance, and altogether from perplexity at the fate that has placed him here. The more one associates with other people, the more one will develop the social confidence and detachment necessary for a hearty sense of amusement at the basic conditions of human life, and that is perhaps why we are more likely to laugh in the presence of our fellow beings than when alone in the company of our private thoughts. Laughter thrives best when a group of varied people are brought together in such a way that their humanity is intensified and their individual differences are minimized as far as possible.

There is perhaps no occasion in which these conditions are better fulfilled than when a theatrical performance is taking place on a stage before an audience, because here the onlookers (except for the professional dramatic critics) are assembled for pleasure rather than for business, and they can relax their attention from the demands of their everyday routine. They can also, if they are intelligent enough, concentrate upon universal rather than personal problems — an ideal situation, congenial to the development of beauty in the abstract. But some heightened awareness of the world outside us is always involved in social entertainment, which is the primary objective of all secular art. At any rate, an audience in the theater laughs easily at playfulness of mind or body and hence, for those interested not only in why but in how and when men laugh, is worth studying. Attendance at a Charlie Chaplin film is one of the best modern methods of testing this principle, and sometimes the universality of the laughter which greets Charlot's pathetic antics seems the only hope of establishing a common ground between classes and nations amid the confusions of our present vigorous but kaleidoscopic civilization. Yet here, too, one realizes that there are limits to the power of art, even when it is aided by the wonders of cinematography, to affect a large group of people, ever increasing in numbers and hence tending to sink in the level of their intelligence.

The movie as an art form is, of course, still in an adolescent stage, but the mimetic impulse is as old as time and has persisted from one generation to another under a variety of guises. In an age of the "talkies" Chaplin has reminded us that words are not needed to make people laugh and that silent pantomime is a mighty weapon in the hands of a skillful performer. But the virtues that lie in words were also discovered early in man's history, one of their chief advantages being that they may be written down and preserved for posterity. They have a special value in the drama, for the art of the actor is a temporary thing at best, even when it can be embalmed in celluloid. In the long run, written dialogue proves to be of greater interest to the race of men than all the other elements of which a theatrical performance is composed. Therefore, if one is to judge the nature of human laughter by observing what has given rise to it in the past, there is no better way than to read the texts of outstanding dramatic comedies; they have brought down to us words, first spoken by actors before an audience of amused people, which have been thought worth inscribing and so perpetuating as a part of the permanent inheritance of the human race.

In this manner, although we may not be able to discover exactly why men laugh, we can get a very good idea of what they have laughed at during different periods of the world's history, and by putting the results together we may be able to learn, in addition, a good deal about mankind's serious problems and some of the classic attempts to solve them. A final solution cannot be achieved through the medium of laughter. Indeed, a study of comedy reminds us that no final solution is probable and that, in any case, no one single remedy offers an infallible panacea for man's afflictions, which will continue as long as there is flesh to be heir to them. Laughter is evidently only one, and not the least, of the aids which have been given man to help him bear the ills he has. It does not necessarily spur him on directly to attack these ills, though it is useful in the essential preliminaries of defining them and promoting a critical attitude towards them. In fact, a sense of humor may even be a deterrent to bold actions, whether virtuous or mischievous ones, and in this connection it should be thought of chiefly as an emergency brake which may well be applied when the human motor is running recklessly ahead at top speed. If laughter is not characteristic of extremists or fanatics, it is least necessary for the men who approach these extreme states. It is a primary function of those who seek the golden mean, and it is most productive when the best balanced and most perceptive people indulge in it. That is why the plays of Molière, the completest expression of the attitude held by the *honnête homme*, are the most perfect examples of social comedy to be found in the literary history of the world and why they still stand as touchstones for an intelligent, cosmopolitan sense of humor.

Humor should be a lighthearted, involuntary affair, which need not be analyzed to be enjoyed, but which is so fluid that it must be caught and imprisoned in some heavier substance if it is to endure for longer than the minute point of contact between the past and the future. If you are going to make a joke, you must think about it at least for a moment beforehand, and, if you are going to recall it, you must also put your attention on it; the process of thought which transforms humor into comedy is not an extremely forced or artificial operation. The danger in it is that, if you have thought about the joke more than its character warrants, the humor becomes heavy-handed and labored. If the thought given to it has a critical sting, the intellectualized product emerges as satire, which is as far from a sense of just proportion on the one hand as the loud laugh that bespeaks the vacant mind is on the other. The laughter of a child or a fool is at the opposite pole from the laughter of a Swift or a Voltaire, but both are necessary ingredients for the composite ideal of laughter in its highest form. One may grant that the more nearly this ideal is approached the more static it becomes, but since perfection can never be completely realized in any department of life there is no danger of a Utopia's being reached in the sphere of comedy. There are too many varieties of human experience for them to be entirely fused in one touch of nature.

A sense of proportion is undoubtedly the most important by-product of intelligent laughter. As we laugh spontaneously at the casual incongruities of existence, our perceptions may gradually grow more discriminating, until we come to appreciate that the slight differences which often appear to bulk so large on our horizon are in reality exceedingly trivial details and that the trivialities of life, when seen with a proper scale of values, become significant straws to show which way the wind is blowing. It is possible to laugh at anything, saying that it doesn't matter that it doesn't matter that it doesn't matter, but there is a *reductio ad absurdum* here also, and to laugh at everything is to be reduced to the status of a gibbering idiot. It is plain that there is a place for everything in this world and that the place for laughter is subordinate to that reserved for full appreciation of love and hate, of birth and death. Yet laughter plays a part in clarifying these great issues. This happens when one laughs intelligently at the wide gap which exists between promise and performance, between what is and what might be, between the animal and the divine elements in human life. A reasonable sense of humor adapts itself continually to changes in the physical conditions of existence, and one need never expect it to be exactly the same in any two individuals or in any two nations, at any two moments or in any two centuries.

The attempt to draw together the social experience of the past, as expressed by the great comic dramatists, has therefore resulted in a book which not only is as painfully serious as most other discussions of humor but also is extremely heterogeneous. It is virtually impossible to see steadily from one all-inclusive point of view the various forms and themes of dramatic comedy which have existed from the time of Aristophanes to the time of Bernard Shaw, and the efforts I have made in that direction have doubtless been too ambitious and not humorous enough; on the other hand, I believe that such an attempt was worth making — at least once, and, so far as I know, no other writer has been sufficiently rash to undertake it.

The first large obstacle in the way is the difficulty of language. To understand the word of the human race in its written form, a linguistic knowledge as vast as that displayed at the Tower of Babel is desirable; and since I lack that endowment I feel sure that many nuances and subtle verbal twists in plays not written in English have escaped my notice and comprehension. Those in Russian I did not attempt to read in the authors' native tongue; the others I read in their original texts, sometimes with the help of translations, with varying degrees of facility. Still I think it may safely be said that the major qualities of comedy reside in something besides dexterous turns of phrase and sparkling dialogue, so that it does not seem impossible to comprehend what the playwrights are aiming to do, even though one must miss some of the details in their work when approaching it with the eyes and ears of a foreigner.

If the linguistic skill desirable for writing a book on dramatic comedy had been completely at my command, I should still, of course, have been embarrassed by the overpowering amount of accessible material. What to include and what to exclude have been most perplexing questions, questions to which no two critics would give the same answers. No doubt many people will disagree even with my selection of the principal dramatists about whom I have written.

From their names, which appear in my chapter headings, Shakespeare's is noticeably absent. Although his work hovers in the background of the discussion, I have omitted a detailed treatment of it, both because to English readers more books are available on Shakespeare than on any other author I have mentioned and because a separate chapter on his comic plays seemed impracticable, for several reasons, within the restricted space and design of this particular book. Shakespearean comedy is almost as many-sided and complicated as human life. It employs every variety of comic experience from knockabout farce to bitter satire, from witty realism to delicate fantasy, from thoughtless *joie de vivre* to transcendental philosophy. Moreover, it is not confined within the limits of this form of dramatic art. It enters into the domain of tragedy, and tragedy treads upon its preserves; some of Shakespeare's most remarkable comic characters appear in plays that are fundamentally tragic, and there is scarcely one of his comedies that does not contain overtones of grief and suffering. Again, so close and complex is the interplay of the imaginative forces in his comedies that it is difficult to disentangle their social themes. When he copied from Plautus the complications that arise from the existence of identical twins, he set the farcical story in a romantic framework which causes one to ponder on the mysterious ways of Providence. Much as he took from his predecessors and from the world about him, he made it thoroughly his own. His work, with its infinite variety and supreme poetry, is, for all its relations to the tradition of comedy, a thing apart. It is best, I think, that it should be so treated; some day I should myself like to make the attempt.

With the exception of Shakespeare, I have tried to place the outstanding dramatists in a historical perspective, indicating their attitude toward social conditions or problems of their times. I have, therefore, followed the chronological order as far as major figures are concerned, although it has been impossible to do so with a number of lesser writers whose plays I have considered. The larger part of the text is devoted to authors who seem to me to be masters of dramatic comedy from the standpoint of both social criticism and aesthetic form.

In any book which covers so much ground, one is brought face to face with the modern problem of specialization, which has been neatly phrased in the remark that a journalist is a person who knows less and less about more and more, and a scholar one who knows

more and more about less and less. The dilemma it suggests is doubtless more apparent than real, and therein lies the humor of the statement, but it has too much truth in it for comfort. Is one to write a
book on dramatic comedy (or on any other comparable subject for
that matter) which attempts encyclopedic minuteness, or is one to
touch upon only the high points of the available material, pleasing
some readers, perhaps, but offending those who know most in detail
about each of the separate items that go to make up the complete
picture? A person trained in the golden mean by a study of comedy
cannot easily bring himself to adopt either of these extreme pro-
grams and finds himself vainly endeavoring to do two irreconcilable
things at once, as a scholar to find out the truth and as a writer to interpret it. This book will doubtless prove too detailed for some tastes
and too vaguely superficial in outline for some others. The one con-
solation to the author if he has fallen between two stools will be
that either one of them alone would have proved a most uncomfortable seat for him.

When the principal dramatists who were to be given the most
detailed study in this book had been selected for its ten main divisions, the next problem was how best to arrange the rest of the material within these divisions. Fortunately for me this difficulty was
partially solved by a circumstance to which I have already alluded,
the diversity of languages represented by the authors I have selected.
Aristophanes is obviously the father of dramatic comedy, as it has
come down to us in written records. Plautus and Terence are the
next great names, and a bridge to them from Aristophanes is provided by Menander, who imitated the latest phase of the one and
provided the raw material for the others to work on by the process
of combining, or "contaminating," plots. The great body of classic
comedy divides itself naturally into the Greek and Roman periods,
and thus an arrangement by language or nationality suggests itself.
This arrangement is harder to carry out in more recent history, but
it can be adapted freely, as all systems must be if they are to maintain
their usefulness, to meet the demands of unexpected situations as
they arise. I have chosen for each of my ten chapters the preeminent
contribution of a different nation, within each chapter following
chiefly national tendencies, but digressing now and then to pick up

The rough scheme having been set by the chapters on classic comedy, the next problem was how to handle the period of the Middle Ages when nationality, as we now know it, scarcely existed. But this was not a serious problem, since there was no superlative body of dramatic comedy composed during this period, possibly because men's thoughts were too much upon heaven for them to be continuously aware of the incongruities plentiful upon earth. Social comedy has in it a large degree of humanism, and it does not flourish when man is thought of predominantly as a domesticated beast or as a creature whose earthly term is merely a novitiate for life after death. There was Hrotswitha, applying the technique of Latin comedy to moral and religious subjects, and there were the medieval folk plays, sometimes intruding their elements into the liturgical drama; but it can be fairly maintained, I believe, that no writer of dramatic comedy so creative as Terence existed between his time and that of Ben Jonson, who reformulated the classic tradition in a Renaissance pattern and gave firm shape to the comic material which had been drifting about western Europe during the medieval period. I do not mean to say that there are not other literatures to reckon with throughout these times, but Ben Jonson takes up the comic tradition where the Roman dramatists left it off and so provides a slight clew to guide one through the confusing maze of dramatic history.

Although there was literary comedy in Italy before Ben Jonson, Italian comedy did not reach its height until the works of Goldoni in the eighteenth century, so that here, as in some other instances, I have departed from chronological order to hold to national divisions, leaving the plays of Bibbiena and Ariosto, of Machiavelli and Giordano Bruno, to be considered in the later chapter on Goldoni and Italian comedy. The height of literary comedy in Spain coincided almost exactly with the period of Jonson's dramatic activity, and the question arises whether Lope and his great successor, Calderón, as well as his other followers, should be treated before or after their English contemporary. This question is complicated by the fact that, while the spirit of the Spaniards is certainly more medieval than that of the Englishman, Calderón came later than Jonson, and Lope did not pretend to follow classical theories, though he was familiar with them. On the whole, it has seemed wiser to put Jonson first in order to achieve two objects: to keep more closely to the chronological order; and to show the changes that Lope made in the tradition of comedy as seen against the intellectual background of his own day. In France, comedy emerged somewhat later than it did in England, in Italy, or in Spain, and then culminated rapidly in the work of Molière, who must be regarded as the climactic figure in any consideration of thoughtful comedy, whether one is approaching the subject from the social or the purely aesthetic standpoint.

After Molière there was a falling off in the quality of comic drama, and an increase in its quantity, as is likely to be the case when the impulse to any art form has reached its highest point and mechanical competence succeeds inspiration. Molière's imitators were legion not only in France and England but also in Denmark, where Holberg, probably his most distinguished disciple, found fresh dramatic material in the peculiar nature of local conditions, and in Italy, where Goldoni did much to alter the form of literary comedy by incorporating it with the tradition of the *commedia dell'arte*, which in turn had sprung from decadent Latin comedy. In the plays of both Holberg and Goldoni there are reflected the changes that were taking place in the structure of organized European society, and the humanitarianism which creeps into the latter's work is a fitting prelude to his death in the Paris of the French Revolution. The wave of idealism which swept over Europe at the end of the eighteenth century was far more conducive to sympathetic warmth than to astringent laughter and that is probably one reason why the greatest master of German comedy, Gotthold Ephraim Lessing, mixed a large amount of saccharine with his gall. His comedies, even more than those of Goldsmith, Sheridan, and Beaumarchais, are addressed to the goddess of the woeful countenance rather than to the muse of detached comedy. Lessing's plays are a portent of the times, exquisitely adapted to the German temperament, and attaining a nice balance of antithetical elements that in *Minna von Barnhelm* resulted in an enduring masterpiece.

As there is little dramatic comedy of importance in western Europe between the French Revolution and the rise of Ibsen's influence in the late 1870's, it has seemed convenient to fill in this gap with plays drawn from the literatures of Austria and Russia. I have associated the Austrian authors, distinguished by their delicate fancy and dexterous wit, with the Germans (from whom they differ sharply) because both groups wrote in the same language and neither one alone seems to be of first-rate aesthetic or social significance. The case of Russia is more distinctive and, barring the difficulty of language, more easily disposed of. Germany did not take naturally to comedy, perhaps because the Teutonic mind was bent on more serious problems of politics and philosophy, but comic drama throve in Russia, undergoing radical alterations in the process. There can be no doubt that *The Inspector-General* is one of the world's great comedies, but although the plays of Chekhov must be ranked in the first class of drama it is by no means clear that they belong to the accepted comic domain. They contain an occasional death and their general mood is so thoroughly gloomy that it is only by enlarging the definition of comedy that they can be brought under it. The enlargement of definitions to admit the ever-recurring changes of any vital creative art is, however, an important part of the critic's task, and in this instance one should not shrink from attempting to grapple with it.

With Chekhov we have almost reached modern times, and perhaps it would have been the part of wisdom to have closed this book with the veiled prophecy of the Russian Revolution that can be read between the lines of *The Cherry Orchard*; but such an abrupt conclusion would have meant ignoring the most ambitious work of Bernard Shaw. It might have been safer to do so, because it is always dangerous to try to evaluate a contemporary in the same terms that one applies to those already dead, yet immortal, but the fun of making the attempt more than compensates for the risk involved in it. Besides, Shaw has an unmistakable affinity with Aristophanes, the comedies of both men containing a strange amalgam of bitter sarcasm and fervent idealism expressed with felicity, whether of poetry or of prose. In addition, Shaw's work has a social value for us, his contemporaries, that is perhaps more than commensurate with its artistic excellence.

The social value of comic drama is much more closely allied to its artistic effect than is that of tragedy or epic poetry, both of which deal with universals, while comedy must by its nature be particular in the subjects which it treats. It has a social as well as an aesthetic function, and to secure their full effect these functions must be combined on an intellectual plane, even at some loss in power to the more limited and simple ingredients of the mixture. That is why a student of comedy goes to the movies in a critical spirit and why he reads the texts of great comedies with one eye for their historical significance and another for their modern application. As he does so, he becomes aware that every major comic author has some special standard which he applies to the confused affairs of the world to bring out their humorous implications.

Aristophanes makes it very plain that what he desired was a peaceful, just, and honest community, which he could imagine as existing in the Clouds or among the Birds, if not on the busy streets of Athens. Plautus and Terence had a more limited range of vision and contented themselves with the feeling that hope for a better society in the future rests with the younger generation, which must always be considered right in its conflict with miserly old age and selfish parental authority. It is comparatively easy to analyze classic comedy from an objective point of view, because the Greeks and Romans were detached enough to do their work without excessive interference from petty human passions. It is much harder to disentangle the confused threads of the complicated European pattern after the Renaissance had once set in. The comedy of the Middle Ages had been in essence the Divine Comedy of Dante. With the revival of worldly curiosity, an amazing amount of diversity and antagonism arose, and the comic dramatists tend to cloud specific issues by merging too closely human problems that have very little intrinsic connection with one another.

Differences in languages, differences in nationalities, and differences in environment all serve to confuse the issue when an effort is made to see individual authors as representative of the times and the countries in which they lived. If the love of money is a dominant theme in Jonsonian comedy, it is natural, if not wholly safe, to connect that fact with the English utilitarian spirit. In the same way, a generalization may be made for jealousy in Spain and rationality in France. Thus I have attempted to find a unifying theme in the plays of each of the major authors I have treated and to show, sometimes with a national and sometimes with a chronological emphasis, how it served a useful purpose in exposing human weaknesses. By the eighteenth century, nationalism, which had arisen with the end of the

Middle Ages, began to give way before the first rumblings of modern industrialism; the members of the lower classes became gradually liberated, with the result that their enlarged social opportunities had both ludicrous and admirable consequences. The tendency of people to ape the ways of their superiors has always had its absurd side, but their laudable desire to become in every way the equal of those above them may assume tragic aspects, as it has done in many recent revolutions and civic upheavals.

In these successive changes which have come over the atmosphere of western Europe in the last three hundred years may no doubt be found some of the reasons why comic drama flourished most perfectly in the time of Molière and has since his day maintained a somewhat precarious existence as an art form. It has had to compete with sentimentality in the eighteenth century, with romanticism in the nineteenth, and with a new authoritarianism in the twentieth, with no one of which can the spirit of comedy be in perfect accord. It may make a temporary truce with sentimentality, resulting in the impure product we paradoxically call sentimental comedy; it may become fused with romanticism in such a way that its nature is transformed into an ironic and bitter commentary upon a decaying civilization; and it may assert itself in a period of rapid change to point out the advantages and the dangers attendant on society's moving in one extreme direction or another. Under none of these forms does it have a great deal of free scope for its operations, but in each of these cases human beings would have been worse off without its chastening influence. It is perhaps most necessary of all in a time of violent upheaval, such as the present, when it is extremely difficult to maintain a reasonable detachment towards its exciting events and to judge their artistic manifestations with coolness and with candor.

It may be argued that no such detachment is possible or desirable, since in all successful art the material and the manner of its communication are inextricably bound together, but I believe that an effort to see the strength and weaknesses of comedy is a positive benefit not only to the development of an individual but to the growth of the community in which he lives. On this confident hope I pin whatever value my book may have for its author and its readers. If it should persuade any of them to turn, or turn again, to the comedies that are here discussed, I should feel that, so far as others are concerned.

my work had been more than justified. It has already rewarded me by enlarging my personal experience in time and space, from the Athens of Plato to the London of the Fabian Society, and by permitting me to look at social history through the eyes of the comic muse.

MASTERS OF DRAMATIC COMEDY
AND THEIR SOCIAL THEMES

CHAPTER I

The First Literary Comedy: Aristophanes and Menander

I

THE ORIGINS of dramatic comedy are shrouded in the dark abysm of time. Like the individual human being, the race of men must have laughed in its infancy, but no written records have come down to us that tell exactly when the process started or how it was first transformed into literary art. Aristotle is astonishingly vague about the beginnings of comedy, but we are now reasonably sure that its chief source was a village revel, or *comos*, and that it is connected with the rites of fertility, which in turn are associated with the worship of Dionysus, the god of fruitfulness and vegetation.

It is natural for human beings to rejoice in the spring of the year when the fig tree puts forth her green shoots and a man calls to his beloved to come away with him and replenish the earth. Then the animal joy in existence, which flourishes when the winter is past and gone, expresses itself automatically in eating, drinking, and making love, regardless of the fact that the cycle of the seasons will bring death and destruction to every living thing. In this exultant mood man's body glows, and he laughs spontaneously and wholeheartedly without realizing just why he does so. To celebrate his happiness, he must develop some sort of ritual that has more than a momentary meaning; and from such a ritual, when its old associations have been lost, may rise new forms of artistic expression.

At any rate, the texts of the earliest literary comedies that still exist are explicable only if we admit some such connection between their gross realism and their moments of inspired vision. From the beginning of time men have associated states of mind and emotion with some organ of the human body, thinking of it symbolically and often associating it with religious rites. Thus the phallus, as the symbol of procreation, became an object of divine worship in ancient Greece, as it still is in some parts of the world. Its worship expressed man's gratitude for the gift of life itself; here we come close to the mystery of the true nature of comedy. We are glad to be alive, and we show by laughter our sense of exuberant well-being. Throughout its history, comedy has leaned heavily upon vulgarity and coarseness, because, like the Greek phallus, they have a logical relation to vitality and animal high spirits.

Aristophanes occasionally apologizes for the use of the phallus and states that he has attempted to abolish it from his plays, though, doubtless because of its popularity, it appears throughout his dramatic work; probably it seemed the funnier to his audiences because an effort had already been made to suppress it. There is no reason to suppose that Aristophanes objected to vulgarity on moral grounds. Whatever objection he had to it sprang from aesthetic reasons. In the *Clouds*, the use of the phallus is mentioned in connection with other stock devices of slapstick comedy, such as making fun of the bald-headed and having a silly old man strike at people with a staff, the implication seeming to be that all these comic devices are cheap rather than disgusting. From the first, Aristophanes' aim was to take the material that came down to him from popular comedy and to raise it to an intellectual, artistic level, as he did with remarkable success considering the tradition that he inherited.

The raucous, unorganized nature of the Dionysiac revel may have been somewhat modified by the intrusion of narrative material from the Dorian farces that flourished in Sicily, before the archon of Athens first granted a chorus for the performance of a formal comedy about 487 B.C., only some forty years before Aristophanes' birth. Of his immediate predecessors in the comic field, Magnes, Crates, and Cratinus, Aristophanes writes most sympathetically in the *Knights*. We may be sure he appreciated the high quality of the small amount of work done before his time and known to him. From the hands of the men that had preceded him, he received a rather definite comic formula, which had come from the religious ritual of the Dionysiac feast. This he made over into a freer, more malleable shape, much nearer to modern drama, but with features not easily understood by readers unacquainted with researches into the origin of Attic comedy.

In his invaluable book on this subject, F. M. Cornford shows that the form of the so-called Old Comedy, as well as its phallic motive, grew out of a festival procession celebrating the rites of fertility.

Originally, at this festival, a band of revellers made their appearance in a group as an organized *comos*, a feature which is preserved in the formal entrance, or *parodos*, of the Chorus in an Aristophanic comedy. Next came an exchange of abuse between the bystanders and the members of the *comos*, who probably attacked specific individuals that they felt were antagonistic to the nature of their performance; these individuals replied in kind, and there followed a battle of invective, which developed into a formal contest, or *agon*, sometimes shared in by subdivisions of the Chorus. Then the *comos*, which had won the contest and become unified in the course of the *agon*, would gather together all its forces and make a concerted defense of its position, telling of the specific problems with which it was concerned in order to accomplish its double ends of winning the favor of the god Dionysus and of obtaining protection against the evil influence of unfriendly powers. The literary equivalent of this practice is the *parabasis* of an Aristophanic comedy, in which the Chorus departs from its assumed character and speaks for the poet, addressing the audience directly. Finally, after some minor horseplay, the *comos* left the scene of the festival to participate in a feast and in a general union of the sexes, or *gamos*, which was supposed to follow. In the Old Comedies that have survived, the Chorus usually delivers a formal speech of farewell, or *exodos*, when it leaves the stage to take part, as it announces, in some expression of the triumphant success that has come to it and its partisans, the protagonist and his friends.

The most important feature of this dramatic development is the unmistakable identification of the Chorus with the *comos* and the fact that the author is in sympathy with the point of view that the Chorus eventually expresses. Because of this convention, one has at the end of each comedy an almost infallible guide to the trend of the author's own opinions, which is extremely useful in attempting to interpret such subtle distinctions as constantly play through the mind of Aristophanes. By the time he began to write, a consciousness of the ritual origin of comedy must have largely disappeared, and an author could turn his attention to whatever specific evil he had decided most needed to be attacked for the good of the community. He was allowed as complete freedom in personal invective as in indecorous references to parts of the human body, but stage convention required him to take sides in a controversial issue and to indicate to the audience his general attitude towards it. Aristophanes never diverged from that necessary condition of his art, but he sometimes applied it in such an indirect and elusive way that it is difficult to determine his exact ideas on the particular subject under discussion.

We are fortunate in having eleven plays of Aristophanes, varying from the *Acharnians*, produced in 425 B.C., to the *Plutus* of 388, and from them we receive most of our light on the nature of the Old Comedy as well as on its artistic possibilities. There are also some fragments of two previous works, the *Banqueters* and the *Babylonians*, the former produced two years and the latter one year before the *Acharnians*, which was the earliest of Aristophanes' plays to win the first prize in a dramatic competition and so to establish him as a comic poet of significance.

The *Acharnians*, largely a political comedy, is somewhat limited by its subject to matters of local interest to the Athenian audience. A wider view of its author's thought can be obtained by what remains of his first drama known to us, the *Banqueters*, which deals with private, more than with public, life. Its central figure seems to have been an old countryman who has tried out different ways of educating his two sons: one has been sent to Athens to learn from the wise men of the metropolis, while the other has stayed on the farm. The contrast is all in favor of the home-keeping son. The old man, a type of the Greeks who fought at Marathon, is completely disgusted with the town-bred boy's effeminacy and lack of filial feeling. He criticizes these weaknesses, railing against the degenerate life of contemporary Athens and praising the simple manly existence of an earlier age.

From the fragments we have of the *Banqueters*, the father appears to be the protagonist of the comedy, and so we may take him to be the mouthpiece for the ideals of its author. Considering him in this light, we find that Aristophanes disapproves of lawsuits and decrees, money-changing and the use of perfumes, debauchery and blackmail, all of them practices that the play associates with the life of the city. Like all clever satirists, Aristophanes is more occupied with describing what is wrong than what is right, but we can gather from the fragments of the *Banqueters* that he admires an education which puts emphasis upon heroic poetry and music, upon physical exercise and such homely virtues as courage and obedience. He must have known something of both the city and the country. It is clear that at about the age of twenty, when he wrote the *Banqueters*, he had already made up his mind what were to be to him the principal values of human life. That he was an old-fashioned idealist is evident enough from the surviving parts of his first play.

His second play, which was produced the next year and of which, again, we have only fragments, leaves no doubt that Aristophanes heartily disapproved of conditions in the Athens of his day. The *Babylonians* is a public and political comedy, as the *Banqueters* had been a private and domestic one. It takes its name from the subject people who had been severely punished by Darius for rebelling against him, just as, according to Aristophanes, the allies of Athens had been harshly treated for their lack of loyalty in the Peloponnesian War against Sparta. From the few and obscure passages of the *Babylonians* which have come down to us, it appears that Aristophanes was here attacking the hollow eloquence of ambassadors to foreign countries and criticizing the orators at home for their share in the oppression of the Athenian allies. Chief among the orators in Athens at this time was Cleon, who had persuaded the government to proceed harshly against the city of Mitylene after its capture in 427. Cleon became enraged at what he considered, quite rightly, to be a personal attack in the play on himself, and he had Aristophanes brought before the City Council. He seems to have been unable to secure a conviction against the rising young poet, but as a result of the incident Aristophanes harbored a lasting grudge against the most powerful demagogue of his day.

With his honesty and justice, he could not have failed to disapprove of the demagogues and what they stood for. The recent misfortunes of Athens, which had included the plague of 430 B.C., the death of Pericles in the next year, and the war with Sparta, still dragging on its painful course, opened the way for unprincipled but dynamic leaders who could dominate the people by their rhetoric and specious arguments, judiciously mixed with flattery and promises of material advantage. For a leader of this type, a foreign war is a good risk when local conditions are bad, because it distracts attention from troubles at home and provides an emotional release, with the hope, easy to take advantage of, that victory will bring glory to the nation and enrich the people with spoils taken from the enemy.

Therefore it was natural that Cleon, the ambitious son of a tanner, should become the leader of the militaristic party in Athens from practical rather than from idealistic motives. He stood to gain everything if Athens was victorious in the war, and to lose nothing, since originally he had had nothing to lose, in case she was defeated. In other words, he was a shortsighted, if not a self-seeking, dictator, who seemed to Aristophanes to lack the poise and balance which were to him fundamental qualities for any useful member of society, whether statesman or private citizen. The comic poet made his social position very clear in the *Banqueters* and the *Babylonians* before he achieved his first acknowledged success with the *Acharnians* in 425.

II

The *Acharnians* takes it name from the Chorus, composed of old men from Acharnae, who at the beginning of the play are ferocious and militant but who in the course of the action are convinced by the author's protagonist, an honest citizen fittingly named Dicaeopolis, that they are entirely mistaken in their love of war. Dicaeopolis' method of persuasion is chiefly argument but partly action, as when he seizes a hamper of charcoal, a kind of fuel vital to the Acharnians, and extravagantly threatens to kill it with his drawn sword if they will not listen to his reasons for opposing the war. His arguments have chiefly to do with the insignificant causes of the conflict then splitting up Greece, and half of the Chorus is immediately convinced. The other half is at first recalcitrant but is won over when Dicaeopolis makes fun of Lamachus, a professional soldier, who, he says, receives large pay and holds an exalted position without doing enough work to justify such rewards. In the *Acharnians*, Lamachus, who was a real person, is used rather than Cleon as a representative of the war party, probably because Aristophanes thought it was not prudent to bring Cleon himself on the stage at this particular time, but Cleon is frequently referred to in the play and it is obvious that he is the motivating force behind the war spirit which Dicaeopolis is attacking in the person of Lamachus.

Dicaeopolis, the sympathetic protagonist of the *Acharnians*, is an old farmer disgusted with the conditions in Athens which gave rise to the war as well as with the war itself. Finding that the As-

sembly is unwilling to put an end to it, he determines to take matters into his own hands and make a private truce with Sparta. This
imaginative conception, the central point of the *Acharnians*, is typical
of the genius of Aristophanes: he supposes that the impossible can
occur, and then, in a perfectly logical way, he works out the fantastic situation he has created. The truce is negotiated, Dicaeopolis begins to reap its advantages, and everyone in the community becomes
anxious to share in the commercial benefits of a peace. The resump-
tion of business after a period of fighting leads to a series of market
scenes, amusing on the surface but motivated by a hatred of the horrors of civil war and, incidentally, of informers. Dicaeopolis opens
his market to allies of the Spartans, with whom he has made peace,
but he will not allow Athenians like Lamachus, who are still at war,
to trade in it. Lamachus is the chief representative of the martial
spirit in the *Acharnians*, and near the end of the play he is again summoned to combat, as Dicaeopolis goes to the Dionysiac feast that
has been prepared for him. Lamachus returns from the battlefield
wounded and exhausted, discouraged and humiliated; Dicaeopolis
comes from the revel satisfied with food and drink, and happy in the
attention of two courtesans. The way of the man of wrath is shown
to be suffering and death; that of the man of peace, gaiety and happiness in a more abundant life.

So Aristophanes pictures in a somewhat extreme form the intelligent pacificist's contention that the destructive nature of war always
returns to plague the inventor, and he implies that peace is good for
human society as well as pleasurable for the individuals affected by it.
There can be no doubt that, as far as Aristophanes is concerned,
Dicaeopolis has chosen the better part, and the honest citizen's ability is made equal to his wisdom. He can convert his reasonable op-
ponents, the Chorus; he can better his own lot and that of his friends,
as he does in the market scenes; and he remains a standing example
of satisfaction and success to the obstinate militarists, like Lamachus.
With all its horseplay and nonsense, the *Acharnians* is essentially a
plea for the wisdom of loving one's Greek neighbor as oneself. It
is a comedy, but a comedy with a purpose and that a highly patriotic
one, although it could not have seemed so to Cleon and his supporters, prejudiced as they were by the narrow range of their own immediate interests. As a work of art, the *Acharnians* is somewhat

sprawling and diffuse, but it has great variety in its invention of comic incidents, it is typical of Aristophanes' literary method, and it furnishes an admirable introduction to the body of his work. The playwright himself seems to have been sufficiently encouraged by its reception to redouble the vigor of his thrusts, for in the next year, 424, he produced the *Knights*, a much more powerful and compact piece of drama, directed openly against the personality and career of Cleon.

In the *Knights*, Cleon himself is brought on the stage as a blustering Paphlagonian slave in the house of Demos, an old man who represents the people of Athens. Cleon is the object of the envy and hatred of two other slaves in the household, called Nicias and Demosthenes, the names of the two Athenian generals from whom Cleon had by a lucky chance wrested some of the honors recently won in the Peloponnesian War. These two jealous slaves learn from a stolen oracle that the Leather-seller (a reference to the lowly trade of Cleon's father) can be ousted from his favored position only by a seller of sausage meat, and when they have found a person in such a business, whose ignorance and impudence can worthily compete with Cleon's, they set him up as the opponent of the man that has made them his enemies. As is generally the case in a work of art stimulated by local conditions, the references to specific abuses perpetrated by Cleon and his associates detract immensely from the pleasure to be gained from the *Knights* by a reader of a different time and place, but at bottom the play is sufficiently inspired by its author's deep human sympathy to justify the high position among his comedies which has generally been assigned to it by literary critics. The course of its action is one continuous struggle between Cleon and the Sausage-seller, in which the latter is egged on and abetted by the Chorus of Knights, young men drawn from the wealthier and more educated members of the community and therefore hereditary enemies of uncultivated upstarts like Cleon.

At the end of the *Knights*, Cleon is completely discomfited. The extraordinary element in his overthrow is that the Sausage-seller, who is supposed to be the admirable hero of the play, can get the better of the Leather-seller only by outdoing him in villainy. A formal *agon* takes place between them with Demos acting as judge, and at its conclusion Cleon has come to realize that in the Sausage-seller he has met his match in underhanded practices. During the course of this debate there are so many specific allusions to Cleon's unjust actions, so much personal invective, and such an endless flow of billingsgate, that the final defeat of Cleon is not reached until the play is nearly over. Ultimately the demagogue admits that he is beaten and agrees to resign his position.

After the catastrophe of the *Knights*, there follows an important statement of the constructive social ideals which Aristophanes believes will expose the expedients of his shortsighted contemporaries to the ridicule that they deserve. Here, after Cleon has been destroyed, the Sausage-seller, who until now has outdone his rival in baseness, suddenly changes his character, reveals his name to be Agoracritus, a man chosen by the Assembly, and becomes the benefactor of Demos. He subjects the old man to a stewing process in the manner of Medea and restores him to what had been his youthful condition in the prime of past Athenian glories. He appears clad in the old national costume, his hair adorned with golden cicalas, his person fragrant with myrrh. His nature is equally changed, and he proceeds to lay down principles as to how the state should be administered in the future as it had not been during the supremacy of Cleon: no flattering eloquence or bribery is to be allowed to get men into power; the sailors are to be promptly paid in full on their return home from foreign service; the muster-rolls of the army are not to be tampered with; effeminate young men are to be kept out of the Assembly and forced to devote themselves to strenuous physical exercise; above all, peace is to be made with Sparta by a truce that shall last for thirty years.

The thirty-year truce is symbolized on the stage by a group of beautiful young girls, whom Cleon has kept from his master but who can now accompany him to the country. The play ends with their triumphant appearance, their union with Demos, which is to be productive of more plentiful life for the state, and the mock funeral procession of Cleon, who is carried off on the shoulders of the attendants to take up the Sausage-seller's loathsome function at the gates of the city. There is a farcical inconsistency involved in this denouement. Although it is entirely logical for Cleon to be debased to the level of the Sausage-seller and for the Sausage-seller to take the place of Cleon, it is unnatural that the Sausage-seller should change his

character for the better so quickly after he has succeeded in his underhanded schemes. This abrupt shift is theatrically effective, however, and it can be further justified by Aristophanes' attitude toward
the Athenian government of his day.

The *Knights* was written at the height of Cleon's popularity, but
the comic poet had sufficient affection for his fellow citizens, and
sufficient confidence in them, to feel that some day they would free
themselves from the spell of the demagogue's magnetic personality.
To make this point, which he hoped would help to bring the people
to their senses, and partially to offset the inconsistency of the Sausage-
seller's conversion, Aristophanes attempted an extremely subtle piece
of characterization in his treatment of Demos, the embodiment of the
Athenian Commonwealth.

Demos is a silly old man, but even before his rejuvenation he remarks that he is not so foolish as he has seemed. He bears with demagogues like Cleon only until they grow fat enough to be worth being
swallowed by him. The process by which Cleon is to be proved fat
enough to be eaten demands a person who shall be able to expose the
success of the demagogue's deceitful arts; throughout the first part
of the play the Sausage-seller is shown out-Cleonizing Cleon in a
way that must have sent contemporary Athens into gales of laughter.
Aristophanes' inventiveness could pile a Pelion upon an Ossa of ridicule, with devastating results as far as Cleon's rascality was concerned,
but the dramatist's brilliant observation would have been trivial and
pointless if it had not been informed by clear thinking as to the best
way to improve conditions in contemporary Athens and by a firm
belief that it was possible to do so.

Aristophanes was attempting to appeal to the better impulses of
human nature, which seemed to him to be overlaid with a vast
amount of laziness and stupidity, but which he was confident could
be made to assert themselves when the occasion demanded it. Such
is the explanation of his curious picture of Demos, at first a silly old
man of the present and afterwards a noble youth of the past. Demos
sloughs off this old skin and emerges in a sort of resurrection, which
fits in extremely well with the ritual practices that lie behind the
technique of early drama. In it the destruction of one individual is
the prelude to the emergence of another nobler one, just as the dis-
tressing situations caused by political corruption in any time and

place can be transformed by an artist with wide vision until they appear as transitory phenomena on the vast stream of human consciousness. The populace, like Demos, are in the long run wiser than the dictators who temporarily dazzle them. Demagogues may succeed one another, but none of them will be permanent, until a leader arises who, like Agoracritus, is a true representative of the people with the welfare of the community at heart. War cannot continue eternally, because there will always be some honest citizens, like Dicaeopolis, to see through the superficial success of deluded warriors, like Lamachus, and to be able to convince quarrelsome people, like the Acharnians, that in the long run it is to their advantage to be at peace with their fellows.

The evils of war and the allied evils of dictatorship are still crucial problems for human society. Both of these evils seem to be based upon a lack of balance in economic forces, which needs to be righted by some violent method of readjustment and upon which intelligence should be brought to bear, if intelligence can be diverted into important and useful channels. Theorists were as much distrusted in Aristophanes' time as they are today, and the comic poet associated an excessive development of the mind with impractical behavior, which in a time of crisis is itself a wasteful indulgence, if it is not a dangerous threat to national prosperity. The chief representative of this nationalistic tendency in the Athens of Aristophanes was the philosopher Socrates, the focal point of the type of sophisticated education which the comic poet had already ridiculed in his early play, the *Banqueters*; and after he had to all intents and purposes demolished Cleon upon the stage in the *Knights*, he turned his attention, the next year, to Socrates, a personal associate of his, and attempted to indicate his divided opinion towards him in the *Clouds*. To Aristophanes' great disgust, this subtle play appears to have proved too difficult for its audience to understand and appreciate. It received only third place in the dramatic competition of 423, at which it was first produced, and later its text underwent a revision to the form in which it has come down to us.

As it stands, the *Clouds* is a confusing work, but its fascination is so great that one continues to read and reread it in an attempt to pluck out the heart of its mystery. Not the least of its virtues is that its indirect method of approach is so perfectly fitted to its complicated subject that the result proves to be an ideal combination of form and substance. If the *Clouds* is not Aristophanes' masterpiece, it is certainly the most ambitious play that he had yet undertaken. His lack of complete success with it is, like that of Shakespeare with *Hamlet*, all the more provocative because there was more in the author's mind than he has been able to put down coherently on paper. Socrates in the *Clouds*, like Demos in the *Knights*, is not the principal figure of the play, but these are the characters who most interest Aristophanes. They are alike in the ambiguity of the position in which the author places them. Socrates is pictured in the *Clouds* as at the head of a Thinking School. He first appears ridiculously suspended in a basket high up in the air, and he explains his position, physical and intellectual, in the striking line, "I walk on air and contemplate the sun." Whether Aristophanes thought of Socrates as a person dangerous to the state or merely as the representative of a dangerous tendency, it is clear that in the *Clouds* the philosopher stands for that overdevelopment of the intellectual processes which the comic dramatist distrusted when it interfered with mutual cooperation between human beings on the level of everyday experience.

The leading character in the *Clouds* is trying to make use of Socrates' wisdom for his own selfish purposes. He is an old rustic, called Strepsiades, anxious to wriggle out of the unfortunate circumstances in which he finds himself placed, no matter how shifty the necessary means may be. He has married a woman of fashion, and she has pushed their son into Athenian high society, with the result that the boy, Pheidippides, a lover of horses, has run through his father's estate and that when the play opens Strepsiades cannot sleep for thinking of his debts. The only remedy for his condition that occurs to him is to have his son learn logic from Sophists like Socrates and thus become able to outargue all pressing creditors. Pheidippides refuses to submit himself to intellectual discipline, and Strepsiades himself decides to attend the Thinking School. In this way the central figure of the *Clouds* becomes a disciple of Socrates in his effort to learn how to avoid paying the debts which he has incurred because of his son's extravagance. Strepsiades disapproves strongly of modern city life, but being a born equivocator he is willing to right one evil by indulging in another and perhaps a greater one. He erroneously supposes that two wrongs make one right, and he attempts to commit the second wrong by extracting from Socrates dangerous information about how to make the worse appear the better reason. This ability is an integral part of intellectual development, but it may have serious practical obstacles, as Strepsiades finds to his sorrow. Socrates cannot justly be held responsible for the misuse of mental power which a capable person learns to develop in an academic institution like the Thinking School.

The difficulty for Strepsiades is that he is too innately stupid to be able to master the refinements of logical argumentation. In despair, he summons Pheidippides to take his place in the difficult art of thinking. At first Socrates thinks that the son appears to be as stupid as the father, but, on being urged, the philosopher agrees to show the boy Right and Wrong Logic, who accordingly appear in person upon the stage and debate their respective merits. This scene, which at first sight appears to be an episodic one, is really the central point of the *Clouds*, for it indicates quite clearly the principal issues which, as Aristophanes thinks, lie behind the confused and distorted problems presented by the position of philosophic education in a world peopled by such ignorant fools as Strepsiades and by such clever rascals as Pheidippides. Right Logic sets forth all the best Aristophanic principles: the subservient position of children, the patriotic feeling of a good Greek, the happy mean in dress and food. One would think from his argument that all men would follow the example of their ancestors in order to become useful and happy, until Wrong Logic proves that now enervating warm baths, deceptive oratory, and open adultery are the order of the day in Athens. Then it is seen that what should be cannot stand against what is, and Right Logic acknowledges the superiority of his opponent. Aristophanes himself does not approve of this position, but it is a necessary part of the paradoxical nature of the *Clouds* to make the worse appear the better reason. Not until the end of the play are Strepsiades' deluded eyes opened and Aristophanes' convictions plainly revealed to the audience.

Strepsiades' conversion is brought about by his son's great skill in assimilating the doctrines of Socrates. Pheidippides easily absorbs the principles of the Wrong Logic; by means of them Strepsiades routs his creditors as he had planned to do; and then the son turns his newly acquired ability against the father. At a banquet he insists upon singing an erotic song by Euripides instead of a dignified one by Aeschylus as requested by Strepsiades, and in the quarrel that follows he justifies his right to strike his father in accordance with Goneril's theory,

> Old fools are babes again, and must be us'd
> With checks as flatteries, when they are seen abus'd.

Strepsiades is angry at this attitude on the part of his son, but he acknowledges the justice of the position; when, however, Pheidippides threatens to beat his mother for the same reason, the father's wrath knows no bounds. He seizes a torch, climbs to the roof of the Thinking School, and sets fire to it. When Socrates in amazement asks him what he is doing, Strepsiades neatly replies, "I walk on air and contemplate the sun." At last Strepsiades has come to take Aristophanes' view that Socrates and the Sophists are dangerous members of human society. The study of philosophy, which at first seems merely a harmless waste of time, in the end becomes the cause of moral degeneration: debts go unpaid, sons lord it over their fathers, and anarchy rules to such a degree that the worse reason can no longer be proved the better one.

One of Strepsiades' final objections to Socrates is that the philosopher has blasphemed against the gods, and it is obvious that a rational point of view like his will always be opposed to any organized system of religion. The criticism brought against the skeptical position is that it tends to remove from the rank and file of mankind the incentives to moral conduct; the chief point in its favor is that it may predicate a deity superior to the one ordinarily accepted by conventional people. For instance, Socrates is ready to displace Zeus in favor of the Whirlwind, an explanation of the divine force which is partly scientific and partly mystical in its nature. In either case it is not adapted to the mentality of stupid people like Strepsiades, who completely misunderstands Socrates' discourse on the supernatural powers that rule the universe, to which the philosopher also gives the general name of Necessity. The height of Strepsiades' bewilderment is reached when these mysterious forces become embodied in the Clouds. He is able to understand that clouds cause thunder and rain, but he is dumfounded when the Clouds appear on the stage in person and take the part of the Chorus in the comedy to which they give their name. In the Chorus of Clouds, Aristophanes has embodied his poetic conception of the wonders of nature, which cannot be entirely explained by the speculation of philosophers, but which are not essentially antagonistic to it. In fact, the Clouds are Socrates' chief allies, and their unsubstantial mistiness is a good symbol for the practical weakness of abstract reasoning.

On the other hand, the Clouds are of the utmost assistance to the philosopher in the sophistical dethronement of Zeus, which is his chosen task. They may be shifting and tenuous, but they are also strong and influential. Aristophanes wrote for their mouths some of his most exquisite poetry, and there can be no doubt that, according to the comic convention, they express the sentiments of their creator. There is no question of conflict among the Clouds, because from the first they are in agreement with one another; they take part in no *agon*, and in general they support the position upheld by Socrates. They encourage Strepsiades to embark on the course which proves so injurious to him, and yet they are supposed to speak words of truth and wisdom. The clue to their paradoxical nature, which is artistically true to a play that is obscure in its purpose and indirect in its method, is probably to be found in one of their last speeches, after Strepsiades has blamed them for his downfall. They then explain that, like Demos in the *Knights*, their way of promoting righteousness is to lure an evildoer on until he overreaches himself, "in order that he may learn to fear the gods." So, after all, they are not the atheistical creatures that they seem, but servants of the gods, perhaps of greater gods than Zeus and his fellows.

Aristophanes wisely leaves the miracle of primitive creation in the sphere of the imagination, and he implies that poetry is necessary to explain our existence satisfactorily to the human emotions. Philosophy makes an attempt to appeal to the mind. When poetry and philosophy work together harmoniously, as do the Clouds and Socrates, the combination is irresistible. If, however, philosophy divorces itself from poetry and attempts to meddle with the affairs of daily life, it is fallible in the extreme. When Socrates sets up a Thinking School and his pupils learn to oppose the normal social relationships of debtor and creditor, of parents and children, then the wise man has exceeded his natural limitations and he deserves to have his house burned down above his head, that he too may learn to fear the gods. Such appears to be the distinction which Aristophanes draws between the Clouds and Socrates. He can praise one of the two allies and yet, at the same time, show that the other member of the partnership is in an insecure and ridiculous position.

It is no wonder that this finespun distinction has proved confusing to an interpretation of the *Clouds*, and perhaps its author was not absolutely sure of his own attitude towards Socrates. Strepsiades is definitely absurd until his conversion, and the Clouds are as definitely superior creatures; but Socrates is in an ambiguous situation, which Aristophanes refuses to defend. Much as the poet may have liked Socrates personally and much as he may have admired his intellectual dexterity, he believed that the philosopher's example was harmful to the state and therefore should be condemned. The conservative element in Aristophanes' nature caused him to distrust individual initiative when it actively came into conflict with well-established traditions, and Socrates was in his own way as extreme an individualist as Cleon. It had required courage to attack Cleon, but it took skill to oppose Socrates, and, perhaps partially as a result of the difference in the caliber of their subjects, the *Clouds* is a much richer and more intricate piece of work than either the *Acharnians* or the *Knights*. It has the breadth of the former comedy and the depth of the latter one, although these qualities are not yet so expertly joined as they were to be when the genius of Aristophanes had reached its full maturity.

III

The increase in Aristophanes' artistic stature which is evident in the *Clouds* becomes more marked in the play which he produced one year later, the *Wasps* of 422. Superficially this comedy appears to be a return to the subject and spirit of the *Knights*, but it proceeds more obliquely to its goal. It is another anti-Cleon comedy, but in it Cleon is not brought upon the stage; instead he is attacked indirectly through the medium of the dicasts, or jurymen, whom the demagogue had made his creatures by playing upon their love of litigation and their desire to be paid well for doing little. The most important character in this play, but not its nominal protagonist, is Philocleon, a lover of Cleon, the end and aim of whose existence is to pass his time trying cases in the law courts. His son, the protagonist, called Bdelycleon, a detester of Cleon, is trying to wean his father away from the object of his devotion. Before the play begins, he has locked his father in the house to prevent him from indulging his absurd mania of attending the courts. The first part of the action is occupied with Philocleon's farcical attempts to escape from his imprisonment, which are unsuccessful because of Bdelycleon's watchfulness and strategy. The son has also to cope with the Chorus of Wasps, his father's fellow dicasts, irritable stinging old men who were warriors in their prime but who are now reduced to serving for dicastic pay as a means of livelihood. To get their meager three obols a day they are forced to attend the courts, and, since Cleon is responsible for their employment, they are only too ready to convict anyone whom he considers his enemy.

Their immediate zeal is somewhat abated by Bdelycleon's attack on them with smoke, which is destructive to wasps, and they agree to act as arbiters in the dispute that is to take place between father and son. In it the rights and wrongs of the dicastic life are thoroughly debated. Philocleon naturally thinks that such a life is useful and agreeable, and he praises Cleon for making it possible. Bdelycleon shows how poverty-stricken the dicasts are in spite of their pay and criticizes the selfishness of Cleon's motives. These latter arguments go home to the bosoms of the Chorus, which now decides to reverse its previous attitude and to favor the side of Bdelycleon. Even his father admits somewhat grudgingly that he has been mistaken in idolizing Cleon, and from this point on in the play there is no real conflict of ideas such as that which continues throughout the *Clouds*. The *Wasps* does contain a number of good incidental hits at the inherent weaknesses of the law, its rigidity, its formality, and its technicality, phases of the subject which are as alive to us as they were when, in the seventeenth century, Jean Baptiste Racine drew on the *Wasps* for the plot of his legal comedy, *The Litigants* ("Les Plaideurs"). The French play omits the personal satire indulged in by Aristophanes, and the result is a work of art much less vigorous and pointed than the original Greek comedy.

The Litigants falls far short of the *Wasps* in the mock-trial scene, where the representatives of two dogs dispute a legal suit, with Philocleon acting in the capacity of judge. Besides containing a slurring reference to Cleon's most recent misdemeanors, Aristophanes' version of this scene is a mirth-provoking parody of the course of a case in the Athenian law courts. It is finally won, rather trickily to be sure, by Cleon's enemy, who urges Philocleon to vote honestly in the future and also to enjoy life, as they did in the brave days of old, by dressing respectably, talking intelligently, and mixing in society like a genial human being.

As in the *Knights*, Aristophanes advocates a return of the state to its former glories, although he also illustrates the difficulty of turning back the clock of progress in the farcical scenes with which the *Wasps* ends. A first-rate comic poet can never resist pointing out the absurdities of any extreme behavior. Excessive ill temper having been ridiculed during the first part of the play, Philocleon's new-found sociability later comes in for its share of satire. Somewhat against his will, the old man is taken by his son to a banquet, where he gets uproariously drunk, and on his return to the stage openly disgraces himself before the audience. We do not entirely lose sympathy with Philocleon, for even in his wanton dancing he is superior to the degenerate men of his day, but it is made clear to us that it is difficult to change old habits, even bad ones, without erring too far in the opposite direction. In this case the opposite direction must have tickled the ears of the groundlings, and it certainly gave rise to the uproarious merriment suitable to the end of a comedy. Philocleon rather overdoes his hilarity, but Bdelycleon is not very much disturbed, while the Chorus is frankly delighted to see its old companion kicking up his heels in such an unceremonious and indecorous manner. It is not necessary to take Philocleon's debauch too literally, even in a serious analysis of the play; it is a comic elaboration of the *joie de vivre* for which Aristophanes is pleading against the bigotry of legal zealots like the dicasts and the tyranny of self-appointed legislators like Cleon.

Cleon's supremacy in the legal and military functions of the Athenian state was to be short-lived, not because of Aristophanes' attacks upon him, but because in the latter part of 422, the year in which the *Wasps* was first presented, the demagogue was killed at the battle of Amphipolis, after seven years of the dictatorship which the comic poet had feared and distrusted. In the same battle Brasidas, the chief military leader of the Spartans, also lost his life, and the next year prospects were bright for the establishment of a Peloponnesian peace, which in fact was soon negotiated through the efforts of

Nicias, a statesman as well as a general. In 421, during the few months that elapsed between the death of Cleon and the Peace of Nicias, Aristophanes wrote and produced a drama, the *Peace*, which is really more a song of triumph than a comic interpretation of the problems that were disturbing Athens at the moment. The protagonist of the *Peace* chimerically sails to heaven on a beetle, finds that the gods have left Olympus in the hands of War, and with the help of a Chorus of Farmers succeeds in extricating Peace from her imprisonment. The Greeks are unanimous in desiring the return of Peace to earth and unrestrained in their expressions of pleasure when she has been safely restored to them.

Aristophanes was as much a poet as he was a comedian, and in the *Peace* his patriotic feelings definitely get the better of his critical detachment. He may have had an uneasy apprehension that the Peace of Nicias was not to prove a durable one; worldly priests and successful munition makers, he seems to say, will always be on hand to disturb the efforts of broad-minded men to establish friendly relations between people whose fundamental interests are not really so opposed as they often seem to be upon the surface. But he seems to have been filled temporarily with such high hopes for the future of Greece that his gloomy forebodings were submerged, or at least reduced to a subordinate position. The tone of the *Peace* is infinitely more optimistic than that of the *Acharnians*, written four years before, but it is also a much less impressive piece of work, because it does not contain any hint of violent opposition to a truce which should herald the return of prosperity, with its double benefits of production for the country and consumption for the city.

Unfortunately, the joy of Aristophanes could not have lasted long. The Peace of Nicias was concluded in 421, shortly after the performance of the *Peace*, but within three years Athens and Sparta were again fighting each other, and by 414, when the dramatist produced his next extant play, the *Birds*, the war was once more in full swing. Athens, which had been successful in taking and destroying Melos, was then launching an immense naval expedition under Alcibiades against the city of Syracuse in Sicily. This expedition, which was destined to be a gigantic failure, had not yet met with any serious setbacks, and in spite of the fact that its start had been made under somewhat unfavorable auspices, it is not probable that, at the moment when Aristophanes was writing his play, discouragement prevailed in Athens. There is, however, every reason to suppose that Aristophanes himself disapproved heartily of any such imperialistic policy as Alcibiades' and that he judged the entire Sicilian expedition to be the height of arrogant folly. He had frequently expressed his hatred of the horrors of an aggressive war, and in the *Birds* this hatred is again implied, if not formally stated. On the other hand, there is no evidence that this comedy was directed specifically against Alcibiades' expedition, although there seems to be some relationship, obscure to us, between the course of events in the real world of Athens and in the imaginary world of the play.

The *Birds* has often puzzled literary critics, as well as political historians, but in the light of Aristophanes' other comedies its general poetic intention should be sufficiently clear. It is not, like the *Clouds*, a play in which the author has difficulty in communicating a consistent attitude toward his material because he himself has not become entirely convinced by its emotional implications, but a play in which the fictitious structure, although suggested by the events of real life, departs from them so far that a realistically minded person has trouble in detecting where the similarity between fact and fancy begins and where it ends. It is a delightfully whimsical comedy, but it is also an intelligent one; and the combination of these two elements makes it as impressive as the *Clouds* is tantalizing. It is probably Aristophanes' greatest play, and there are a number of reasons why it should be ranked as his most important single contribution to the history of literature.

The *Birds* holds the strategic position of being chronologically the sixth of the eleven extant comedies by Aristophanes, it is by far the longest of them all, and it contains the last complete *parabasis* to be found in any of them. It was written at the height of its author's career, when the community in which he was living appeared to be at the peak of its development. At this period Aristophanes had had enough successes to give him some confidence in his ability as a dramatist, and his failures, as with the *Clouds*, had not yet been so pronounced as to weigh heavily upon him; he had perfected his technique to the point where he was able to express what was in his mind, and he had not yet begun to grow careless of his means because of concentration on his ends. In the *Birds* Aristophanes may be said for the first time to have set himself a definite task on a large scale, without expanding his material to the point where it is vague and unmanageable. In it he has risen above petty local interests, and yet he has not entirely lost touch with the everyday world, which provides the vitality that is needed by a masterpiece of comedy. The *Birds* is not lacking in the high seriousness with which Aristophanes regarded specific conditions in Athens at the beginning of his career, but it has already entered into the sphere of universals, with which he was to be more and more concerned in his later work. One suspects that in this play lies the core of its author's artistic achievement; if it is to be appreciated as fully as possible, it should be read in its chronological position among his other plays; to understand it in every detail would be to perform the miracle of comprehending completely the extraordinary range of Aristophanes' comic inventiveness.

The plot of the *Birds* begins with deceptive simplicity. Pcisthetaerus, a man who can easily persuade others, and his side partner, the possessor of a hopeful disposition, have fled from Athens to escape the lawsuits that are rife there. They are seeking some place where they can avoid their creditors, and they hope to be directed to such a quiet spot by Tereus, King of Thrace, now turned into a bird, a hoopoe. They tell him that they do not desire an aristocratic community, but one where they may enjoy life by bathing, feasting, and indulging in social intercourse, without regard to how much these pleasures cost. In the land of the Birds there is to be found neither money nor any other practical obstacle to the higher delights that come from pleasant dalliance in fair gardens, a state of affairs which appeals so much to Peisthetaerus that he proposes the establishment of an ethereal city to be called Cloud-Cuckoo-Land, or Nephelococcygia. He explains to the Hoopoe that by constructing city walls in the air they can starve into subjection the gods, who are dependent upon the steam from earthly sacrifices for their subsistence. The Hoopoe is fascinated by the plan; he summons his mate, the Nightingale, from her sleep in a near-by thicket, and together they call upon the land-birds, the marsh-birds, and the sea-birds, who make up the Chorus of the play. The Birds of the Chorus are at first angry to find two fallible mortals in their country and threaten to peck out the intruders' eyes with their beaks, but the Athenians prepare to defend themselves with pots, spits, and platters, while the Hoopoe persuades the other birds to listen to the plan of Peisthetaerus.

At this point in the action the physical warfare ceases, and Peisthetaerus has an opportunity to show his ability in argument. He ingratiates himself with the Birds by telling them that they were sovereigns before the present earth and its gods existed; they may be so again, if they will follow his instructions. They must build walls between heaven and earth and then send a message of defiance to Zeus, warning him that the gods will no longer be permitted to go through the air on their way to illicit love affairs with mortal women. At the same time they must assert their claims to divinity in the eyes of men by devouring grain and plucking out the eyes of oxen. They are also to aid their adherents in various birdlike ways, which are extremely picturesque and give an excellent opportunity for the free play of the poet's fancy; the ingenious uses to which Aristophanes puts his extensive knowledge of birds, in both a witty and a lyric fashion, are strikingly original, but they should not be allowed to obscure the fundamental issue of the comedy, the possibility of a new heaven and a new earth, purer and less material than the conventional ones of the dramatist and his countrymen. The implication of the *Clouds* that the Olympian gods are inferior to vast forces of nature, like the Whirlwind, and the suggestion in the *Peace* that they would take flight before the inroads of War, are here further clarified and elaborated. The Clouds were superior in force to Zeus, but they were vague and impalpable; the Birds may be weaker physically than the Clouds, but at least they are more concrete and reliable. They need only to be organized and disciplined to reduce the gods to a ridiculous state of subjection.

The Birds finally agree to try the experiment, and in the choral ode which follows they dilate upon the two phases of Peisthetaerus' proposal that have most appealed to them, the antiquity of their glorious lineage and their ability to aid mankind. They also extend an invitation to all people who are unhappy at Athens to migrate to the Kingdom of the Birds, even if they are intrinsically undesirable members of society. In this dangerous proposal they are probably actuated by a zeal for proselyting and by the hope that in their ideal community even criminals may be reformed. Their impulse must have been a momentary one that came to them in the first flush of their pioneering enthusiasm, and they soon have good reason to regret their indiscriminate hospitality. It was not too few, but too many, immigrants that Cloud-Cuckoo-Land had to fear. Even before its walls were finished, a crew of discontented Athenians jumped at the opportunity presented by the new social state, but they are all rejected by Peisthetaerus, now himself arrayed with wings like a veritable bird. The many short scenes in which various undesirable visitors are dismissed serve the double purpose of showing the sort of people whom Aristophanes would not allow to enter his Utopian community and of indicating the success with which the project of the Birds has been meeting upon earth.

Among the gods it is no less effective. As soon as the city walls are completed, the process of attrition sets in. At first Zeus is puzzled by the fact that sweet odors no longer come to him from the earth, and he sends Iris to command men to resume their former sacrifices; but the messenger of the gods soon learns to her sorrow the true nature of the Birds' revolutionary undertaking. Then Prometheus appears, well wrapped up to escape Zeus's observation, with the news that the Olympians are starving, that the barbarian gods are rebellious, and that an embassy will soon be sent from heaven to make peace with Cloud-Cuckoo-Land. Prometheus, who is so much afraid of Zeus that he constantly cowers under an open umbrella in order not to be seen from on high, explains that he has always been an enemy of the old gods and that he now considers himself an ally of the new divinities. His advice is not to cease hostilities until, as a sign of utter submission, the gods restore the royal scepter to the Birds and hand over Sovereignty to be the bride of Peisthetaerus. Accordingly, when the envoys arrive, the Birds insist upon these terms and gain them by playing on the greediness of Heracles, one of the ambassadors from the immortals. Peisthetaerus is making the oligarchical birds who have opposed a democratic form of government into a stew, the fumes of which are so pleasing to Heracles that he is willing to accept any conditions. He finally wins over his fellow envoys, not without a struggle, and the *Birds* ends with the customary feast in celebration of a victory. Peisthetaerus' rash plan has been entirely vindicated. In the Kingdom of the Birds, people are to live happily forever after.

The treatment of mortals in this play is quite according to Aristophanes' usual attitude of amused toleration for their weaknesses, but the question of the gods is more complicated. The dramatist has been charged with impiety in the *Birds*, as he was charged with obscurantism in the *Clouds*, but these charges can be sustained in only a very modified form. No doubt the gods are treated with scant courtesy in this comedy, but their existence is never questioned. They rule supreme in the affairs of the world, and they will continue to do so as long as they fulfill a useful function. Meanwhile it does no harm to subject them to tonic satire from a superior individual like Peisthetaerus, who has ascended into a sphere that is halfway between heaven and earth. To human beings he and his birds appear as godlike, and to himself he appears as godlike, too, after he has received Sovereignty for a wife. If, as Aristophanes seems to imply, human nature can be raised to the level of the ideal, there is no longer any logical necessity for divine guidance, and then the gods, whoever they may be, must capitulate to human perfection as it will be revealed in the institutions of a Utopian society.

The creation of such an ideal world as that humorously portrayed in the *Birds* demands unusual powers of penetration. When this insight is expressed in a form precisely suited to the nature of its subject, the result may be justly called a work of genius. Apparently Aristophanes did not anticipate the immediate destruction of the Olympians and the rise of other deities, themselves to be superseded with the passage of time, but his conception of a supernatural force greater than any yet apprehended by men offers such a prospect to the human imagination. Above Zeus and his followers, there may be the Birds; above the Birds, what may there not be? It is the same sort of inquiry that is presented to our minds by the position of the Clouds in the comedy named after them. They have taken the place of Zeus, it appears, but at the end of the play they are represented as instruments of ultimate good. Again it is faintly hinted that, powerful as are the old gods, mankind may in the future know still mightier divinities. Aristophanes nowhere formulates such an exact statement of his intellectual position, but the *Clouds* and the *Birds* both seem to be fables that bear this interpretation. If one remembers the part taken by the Choruses of these plays in the dramatic framework that surrounds them, and if at the same time one thinks of birds and clouds as "blithe spirits" and "nurslings of the sky," after the manner of Shelley, new attitudes toward religion, art, and life are suggested to the consciousness by the comedies of Aristophanes. Above the theology of his day there are suddenly seen to loom such larger issues as the nature of Truth, Justice, and Wisdom.

The difficulty for the dramatist is that these abstractions tend to become formless, unless he can associate them with impressions and symbols that can be conveyed objectively, through devices that are effective on the stage. In making this attempt he may lose something of the force in his original impulse, as to the modern reader, at least, Aristophanes sometimes seems to do. When he indulges in excessive horseplay, coarseness, and superficial absurdity, his central purpose is obscured and dulled. Yet with all the boisterousness and confusion characteristic of his comedies, the sense of a consistent underlying intention emerges, and it is this sense which puts the *Clouds* and the *Birds* in the front rank of his literary work. As we look back on the *Clouds* it is difficult for us to forgive the injustice done to Socrates or the devious methods by which proposals for the public good are set forth; but in the *Birds* the dramatist seems largely to have freed himself from the limitations of time and space. He has soared into the air on the wings of his own Birds and created in Cloud-Cuckoo-Land one of the few really attractive Utopias, none the less attractive because it belongs to the realm of pure fancy.

Aristophanes has Peisthetaerus embark on an impossible aerial voyage with much the same enthusiasm as that of Alcibiades when he set out on his expedition to Syracuse, although in his heart the writer of comedy feels sure that such presumption can have only the most disastrous efforts. It is necessary to go beyond the confines of our material universe and to enter the territory of the poet's imagination in order to find a new and ideal community that may meet with undisputed success. Within the bounds of three dimensions, the failures of actual existence can always be most vividly presented by comparison with what might have occurred under a set of ideal circumstances. A comedy's reach should exceed its grasp in order to expose the insufficiency of mortal attainments and the standards by which they are ordinarily judged. It is an ironical commentary upon the truth of this critical principle that the *Birds*, which is the highest flight of Aristophanes' comic genius, should have received only second prize in the dramatic competition at which it was first presented.

IV

Three years elapsed between the *Birds* and the next play by Aristophanes that has come down to us. The *Lysistrata*, which was produced in 411, is the third and last, and also the least hopeful, of Aristophanes' antiwar comedies. In the interim between the *Birds* and the *Lysistrata* the Syracusan expedition of Alcibiades had been overwhelmingly defeated, many of the Athenians' allies had revolted in consequence of that crushing disaster, and the treasury at Athens had become greatly impoverished. In such a situation it would have been as hard to win peace from Sparta on honorable terms as it had been easy at the time when the *Peace* was written. To propose a general pacification of Greece at this moment was a heroic expedient, and one which required cleverness as well as courage, but Aristophanes did not shrink from the difficult task of once more setting his constructive proposals before the citizens of Athens.

The more desperate the situation became, the keener grew Aristophanes' wits and the stronger his convictions. All Greece was suffering from a protracted war, and the sanest sufferers from it were the women, less blinded than the men by military glory; so it seemed natural to suppose that in an appeal to women's intelligence might lie the least forlorn hope of peace, and that their rejection of war as a sensible means of solving human problems might, in turn, reflect upon the intelligence of men. At any rate, such an idea seems to have been in the back of Aristophanes' mind when he made the protagonist of his next comedy a woman, called Lysistrata, a Greek name which means the releaser of armies. Lysistrata wishes to band together all her sex in a league against the warlike men by an ingenious plan, which, if it is more physically possible than those adopted by the heroes of the *Acharnians* and the *Peace*, is scarcely less psychologically improbable. She persuades her cohorts to swear an oath upon a jar of wine (which Aristophanes takes as a symbol of the weakness for strong drink prevalent among Greek women) that, until peace is restored, they will refrain from all intercourse with men, whether husbands or lovers. The men find it increasingly painful to abstain from association with women, and, as the play progresses, the phallic element in it grows to extravagantly comic proportions. Upon our stage today, from Moscow to New York, the *Lysistrata* is the most familiar of Aristophanes' plays; if its superficial attraction depends largely upon pandering to a modern interest in the animal functions of life, it has also appealed deeply on its serious side to a generation disillusioned and burdened by the results of a destructive war.

As a dramatic narrative, the *Lysistrata* is far more exciting than the poet's two earlier attacks on war; one is kept in suspense until the very end of it as to the outcome of the heroine's daring experiment. In addition to that major uncertainty, the Chorus is divided against itself. It is composed half of women, who have seized the Acropolis, and half of men, who are trying to regain possession of it. Not until the end of the play do these two opposing parties become reconciled, by the men's capitulation to the blandishments of the women, and arrive at a unity of purpose in line with Aristophanes' fundamental beliefs on the subject of human welfare. To him peace is more important than relations between the sexes, but, since some sexual gratification is necessary for the happiness of men and women, it follows logically that the maintenance of peaceful conditions in the world should be a matter of primary importance to both sexes; to men because they desire to beget children, and to women because they wish to protect them after they have been born.

With the exception of one brief scene near the end, the *Lysistrata* is a carefully integrated and logically worked-out comedy, much more restricted in range and unified in spirit than are Aristophanes' earlier plays. In them there is a more wanton prodigality of material and a freer treatment of subject matter, qualities which help to make the plays written before the *Birds* seem rich and at the same time confused. The idealism of Peisthetaerus imposed some kind of restraint on the strange candidates for admission to the Kingdom of the Birds, and in much the same way Aristophanes began to limit his artistic canvas in the interests of law and order. Perhaps the desperate nature of the contemporary situation at Athens increased the power of the dramatist's attack upon that evil which he considered at the root of all human suffering, but, whatever the reason, the *Lysistrata* is the most effective and concentrated of all his peace plays. While it provokes hearty laughter at the physical inconveniences of war, it drives home at the same time the serious idea that war is a crime, because bloodshed is in direct opposition to the creative impulse of the human race.

The capacity of women for producing new organisms to inherit the earth brings them close to the source of life and consequently gives them an important part to play in all drama concerned with humorous comment upon social conditions. In the *Lysistrata* Aristophanes found it a useful device to make his protagonist a woman, hostile to those practices of men which he most deplored, and almost immediately afterwards he composed a new variation on this same theme in the comedy of the *Thesmophoriazusae* ("The Women Celebrating the Festival of the Thesmophoria"),[1] produced for the first time in 411 or 410 B.C. This amusing farce represents the women at the festival as outraged because of the attacks that they feel have been made upon their sex by the tragic dramatist Euripides, a contemporary artist whom Aristophanes distrusted almost as much as he did Cleon, the demagogue, or Socrates, the philosopher. In the *Clouds* Aristophanes had already pictured an unscrupulous pupil of Socrates as insistent upon singing a song by Euripides and so precipitating a quarrel with his old-fashioned father. Evidently to Aristophanes' mind the plays of Euripides were a preponderant influence in the movement towards degeneracy that was threatening the ancient glory and nobility of Athens.

In the *Acharnians*, his earliest extant play, Aristophanes had made it plain that in his judgment the characters created by Euripides fall far short of the elevation and splendor demanded by tragedy. The *Thesmophoriazusae*, produced fifteen years later, is chiefly an amplification of the minor episode dealing with Euripides in the *Acharnians*, and it is generally held to be one of Aristophanes' lesser efforts. Its intellectual content seems slight unless one realizes the seriousness of its author's criticism of Euripides as an exponent of vicious contemporary tendencies comparable to Cleon and Socrates. The only difference in the critical attitude of the comic writer toward these three men is that, while he attacks the politician as more dangerous to the state than the philosopher, he shows that the philosopher may be more dangerous and yet more honest than the imaginative artist. Thus Aristophanes treated Euripides with a mixture of scorn and toleration: toleration because, as one dramatist to another, he had

---

[1] I have used an English translation of the titles of plays mentioned in this book, except where (as in the case of the *Thesmophoriazusae*) the English is more awkward than the original language.

to admit the frequent skillfulness of Euripides' art; scorn because of
his rooted objections to the intellectual concepts, which he considered demoralizing, that underlie it. Although he did not charge
Euripides with originating these concepts, shared by many, he held
him responsible for making them seem attractive and thereby further
debasing the taste of his audience.

Above all, Aristophanes blamed Euripides for presenting women
in his plays as the victims of romantic love. The playwright who
could show Lysistrata rallying the members of her sex, for the good
of the entire community, against an overpowering desire to join
their mates, could not be expected to be very sympathetic to a
writer who had devoted his major talents to portraying the pangs
of a Medea or a Phaedra. Aristophanes was scarcely a conventional
feminist, but he was a humanist with an unusually broad social platform, the object of which was to make women, like men, into
worthy citizens and not to encourage them in undisciplined passion
that would work against the general welfare.

Aristophanes' treatment of women is not based upon a close study
of their psychology, as is that of Euripides, but upon an elaborate
idealism, which is a part of his general view of the world as a place
where healthy physical appetites need not interfere with moral sub-
limity. A rationalized synthesis between the body and the soul he
seems never to have contemplated; but doubtless he did not disas-
sociate them as completely as some later moralists have tried to do.
As it was, he liked to laugh good-naturedly at the bondage of the
flesh and also to preach a refined code of ethical conduct for the individual as a member of society. He is, at the same time, a patriot
and a pacifist, a *bon vivant* and a poet who "on honeydew has fed,"
a man of the world and a philosophical thinker. It is the conventional
element that predominates on the surface of his plays, with their
praise of Marathon, their scenes of wild drinking, and their delight
in courtesans. It is the more idealistic factor that provides their basic
fiber, an incessant yearning for peace, a desire for good government
and social harmony, and an unquenchable faith in the ultimate possibilities of human nature.

In the *Thesmophoriazusae*, Aristophanes has the women at their
festival planning to try Euripides for the evil about their sex that he
has disseminated in his erotic tragedies. They admit that there may

be some truth in the charges of immorality which he has brought against them, but their occasional falseness toward mortal man is as nothing compared to the essential impiety of Euripides' teaching. This part of the play, which is developed with resourcefulness and amusing vulgarity, leads into a series of scenes that deftly ridicule the literary weaknesses of Euripides as exhibited in some of his least impressive tragedies. The *Thesmophoriazusae* ends gaily with Euripides' promise to stop slandering women in his plays, but its intellectual implications are not to be taken very seriously. They point in the general direction of Aristòphanes' hopes that tragedy will return to the simpler and more elevated tone of Euripides' great predecessors, Aeschylus and Sophocles. Sophocles seems to have been greatly admired by Aristophanes, but when the comic dramatist wanted an exaggerated foil for the hairsplitting Euripides, he went back to Aeschylus, the father of Attic tragedy.

In the plays of Aeschylus, the *Persians* and the *Seven against Thebes*, for instance, one finds the old unquestioning love of country, the lofty idealism, and the stern moral code which Aristophanes admired above all things. Here were no verbal jugglings, no studies in abnormal psychology, no quibbling chop-logic of the schools, such as were evident in the famous line from the *Hippolytus* of Euripides, "My tongue swore; my mind remains unsworn." No doubt Aeschylus had his weaknesses — to the penetrating eye of Aristophanes what human being was without them? — but they were nothing more weighty than a bombastic phraseology, a monotonous rhythm, and an occasional repetition or ambiguity. These were but slight errors of style and could easily be overlooked; the subject matter which they enclosed was pure gold, and therefore the work of Aeschylus could justifiably be opposed to that of Euripides as a model of what tragic drama ought to be. This point of view is expressed by Aristophanes in his comedy of the *Frogs*, acted in 405 B.C., five or six years later than the *Thesmophoriazusae*, and much the more pretentious of the two plays that Aristophanes directed primarily against his particular literary aversion. Euripides had died in 406, but Aristophanes apparently felt that the tragedian's influence was still too much alive for the good of Athens. He therefore attacked it again in a comedy which was half horseplay and half dramatic criticism.

The plot of the *Frogs* starts with the premise that Dionysus, god of wine and of the theater, is very much upset by the death of Euripides. Dionysus has read with such pleasure the *Andromeda* of Euripides (a play already parodied in the *Thesmophoriazusae*) that now, four months after the tragedian's death, he determines to go to Hades and bring his hero back to earth. This information he imparts to Heracles, who, by disagreeing with the god's literary judgment and implying that he prefers Sophocles to Euripides, suggests to the audience that, even though Dionysus is an immortal, his views on art may be a trifle erroneous. This foreshadowing of the main conflict in the *Frogs* is structurally important, because it prepares one for a change in Dionysus' attitude toward Euripides similar to the change in the protagonist's attitude toward Socrates in the *Clouds*. In both cases the dramatist brings his main character around to his own unfavorable point of view, but he manages this conversion less abruptly and more effectively in the later play than in the earlier one.

After the Heracles scene the subject of the respective merits of the three great tragedians is dropped until the second half of the drama, and in the meantime the author's attention is devoted almost exclusively to Dionysus' ludicrous adventures on his trip to Hades, adventures that have more in common with the scant reverence shown to the gods in the *Birds* than with the anti-Euripidean material of the *Frogs*. In this play, contrary to his usual practice, Aristophanes does not make a very well-integrated connection between his serious ideas and the amusing incidents that should logically spring from them. Possibly he felt that the *agon*, when it was finally reached, was to be of such a highly specialized nature that the spectators must first be thrown into a state of good humor. He seems to have been pleased that the audience at the *Frogs* was furnished with a book of the play, apparently because he thought that familiarity with the text would help people to appreciate his meaning and prevent them from being confused by his subtleties, as they had been in his artistic masterpieces like the *Clouds* and the *Birds*.

The *Frogs* has always been one of Aristophanes' most popular plays, no doubt chiefly because of the large proportion of low comedy that it contains. Frivolity holds the stage after the scene with Heracles throughout Dionysus' absurd interviews with a corpse, with Charon, and with the unseen Chorus of Frogs, who keep up their constant croaking of *brekekekex ko-ax ko-ax* while the god is crossing the

Styx. Much of the humor in this part of the play is due to Dionysus'
slave, Xanthias, the first important servant in recorded comedy, who
plays outrageously upon Dionysus' fear of the dark, which he shares
to some extent, changes clothes with his master, when Heracles' gar-
ments prove to have a disagreeable connotation for the porter of the
underworld, and later compares professional notes with this porter:
what fun it is to curse one's superiors, to grumble after being
whipped, to pry into the private affairs of the great, and so on. This
dialogue between the two servants contains all the elements of social
comedy as it was to develop after Aristophanes' time, but here it
is merely an incident leading into the formal argument between
Aeschylus and Euripides, which comprises the dramatic core of the
Frogs.

The immediate provocation for this dispute is that Aeschylus had
formerly held the principal tragedian's seat in Pluto's assembly hall,
but that Euripides now claims precedence over the elder dramatist.
Sophocles has been more modest, but he too is opposed to Euripides
and will challenge him if Aeschylus loses the present contest. It is
decided to make Dionysus the judge. Although he was originally in
favor of Euripides, he is the patron god of drama and should be unbiased enough to listen to reason, a situation not unlike that in the
Wasps, where the old dicasts decide the *agon* in favor of their acknowledged opponent. In the *Frogs* the Chorus does not have the
judicial position, and it is not, as sometimes, one of the parties to the
dispute; it is used solely to encourage the rivals and to clarify their
arguments. It is composed of Mystics, who on their entrance celebrate the ritual of the sacred procession to Eleusis and in a much ab-
breviated *parabasis* express their opinion that citizens who had been
disenfranchised for a single political mistake should receive the vote
again, now that it has been given to the slaves who fought at Argi-
nusae. The lack of coherent relationship between the Chorus of the
Frogs and the rest of the play is a sign that, at this time, the function
of the Chorus in comedy was rapidly shrinking and a warning that
its prominence might soon be still further reduced. Without the
songs of the Mystics the *Frogs* would lose some of its most beautiful
poetry but the debate between Aeschylus and Euripides could very
well have gone on just as it does.

Euripides, in the role of plaintiff, opens his case brilliantly. He objects that Aeschylus has introduced into his tragedies silent veiled figures, elaborate choral odes, and unwieldy compound words, while he himself has toned down his vocabulary, showed scenes of common life, and encouraged his audience to attempt to solve the problems that arise in everyday experience. This program is just what Aeschylus criticizes, for he claims that, by debasing mankind and humanizing the divine, Euripides has set a bad example of impiety and skepticism to the Athenian public. The combatants, having thus canvassed their general theories, then take up particular details, like the technique of prologues and choral songs. Ultimately there is a contest over the weight of the two poets' lines, during which a pair of scales is brought on the stage to weigh them. In this absurd test Aeschylus is of course overwhelmingly successful, because his ponderous philosophizings are obviously heavier than the delicate fancies of Euripides.

The artistic merits of the two dramatists are so nearly equal that Dionysus is puzzled as to which has the better claim to superiority, and, in accordance with Aristophanes' fundamental social principles, he proposes a question based on subject matter rather than on form: what does each contestant think of Alcibiades, now for the second time in exile? Euripides speaks enigmatically against this once idolized Athenian, Aeschylus halfheartedly in his favor. Dionysus is still uncertain and asks what plan each has to offer for the safety of the state. Euripides eagerly gives the negative advice that the opposite course to the one then being pursued would be the best; Aeschylus reluctantly states his belief that Athens should trust in its ships, which are its true wealth. This was exactly the counsel of Pericles in the good old days, and it meets with the approval of Dionysus, who now speaks with the tongue of Aristophanes. He decided that Aeschylus is the victor and bears him away in triumph to the upper world, while Euripides, whom he had come to seek, falls to the ground discomfited, as Cleon did at the end of the *Knights*. Sophocles is left to sit temporarily on the vacant throne of Hades. It is implied that, although he is inferior in grandeur to Aeschylus, he is also free from the extravagances likely to accompany an excess of inspiration.

Such is the comic dramatist's conclusion as to the comparative merit of the three great Greek tragedians, a conclusion which is arrived at only after much buffoonery and satire, but which depends fundamentally upon the differing points of view that they take toward contemporary public affairs. For Aristophanes the time was out of joint, and he looked backwards toward the golden age of Athens for the fulfillment of his romantic dreams. Compare the heroism of the Persian Wars with the pettiness of that now being waged against Sparta. Compare the glorious leaders of the past, like Miltiades and Aristides, with the pitiful insufficiency of Cleon and other demagogues. Compare Aeschylus and Sophocles with Socrates and Euripides in the realms of art and thought. It is plain that, on the whole, Aristophanes despaired of finding a solution for the immediate difficulties of Athens. He realized, too, that, much as he might have preferred to live in an earlier historical period, it is not possible for any individual to turn back the wheel of destiny. His way out of this dilemma was to create by the poetic imagination a dream world, as he did when he dramatized the attempt to found a model community in the Kingdom of the Birds.

Cloud-Cuckoo-Land met with the complete success that all such airy undertakings can achieve in the realm of the imagination, but its triumph seems somewhat unsubstantial when viewed in the harsh light of physical reality. Freedom from the material restrictions of finite time and space is the glory of all artistic effort, but the abuse of this freedom is also its besetting weakness, as may be seen in Aristophanes' literary development. The comedies written after the Birds have greater clarity of vision but much less dynamic power than the early ones which were completed before their author first formulated his plan for a Utopia. The audacity of the Lysistrata does not conceal its lack of confidence, the gaiety of the Thesmophoriazusae does not alter the triviality of its central theme, and the variety of the Frogs does not compensate for its diffusenesss. All three of these plays show some evidences of technical originality, but their distinctive characteristics were to appear to still better advantage in the two doctrinaire comedies that have come down to us from the last period of Aristophanes' dramatic career.

V

Twelve or thirteen years elapsed between the triumphant production of the Frogs and the first performance, in 393–392 B.C., of the Ecclesiazusae ("The Women in the Assembly"), years in which

Athens had fallen, the Long Walls had been destroyed and rebuilt, the Thirty Tyrants had arisen and been defeated, Socrates had been condemned to death, and Plato had outlined at least a portion of his ideal commonwealth as it exists for us today in the pages of the *Republic*. The *Republic* had probably not yet been completed in its present form, but Aristophanes seems to have been conversant with many of its leading ideas and to have put them to daring use in the *Ecclesiazusae*. Perhaps he felt that it was time for his comedies to descend from the Clouds and the Kingdom of the Birds, in order to point out to men more directly the path which they should travel if they intended to preserve the remnants of their shattered civilization from the inroads of barbarism. Furthermore, the demoralization in Athenian politics made specific references to living individuals much more dangerous to the community than they had been in the prosperous days when it was customary to scatter personal abuse freely throughout the *parabasis* of an Old Comedy. Now the Chorus was no longer allowed to step out of its dramatic role and address the audience on intimate terms, with the result that the application of comic principles to local conditions had to be managed in a devious, often an elusive, way.

Aristophanes himself seems to have been divided in his own mind about his artistic mission during the composition of his last plays. No doubt his own increasing age and the difficulties of the situation around him in Athens united to produce the strange combination of resignation and superficiality that can be detected in his latest comedies, where he is principally concerned with general theories and the remote possibility that they might some day be applied to ordinary life. In these circumstances it was not unnatural for Aristophanes to adopt the ideas of Plato, which were doubtless widely current in the Athens of that time, and to imagine that they had been literally put into practice by the government of the city. It was also entirely logical, from a topsy-turvy point of view, for the comic poet to imagine that such perfection would have to depend ultimately upon the contrivances of women.

Praxagora, the leader of the Assembly, in the *Ecclesiazusae*, is the direct successor of Lysistrata in advocating that women should control Athenian politics. Instead of using the peculiar strength of her own sex to attain her ends, as Lysistrata did, Praxagora obtains the power by disguising herself and her followers as men and then persuading the Assembly to try an idealistic feminine experiment. She rehearses her arguments among the women before the formal legislative meeting takes place, touching lightly upon certain elements in the contemporary scene which Aristophanes regarded as the flagrant abuses of Greek civilization: the league against Sparta is unpopular; the three-obol fee for attending the Assembly is demoralizing; and the vacillation of the present government is notorious. Would it not be better, on the whole, for the men to hand over public affairs to the women, who are conservative by nature and clever in compensating for their physical inferiority? The disguised Chorus gleefully assent to Praxagora's arguments. Swept away by enthusiasm for their cause, they carry her motion through the Assembly with an overwhelming number of votes.

It remains to be seen in what the "conservatism" of the women will consist. The meaning of this term, which Praxagora explains in an argument with her husband about the new government, turns out to be quite different from what one might have expected. To Aristophanes, a conservative because he disapproved so strongly of the deplorable tendencies of his own time, a return to the past meant a return only to the best things in the past. Just as the democracy of the *Birds* is a perfect democracy, so the conservatism of Praxagora is a perfect conservatism, an attempt to reach far back into history for ideal conditions and, by putting them into practice, to restore the golden age again to earth. In this way the ultraconservatism of the comic poet joins hands with the ultraradicalism of the philosopher, extreme political views seem to meet, and Aristophanes can offer, as Praxagora's program, proposals that are almost identical with those made by Plato in the *Republic*. If anything, they go a little farther, for Praxagora sponsors a communistic system for all Athenians except the slaves. Property, both personal and real, is to be owned in common, with the government furnishing food and maintenance for all. Husbands and wives are to be held in common, with the provision that the ugly must be loved before the beautiful can be enjoyed. On these two points hangs Praxagora's entire gospel, which also teaches that lawsuits and gambling are to be abolished, that there is to be complete ignorance of one's parentage, and that there will be throughout the community a consequent increase in benevolent and constructive philanthropy.

Although it has generally been said that Aristophanes mentioned these hopes only in order to ridicule them, such a hypothesis does not seem to be warranted. Absurdities are bound to arise in the practical effort to work out any idealistic program, and a comic dramatist would be the last person in the world to neglect to make use of them. Lysistrata's plan had had its obvious inconveniences, and yet no one would assert that Aristophanes had not wholeheartedly supported the attempt to do away with war. Likewise, Praxagora's scheme must be given serious consideration, even if the method of putting it into effect appears at certain points crude and undignified. It is amusing to see the women in the *Ecclesiazusae* adorning themselves with beards and tanning the color of their skins, or to watch the men dressed in their wives' clothes, particularly when occupied in the most personal of domestic duties, but these are simply comic means to express the different attitudes held by the two sexes on both public and private matters and to put the men to shame. The most blatant absurdities in comedy are usually those that offend against some ideal, stated or implied, an ideal which in Aristophanes is set forth by the protagonist and which the Chorus sooner or later accepts in lyrical outbursts that reveal the poet's deepest feelings.

From the *Ecclesiazusae* some of the choruses have disappeared, if they were ever written, but it is clear from those which have come down to us that, from the start, Praxagora's companions enthusiastically favor their leader's plan, in spite of the many ludicrous situations in regard to money and sex that grow out of it. Of these Aristophanes makes full use in the second and episodic half of the play, ridiculing the superficial follies of people whose fundamental position he upholds. The *Ecclesiazusae* ends with a paean of rejoicing at the success of Praxagora's experiment and a word of advice from the Chorus to the judges, stating that this play should be considered wise as well as amusing. It concludes, in the vein of Aristophanes' other dramatic works, with universal exultation over an improved condition in society, not with mocking laughter at a heroic attempt to point the way toward a brighter future for mankind.

Praxagora's experiment is conducted on a purely rational basis, which makes it at once both less charming than the fantastic proposal of the *Birds* and less convincing than the divine portents that come to the assistance of the virtuous in Aristophanes' last play, the *Plutus*, performed in 388. In this swan song of the Old Comedy, Chremylus, the protagonist, enlists the aid of two gods, Apollo and Asclepius, in his desire to keep his son on the straight and narrow path. Chremylus has always lived honestly himself, but, as he has gained nothing by doing so, he decides that he will attempt to alter human institutions in the interests of morality. He finds that Plutus, the god of wealth, is a blind old man, made incapable by Zeus of recognizing good from evil, and he undertakes to cure this physical infirmity, in spite of the fact that Wealth himself fears to encounter the wrath of Zeus, the jealous lord of things as they are. The god of riches has to be convinced that he has greater resources at his command than the ruler of Olympus and that, if he could see, he would make a far more just and powerful king. Zeus's unfairness and weakness had already been touched on in the *Birds*. Here, in the *Plutus*, Aristophanes seems to say even more straightforwardly that it is high time for a new theology, which should assist in reforming present abuses and in developing a more idealistic attitude toward human affairs.

This new idealism Aristophanes associates as usual with the return to a simpler, more primitive way of life. His counsel of perfection is always conservative in its nature, as can be seen when in the *Plutus* he selects a group of needy old farmers to be the Chorus. Throughout all his plays, from the *Banqueters* and the *Acharnians* on, country people are held up to admiration because they keep the old traditions purer and more undefiled than do the restless citizens of Athens. The Chorus of the *Plutus*, which is even less important than that in the *Ecclesiazusae*, has very little connection with the action of the piece, but the quality of the persons who compose it bears witness to the fact that there is a basic unity in Aristophanes' work, in spite of the numerous inconsistencies that appear upon the surface of it. It deals at different times with different subjects in a variety of artistic forms, but at bottom there is always a steady and continuous protest against the trends of city life in politics, in philosophy, in literature, and in social relationships at large.

In the *Plutus* the chief opponent of the protagonist and hence the chief apologist for existing economic conditions is the goddess

Poverty herself. She offers Chremylus a logical and impassioned argument to justify her own position, which is in great danger as the result of his novel experiment. If all good men become rich, all men will become good, and poverty will perish with vice. Ideally this is a noble theory, but how will it work out in practice? Poverty explains that, if wealth is made common to all, no one will work in either the arts or the sciences, and each man will have a much more painful life than he ever had under the old dispensation. She contrasts the decency of the poor with the miseries of beggars and the bloated arrogance of the rich. In short, she states all the neat and limited arguments which can be advanced against any proposal for economic change, even if it might bring about a marked improvement in human welfare. What is more, she outargues Chremylus, as the intellectually keen frequently outwit pure idealists, and she would have won the debate if it had been decided upon purely rational grounds. Chremylus, however, will not be persuaded against his will, and he drives Poverty from the stage in disgrace. He is still determined to effect a just distribution of wealth, which it may be impossible to achieve in real life, but which by sheer force of the imagination Aristophanes establishes in the mimic world of his comedy.

The machinery by which this financial revolution is accomplished in the *Plutus* is to have Wealth pass the night inside the temple of Asclepius and there take part in an elaborate ritual by means of which his sight is restored. The process is described at length by Chremylus' slave, who succeeds in stealing for his own use a portion of the broth that had been intended for the god. He recounts his exploit to his master's wife, and she is as naïvely horrified by the slave's impudence as she is properly impressed by the god's miraculous powers. This domestic scene between the servant and his mistress is an amusing bit of incidental genre painting, and it also advances the play's action by giving the audience some necessary information. It takes the place of a formal announcement of events which have occurred off the stage, like that often to be found in a messenger's speech, substituting for this artificial convention of Greek drama a piece of realistic dialogue based upon firsthand observation. The social comment in this scene is slight and vague, but its novel features were to become extremely important in subsequent modifications of the technique and subject matter used by dramatic comedy. For the time being, its function is to delight Chremylus' wife with the success of her husband's experiment and to herald the dawn of a new order, which like Praxagora's Utopia will not be without its temporary embarrassments as to finances and relations between the sexes.

Chremylus' innovation is on the whole a satisfactory one, however, and in the end it meets with the same success that attended the establishment of Cloud-Cuckoo-Land. As, in the earlier play, Heracles capitulated to the Birds because the Olympians had been cut off from the sweet aroma of sacrifices to which they were accustomed, so Hermes, in the *Plutus*, finds that people no longer give tribute to Zeus but to Wealth and begs to be received into the service of the new divinity. His request is granted, not because he is the god of commerce and craftiness, qualifications which have no place in an ideal community, but because he is the god of games, and men must have some recreations with which to fill their leisure time. In addition, a Priest of Zeus, who is anxious to desert his master and join the new organization, finds that Zeus himself has succumbed to the strongest force in the world and already offered his allegiance to Wealth. All that remains is to replenish the exhausted treasury at Athens and thus to apply the abstract principles of the situation to the demands of contemporary politics. Politics, however, is relegated to the distant background of this play, which in spite of its divine machinery is concerned with morals more than with religion and therefore with the intricacies of social life more than with the larger issues of man's destiny upon the earth. As the importance of Chremylus' slave in the action of this play suggests, the Old Comedy was gradually shifting its material and its form into a new hybrid product, to be known as Middle Comedy.

VI

The change in the form and matter of comedy that took place during Aristophanes' lifetime may be seen in an extreme form by comparing the *Acharnians* with the *Plutus*. It goes much deeper than the abolition of *parabasis* and the inevitable reduction in the importance of the Chorus which accompanied that suppression. It goes deeper than the increased part played by slaves and their antics in the later dramas, although that is a logical effect of the alteration. Its essence is an enlargement in the scope of the dramatist's subjects, which, in turn, opened up possibilities of new technique. In its earliest form comedy was an informal dramatization of local comment and criticism, arising out of temporary conditions in the community where it was acted. When Aristophanes began to write, it was much the same sort of thing, slightly developed to provide the structure necessary for a permanent work of art: there had to be the sympathetic protagonist and his rival to engage in a formal debate, always to be won by the author's favorite; there had to be the Chorus to discuss this conflict and sometimes to share in it, but always on the right side; there had to be a working-out section to show through incidents suited to the stage the results of the protagonist's victory; and there had to be a triumphant conclusion related to the satisfactory upshot of the plot. This was the skeleton of the original formula, which was first applied to attacks upon particular abuses and then extended to embrace theoretical remedies for universal injustices. Beginning as sharp personal invective, in a loosely integrated series of topical hits, comedy came to be used with more disinterestedness and with greater artistic invention as an index to the chronic foibles of organized society. The *Plutus* is as different from the *Birds* as the *Birds* is from the *Acharnians*, but the *Birds* binds the two types of drama together and must be considered the central event in the history of Old Comedy.

After Aristophanes came the so-called Middle Comedy and then New Comedy. Middle Comedy, which flourished roughly during the fifty years between the *Plutus* and the conquest of Greece by the Macedonians in 338 B.C., was probably something like that play with its original features still further elaborated. We know little about it except that it rarely employed a Chorus, that it was prone to burlesque mythological stories and old-fashioned beliefs, and that it often introduced such typical characters as the clever servant, the boastful cook, and the talkative woman. New Comedy went still further in the same technical direction, abandoning altogether the Chorus with its poetry, reducing the superhuman element to a minimum, and enlarging the range of characters to include any figures that could be frequently observed in everyday life. In other words, the movement in comedy was away from the rhapsodic and poetic toward the critical and the prosaic. A form much nearer our modern social comedy arose, concerned more and more with the affairs of this world and without Aristophanes' powerful combination of idealism and horseplay.

Horseplay can never be wholly absent from comedy, however, and some form of idealism is always implied in its ridicule. Misunderstandings, mistakes in identity, and the ingenious use of language for puns and double meanings are to be found in New Comedy as well as in Old. In New Comedy, too, a kind of distorted idealism is present under the surface. It is hard to explain the conventional happy ending which occurs in New Comedy as anything but a bowdlerization of the final victorious celebrations that take place in Aristophanes' plays, celebrations in which food, drink, and a union of the sexes remind one constantly of the drama's origin in early religious ritual. In New Comedy there is seldom any intervention of divine powers in the affairs of men to make the will of the gods prevail, but the most extraordinary coincidences bring about a harmonious solution of incongruous events and awkward complications. The complications caused by the exchange of children in infancy, by the confusion of identity that might occur under peculiar circumstances, and by the mounting cross-purposes of human delusions are frequently straightened out in a recognition scene, which is quite incredible unless one remembers that it represents the survival of a belief that occasionally the gods are moved to interfere in the affairs of men. The treatment of sex follows a similar line of development, with less emphasis on the social and more on the personal side of the question; a general union of men and women for the purpose of glorifying fertility and propagation gradually gave place in comedy to a highly individualized and romantic love story.

VII

Evidently the technique which we associate today with dramatic comedy had become vaguely formulated in Athens soon after the Macedonian conquest of Greece, for it was at hand to be used by Menander, who lived from about 343 to 291 B.C. In the hundred years after the first performance of the Plutus both Middle and New Comedy had been born, had reached their highest points, and had begun to decline. For both of them Aristophanes must be given a considerable share of the credit, although the influence of Euripides can also be distinctly detected. The humanitarian spirit of Euripides breathes through the fragments of Menander's plays that have come down to us, but they lack the lofty inspiration that Aristophanes admired in Aeschylus. Whatever the misfortunes of the characters, one is conscious that they will come out all right in the end, and therefore one is diverted rather than seriously distressed by them. In what is probably his best known line Menander wrote, "He whom the gods love dies young," but in his plays few people seem to die at any age. His audience must have been more sentimentally than profoundly moved by the human suffering which he depicts. Its members were no doubt happy to relapse at last into a mood which was less hilarious, but no less contented, than that which dominated the end of a comedy by Aristophanes.

It is extremely difficult to generalize about Menander because we know so little of his life and works. He is supposed to have written over one hundred plays within about thirty-three years, but no one of his comedies has come down to us with its text complete. We must judge him, as best we can, from a large number of disconnected fragments, from the Latin plays in which Plautus and Terence some hundred years later imitated his work, and from a few substantial consecutive passages which give us a passable idea of the main action in three of his comedies. These three, the *Epitrepontes* ("Those Who Submit Their Case to Arbitration"), the *Periceiromene* ("The Girl Whose Hair Is Cut Off"), and the *Girl from Samos*, resemble one another enough for us to feel that they must be fairly representative of Menander's literary art. The chief thing that one notices about them is the narrowness of their range compared with the variety of material in Aristophanes. There is a marked similarity between these three examples of New Comedy in plot, in characterization, and in general atmosphere. The distinction between them lies in the ingenuity with which stereotyped characters are combined in conventional situations and the delicacy with which the predicaments of the various persons are expressed in the neatest and most finely modulated words. Menander is one of those artists in miniature who make up for the limitation of their canvas by the exquisite precision with which every detail in the whole design is arranged. The weakness of such work, particularly in the realm of dramatic comedy, is a tendency to emphasize external trivialities at the expense of underlying problems, like those that had engrossed Aristophanes in an earlier and more vital period of Athenian history.

By Menander's time Greece was firmly under the heel of the Macedonian conqueror. The people he describes were no longer fired with ambition to pluck glory from heroic exploits. As Menander depicts them, they were satisfied to fill their time with minor personal troubles and the moments of relief which provide excellent material for comedies of contrasting social manners. The chief cause of anxiety, to judge from these comedies, was the unfounded jealousy that played havoc with many a household, not always one based on the union of man and wife; Athenian citizens, not being permitted to marry outside their own class, sometimes contracted perfectly respectable alliances with women who were foreigners or foundlings. A free and easy relationship between the sexes, with little sense of general social responsibility, is one of the distinguishing features of Menander's comedies, in which all sorts of irregular love affairs seem to have been accepted as a matter of course. People lived together quite openly when they were not formally married, and unwanted children were exposed to the elements by parents who wished to abandon them, a situation which is frequently of great importance in the plots of Menander.

It is the reactions of various characters to the highly colored events of their lives, not the events themselves, which give Menander's work its peculiar quality. The *Epitrepontes*, for instance, contains a rather careful analytical study of the question whether men and women should be subjected to the same moral standard in matters of sex. The young husband has been horrified to learn that his wife had had a child five months after their marriage, and he is too conventional to face the fact honestly. Instead he embarks upon a course of wild dissipation as a sort of compensation for the wrong that has been done him. Later, when he finds that he himself is the father of the child in question, he is plunged into the depths of gloomy self-abasement. His uneasy sensibility is very different from the hotheaded but decisive temper of the young soldier in the *Periceiromene*, who when he suspects his mistress of infidelity quickly draws his sword and angrily cuts off her hair, or from the uncontrollable fury of the middle-aged householder in the *Girl from Samos*, whose illusions about women have been shattered because he thinks that his generosity to the heroine has been abused. These three plays are studies in contrasting types of jealousy, and in each case the jealousy proves to have been ridiculous because it was founded upon a misapprehension. If we may take the fragments we have of these dramas as exemplifying fairly well their author's attitude toward his characters, we can draw the conclusion that, although he is conscious of human defects, he is anxious to make every possible allowance for them. Jealousy may bring out the worst side of a noble nature, but under favorable circumstances man's better impulses will assert themselves and in time adversity will give place to a more congenial environment.

Menander seems to have been of a predominantly optimistic disposition; at least, he composed cheerful comedies. It was perhaps lucky for him that he lacked the deep penetration necessary to probe into the heart of large social issues and that he possessed the broad human sympathy which enabled him to enter into the personal problems immediately before his eyes. He excelled at picturing romantic young men and women. His portraits of them give a delightfully sunny tinge to his plays, which, because they deal so much with buoyant youth, are deficient in the strictly critical spirit of comedy. Besides the romantic lovers there are many other types of people in these dramas, most of them decidedly ingratiating if not always impeccable in conduct. It is a varied group of characters that Menander sets before us, but it may be observed that the persons in his plays fall into definite categories as those in the great Greek comedies rarely do. In Aristophanes the protagonist can always be easily recognized, and there is rarely any doubt as to where the author's sympathies lie, with the result that his figures become symbolic of social forces rather than typical of social classes. Menander's broader but less judicious tolerance made him an admirable creator of character but hardly a first-rate comic dramatist.

A steady social point of view is necessary for the writer of comedy if he is to see clearly and express vigorously what is ridiculous in human activity and how it might be remedied. This intellectual stability Aristophanes had, and he carried his work to its logical extreme with withering scorn and devastating effect. Sometimes he cloaked his meaning so subtly that it is difficult for us to disentangle it, but he never swerved from what must have seemed to him a consistent and sensible set of principles. Like all reasonable people, however, he altered his ground slightly from time to time. He attacked Cleon, when he felt that a demagogic dictator like Cleon was representative of the worst tendencies of the time; he did not hesitate to ridicule his friend Socrates, when he thought that a subversive theorist like Socrates was a disturbing influence upon the youth of the day; he poked gentle fun at Euripides, when contemporary poetry like that of Euripides seemed to him, for all its undeniable charm, more flashy than sound. Throughout his entire lifetime he bitterly opposed any war which he considered petty in its motives or brutal in its methods.

As Aristophanes progressed in his career, he gradually took higher and higher ground until he ascended into the airy regions of Cloud-Cuckoo-Land, in much the same way that Shakespeare followed the flight of Ariel beyond the cloud-capped towers of this transitory world. Then, when he could go no farther in three-dimensional space, the Greek dramatist attempted to apply his ideals literally to practical affairs, and he ended by dreaming wistfully that Plato's Utopian Republic had been established on the unsteady foundation of his own Athens. Here the absurdities thrust themselves forward so violently that Aristophanes might have seemed to be undermining the values which all his life he had most striven to support. At any rate, he was preparing the way for a better balanced and more human type of comedy, the remains of which are preserved in the fragments of Menander. Obviously it did not have the Old Comedy's vigor and drive as social criticism, or its poetic beauty, or its brilliant stagecraft, but within narrower limits it appears to have had a poise and serenity which the work of Aristophanes often lacked. It was less concerned with burning public problems than with the limitations of private citizens, which it exhibited but on which it passed no arbitrary judgment. It may not be permeated with the sane detachment which characterizes comic drama of the first order, but it was the natural consequence of Aristophanes' descent to earth in the last phase of his writing for the theater. The themes it contained were to be reworked, always with new variations, by Plautus and Terence and their literary descendants during the course of two thousand years.

CHAPTER II

Roman Imitators: Plautus and Terence

I

LESS THAN a hundred years elapsed between the death of Menander and the beginning of the career of Titus Maccius Plautus. During this period the glory that was Greece became much dimmed, and the grandeur that was to be Rome commenced to shine with noticeable brightness. Latin took the place of Greek as the dominant language of the western world, but Greek art and literature were still supreme as masterpieces and as models. It is not surprising that Latin authors began their work in imitation of their Greek predecessors, or that Plautus and Terence depended for their inspiration largely upon the comedies of Menander and his contemporaries. The literary, or *palliata*, comedy of the Romans laid its scene in Greece, and in it Greek customs were overlaid with bits of Roman local color.

The exact degree of this similarity is difficult to determine, since we do not possess a single complete play by Menander, although we have twenty of the mythical hundred and thirty by Plautus as well as all six comedies left by Publius Terentius Afer when, at the age of about thirty, he set out on the sea voyage from which he never returned. It is true that the *Mother-in-Law* ("Hecyra") of Terence has a plot extraordinarily like that of the most extended fragment by Menander, the *Epitrepontes*; that four of Terence's five other comedies seem to be taken from one, or sometimes two, of Menander's plays; and that of Plautus the *Bacchides* ("The Bacchises") and perhaps the *Stichus* come from the same source. On the other hand, the debt of the Latin writers to Diphilus, to Philemon, and to Apollodorus, although acknowledged, is still more shadowy, and we have not enough of Menander's work to determine how much of what we accept as Plautine or Terentian should be credited to him. We may safely say, however, that he is responsible for the general outlines of Roman comedy, with its emphasis upon the ludicrous adventures that may befall ordinary people in an ordinary world.

When comedy left the fantastic realm of Aristophanes, where'in politics it had become dangerous and in philosophy it had become abstract, it seized upon the momentary happiness of young lovers as the only suitable substitute for its previous jubilant hilarity. The obstructions to such happiness must be met by ridicule, and the enemies of it must be tricked and deceived, if necessary, until every Jack shall have his Jill and all shall be well. In this way there arose the convention of the romantic ending, which in later times developed into having the actors pair off and stand in a neat semicircle before the falling curtain. The irrelevant question of whether the various couples lived happily ever afterwards is one to be treated by a dramatic art more sophisticated than that to which Plautus and Terence attained. They did not have any hesitation in presenting elderly husbands and wives in uncomfortable situations, but to their minds domestic difficulties had no connection with the moment of radiance in which the actors stepped from their parts and asked the audience to applaud the particular play that had just been played out. The Latin dramatists had not yet reached the point of showing the lovers in each other's arms, but they had learned from their predecessors, who had gathered it from Aristophanes, that universal rejoicing was needed at the end of a comedy, and in this uneven world there is never more general joy than that which surrounds marrying and giving in marriage.

The progress of a romantic love affair constitutes the plot of most Roman comedies and may be regarded as the mainspring of their action. To this scheme there were, however, certain hindrances, the most important having to do with the status of the heroine. Since Latin comedy was conventionally represented as taking place out-of-doors in a public street, and since Roman, like Greek, girls were seldom allowed to mix freely in the life of the outside world, it was a difficult technical matter for Plautus and Terence to give leading parts to their respectable heroines. This problem the dramatists solved in a variety of ways: the most common expedient was to make the young lady a freewoman, stolen from her parents in childhood, who has fallen into the hands of a slave-merchant; sometimes she is a freewoman who has been violated in the confusion of a religious festival; at other times she is a slave-girl, for whom there can be no question of marriage with a Roman citizen but merely an uncertainty as to which lover shall temporarily possess her. In any case, the efforts of a young man to secure the person of a girl whom he loves occupy the primary attention of the dramatist, and the lovers are seldom already married when the play begins. The exception to this rule is the play by Plautus which most closely resembles what we imagine the Middle Comedy of the Greeks to have been like; the *Amphitryon* ("Amphitruo") deals with impediments to the continued welfare of a happily married husband and wife.

We have very little definite information about the exact chronology of Plautus' twenty comedies. The earliest date suggested for any of them is 214 B.C., and 184 has been generally accepted as the year of Plautus' death. Ordinarily no attempt has been made to arrange the plays in chronological order, and they are usually listed alphabetically, beginning with the *Amphitryon* and ending with the fragment of a twenty-first comedy, the *Vidularia* ("The Comedy of the Traveling-Bag"). Logically as well as alphabetically the *Amphitryon* comes first in Plautus' work. Its main complications are caused by the intervention of a divinity, and as no other gods appear in Plautus' plays, except for an occasional prologue figure, the *Amphitryon* alone belongs to the legendary world of Middle Comedy. Jupiter and Mercury are the supernatural agents, and it is a coincidence that both these characters take part in the *Plutus* of Aristophanes. In neither play do they appear to great advantage: in Aristophanes, Zeus and Hermes are represented as capitulating to the new order established by Wealth; in Plautus, Jupiter and Mercury are engaged in most undignified adventures.

The laughter in the *Plutus* is at the expense of imperfections in human society, that in the *Amphitryon* is directed at a pair of lovers, and therein lies the chief difference between Old and New Comedy. The restricted range of the Latin playwright is evident from the fact that his gods are not merely subjected to a power higher than themselves but are degraded to taking part in a low love intrigue. At the end of the piece the purpose of the legend, which is intended to explain Jupiter's parentage of Hercules, emerges for an instant, but the glory of the demigods, those supermen in whose begetting divinity took part, is almost disregarded for the sake of showing the ridiculous plight of the mortals involved in the affair. The *Amphitryon* is rather like a Christian play on the Nativity with the emphasis upon Joseph's comic position in the story and with repeated visitations from the Holy Ghost. Plautus frankly disavows all serious intentions and reveals himself as a professional comedian, whose sole purpose in writing his plays is to entertain an exacting audience. That he felt slightly uncomfortable with his divine material is clear from the elaborate way in which the Prologue describes the piece as a tragicomedy, or *tragicomoedia*, but the tragic element implied in it is subordinated by making the gods involved act quite like ordinary mortals.

The comic side of the plot is carried out and intensified by a nice alternation of the visits from husband and masquerading god. Amphitryon and Jupiter disguised as Amphitryon (with a gold tassel on his hat to mark the difference for the audience) appear successively to the troubled Alcmena, and at last both men stand side by side, each claiming to be her true husband. In addition, as if this confusion were not ridiculous enough, Plautus makes still further play with Mercury disguised as the slave Sosia. In Mercury and Sosia we have the two typical roles played by low-life servants in New Comedy: Mercury is the mischief-making assistant of the lover; Sosia is the cowardly, lazy, drunken slave, impudent when all is going well with him, grumbling because he has to work hard, and cringing before inevitable beatings from his master. The fact that into Sosia's mouth is put an extended humorous account of Amphitryon's heroic victory indicates to what lengths Plautus was willing to go for the sake of comic effects. Not even the sufferings of the noble Alcmena raise the *Amphitryon* above the level of farcical intrigue; in that respect it is typical of Plautus' whole activity in the theater.

The other play by Plautus which depends solely upon a misunderstanding is the *Menaechmi* ("The Menaechmuses"), as well known to modern readers from Shakespeare's use of it in *The Comedy of Errors* as is the *Amphitryon* from its thirty-eight versions through Molière to Jean Giraudoux. The *Menaechmi* dispenses with divine machinery, unless the appearance of identical twins on this world's stage can be considered as a supernatural event. The two Menaechmuses look as much alike as Amphitryon and Jupiter and cause as much trouble by their alternate interviews with wife, courtesan, and parasite. The complications caused by mistaken identity accumulate, until, in the lengthy last act, there are doubts of the husband's sanity and confusion over the brother's slave, from the latter of which (or from Mercury and Sosia) Shakespeare took a hint for his addition to the story of the twin Dromios. The resolution is brought about as in the *Amphitryon* by the simultaneous appearance of the doubles, but one striking difference between these two dramas may be noted. Jupiter was aware of the deception and revealed it with divine machinery at the end of the play; neither Menaechmus understands the cross-purposes in which he is involved, and not until the brothers are confronted can their entanglements be naturally straightened out. The humorous possibilities of twinship are alone responsible for the logic and clarity of this justly famous comedy.

All that is needed to execute the plot successfully is a certain hardness in the characters of the Menaechmuses, which contrasts vividly with the good intentions of the Shakespearean Antipholuses, but which is quite in accordance with the comic tradition of healthy social criticism. The brother is anxious to benefit as much as possible from hospitable strangers, and the husband steals from his shrewish wife; the courtesan and the parasite live up to their professional reputations for greed and gluttony; even the courtesan's maid and a doctor (the only one to appear in Plautus' plays) are chiefly concerned with how to profit from their strategic positions at little cost to themselves. This gallery of self-seeking characters, among whom not a single noble soul is to be found, is in direct contrast with the kindliness that pervades Menander's work, but it bears out Aristotle's dictum that the ludicrous consists in some defect or ugliness that is not painful or destructive. In the *Menaechmi* no just person, but chance itself, is the means by which the ludicrous is shown to be a subdivision of the ugly. When the artificial basis of the plot has been accepted, fate plays its tricks upon the characters, who because of their grasping natures deserve to be ridiculed.

Apart from the predatory atmosphere of the *Menaechmi*, the play is principally concerned with the relations between husband and wife. The Menaechmus ménage is very different from the idyllic domesticity of Amphitryon and Alcmena before the intrusion of Jupiter. Menaechmus considers his wife an inquisitive, faultfinding virago, and he has certainly given her cause for complaint by his eager attentions to the courtesan. His father-in-law defends him, however, and blames his own daughter for the pride which he thinks that her dowry has given her. One would conclude from the father-in-law's testimony that Plautus' sympathies were chiefly with Menaechmus, if it were not necessary to remember that married men are expected to stand together. Wives may be jealous and ill-tempered, but husbands are apt to rove afield; we should have liked to know what Menaechmus' mother-in-law thought about the rights and wrongs of her daughter's position. As it is, the dramatist expounds the two sides of marital friction and furnishes amusement to both husbands and wives in his audience. He does not support warmly either party to the dispute but lets the misunderstandings of the plot gall Menaechmus and his wife alike.

II

Occasionally the dramatist can hit upon a perfectly balanced comic situation like that in the *Menaechmi*. More frequently he must take sides in the dramatic conflict in order to evolve complications and to reveal absurdities. The relationship between Menaechmus and his wife is repeated many times in Plautus' plays, never more entertainingly than in that uproarious and indelicate farce, the *Casina*. In this piece the husband is anxious to marry the slave-girl Casina to his bailiff, that he himself may have an affair with her. His wife, who is no more kind and sympathetic than Menaechmus', prevents her spouse's intended liaison by disguising a man as the bride, with the result that both the husband and the bailiff suffer humorous indignities in prosecuting their love affairs. The husband's unfaithfulness is openly disclosed to his wife, who grants him her pardon rather abruptly, that, as she says, "we may not make this long play longer." The husband's amorous inclinations are exposed and punished to make a Roman holiday; the wife, however bad her disposition, is left complete mistress of the field.

She might easily have forfeited our sympathy, like the wife of Menaechmus, if it were not that her scheming serves a double purpose: it teaches her husband a much-needed lesson, and it helps her son in his love affair. The son is in love with the same girl as his father and wishes to marry her to his servant, so that he may have her within his power. The plans of father and son are exactly alike in substance, but the son's appears much less ridiculous because he is of a suitable age to engage in a love affair. Moreover, it is promised by both the Prologue and Epilogue that the slave-girl will turn out to be freeborn, so that after the play is over the son may be united to her in matrimony. This highly artificial outcome of the intrigue gives a satisfactory excuse for the father's undignified rivalry with his son; that it is only an excuse is clear from the circumstance that neither the son nor the slave-girl, the logical hero and heroine of the comedy, appears upon the stage. Plautus deliberately keeps them out of sight, because he is not interested in their affection except as an opportunity to make the father appear absurd. There could be no better illustration of the way in which Plautus uses romantic love as the core of his plots but puts his emphasis upon the comic plight of all those who oppose the union of two conventionalized lovers.

It is not possible for the hero to marry his young lady unless she turns out to be a legal citizen, but it is necessary for him to obtain possession of her if the proper rejoicing is to prevail at the end of a comedy. The Epilogue of the *Merchant* ("Mercator") makes an elaborate defense of a young man's procuring his mistress and at the same time ridicules the similar ambitions of old men. In this play, as in the *Casina*, father and merchant-son are rivals for the same girl, but here the father withdraws his attentions as soon as he learns of the son's feelings. The lovers, both of whom appear on the stage, are also sympathetically presented. Compared with the *Casina*, the *Merchant* gains in human tenderness what it loses in comic impartiality.

In the *Asinaria* ("The Comedy of the Asses") father and son are allies, or at least the son is compelled to accept the father's aid in obtaining his mistress. Money is needed for the transaction, as the heroine is the daughter of a mercenary bawd, and the first part of the play is taken up with the fraudulent sale of some asses, by means of which the required cash is procured. Two wily slaves are the father's agents in the transaction, which is successfully accomplished just as the young lovers, in despair, are threatening to kill themselves. The slaves watch the lovers with great amusement and then proceed to tease them unmercifully before handing over the required funds. They demand embraces from the girl as a reward for the money, and one of them in a farcical bit of boisterous horseplay makes his young master carry him about on his back. This entire episode shows how young lovers are at the mercy of clever slaves, who by their wanton trickery often furnish the chief entertainment in a Plautine comedy.

The *Asinaria*, curiously, breaks in two at this central scene of the play, and a new element enters the plot. It has already seemed strange, considering the usual antipathy between youth and age in Plautus, that the hero's father was willing to help his son secure a beautiful young girl. The father's ulterior motives are revealed when the slaves tell the lover that his father has sent him the money on condition that he himself be allowed one evening with the girl. The son reluctantly consents to this imposition, and we are treated to an amusing scene where the father enjoys himself at a banquet *à trois*, much to the disgust of the young lovers. Fortunately for them, the hero's disagreeable mother interrupts the proceedings and drags her husband home by the hair of his head, leaving the lovers together at last. They have had to suffer humiliations from the slaves and the lecherous old man, but in the end they have triumphed over all comic embarrassments.

The lovers in the *Bacchides* are not so fortunate. There are two heroes in this play, each in love with one of the Bacchis sisters, courtesans of dubious origin. One of the sisters has been hired to a captain, who demands his price if he is to release her from the engagement, a price that a clever slave ultimately secures by trickery from the hero's rich father. The slave's somewhat monotonous stratagems occupy the greater portion of this play, but in the last act it takes a turn quite as unexpected as that in the *Asinaria*. The fathers of the two heroes, having at last learned the true state of affairs, plan to remonstrate with the courtesans who have enticed the sons, and themselves fall victims to the charms of the Bacchises. The sons must have been somewhat annoyed at being compelled to share the favors of the courtesans with the fathers, but the Bacchises do not object to senile embraces, provided they are properly paid for. In the *Bacchides* the conventional happy ending for young lovers gives place to the triumph of two unscrupulous and mercenary women, a realistic conclusion with a slightly cynical tone which gives this drama its special pungency.

Four-fifths of the *Bacchides* deals with the efforts of a young man and his slave to get money for a love affair from his father, a situation which is frequently treated by Plautus. In the *Epidicus* the hero has two girls on his hands, and his slave, Epidicus, as well as the audience, has to make an effort to keep the entanglements clear. The hero turns his attentions from one girl to the other, only to find that the second girl is his long-lost sister, a discovery which necessitates a change in the nature of his feelings toward her. He reverts to his first lady as easily as he had apparently left her, but the *Epidicus* remains an unsatisfactory comedy because the romantic discovery of the sister's parentage has deflected the course of true love. Circumstances force upon the hero the unattractive role of a light-o'-love, and the slave who gives his name to the play triumphs incongruously by effecting the discovery rather than by ingeniously defrauding the hero's father of the money necessary for his son's complicated love affairs.

Tranio, the slave of the *Mostellaria* ("The Comedy of the Ghost"), has almost as hard a task as Epidicus. At first it appears easier, since it is not to obtain a mistress for his young master but to keep one who has already been secured. In his father's absence the hero has bought a slave-girl and turned the parental home into a scene of gay dissipation, which Tranio explains by saying that the house is haunted. This lie is successful for a time, but its consequences make final detection inevitable, and Tranio has not, like Epidicus, a romantic discovery to bring to his aid. He has courage, however, and at the end of the play he calmly takes refuge on an altar and explains to the old man just how he has been fooled. The conclusion of the *Mostellaria* is singularly ineffective. It depends upon the intervention of one of the son's friends, who persuades the father to forgive everyone, including the deceitful servant. Perhaps Plautus thought that the lie of the haunted house was sufficiently novel to make a logical ending to the elaborate intrigue superfluous.

The *Mostellaria* does not depend wholly upon its central idea for its success. It contains a large amount of interesting characterization, some of which is quite incidental to the plot. A country servant, who, in the first scene, denounces the demoralizing life of cities, is most vividly drawn, and one regrets that he figures only in the opening exposition.[1] The hero is introduced with a lyrical passage which

---

[1] This servant is called Grumio, a name to be used by Shakespeare (like Tranio also) for a servant in *The Taming of the Shrew*.

forms a link between Plautine comedy and the choral odes of Aristophanes; the comparison of man's body to a house is not exactly in keeping with the hero's character, but it fits remarkably well into a play largely concerned with human habitations. The heroine is an odd mixture of the noble courtesan of the *Asinaria* and the designing ones of the *Bacchides*; she is devoted to her lover, but she does not hesitate to adorn herself with the arts of a professional coquette. Her maid represents a more material point of view. She has been deserted by her lover in youth and has learned to her sorrow how shifting the impulses of men may be. A crusty old neighbor, interested in the possessions of his rich wife, is keenly, if slightly, sketched into the picture. Finally the hero's friend has a delightful drunken scene, which does not agree very well with his part in resolving the action but is one of the numerous evidences that the literary excellence of the *Mostellaria* consists far more in individual details than in the stereotyped plot of deceiving an old man.

III

The *Casina, Merchant,* and *Asinaria* are concerned with a son's getting a young lady away from his father; the *Bacchides, Epidicus,* and *Mostellaria* deal with extracting money for a love affair from a reluctant parent; in all six of these plays the older generation is set up as the main obstacle to youthful happiness and is ridiculed accordingly. Age appears absurd either when it tries to emulate youth or when it has fallen prey to the "good old-gentlemanly vice" of avarice; in both cases it is a proper target for the shafts of a comic dramatist. Plautus' lovers have also to face the opposition of two less universal types, the *leno*, a combination of slave-merchant and procurer, and the *miles gloriosus*, or boasting soldier. The latter corresponds to the successful business man who can afford to purchase a love that is inaccessible to the poverty-stricken hero; the former has its equivalent in the powerful relative who opposes a girl's marriage to anyone not well endowed with this world's goods. Since many of Plautus' heroines are slave-girls or courtesans, the part which in normal life would fall to the girl's parents is played by the *leno*, invariably represented as an odious person, whose mercenary aims stand in the way of love's fulfillment. The female of the species is shown in the *Asinaria*, and her male counterpart fills an important place in five of Plautus' other plays.

In the *Persian* ("Persa") there is such a person, a brutal, scheming fellow, whose desire to drive a shrewd bargain proves his undoing when he buys from a supposed Persian a mysterious slave-girl, who is really the freeborn daughter of an Athenian parasite. The girl has had enough experience of the world to realize the dangers of being sold to a *leno*, even temporarily and as part of a trick. She offers her father various good and sufficient reasons against the plan but at last dutifully capitulates to his insistence. During her interview with the *leno* she shows a delightful reluctance to tell an outright lie about her status and a skill with words that steers a middle course between deceit and truthfulness. The scenes in which she appears and the vivacious dialogue between a pert boy and a perter maid distinguish the *Persian* among Plautus' *leno* plays.

The *Young Carthaginian* ("Poenulus") is another comedy which depends upon the tricking of a *leno*. It is an incongruous mixture of intrigue and romance; in addition to the main plot, it contains the hero's uncle, Hanno, who is seeking his two lost daughters and ultimately finds them in the possession of the slave-merchant. The *Young Carthaginian* is composed of such divergent elements as satire upon Hanno's outlandish Carthaginian dialect and his wanton teasing of his daughters, set against the background of the father's wanderings and the Feast of the Aphrodisia which the girls have been attending. All these varied interests converge upon the overthrow of the *leno*, which furnishes the central theme of this lengthy play.

The *Rope* ("Rudens") is likewise a mixture of romance and intrigue, but in this case the slave-merchant plays a subordinate role. He is forced to hand over the girl whom he has dishonestly tried to keep from the hero, and he meets his match in trickery in the person of a greedy fisherman, from whom he parts with the honors in roguery evenly divided. He is treated with more mercy than the *leno* in either the *Persian* or the *Young Carthaginian*, as is suitable to the fairy-story mood that dominates the major portion of the *Rope*. Its scene is laid upon a rocky coast, with the exteriors of two buildings, the conventional background of classical comedy, visible upon the stage. One is the Temple of Venus, presided over by a dignified and benevolent priestess, the other the house of a hospitable old man, who turns out to be the father of the shipwrecked heroine and whose only pretense to serving as a comic character is that he has a jealous wife at home. His servant, who thinks that no woman can resist him, also provides incidental humor in a drama that would have been dominated by a heavy emotional atmosphere if it were not for the familiar situation of a *leno* worsted by his enemies.

The most detailed of Plautus' studies of the *leno* is Ballio in the *Pseudolus*. This slave-dealer's cold-blooded treatment of the human beings whose bodies he owns and his calculating mode of life are shown in loathsome detail. Although Ballio is strictly honest in his business dealings, the sympathy of the audience is roused against him and in favor of Pseudolus, the liar, who is to outwit him. The slave Pseudolus is more than a trickster; he is an artist in deceit. When caught in a quandary, he attempts to extricate himself by ingenious and imaginative lies, saying, "As a poet, when he takes his tablets, seeks what is nowhere in this world, yet finds it and makes what is false like the truth, so now I will become a poet."

> sed quasi poeta, tabulas quom cepit sibi,
> quaerit quod nusquam gentiumst, reperit tamen,
> facit illud veri simile, quod mendacium est,
> nunc ego poeta fiam.

The hero's father in the *Pseudolus* is an unusual figure, halfway between the censorious old gentlemen of the *Epidicus* and *Mostellaria* and the kindly graybeards of the *Young Carthaginian* and *Rope*. Simo has been a gay fellow in his youth and looks with understanding on his son's escapades, although he cannot bring himself to approve of them. He wins a bet of twenty minae from the *leno*, but he loses the same sum to Pseudolus, who succeeds in fooling both Ballio and Simo. Simo is superior in adroitness to the slave-merchant but inferior to the slave, at the end joining Pseudolus in an entertainment that is to be paid for out of the twenty minae; Ballio is utterly discredited and slinks out of sight before the rejoicing at his defeat is well under way.

The fifth of the *leno* plays is the *Curculio*. In it the slave-merchant is a fellow with a huge stomach which causes him much trouble. His physical uneasiness makes him a more amusing person than the other slave-dealers, but his character is not so repulsive as theirs. The part of the clever servant in this comedy is played by Curculio, the weevil, a one-eyed parasite, who is much less shrewd than Pseudolus, but fluent and plausible enough. He skillfully secures the heroine for his patron until she is claimed by a captain, who has already purchased her but who luckily turns out to be her brother. The *leno* is, as usual, left miserable at the end of the play, but the captain fares better than a *miles gloriosus* generally does.

The soldier, who, like the *leno*, is a stock character in Plautus, represents an obstacle to true love but not an insuperable one, because he has no legal right to interfere with the union of hero and heroine. He is not a parent or an owner, but by virtue of his wealth he is in a position to buy the girl whom the impecunious hero desires. At the end of the play he must be reimbursed for his loss of the heroine, and therefore he suffers from the lovers' victory less than the father or the *leno*. He is often a subordinate character in the plot, but once at least he figures as the principal target for ridicule. Pyrgopolynices in the *Boasting Soldier* ("Miles Gloriosus") is the most splendid example of his famous species in the range of Latin comedy.

Like other captains, Pyrgopolynices has accumulated his wealth as a hired mercenary. At the moment he is engaged in raising recruits, but he is not contented with looking forward to new exploits. He exacts from his parasite a catalogue of his past successes, a catalogue in which it is extremely difficult to disentangle the facts from his henchman's flattering exaggerations. Pyrgopolynices is said to have fought against Silicians, Sardinians, and Macedonians, to have killed seven thousand men in one day, and to have broken the foreleg of an elephant with a tap of his fist. He delights in hearing the parasite's account of his incredible adventures; he commands his orderlies to make his shield shine like the sun; he brandishes his sword that it may not grieve from inactivity. He is as proud of his successes with women as with men; he is amorous as well as boastful and ready to believe any story that redounds to his prowess in love or war. His high-sounding name, which signifies Tower-Town-Taker, is outdone by that of Polymachaeroplagides in the *Pseudolus*, but Pyrgopolynices states that he has fought in battle with Bumbomachides Clutomistaridysarchides, who was no doubt a worthy opponent. The exaggeration of these titles shows what an artificial figure the *miles gloriosus* has become. Originally suggested by actual soldiers with their tall tales of military and philandering exploits, he has transcended the sphere of real life and even more than the *leno* has become a conventional butt for the wit of a comic dramatist.

Plautus shows his wisdom in not employing this lay figure too prominently in his plays; even in the *Boasting Soldier* Pyrgopolynices does not always dominate the action. After the short first act, which is entirely devoted to an exposition of his character, he falls out of the drama until it has run half its course. The *Boasting Soldier* is really two comedies in one and may very well be the result of *contaminatio*, or the combining of two Greek sources into a single plot. In the first half of Plautus' rambling play the antagonist of the lovers is Pyrgopolynices' slow-witted old servant, who, when he is set by his master to watch the heroine, is tricked into believing her to be her own twin sister. He apologizes for the mistake that he thinks he has made and leaves the stage, fearing that his master will blame him for his stupidity, although his only stupidity consists in believing that he has made a mistake.

At this point, the *Boasting Soldier* takes a new turn, and Plautus separates the two parts of its action by an interlude that has little connection with either of them. It displays the character and philosophy of Periplecomenus, an old gentleman at whose house the hero is living. Periplecomenus is one of the most arresting characters created by Plautus. He is entirely outside the class of amorous, stingy old men treated as dupes, and he is not one of the noble, self-sacrificing parents rewarded for their virtue. He is a detached and complacent individual, master of his own destiny and willing to aid young love as long as his efforts do not inconvenience him too greatly. He is fifty-four years old, and he does not wish to be considered antiquated. He is a social being and enjoys going out to dinners, where he is still good company; he knows how to crack a joke and when to be silent; he can give sound advice or entertain with a seductive dance. He attributes his vigor to his never having married and thus not having had to worry over wife and children. He has money to enjoy himself without supporting a family, and he secures additional income from the relatives who ingratiate themselves with him in the hope of being made his heirs. In short, he is a sophisticated man of the world and believes in the gods of things as they are. His creed is expressed in the line, "He who blames the plans of the gods would be foolish and ignorant." Periplecomenus takes his good where he finds it and as a result is an agreeable, if static, member of human society.

The delineation of his character does not advance the plot of the *Boasting Soldier*; in fact, it retards it. With all his pleasant qualities Periplecomenus is inconsiderately loquacious and fond of talking about himself. However, he is willing to help young love by allowing a clever and unscrupulous courtesan to pose as his wife. Pyrgopolynices is told that Periplecomenus' wife is dying for love of him, and when, in the fourth act, he again appears upon the stage, he is completely taken in by the supposed wife's advances. Having been told that her husband is away from home, he is easily caught by Periplecomenus and subjected to a most humiliating punishment for his attempted adultery. At the end of the play he admits that he has been justly treated, and one might expect a change in his way of life if Plautus were not more concerned with ridiculing the enemies of his lovers than with reforming them. The *miles gloriosus* is the easiest possible sort of person to make absurd. He is an obvious excuse for laughter, and the only danger is that his patent artificiality may in the end become a bore. Plautus was not capable of creating a character with the variety of Falstaff or the solidity of Bobadill, but his Pyrgopolynices is the father of them both.

In another of Plautus' comedies, the *Truculentus*, a leading part is played by a boasting soldier. He attempts to differentiate himself from other examples of this type by stating on his entrance that he likes to do great deeds instead of talk about them, but this statement proves to be merely a more subtle means of showing a character similar to that of Pyrgopolynices. Like him, the captain in the *Truculentus* is deluded by a courtesan, the most complete portrait of a designing woman in Plautus' works. She pretends to have had a child by the soldier in order to make exorbitant financial demands upon him, and at the same time she encourages other lovers. At the end of the play she is possessed by both the soldier and a rich fellow from the country, whom she has just snared. Furthermore, the countryman's surly slave, Truculentus, the savage fellow from whom the play takes its name, has unexpectedly succumbed to the wiles of the courtesan's maid, who is quite as callous as her mistress in making money from all sorts and conditions of men.

There is another aspect of the *Truculentus* which distracts attention from the disgrace of the boasting soldier. The courtesan has a third lover, whom she has no necessity of entrapping because he is already hers in body and soul. He has wasted all his property upon her, and when the comedy begins he is in the pitiable condition of still desiring the favors he is no longer able to purchase. The courtesan is relentless in her attitude toward him, accepting his attentions when he is able to gather together a little money and leaving him abruptly as soon as she has exhausted his resources. She congratulates him scornfully on his approaching marriage to a respectable girl, into which he has been forced against his will, and she invites him to come to see her when conditions at home become intolerable. He promises to do so, and we leave the poor wretch, as we found him, completely infatuated with the worthless courtesan. He is a figure that suggests Plautus' ability to deal with ironic comedy in a play that is his most thorough study of vice and degradation.

IV

If the *Truculentus* is the somberest of Plautus' works, the *Captives* ("Captivi") is his comedy that presents life in its most cheerful mood. All the characters in this play are uniformly honorable, except a runaway slave whose role is of slight importance. We are introduced to a father seeking to ransom his captured son; the honest captive who effects this ransom; the captive's servant, devoted to his master and willing to sacrifice himself in the cause of loyalty. The mischief made by a subordinate character is quite unintentional, and the slave-overseer presented exhibits a surprising amount of compassion for his charges. It is no wonder that this play was a favorite of the sentimental Lessing's and that it is often presented to young students as typical of Plautus' work, which it most certainly is not. The author himself mentions the absence from it of courtesan, *leno*, and *miles gloriosus*; and at the end he significantly remarks, "Poets find few comedies of this kind, where good men are made better."

There is no love interest in this piece, which contains only affection between father and sons, between master and servant. It is artistically satisfactory that in such an atmosphere all family relationships should be straightened out, that the father should have his captive son restored to him, and that he should find in the ransomer's servant his long-lost younger son. Here, for once in Plautus, universal benevolence is crowned with universal rejoicing.

In fact, the *Captives* almost escapes from the category of judicial comedy. That it does not do so entirely is owing to the incidental figure of a parasite, who has a more important role than that usually given to a person of his class. In most of Plautus' plays the parasite is a hanger-on and does not take much part in the main action. He is principally ridiculed for his vast appetite and the difficulty he has in satisfying it. In the *Captives* he creates great havoc in the kitchen, after he is awarded a meal for having brought the good news of the captive son's return. For him, as for the leading characters of the play, there is a happy ending after all afflictions.

The only other of Plautus' comedies where, it might be said, good men are made better is the *Trinummus* ("The Day of the Three Sesterces"). Its plot, which is too complicated to be easily followed, is chiefly a vehicle for the depiction of admirable characters. There are two heroes, one a spendthrift with fine instincts misdirected and the other a serious-minded fellow who puts the temptations of youth behind him. The interest lies in the contrast between the conduct of these two young men, as the prologue figures of Luxury and Poverty indicate. In the end the spendthrift reforms and both heroes are rewarded with the hands of suitable young women, neither of whom appears upon the stage and one of whom is not even mentioned until the final curtain. The *Trinummus* is a man's play. The old men in it are more prominent than the young ones. The characters of the heroes are accentuated by their respective fathers, and there are two other elderly gentlemen who concoct an elaborate scheme to help out the young people. The conspirators are intimate and affectionate friends, actuated by generous motives. They are only comic when they complain about their wives and jestingly wonder if an exchange of mates would make them both happier. They overreach themselves, as old men are likely to do, in planning a stratagem which causes more trouble than it is worth, but they are not in the least discouraged when their efforts meet with a temporary setback. Their buoyant spirits are quite able to cope with any emergency.

A less admirable, but no less fascinating, elderly gentleman appears in the loosely organized scenes of the *Stichus*. He prudently urges his two daughters to marry again, because their husbands have been away for three years and have left no money behind them, but the wives refuse to do so and their constancy is rewarded by the return of their husbands with plentiful fortunes. He also asks what kind of second wife his daughters would advise for him, but he can get no satisfaction from them on that score. Later he becomes captivated by a flute-girl brought home by his sons-in-law and tells an extended parable of how a friend of his was rewarded with four mistresses under similar circumstances. He receives the girl, but his further adventures are ignored amid the activities of a parasite and a slave which fill the last part of the play. The slave, called Stichus, gives his name to the comedy, but he is not drawn with nearly so much pains as the worldly father of the two faithful heroines.

Old men are, on the whole, the characters best depicted by Plautus, but they do not always have an importance in the action that is commensurate with the dramatist's interest in them. Only once, and then perhaps by better luck than management, does an old man's character furnish the motivating force in the story. This happy combination of circumstances occurs in the *Aulularia* ("The Comedy of the Little Pot"), which consequently holds a unique position among its author's plays; it is a comedy of character rather than incident, and it is probably Plautus' finest piece of work. Molière showed his true flair for comedy by adapting the *Aulularia* as well as the *Amphitryon*, and, even if Harpagon had never existed, the miser Euclio would have been assured of immortality.

Euclio is an old fellow who has lived in comparative poverty until just before the play begins, when by the agency of a household god he discovers a pot of gold concealed by his grandfather at the family hearth. This unexpected wealth goes to Euclio's head and becomes the mania which causes his absurd actions. He suspects his old maidservant of spying on him; he fears that any affable acquaintance has learned of his wealth; when his daughter's hand is asked in marriage, he is sure that the rich old suitor knows of the pot of gold. The preparations for his daughter's wedding necessitate bringing hired cooks into the house. They are told that Euclio is so stingy he collects the clippings from his nails, but they determine to exercise their traditional rights to perquisites, much to the horror of the miser.

Euclio hears the cooks ask for a pot, and his worst fears for his gold are aroused. He sees an inoffensive cock scratching near his treasure and decides to wring its neck. Finally he cannot endure having his money at home during the marriage preparations and takes it from the house. He tries two hiding-places, but his very anxieties cause his undoing. They attract the notice of the hero's servant, who steals the pot of gold from its last place of concealment. On discovering the loss of his treasure, Euclio goes wild with anger. He appeals to the audience for help and rushes madly about the stage, a strange figure whose obsession has made him at the same time pathetic and amusing.

Plautus develops the comic side of Euclio's plight by means of a scene between him and the young hero, in which they misunderstand each other. From the fact that the word for pot, *aula*, is of the feminine gender, the miser supposes the young man has stolen his most precious possession, whereas the hero is trying to explain that in a fit of drunkenness he has assaulted Euclio's daughter. He is anxious to right this wrong by marrying the girl, and he finally does so. Just how Euclio became reconciled to this unadvantageous match we do not know, for the last part of the *Aulularia* has not come down to us. There does not seem to be much likelihood that the avaricious man would have repented his evil deeds, as he is made to do in one of the efforts to complete this drama. His reformation would have been quite foreign to his character and also contrary to the general spirit of Plautus' comedies. It is more probable that the hero was to obtain possession of the gold from his servant and agree to restore it if allowed to marry Euclio's daughter. In this case the miser's greed would have been the means by which, with poetic justice, the lovers were ultimately united.

The scene of verbal misunderstanding between Euclio and the hero is extremely laughable, but it is not so subtly amusing as the scene in which the rich suitor, Megadorus, proposes to Euclio for his daughter's hand. Megadorus has determined to marry a girl whom he supposes to be poor, because of the misery that a purse-proud wife usually brings upon her husband. He has selected Euclio's daughter for the opposite reason from the covetous one which the miser fears, preferring poverty and youth in a mate to riches and middle age. The scene between Megadorus and Euclio depends upon a clash of personalities that have been made mellow and eccentric by their many past experiences. It illustrates strikingly the individuality of the miser, from which spring the chief humorous complications in the plot of the *Aulularia*.

Many of the fathers in Plautus are parted from their money with difficulty, through the wiles of an intriguing slave, but only in the case of Euclio is the dominant vice of old age minutely analyzed. The crusty neighbor in the *Mostellaria* is a similarly greedy person, but he is a minor figure in the plot. Periplecomenus in the *Boasting Soldier* has an anxious regard for worldly possessions, but he is, like Megadorus, a predominantly sympathetic person. Euclio is shown in the same play with Megadorus, as if Plautus wished to suggest that carefulness in financial matters may easily become avarice when carried to an extreme. The dramatist probably did not realize that in .writing the *Aulularia* he was creating his masterpiece, and perhaps it would not seem so to us if the play's original ending had been preserved and had not harmonized with its central theme. As it stands, this comedy is eminently successful in creating laughter, in picturing old age, and in implying a serious critical interpretation of human life.

V

Plautus' twentieth play, the *Cistellaria* ("The Comedy of the Casket"), is frankly a romantic story rather than a humorous one. It is the extreme development of a situation that occurs in many of his plays, the story of a child lost when a baby, who is identified in later life by its grief-stricken parents. Menander had made frequent use of this incident, originally based on actual conditions of Greek life, and after his time it continued to prove a most useful piece of machinery for comic dramatists. It not only provides an effective scene of recognition and straightens out the dramatic conflict, but it is also one feasible solution for the troublesome problem of how to present a freeborn heroine on the stage. Plautus cared too much for laughter to devote himself wholeheartedly to exploring the pathetic possibilities of this theme, except in an occasional isolated case like the *Cistellaria*, but Terence found it very congenial to his temperament. Plautus' primary intention was to amuse his audience, Terence's was to arouse compassion for his characters. By common consent his most famous line has been lifted from its context and made to express his creed: "I am a man; I consider nothing human foreign to me" (*homo sum: humani nil a me alienum puto*).

The ability to understand mankind is a useful attribute for any artist, but when carried so far that to understand all is to forgive all, it becomes a danger to the comic dramatist. The limitations of the stage and the demands of a plot compel a partial view of life, which in the realm of classic comedy means an insistence upon human weaknesses. The comic dramatist may allow himself some attractive characters on whose fortunes to hang his story, but in his foreground he should place people with harmless eccentricities, which may be legitimately ridiculed. Terence's equal interest in the strength and weakness of human beings may make him a greater artist than Plautus (as he admittedly is in the adroit handling of words), but it places him on a lower plane from the point of view of comic gusto. He did not have the capacity to conceive a clear and effective situation and to carry it through logically and unfalteringly, as Plautus did. There is a softness in the atmosphere of his plays which, however ingratiating it may be, does not always help to promote laughter.

It was natural for Terence to exploit that element in the tradition of New Comedy which Plautus had ordinarily subordinated to his sense for humorous effects. Terence is much more like Menander than Plautus is, four of his six plays being based on works by Menander and all of his dramas giving the effect of imitation more than of creative vitality. Unlike Plautus, he had no hesitancy in wringing every possible tear from Menander's situation of the long-lost child. He makes use of it in all but one of his comedies. Plautus is at bottom concerned with the humorous complications that get in the way of his lovers and frequently with the absurd persons who stand in their paths; Terence is obsessed with the harshness of fate. After he has developed throughout five acts the misery that it causes, he finally permits its patient victims to be rewarded, not always inevitably, with unexpected happiness.

What is exceptionally non-Plautine in the *Cistellaria* is typically Terentian in the *Girl from Andros* ("Andria"), the first of Terence's plays, produced in 166 B.C. These two plays have the same basic plot, the love of a young man for a girl who turns out to be the sister of his fiancée. In the *Girl from Andros* a slave tries to break off the formal engagement, but his efforts are worse than useless. If it were not for the romantic discovery of the Andrian's birth, the hero would probably have had to give up the girl with whom he was in love and by whom he had already had a child. In the *Self-Tormentor* ("Heauton Timorumenos") of 163 B.C. the hero has not lived with the girl whom he loves, but again the revelation of the heroine's birth is necessary to clear up all the complications of the plot. The *Eunuch* ("Eunuchus"), 161 B.C., shows the young man anticipating Wycherley's Horner in *The Country Wife*, by posing as a eunuch so that he may secure access to a mistress; libertine though he is, he is anxious to continue the liaison, and the discovery that the girl is freeborn makes marriage with her possible for him. In the *Phormio* (also 161 B.C.) the hero has already taken the girl as his wife and later finds that she is his own cousin, whom his father had intended him to marry. In all these cases the proof that the heroine is freeborn straightens out an intrigue which has progressed to the varying stages of first love, physical violence, parenthood, or marriage.

Terence's fifth play, the *Mother-in-Law*, has a curious history. It was originally produced in 165, which would make it his second piece in chronological order, but it failed and was taken off the boards. In 161 it was performed again, probably in its present form, but it was not until 160 that it finally met with success. As the play now stands, its central plot is a combination of those used in the *Eunuch* and the *Phormio*. As in the former, the hero has attacked the girl; as in the latter, he has married her. The denouement reveals that the unfortunate girl and his wife are one and the same person, a fact which he himself did not previously know. This situation is like that in the *Epitrepontes* of Menander, and the heroes of the two plays are equally sensitive and upright in intention. The young man in the *Mother-in-Law* finds it difficult to give up Bacchis, the courtesan with whom he has lived up to the time of his marriage and who is herself a noble creature. She refuses to let her lover visit her after he is married, she assures his wife and mother-in-law that her intrigue with him is over, and by so doing she is the instrument of the discovery essential to a happy outcome of the plot. She does not appear on the stage until the last act, but her brief scenes establish her as the most unselfish courtesan in Latin comedy, a striking contrast to the two mercenary sisters in Plautus whose names are also Bacchis.

Another attractive figure in the *Mother-in-Law* is the hero's mother. Fearing that the success of her son's marriage is endangered by her presence, she resolves to sacrifice herself by retiring to the country out of her daughter-in-law's way. She is the mother-in-law or *hecyra* who gives her name to the play, unless this title, like those of the *Self-Tormentor* and the *Brothers* ("Adelphoe"), can bear two interpretations. The hero's mother is thought to be the first obstacle to the happiness of the married pair, and the heroine's mother is considered the second one; but as a matter of fact neither of them is responsible for the original misunderstanding, which is brought about by the wife's having given birth to a child before the marriage was consummated. When it is proved that the husband is also the father of the child, the bad luck that has pursued all the characters is dispelled in time for a happy ending. The one comic twist in the story is that the two fathers-in-law are kept in the dark as to the true state of affairs. They blame the trouble first on one of their wives and then on the other, and even at the end they are not enlightened as to its cause. The hero says that it is not necessary to tell everyone everything, as is customary in most comedies, and it is arranged that the unsavory facts of the case shall be concealed by the husband and wife, the wife's mother, and the husband's former mistress. The ironic way in which the fathers are fooled by the women in the *Mother-in-Law* is the only amusing incident in a drama that is otherwise extremely grave in tone.

The *Mother-in-Law* is the most solemn of Terence's comedies, with the possible exception of the *Girl from Andros*, and that early play has its comic moments in the vain attempts of a slave to help the lovers by trickery. The scheming slave is naturally a much less important figure in the sentimental dramas of Terence than in the boisterous farces of Plautus. In the *Mother-in-Law*, he is pathetically powerless. At the end of the play he is almost as ignorant of what has occurred as are the fathers. In the *Self-Tormentor* he has slightly more to do, by suggesting the plot which temporarily comes to the aid of the second lover. All Terence's dramas except the *Mother-in-Law* have two pairs of lovers whose fortunes are at stake, and it is generally the affair of the secondary hero which provides the comic situations needed to sustain the serious primary action. Terence's plays would not fall into the sphere of comedy if in all of them there were not occasional opportunities for laughter, or at least for quiet smiles.

The hero's jealous friend in the *Girl from Andros* is not sufficiently prominent to produce much merriment, but the secondary hero of the *Self-Tormentor* is amusing in his efforts to get money enough to buy the favors of the courtesan whom he loves. He succeeds for a time, but finally his ruses are discovered by his father, who threatens to disinherit him unless the son will agree to reform his conduct and settle down in matrimony. He does not like the first girl proposed for him, but he is willing to accept his father's second choice for a suitable but not very joyful marriage. In a true comedy the son would not only have secured the money for the courtesan by cheating his father, but he would have been left with her at the final curtain to enjoy his momentary happiness. His repentance is much less plausible than that of the reformed spendthrift in Plautus' *Trinummus*, who was not in love with any specific courtesan, and this abrupt reformation is a striking evidence of how unwilling Terence was to let the events of his plays work themselves out to a logical comic conclusion.

The outcome of the secondary plot of the *Eunuch* is no better prepared for than is that of the *Self-Tormentor*, but its unexpected turn is in the direction of comedy instead of towards conventional morality. The brother of the supposed eunuch is in love with a courtesan who really cares for him, and his father agrees to the liaison; but even a sincere courtesan has expensive tastes that must be gratified. At the end of the play the courtesan's lover agrees to share his mistress's favors with Thraso, a wealthy captain who has been pursuing her, with the result that the secondary plot of the *Eunuch* closes in a sardonic mood. Thraso is the best example of the Terentian *miles gloriosus*, differing from the similar figure of Plautus in that he boasts of his wit rather than of his valor. Terence's conception is characteristically more subtle than Plautus', but Thraso lacks the astonishing verve of Pyrgopolynices.

To the secondary plot of the *Phormio* Terence gives an ending that is in accordance with the best traditions of classic comedy. The hero of this part of the play is in love with a slave-girl owned by a *leno* and is successful in obtaining the money necessary to secure her. The

leno is not tricked, as is generally the case in Plautus, but fairly receives the money, which is wrung from the hero's father by the
taunts of his jealous wife. The agent in this transaction is Phormio, a
parasite, who plays the part generally taken by the clever slave in
Plautus. Terence here challenges his predecessor on his own grounds,
and he has succeeded in creating a drama as truly comic as any by
Plautus. The double plot in the *Phormio* is a little too complicated to
follow easily, but its parts are fitted together with the technical skill
of which Terence was a master. In the course of his career he had
gradually developed from the romantic author of the *Girl from
Andros* into a comic dramatist able to evolve original variations on
the traditional theme of a crafty servant deceiving a father in the
interest of a pair of young lovers.

VI

The father is the principal dupe in the *Phormio* and, as we have seen,
the main humor of the *Mother-in-Law* comes from the ignorance in
which its old men are left at the close of the intrigue. Is it possible
that Terence introduced that comic touch into the earlier and more
sentimental version of his play when he rewrote it for a second production? This surmise is given additional weight when we observe
the importance of old men in Terence's last comedy and masterpiece, the *Brothers* of 160 B.C. In this piece the dramatist avoids the
romantic discovery which plays a strategic part in his first five
dramas and concentrates his interest on the lovers and their fathers.
Both young heroes are really the sons of Demea, but Demea's
brother, Micio, has adopted one of them, to whom he acts as a father.
Both of the sons are engaged in love affairs; with the aid of the benevolent Micio each of them finally secures the girl of his choice. The
element of intrigue in the *Brothers* is largely superficial and does not
engage the main attention of Terence.

The point of this play is the contrasted characters of Micio and
Demea. Micio lives in the city, where by knowing the ways of the
world he has been able to accumulate a large fortune. He has not
been contaminated by his experiences, however, and maintains a
kindly spirit toward his fellow men. He is especially sympathetic
with his adopted son and gives him everything he desires. Demea,

on the other hand, has always lived in the country, where he has learned cautious habits from the necessity of supporting a wife and family. He is suspicious and grasping, and he rules his son with a rod of iron. The two methods of life, particularly the two ways of bringing up children, are the opposing forces in the *Brothers*.

In the first meeting between the two brothers at the beginning of the play, the problem is clearly stated: Is it better in this world to be kind or to be careful? Micio is always tolerant toward the escapades of youth, for would not he and Demea have acted in the same free and easy way when they were young, if they had had the necessary funds? Demea complains of the way Micio has spoiled his adopted son and feels that his own strict attitude towards his boy has been far more successful. He has apparent evidence on his side, because the adopted son has just been discovered to have taken part in a disreputable adventure. Still Micio refuses to blame the young man, and in due time learns that the boy's outrageous actions have sprung from high-minded motives.

Demea is much slower to find out the true facts of the case; when the two old men meet at the end of the fourth act, he is at a disadvantage from his ignorance of the situation. As a result he is inexpressibly shocked by his brother's complacent philosophy and unimpressed by its splendid phrasing: "Human life is like a game of dice; if the throw which you most want does not turn up, you must by your skill make the most of the one which has fallen by chance,"

> ita vitast hominum quasi quom ludas tesseris;
> si illud quod maxume opus est iactu non cadit,
> illud quod cecidit forte, id arte ut corrigas.

Micio mischievously refuses to explain to Demea why he can be satisfied with the present state of his adopted son's affairs, but Demea soon finds out the truth, which does not redound to the credit of his own son. This turn of affairs leads into the third scene between the brothers at the beginning of the fifth act, in which Micio is clearly the victor. Facts are now on his side: his adopted son has shown a certain degree of nobility, and Demea's training has brought his son to grief. Micio is able to preach to his brother and remind him that if extravagance is the vice of youth, avarice is the vice of age: "O my dear Demea, in all other things we judge more rightly with age; old age brings to men only this one defect: we all pay more attention to money than we need to."

If the Brothers ended at this point Micio would be completely vindicated, as is the corresponding character in Thomas Shadwell's The Squire of Alsatia, but Terence has a surprise in store for his audience. Often in his comedies a new element is introduced with great effect into the final scene, but never more successfully than in the case of Demea. He proves to be a more subtle and complex character than Micio, for, whereas Micio does not understand Demea's point of view, Demea comes to realize the value of Micio's. Since his treatment of his own son has not restrained the boy from sowing wild oats and has made him dislike his father, Demea resolves to imitate Micio's course of action. He suddenly assumes benevolence and prosecutes it to an absurd extreme. He becomes very polite to his servants; he advises that the wall between two adjacent houses be demolished in the interests of friendship; he persuades Micio to marry an impoverished neighbor, and he urges his brother to free a slave and advance him money. When asked why he has completely changed his attitude, Demea explains that he is simply trying to show where Micio's position logically leads: undiscriminating kindness is sure to cause acts of folly. Demea has not been converted by the action of the play; he has merely been forced to see the weakness of his own views and as a result to appreciate the grain of truth in his brother's code of action. He finds that basically Micio's ideas are as absurd as his own, and that, when all is said and done, there is not much to choose between them.

Such is Terence's conclusion in regard to the problem that he stated at the beginning of the play. The golden mean has triumphed, and any extreme is shown to be dangerous and absurd. The dramatist's approach to the specific question raised in the Brothers is unmistakable. How far he intended that Demea should finally come to share his views is left in fascinating ambiguity. The old gentleman berates his brother for too great indulgence and selfishness in his easy course of life. Then he turns to the boys and assures them that as for himself he will never fall in with all their inclinations, adding, "But if in those matters where because of your youth you have too little wisdom, where your desires are too immoderate, where you take too little counsel, you would have me reprove and correct and aid you at the proper time, here I am to do it for you."

This statement may mean that hereafter Demea will temper severity with sympathy, or it may mean that Demea will revert to his original position, having shown by his own foolish conduct the fallacy in Micio's behavior. For the time being he lets his son have his way, and the comedy comes to a happy ending; but there is a sting in the happiness that leaves no one entirely satisfied. Demea was wrong and Micio was wrong, but the tolerance of Micio comes off a shade worse than the worldly wisdom of Demea. In the *Brothers* Terence has risen above his own innate kindliness and taken a detached view of human imperfections.

The *Brothers* is probably the best comedy written in the Latin language. The breadth of its wisdom and the depth of its feeling set it far above the more obviously uproarious farces of Plautus. Only once, in the *Aulularia*, does Plautus arrange matters so that incongruous incidents seem to spring directly from men's weaknesses. Euclio's avarice is his outstanding characteristic; in fact, it is so outstanding that it becomes impossible to regard the miser as a credible figure. In spite of minor efforts to give life to his characters, Plautus is primarily an entertainer, sympathizing little with human beings and striving at all costs to make his audiences laugh. The playgoers of his day were, to judge from his prologues, a miscellaneous and illbehaved group of people, who cared little for the nuances of life; if they were not entertained in the theater, they would not listen to the play. Plautus had a genius for amusing them. He could construct a complicated plot that would entangle unpleasant old men, vicious slave-dealers, or boastful soldiers. His comic gift extended beyond skill in plot construction to the adroit handling of individual scenes and the writing of brilliant dialogue. He was adept at the use of words and never missed an opportunity for a pun or a double meaning. His immense fertility of comic invention was unflagging; sometimes there does not seem to be sufficient relief from the continuous merriment in his plays.

Terence took a more serious view of life and erred in the opposite direction. His early plays are hardly comedies at all, if by a comedy is meant a humorous picture of human society. They are stories of adventure, which end happily but in which disaster is constantly threatened. Gradually the dramatist developed an increased sense of gaiety, possibly urged on by the failure of his second play, the *Mother-in-Law*. Terence also had to consider his audience, but his prologues suggest that he was far less concerned with pleasing them than Plautus was. Terence was a Carthaginian slave who had been freed by his Roman master and introduced into the most cultivated social circles of his day. He was the friend of Scipio Africanus Minor and Gaius Laelius, and these men are supposed to have helped him in composing his dramas. Whether they did so or not, Terence seems to have cared more for winning their praise than for appealing to the many-headed mob. The fact that he was a foreigner by birth may have made it easier for him to assimilate Greek culture than if he had been a native Roman. The detachment from his audience which his situation gave him influenced his writing both for good and bad. It made his plays more like those of Menander and less a purely Roman product. It enabled him to devote such attention and care to the purity of his language that Terentian Latin became a byword through the Middle Ages and that his comedies were kept alive during a religious period in spite of the worldly nature of their subjects. It caused his plays to be more refined, and less amusing, than those of Plautus; it made him less a pure comedian and more thoroughly a literary artist.

The quality of human sympathy which prevented Terence from seeing life as an unrelieved comic phenomenon made it possible for him once, in the *Brothers*, to surpass anything that his predecessor had done. The characters of Micio and Demea, especially Demea, have more vital reality than Euclio remotely suggests. For one thing, the contrast between the brothers in Terence is much more striking than that between Euclio and his foil, the generous Megadorus. Micio and Demea embody in themselves the opposing forces that are at work in the *Brothers*; the conflict between Euclio and Megadorus seems more superficial than structurally fundamental. Moreover, Terence understood his characters and was anxious to have his audience do so. Plautus was a much less humane person. His lack of humanity reveals itself in the unnaturalness of the exaggerated figures in his plays. They make up in number and variety for what they lack in carefully observed detail, but they move on a lower artistic plane than Terence's most masterly creations.

The broad sweep of Plautus and the refined sensitivity of Terence both emphasize the personalities of old men. Micio and Demea, Euclio, and Periplecomenus in the *Boasting Soldier* are the most memorable figures created by the two dramatists. They stand out from the rank and file of colorless lovers, intriguing servants, and foolish dupes. They help or hinder the lovers, they are themselves deceivers or deceived, but they maintain their own individualities irrespective of the plots in which they appear. That this should be so depends partly upon social conditions in Greece and Rome, where the older generation exerted a powerful influence upon the lives of younger people. Old men held the purse strings and exacted obedience to parental authority as the price of their compliance with youthful inclinations. They could not be laughed off the stage as palpably absurd, like boasting soldiers; they could not be treated as utterly despicable, like slave-merchants. They must be given a certain amount of consideration, and yet they should not be allowed exclusive domination over the lives of the young.

Old age has its power and respect is due to it, but it also has its foibles and peculiarities. An old man who keeps youthful impulses in a decaying body is ridiculous, and so is one who has succumbed to the lure of worldly treasure. He who has lived his life without affections is no less badly balanced than he who loves his fellow men and women without discrimination. Advancing years have pitfalls for men of whatever temperament, and a comic dramatist must be expected to make the most of them. Plautus shows us old men who err by being too selfish, Terence shows us old men who err by being too blind; they unite in ridiculing old age as that period in life when a man's personality, having reached its fullest development, is at its most rigid and absurd. Social comedy under the conditions prevalent at Rome in the pre-Christian era had come to the conclusion that youth is always right and that with age comes a loss of the perspective essential to appreciating the proper human values.

CHAPTER III

The Revival of Classical Comedy: Ben Jonson

I

AS THE comic spirit is no more a respecter of institutions than of persons, it is not surprising to find that there has usually been an antagonism between comedy and the Christian Church, even though the Church has sometimes made use of it. Tragedy at its most elevated provides an unmistakable link between mortality and immortality, but comedy, being a more mundane affair, can bridge the gulf only indirectly and by implication. It is primarily occupied with human beings and their foibles, which it judges by a set of ideal standards that must always be expressible in physical terms. Philosophy, rather than religion, is at the core of comedy. Thus, quite naturally, comic drama languished during the Middle Ages. From the fall of the Roman Empire to the Revival of Learning there is no comic dramatist of literary importance, except Hrotswitha, the nun of Gandersheim. Her plays are frankly propaganda for Christianity, but it is notable that she had read, and professed to imitate, the works of Terence. It was his style which she thought worthy to be copied, not his matter, but the fact that Terence was known and tolerated in the convents and monasteries of the tenth century makes the miracle of the Renaissance a little less inexplicable.

When the movement to which we give that name swept over Europe from the fourteenth to the sixteenth century, the time was ripe for a revival of classical culture. The fall of Constantinople had its effect in the dissemination of Greek letters, and an increased knowledge of Latin literature followed in the wake of these events. The works of Plautus as well as those of Terence were rediscovered by educated Europeans, and as a result the soil of literature again became fertile for the growth of comic drama. The reëstablishment of classical learning meant among other things the revival of comedy. In all countries touched by Roman civilization the process went on, but like much else in the Renaissance it had its beginnings in Italy. The Italian comedies of the early sixteenth century show a definite knowledge of the Roman comic dramatists and make a faltering attempt to translate their classical formulas into terms of contemporary Italian life. In Spain, Lope de Vega knew the plays of Plautus and Terence, but by his own confession he disregarded them in his writing, because he feared that their practice was too severe for the popular audience to which he wished to appeal. In England, Nicholas Udall's *Ralph Roister Doister* (*c.* 1553) was probably the first drama based on a Latin comedy, the *Boasting Soldier* of Plautus, but it was Ben Jonson who must be credited with reviving the tradition of classical comedy and adapting it to the conditions of his time in such a way as to give it new vigor and endurance.

Unlike Lope de Vega, Jonson was not so anxious to please his audiences as he was to please himself. The intelligent methods of classical comedy made an irresistible appeal to him. He had a well-trained mind, stored with a knowledge of ancient culture and ready to use it in interpreting the society of his own day. From his education at Westminster School under that "most reverend head," William Camden, he gained a firm grounding in the languages and literatures of Greece and Rome, which was to be strengthened and extended throughout the course of his life. His classical background was not, however, so rigid and unyielding that it prevented him from distinguishing between theoretical wisdom and the rigors of necessity, with which he had some actual experience. He passed through a disagreeable period of employment at his stepfather's trade of bricklaying; he took part in a military expedition to Flanders, where he killed a man in single combat on the field of honor; and he gave hostages to fortune by marrying at an early age, without any visible means of supporting his wife and children. When in the 1590's, at the age of twenty-odd, he entered upon the London stage as actor and then as playwright, he was in a position to know the abuses and demands of the world. Ben Jonson was from first to last a realistic man, but his strength of character enabled him to keep his personal and artistic integrity unimpaired among the eddying currents of Elizabethan life and letters.

The Renaissance implied a revaluation of ideals, both intellectual and aesthetic; a man of marked individuality, like Jonson, was sure to be an influential factor in shaping and establishing new standards. He sometimes erred in his judgment and confused the ephemeral with the eternal, but he always made an honest effort to support the views which his training and experience recommended to him as most sound. He frequently became involved in petty quarrels, and personal animus often drove him into unworthy attacks upon individuals, his abundant energy asserting itself with violence after his rationalizing faculty had ceased to do its work. Generally he was able to reconcile his a priori ideas with his keen interest in the world about him, although a certain self-consciousness can be observed in the result — especially at first. Both his success and his failure came from his reliance upon the rich experience of the past, which in comic drama meant chiefly the plays of Plautus and Terence. He never lost sight of these authors as models; but he came to depend on them less and less as time went on, and he never felt constrained to limit himself to their narrow range of observation. His particular gift was the ability to adapt classical precedents to the variety and profusion of life in Elizabethan England.

Since Ben Jonson was an avowed classicist with a difference, it is entirely fitting that one of his first extant plays should be an amalgamation of two of Plautus' plots. *The Case Is Altered*, probably produced in 1597–98, is based on the *Captives* and the *Aulularia*, and it is a remarkably successful combination of the two stories. One was essentially romantic, the other a comedy of character. Out of them Jonson made an elaborate tragicomedy which would appeal to many tastes. To bring the two plots into agreement, he added a romantic strand to the *Aulularia* exactly parallel to the main argument of the *Captives*, making the miser's daughter turn out to be not the miser's daughter at all, but a girl whom he has stolen when a baby. With this structural change in the story Jonson seems to be contented. He gives little attention to the emotional complications that might be contained in his new version of the situation. In fact, he does not go so far as Plautus in wringing dramatic effects from the romantic plot of the *Captives*, making use of it only to connect and set off elements in the story which seem to him to be of greater interest and importance.

Of these the chief is the miserliness of Euclio, or, as he is called by Ben Jonson, Jaques de Prie. Like all comic dramatists, Jonson saw in the love of money one of humanity's basic weaknesses. During his entire career he was greatly engrossed by its insidious effects. His inability to stabilize his own business affairs may have had something to do with his scorn and hatred for the cursed greed of gold in others. Another reason for his preoccupation with the subject may have been the growth of capitalistic finance during the Renaissance. Greed, pure and simple, is the quintessence of worldliness and may thus be a prime source of the ludicrous in society. Jonson characteristically treated this human defect in *The Case Is Altered*, where Jaques de Prie, like Euclio and like Shylock, gives instructions how his house is to be guarded in his absence. In both Plautus and Jonson, the household fire is to be extinguished, but the depiction of Jaques lacks many of the details which go to build up the character of Euclio. For one thing, Jonson has too many strands of narrative in his plot to develop even the principal story as thoroughly as more unity of action would allow. We get one pleasant new touch in the mention of Jaques' watchdog, Garlick, but in general the characterization loses force because of the romantic tone of the whole play. Jaques rhapsodizes in poetic verse about the divinity from whom gold comes, and at the end he is allowed to retain the money he had stolen as a reward for having revealed the true parentage of his supposed daughter. The case is never so much altered from Plautus as when the story of the miser's gold is crowded off the stage by attention to his daughter's fate.

In the *Aulularia* the heroine had two suitors; in Jonson's play she has no less than five. The Elizabethan dramatist is interested in the variety, not in the intensity, of romantic passion. For him, as for Plautus, a love affair is a convenient peg on which to hang developments of plot, but, whereas the Latin dramatist concentrated all his fire upon the heroine's father, Ben Jonson brought in a score of diverse subjects. Those most to his taste are the farcical adventures and rare high spirits of the cobbler, Juniper, and the groom, Peter Onion, elementary studies in realistic comedy. *The Case Is Altered* opens with Juniper singing at his work, and we soon realize that Jonson entered into the life of his own day much more easily than into the Greek setting of a Roman play, the scene of which has been transferred to Renaissance Italy. After Juniper and Onion have stolen the miser's gold, they appear richly dressed and drunk as lords, with pages in attendance. Their overdisplay leads to their apprehension for the theft; we take leave of them about to be set in the stocks.

Onion is panic-stricken, but Juniper carries off the situation with bravado: "Away, scoundrel! dost thou fear a little elocution? shall we be confiscate now? shall we droop now? shall we be now in helogabolus?" To the end he is the stronger of the two knaves, in personality as well as in vocabulary; he uses vastly more words than he understands, and Onion adopts his confederate's fine language in his own more illiterate way. Onion and Juniper are a humorous pair of clowns who by their parade of mock grandeur throw a satiric light upon the serious love-making and money-seeking of the principal characters in the play.

Besides these two hilarious figures, Jonson inserted other foreign elements into the patchwork of *The Case Is Altered*. A sad sister and gay sister are obviously contrasted, and there are two sprightly pages who practice polite salutations with dignified ceremony, both themes that were to be touched on again in later plays, but neither of which was to become an outstanding feature of Jonsonian comedy. More characteristic were the satire on Anthony Munday as Balladino, probably a late insertion into the text, and the comments on dramatic conditions placed in the mouth of a much-traveled servant:

But there are two sorts of persons that most commonly are infectious to a whole auditory. . . . Marry, one is the rude barbarous crew, a people that have no brains, and yet grounded judgments; these will hiss anything that mounts above their grounded capacities; but the other are worth the observation i' faith . . . a few capricious gallants. . . . And they have taken such a habit of dislike in all things, that they will approve nothing, be it never so conceited or elaborate.

This is an authentic Jonsonian utterance, which, like much else in *The Case Is Altered*, foreshadows the greater dramatist that its author was to become. Later, in his masterpieces, he was to subdue the animosity which he felt towards certain specific individuals, to soften his general scorn for unintelligent audiences, and to elaborate the outstanding excellences of his early play. These were, first, the tradition of classical comedy, as manifested in the Plautine figure of Jaques de Prie, and, second, the lusty veracity of Onion and Juniper. Of these two elements the former predominates in *The Case Is Altered*, if any single thread of interest can be said to stand out among the collection of heterogeneous scenes of which it is composed.

In the other play of Jonson's which modern criticism supposes to have been written for the most part before 1598, the English atmosphere far surpasses the classical influence, as it had done more than forty years earlier in *Gammer Gurton's Needle*. Jonson's *A Tale of a Tub* has its scene laid in Finsbury Hundred on the outskirts of London; its characters belong to a stratum of rural society in which Onion and Juniper would have been at home. When, at a much later date, the author decided to introduce into this comedy a satirical portrait of Inigo Jones, Jones's humble origin added point to the representation of the court architect as In-and-In Medlay, cooper and headborough (petty constable) of Islington. In *A Tale of a Tub* Jonson is drawing a picture of suburban life, suburban life as seen by a detached and slightly supercilious city man. The self-complacency and illiteracy of the yokels are not exposed by their association with persons superior to them in social position and intellectual development, as are the weaknesses of Onion and Juniper. Instead Jonson has made use of an intrigue in which one incapable faction is defeated by another, which in turn yields to a third, the third to a fourth. Each new group is of a little higher mentality than the preceding one, but the final victory is attributable more to good luck than good management.

The object of the struggle is to see which of four men shall win the hand of Awdrey Turfe, a high constable's daughter, whose practical sentiments on marriage are expressed in the lines:

> Husbands, they say, grow thick, but thin are sown;
> I care not who it be, so I have one.

This realistic attitude is in striking contrast with the high-flown notions of the heroine in *The Case Is Altered*, who also has many suitors but has given her heart devotedly to one of them. *A Tale of a Tub* is, in subject matter, like a low-life parody of the earlier play; in form, it is a much better constructed piece of work. Its entire action converges upon the business of Awdrey's wedding. In the first half of the play she is about to be married at different times to three separate men, but each of them loses her and she returns home to her father without a husband. The latter half of the action is composed of variations upon the same theme, with a fourth suitor introduced in the person of an upstart usher, under whose protection Awdrey is temporarily placed and who weds her out of hand. Each section of the plot is a logical and well-integrated whole, but this play contains so many characters of a similar type that there is little chance for contrasting effects. The suitors are all stupid in their different ways, although each new one introduced is slightly more able than his predecessor; they all have supporters in their efforts to gain Awdrey, and their supporters are graded in a similar fashion. No one of these persons is so vivid as the passive Awdrey, and the most brilliant figure in the comedy has almost nothing to do with the plot.

Hannibal (Ball) Puppy, the high constable's man, stands out from the ineffectual crowd as a fellow of wits and capabilities. He is a faithful servant, in great things as well as small, going about his business with speed in his legs and a jest on his tongue. He is not above his station in his love of good food and his superstitious terror of the devil, but his immense vitality overrides all obstacles and wins for him the hand of a jolly maidservant. His repartee is excellent, and he has no illusions about pretenders to learning:

> Why, all's but writing and reading, is it, Scriben?
> An it be any more, it is mere cheating, zure,
> Vlat cheating; all your law and poets too.

It is no wonder that both the maid and the maid's aristocratic mistress seize on Puppy to be their valentine: he embodies excellently the merry spirit of the fourteenth of February, the day on which all the amorous contretemps of *A Tale of a Tub* occur.

Ball Puppy expresses very well the mood of this drama, realistic and gay, without the somewhat heavy standard of judgment implied in classical comedy. All the unsuccessful lovers and their allies are willing to participate in the celebration of Awdrey's wedding and share in Puppy's joy at his own marriage. In this respect they differ from the similar characters in *The Case Is Altered*. Onion and Juniper are ridiculed throughout the play and at the end are dismissed with infamy as the reward of their dangerous follies. In them Ben Jonson was picturing the life of his time, but in their case he was emphasizing the defects of their characters. The laughter in *A Tale of a Tub* is much more spontaneous than that in the more pretentious play, but it is also much less pointed. In the story of Awdrey's lovers there is no such solid figure as the miserly Jaques de Prie, no romantic lovemaking, and no discovery of lost children. The only departure from the genial mood of the piece is the episode of In-and-In Medlay, and that was apparently an afterthought. The "Scene Interloping" and the redundant masque at the close, which are biting satires upon Inigo Jones, do not interfere with the tone of harmless mirth that prevails throughout the story. In the course of it Jonson has portrayed a number of fools and rogues, but he has refrained from passing judgment on them as he did in his less coherent and amusing, but more significant, early play, *The Case Is Altered*.

II

Both *The Case Is Altered* and *A Tale of a Tub* are now thought to have been composed in large part before September 1598, when Jonson scored his first pronounced success as a playwright with *Every Man in His Humour*. This comedy was largely rewritten at a later date, when the scene was changed from Italy to London, but even in its early form it marked a distinct advance over anything he had yet produced. In it for the first time he used the theory of humours which was to run through all his later work and which was to be his chief contribution to the history of dramatic comedy. The application to comedy of the word "humour" was more novel than the idea contained in it; certainly the germ of everything that it meant to Jonson is to be found in his previous work. In *The Case Is Altered* he had accepted the classical convention of embodying a universal trait in a particular human being; in *A Tale of a Tub* he had already begun to draw people from his observation of the life about him.

In *Every Man in His Humour* he combined these two methods of comic portraiture, when he created a cross between the conceited Juniper and the genial Ball Puppy, in the person of Oliver Cob, the water-carrier. Like Juniper, Cob has pretensions above his position, which he glorifies unduly; like Puppy, he is a gay and carefree, if ignorant, member of society. His fate is halfway between the severe punishment of Juniper and the reward meted out to Puppy. His vulgar scorn of tobacco wins for him an incidental beating, but his unforced good nature keeps him free from criticism at the judicial close of the play.

In the artistic structure of *Every Man in His Humour* Cob serves the purpose of mirroring in a slight degree the humour of jealousy, which is treated more thoroughly in the case of Kitely. Kitely is drawn in the vein of Jaques de Prie, although with less debt to Plautus and Terence, who were not given to describing the pangs of jealous husbands. The jealous husband, who had already appeared in Greek drama and was a common figure in the popular plays of the Middle Ages, was frequently depicted by the literary dramatists of the Renaissance, nowhere with more skill than in the character of Kitely. The middle-class merchant with an eye to his financial gains furnishes a realistic exterior into which is introduced the dominant trait of jealousy. Kitely's absurd foible causes him a proper amount of unhappiness, but he is finally purged of his fault and made to see the error of his ways. On the whole, he is treated with a sympathy that is surprising, and so is his wife, who has given her husband no cause for his jealousy but is in her turn unjustly suspicious of him.

The elder Knowell is another example of the nice mingling of classical convention and realistic observation. He recalls the old men of Latin comedy in his blind distrust of youth's follies, but he also mixes much shrewd common sense with his unnecessary admonitions. In the Folio text there is less emphasis than there was in the original Quarto[1] on Young Knowell's passionate love for true poetry, with the result that, while the son becomes more faintly drawn than he was in the earlier version of the play, his father's dislike for literary tastes is made to appear more human and forgivable. Knowell's re-deeming trait, his extreme love for his son, which is laudable in in-tention, if perverted in expression, is suitably disciplined when it makes him an easy mark for the strategies of his servant, Brainworm.

Young Knowell's shadowy love affair gives *Every Man in His Humour* the superficial structure demanded by a classical comedy, but Brainworm is the real center of a play which depends decidedly more upon character than upon plot. Brainworm, a combination of wily slave and medieval "Vice," engages in his deceits first for the purpose of making money and secondly from sheer love of amusement. This secondary element, delight in mischief-making for its own sake, is a contribution of popular drama to the comic tradition, which adds immeasurably to the zest of a play. It is entertaining to see Brain-

---

[1] The Quarto text of *Every Man in*, in which the scene is laid in Italy and the characters have Italian names, appeared in 1601. The Folio of 1616 contained the revised version, with its English background and names, which is more familiar to us.

worm tricking all the characters indiscriminately, and his exploits give an underlying unity to the motley group of persons represented in this comedy. Occasionally his jests are so ill-judged that they make him liable to punishment by the law, but he is easily forgiven because of the discomfort that he has brought upon the most ridiculous and vulnerable characters in the dramatic action.

The three gulls that are the chief victims of Brainworm are the principal targets for Jonson's scorn. Master Stephen does not even know how to use the hawk he has bought in the country and is quite unable to adapt himself to city ways. A cheap rapier is easily palmed off on him as a pure Toledo blade, and he soon becomes a devoted follower of the town gulls. Master Matthew, the son of a fishmonger, wishes to be thought a gentleman of fashion and a poet into the bargain. He borrows his verses quite brazenly from Marlowe or Daniel, and he learns something about the art of fencing from Bobadill. He is as successful in his imitation of that mighty warrior as Stephen is pathetic in his vain attempts to adopt fashionable oaths and the habit of using tobacco. The country gull's absurd efforts to improve his social status are so inefficient that his only punishment is to be left in his native simplicity. He dines in the buttery with Cob and his wife, while Matthew for his more serious transgression is sent supperless to the courtyard in company with Bobadill.

Bobadill is the most accomplished of the gulls, and at times he even rises superior to that classification. Like most of the characters in this play, he is a mixture of literary tradition and careful observation. As a *miles gloriosus*, he is connected with the artificial Pyrgopolynices of Plautus and is suitably chastised. As a "Paul's man," he shows wits and some finesse in dealing with his inferiors. He does not boast blatantly about his military exploits until someone has drawn him out. His exploits, as he narrates them, depend not upon prodigious valor but upon extraordinary skill in strategy. The dignified reserve into which he withdraws, although akin to the melancholy of Stephen and more conventional gulls, adds a touch of refined subtlety to a portrait which in its broad outlines is farcical and obvious. Bobadill's stock of oaths bears witness not only to his braggadocio but to his ingenuity. There is a nice variety in his "By St. George! the foot of Pharaoh! the body of me! as I am a gentleman and a soldier!" He drinks and smokes with an air, he fences well, he admires *The Spanish Tragedy*, but his proud words shrivel into nothing before a person like Downright, whose forte is action, not language.

Bobadill is exposed and punished at the end of the play by the jovial Clement, who dispenses both poetic and legal justice. This kindly magistrate (more kindly in the Folio than in the original Quarto, it may be noted) sums up the entire play in the last scene and by his judgments enforces Jonson's views. Bobadill and Matthew, "the sign o' the soldier, and picture o' the poet," are treated most severely because their talents are, when misapplied, the most harmful. Stephen, the simpleton, is paired with Cob, whose good nature about equalizes his absurd pretensions. The other characters are to learn from their experiences and to live saner lives in the future: "Come, I conjure the rest to put off all discontent. You, Master Downright, your anger; you, Master Knowell, your cares; Master Kitely and his wife, their jealousy." Downright's anger is less of an offense than Knowell's cares, as Knowell's cares are less injurious than Kitely's jealousy, but all three are to be pardoned as springing from innately good instincts, not from simplicity or roguery.

Justice is tempered with mercy, or rather with good humor, as Clement chooses his own favorite among the company: "This night we'll dedicate to friendship, love, and laughter. Master bridegroom, take your bride and lead; every one a fellow. Here is my mistress, Brainworm! to whom all my addresses of courtship shall have their reference." This final union of the just but generous Clement with the mischievous Brainworm strikes exactly the right note for the conclusion of *Every Man in His Humour*, a comedy which represents the world as an amusing place where the individual's limitations involve him in laughable predicaments and where the punishment exactly fits the crime. Good intentions ultimately prevail, the brainless suffer only from their own incapacity, and no one is damned except the conscious hypocrites. Bodabill and Matthew fall into this latter class, but in the revised version even they are let off more easily, as if Jonson had come to the humane conclusion that nobody is a conscious hypocrite when every man is depicted in his true humour.

Ben Jonson's first humour comedy contains many brilliant illustrations of its author's aesthetic theory; his second one expounds the theory so precisely that little malleability and almost no charm remain in it. *Every Man out of His Humour* was acted late in 1599 or early in 1600 and, probably in large part because of the success of its predecessor, carried out the germinal ideas of the earlier play beyond reasonable limits. In *Every Man in*, the characters are punished according to the extent of their folly; in *Every Man out*, they suffer so greatly from indulging their humours that they all become reconciled to leaving their imperfections behind them. In *Every Man in*, the nature of a humour is suggested and its serious aspect touched on; in *Every Man out*, it is exactly defined in words that have become famous in the history of comic drama:

> As when some one peculiar quality
> Doth so possess a man, that it doth draw
> All his effects, his spirits, and his powers
> In their confluctions, all to run one way
> This may be truly said to be a humour.

This formula, along with much other critical comment, appears in the elaborate Induction, where Jonson in the words of Asper explains the general drift of the play. Not content with this marginal comment, the author prefixed to the printed edition a careful description of the various persons in the comedy, after the manner of the *Characters* of Theophrastus. No one after reading these trenchant characterizations could be ignorant that all the figures in Asper's play were set up to be ridiculed and reformed. The difference in mood between the two humour plays is aptly expressed at the beginning of each. *Every Man in* will be concerned not with romantic complications,

> But deeds, and language, such as men do use,
> And persons, such as comedy would choose,
> When she would shew an image of the times,
> And sport with human follies, not with crimes.

Asper in *Every Man out* says he will not compromise with humanity,

> Not I: my language
> Was never ground into such oily colours,
> To flatter vice, and daub iniquity:
> But, with an armed and resolved hand,
> I'll strip the ragged follies of the time
> Naked as at their birth.

Every Man out of His Humour is frankly a "comicall satyre," as the title page indicates, and not, strictly speaking, a comedy at all. It contains no high-spirited people like Brainworm and Justice Clement to unmask the fallible members of society. Instead of the fun-loving Clement there is the envious Macilente, and the gay roguery of Brainworm is supplanted by the surly joking of Carlo Buffone. At the end of the fourth act Macilente and Buffone conspire to punish all their acquaintances, as they succeed in doing with remarkable thoroughness. In the course of his exploits Macilente goes to the palace, where Jonson has an opportunity to extend his social range by showing a court lady who prides herself on her wit mistaking a country clown for a gentleman, while the clown, who has been trying to learn the manners of the city, proves utterly unable to adapt himself to fashionable society.

There are three contrasted rural types in this play: the stupid fellow who has money and wants to learn how to spend it; a young student from the country who to his stingy old father keeps applying for more funds; and the father who remains at home, taking pleasure in the bad weather which ruins the crops of his neighbors and makes the poor still poorer. When good weather comes in spite of his almanacs, the farmer resolves to hang himself but is cut down by some rustics, who on recognizing him regret that they have saved him. This evidence of his unpopularity puts the farmer into a penitent mood. His reform is accomplished by a sentimental appeal to his better nature, not by the ridicule which is brought to bear on most of the characters in *Every Man out of His Humour*.

While Macilente was managing affairs at court, Carlo Buffone had been arranging to dehumourize the other misguided persons. Fastidious Brisk, an impoverished but affected courtier, is taken to a debtors' prison, where a citizen's wife, who dotes on him, comes to help him and is found by her unsuspicious husband. The husband, blindly in love up to this point, now suddenly becomes aware of his wife's folly. He will worship her no longer, and she on her side suddenly realizes that it is not wise to antagonize a rich husband in favor of an impecunious fop like Fastidious Brisk, who in turn learns from his imprisonment the folly of empty display. In this fashion all the dupes of the play are driven out of their humours.

Jonson's greatest technical difficulty came with the problem of having the reformers see the errors of their own ways. Nothing less than physical force would impress the hardened Buffone, but his callousness could not be allowed to go unpunished. Jonson made use of a picturesque story current at the time when he had one of Buffone's victims seal his tormentor's lips with wax to shut off the cruel gibes that were issuing from them. The victim was encouraged in his revenge by Macilente, who here turns against his partner and becomes the ultimate force in stripping the ragged follies of the time. To reform Macilente was a still more delicate matter, if Jonson was to keep within the bounds of the rigid scheme which he had imposed on himself for this comedy. Macilente's humour began by his being envious at the good fortune of others, but, as the play progresses, his dominant trait turns into a dislike for the success of fools and rogues. Then by the time that the other characters have reformed, Macilente can truthfully identify himself with Asper and say:

> My humour, like a flame, no longer lasts
> Than it hath stuff to feed it; and their folly
> Being now raked up in their repentant ashes,
> Affords no ampler subject to my spleen.

Macilente's position here is inconsistent with that which he held at the beginning of the comedy, but in no other way could Jonson have carried out his essentially undramatic program, except by introducing a god from the machine, as he had evidently intended to do in the person of Queen Elizabeth. Macilente was to have gone to court and there to have been overpowered by the brightness of his sovereign, but the idea of bringing the Queen upon the stage did not meet with approval and this incident was later canceled in favor of the present forced conclusion.

III

In his next play, *Cynthia's Revels, or The Fountain of Self-Love*, performed late in 1600 by the children of the Queen's Chapel, Jonson determined to amplify the experiment of representing the Queen upon the stage and this time to identify her with Cynthia, the virgin goddess, in a classical legend after the manner of John Lyly. Whether or not the Actaeon story was applicable to the situation of Essex, the conception of the fountain by the side of which Narcissus pined away from love of his own image must have been sympathetic to the Jonsonian theory of humours. Inasmuch as all personal foibles spring from the root of self-love, a mythological story centering in conceit was a natural setting for a satire upon human errors. At the beginning of the drama Echo laments her lost lover, Narcissus, and curses the fountain where he died in the following words:

Henceforth, thou treacherous and murdering spring,
Be ever called the FOUNTAIN OF SELF-LOVE:
And with thy water let this curse remain,
As an inseparate plague, that who but taste
A drop thereof, may, with the instant touch,
Grow dotingly enamoured on themselves.

It was a simple device to make the humourous characters of the play drink from this fountain, the only difficulty being that they were all filled with conceit before they ever tasted the magic draught.

This machinery connected the persons in the comedy with Elizabeth and made a picture of court follies the logical object of its satire. Jonson was beginning to know more of aristocratic life as he attained dramatic success, and it was natural for him, in *Cynthia's Revels*, to compose variations on the themes of superficial courtier and arrogant court lady which he had already announced in *Every Man out of His Humour*. The rough plebeian poet could not, however, sympathize with the fops and coquettes he was depicting; *Cynthia's Revels* is more satiric than any work that had yet come from his pen. The satire is heightened at the expense of dramatic effectiveness by the transposition of the character sketches placed at the head of his previous comedy into the spoken text of *Cynthia's Revels*. Jonson was always inclined to have his characters describe one another at length, but never before this play, and rarely after it, did he venture such elaborate literary portraits as those which are contained in the second act of *Cynthia's Revels*. After the *dramatis personae* have been so carefully described, there is almost nothing further that can be done with them. Drinking at the Fountain of Self-Love will not augment the essential selfishness of their already unyielding natures.

They are all characters such as had appeared in Jonson's earlier comedies. Here skillful literary treatment, not novelty of conception, makes them distinctive. There is "a gallant wholly consecrated to his pleasures"; a brazen fellow "who speaks all that comes in his cheeks and will blush no more than a sackbut"; a traveler "so made out of a mixture of shreds of forms, that himself is truly deformed"; and the traveler's young sycophant, who "sweats to imitate him in every thing to a hair, except a beard, which is not yet extant." In this play Jonson is so intent on satirizing court life that he pays very little attention to the lower and middle classes of society.

At the court, women were more important than in bourgeois circles, and here Jonson encountered another obstacle to his talents. He was never much at his ease in depicting the female sex, especially of the highly civilized variety. In *Cynthia's Revels* he does not attempt much more in characterization than to give the ladies abstract names that will reveal their personal peculiarities. The climax of this method is reached in the character of Argurion (Money), who loves a rich man and swoons when he distributes valuable presents with lavish munificence. Argurion is reminiscent of the Aristophanic conception of Wealth. She focuses for a moment the love of riches which plays an important part in all Jonson's comedy.

The foolish pretenders to elegance are destined to be overthrown, but Jonson makes no effort to invent a logical succession of events which will bring about that conclusion. It is motivated from without by the gracious Queen, with the help of her human instruments, the scholarly Crites and the virtuous Arete, who are set up as contrasts to the various forms of folly represented by the gallants and court ladies. Dramatically the total effect of this exaggerated conflict between vice and virtue is very pallid, but the vigorous invective directed against thoughtless pleasure has a moral and personal impressiveness largely derived from the character of Crites. According to the character sketch of this retired scholar, he is "a creature of a most perfect and divine temper: one, in whom the humours and elements are peaceably met, without emulation of precedency; he is . . . in all so composed and ordered, as it is clear Nature went about some full work, she did more than make a man when she made him." He is the earthly ideal, but the earthly ideal infused with the personality of Ben Jonson, and it is no wonder that the poet's enemies accused him of possessing the self-love which he was attacking in this play. The self-appointed chastiser of society ought to reckon with the mote that is in his own eye before he boldly says of his work, as Jonson does in the last line of his Epilogue, "By God 'tis good, and if you like't, you may."

When one is taking such high ground as that abrupt conclusion suggests, it is the part of discretion to avoid antagonizing one's personal enemies. Jonson did not take this precaution in *Cynthia's Revels*, where two of the gallants, "the one a light voluptuous reveller, the other a strange arrogating puff," have traits which they obviously share with objects of the author's special dislike, John Marston and Thomas Dekker. These two men were further attacked by Jonson in his next comedy, *Poetaster, or His Arraignment*, where they appear under the names of Crispinus, the poetaster of the title, and Demetrius Fannius, a ragged "dresser of plays." The absurd diction of the one and the doggerel meter of the other are subjected to ridicule, but it is their jealous opposition to Horace, the true poet, which is most clearly emphasized. The fact that Marston was a satirist without moderation and Dekker a realist with more high spirits than settled judgment explains clearly enough the underlying causes for the rivalry between them and Jonson, a comic poet who, by the use of his intelligence, succeeded in combining satire and realism. Horace triumphs over his enemies in two contrasting ways: he skillfully purges Crispinus of his unwieldy vocabulary by means of an emetic, and he compassionately intercedes for Demetrius, who was to have been punished by being branded on the forehead.

Poetaster was composed for the purpose of disclosing the frailties of Jonson's enemies as well as of depicting its author's ability and magnanimity. Horace is more cautiously and less idealistically drawn than Crites. He is intended to be Jonson in so far as he has suffered from the attacks of his enemies; his perfection is constantly repressed to avoid giving the appearance of self-conceit. It is extremely curious that Jonson ever thought of representing his own rugged personality under the urbane guise of the Latin poet, with whom he had nothing in common except a gift for satire. In the "Apologetical Dialogue" at the end of *Poetaster* it is stated that the author selected the times of Augustus Caesar as the period for his play,

> To shew that Virgil, Horace, and the rest
> Of these great master-spirits, did not want
> Detractors then, or practicers against them.

The similarity between Jonson and the Roman poets is certainly not a very striking one. The effort to enforce it raised all sorts of difficulties in the construction of the drama.

Virgil is introduced as of higher rank than Horace, in order that Jonson may not be accused of drawing himself as the perfect poet. But whom does Virgil stand for? Is he Shakespeare or Chapman or just an impersonal ideal? Ovid, on the other hand, is pictured as inferior to Horace, although he upholds the profession of literature against his father's love of the law and suggests Ben Jonson's own early struggles to embark on an artistic career. Perhaps Ovid in the first act must be looked upon as the youthful Jonson and Virgil in the last act be considered as embodying the dramatist's exalted ambitions, with Horace, thus robbed of much activity and glory, representing the static Jonson of 1601, without a past and without a future.

Ovid serves another purpose than to develop the threefold literary ideal that he shares with Virgil and Horace. He is engaged in a love affair with Augustus' daughter, from whom he parts in a scene, bordering on tragedy, that is a striking indication of how intensely *Poetaster* is conceived and how ineptly it is executed. One of the reasons for the failure of this scene is that its elevated tone is quite unexpected, after the far from dignified banquet at which the lovers have been diverting themselves. The social group of poets, their mistresses, and their friends are handled throughout in a clumsy and ambiguous way, as if Jonson had never quite made up his mind whether he wished them to be laughed at or admired.

There is a strange quality of indecision about all of *Poetaster*, as if Jonson had started this play with the satire left over from *Cynthia's Revels* and then, to eke out the thinness of his material, had introduced a number of incongruous minor details. Crispinus, for instance, is at one moment the prototype of Marston and at another the foolish lover of a plodding tradesman's socially ambitious wife; he plays the part of the bore whom Horace met on the Via Sacra, and he is the subservient follower of Captain Pantilius Tucca, the most vital figure of the many that occur in *Poetaster*. Tucca is a craven soldier like Bobadill, not quite so subtly drawn, but with more gusto of mind and body. He is not unworthy of comparison with Falstaff; one is inclined to believe that he would be a much more famous person if the play in which he appears had more value as an individual work of art. It is unfortunate that Tucca is connected on the one hand with Crispinus-Marston and on the other with certain actors against whom Jonson had a grievance. Their identities have not been specifically determined, but as enemies of Ovid and Horace they probably belong to the limited range of personal satire which disfigures *Poetaster* and yet is the chief reason for its existence. The dignity of Jonson's total program, which is always hovering in the background, redeems this play from being merely commonplace and badly organized invective.

IV

Five years elapsed between Jonson's farewell to comedy in the "Apologetical Dialogue" of *Poetaster* and his return to working in that genre. In the four plays he had produced in quick succession from 1598 to 1601 he had carried beyond its logical conclusion the theory he had evolved from his early experiments. It had become hardened into a formula, broadened into an allegorical pattern, and narrowed to express personal rancor; it was time for its author to enter a new field of dramatic activity. He had experimented with a Roman background in *Poetaster*, and he had made an approach to tragedy in the parting scene between Ovid and his mistress. It was not unnatural that his next play should be a tragedy with a Roman setting. *Sejanus* bears a certain superficial resemblance to its predecessor, but in spirit it is much more like Jonson's next comedy, *Volpone, or The Fox*, which appeared in 1606. In *Sejanus* the pleasure-loving emperor Tiberius and his ambitious favorite Sejanus are treated in the humour method with a certain dryness and detachment not well suited to tragedy. In *Volpone* Jonson has taken as his central figure a man who, combining the qualities of Tiberius and Sejanus, catches something of the magnificence that comes from their exalted position as historical personages.

Volpone is as sensuous an epicurean as the Emperor and as untiringly active in his evil schemes as the imperial favorite. His worldly desires are fed by the money which it is his pleasure to wring from unsuspecting simpletons, but it is hard to tell whether the physical or mental delights involved give him the greater satisfaction. Jonson has here taken money as the symbol of both man's material and intellectual development; the possession of it has proved his abilities and will procure his pleasures. To need money is absurd; to have it in abundance is equally ridiculous. Both to have it and to want more, as Volpone does, verges on the criminal rather than the amusing. The Fox is a colossal figure of vice portrayed with a Renaissance zest foreign to the classical sources of Lucian and Petronius on which Jonson drew for his story of the cheater of legacy-hunters.

Volpone is represented as a luxurious Venetian, poet, artist, and sensualist. The gorgeous speech at the opening of the play in which he greets the sun and his gold reveals his appreciation of beauty and his ability to express it in words. The dwarf, eunuch, and hermaphrodite who wait upon him are signs of his degenerate taste in seeking out strange and unnatural manifestations of human life, expensive to obtain and curious to observe. His ability as an actor becomes apparent in his pretense of sickness when the birds of prey who hope to inherit his estate are received at his bedside. The Vulture, the Raven, and the Crow are as greedy as the Fox, but they lack his stature and versatility. One cannot help sharing in Volpone's pleasure when, with the aid of his henchman Mosca, or the Fly, he cheats men no more noble and far less clever than himself.

A modicum of sympathy with Mosca and his master having been established in the first act, Jonson is ready to start a train of action which will lead to their mutual undoing. Volpone's impassioned wooing and attempted rape of the noble wife of one of his dupes are interrupted by the entrance of the son of another of them, who is seeking to save his father from the Fox's rapacious clutches. If the wife and the son respectively were more active characters, they might represent the forces hostile to evil in this world, but after the son's momentary heroism they lapse into the position of injured innocence. When they appear as prisoners before the bar of justice, the interest centers not on them but on whether Mosca and his allies can overcome the truth of facts by the sophistry of reason. Jonson here gives a powerful demonstration of how gold can buy out justice. He makes one of the dupes an unprincipled lawyer, who, aided by the false witness of the other legacy-hunters, successfully defends Volpone.

At this point in the play the original situation has been restored, but Volpone is not contented with having retrieved his lost position. He wishes to exploit his talents further by pretending that he has died and left Mosca as his heir. The lawyer, infuriated, confesses his own duplicity to the court, but when he learns that Volpone is still alive he returns to the earlier version of his story. The venality of the law is further emphasized by the avarice of one of the Venetian magistrates, who is less eager to administer justice than to secure a rich son-in-law. The court scenes in Acts IV and V carry to a triumphant conclusion the theme of how in a practical world anything can be accomplished by gold, if it is handled with the proper skill.

The point at which Volpone finally overreaches himself is in trusting his affairs unreservedly to Mosca. From the beginning of this sardonic comedy the parasite has appeared as a faithful servant, living off the craft of his master. Mosca has shown a spirit of his own in inventing new stratagems, but he never attempted to work against Volpone until the Fox made the fatal error of giving out the news that he himself was dead. The opportunity thus offered to Mosca's ingenuity was too great to be resisted, and in this way retribution is brought on Volpone by a member of his own household. Justice can only be maintained when thieves fall out, as they do in the last act of *Volpone*, where a new element is introduced into the play, turning it from a brilliant satire on the love of money into an exciting theatrical duel between master and man, like that which had been the subject of *Sejanus*.

As the complete overthrow of Tiberius' favorite is held in doubt until the end of the tragedy, so the conflict between Mosca and Volpone is not resolved until the very last minute. The Fly and the disguised Fox stand side by side before the court, the one asserting that Volpone is dead, the other that he is still alive. When Mosca is upheld, and Volpone is threatened with whipping, the Fox tears off his disguise, reveals his true identity, and involves Mosca in his ruin. Summary justice is executed upon them both: Mosca is to go to the galleys, Volpone is sent to prison. The play is enough of a comedy to have the servant triumph over the master, but it is tragic in depicting the ruin of an aspiring parasite. It does not purge the audience either by emotion or laughter; its appeal is to horror at the bestial impulses that lurk beneath the surface of human nature. *Volpone* does not fall into any definite artistic category, but its constant emphasis on the subject of avarice gives it an underlying unity of conception that more than compensates for its apparent wantonness in defying the formal rules of comic procedure.

The chief excrescence in this somewhat barbaric and unwieldy play is its most typically Jonsonian feature, the episode of Sir Politick and Lady Would-be. These characters are not entirely unrelated to the main plot, because Lady Would-be is a hanger-on of Volpone's and testifies for him in the trial scene, but in mood they are quite different from the effete Venetian society in which they move. They are English people on their travels, both geographically and imaginatively. They find themselves among a strange company that has sprung from Latin literature and is only partially domesticated in Renaissance Venice. The Would-bes are not at home in the somber half-tragic atmosphere of the rest of the comedy, but they disport themselves in it very unconcernedly. Sir Pol, the pretentious Englishman traveling abroad, has come to Venice only because of his wife's wishes. His chief desire is to get all the news from home as soon as possible. As his name implies, he has first of all the humour of thinking himself a politician and indulging in abstruse plots; to this ·main eccentricity is attached a weakness for projects (chimerical schemes) and diaries. Lady Would-be is a pretender to fashion and culture, who by her extreme talkativeness infuriates Volpone and gives the audience a chance for hearty laughter. At the end of the comedy she and her husband depart from Venice, the wife disgusted by Mosca's trickery and Sir Pol driven out of his humour of plotting as the result of a farcical practical joke that has been played on him by a chance acquaintance.

The Would-bes distract attention from the satire upon avarice. They do something to lighten the gloomy tone of *Volpone*, and they infuse an English element into its fantastic setting. Their presence may have been partially responsible for the great success of the piece, which in turn may help to explain the milder mood of Jonson's next comedy. *Epicoene, or The Silent Woman* (written in prose, in contrast to the verse of *Volpone*) did not appear until 1609, and during the interim Jonson had had increasing success as a writer of masques for the court of James I. When he embarked upon comedy again, he seemed to be more willing to indulge in the genial horseplay of Sir Politick and the obvious humours of his wife than to continue the satiric method he had so brilliantly inaugurated with Volpone, Mosca, and their dupes. The plot of *Epicoene* is as farcical in essence as the scene in *Volpone* where Sir Pol hides beneath a tortoise shell, and the group of Ladies Collegiate is a multiplied and diffused version of Lady Would-be. As a whole, they hit at women's clubs; individually, they are examples of jealousy and lasciviousness in feminine nature. They help to create the noise which Morose hates and which drowns out serious thought in *The Silent Woman*.

The Ladies Collegiate pick up a thread of *Volpone*, and the other incidental characters in *Epicoene* hark still farther back in Jonson's work. Sir John Daw and Sir Amorous La-Foole are a whining coward and a "brave, heroic coward" in the duel scene imitated from *Twelfth Night*. Actually they resemble Bobadill and Pantilius Tucca less than they do Master Matthew and Fastidious Brisk. Sir John is "a fellow that pretends only to learning, buys titles, and nothing else of books in him"; Sir Amorous is proud of his social accomplishments and positively lyric about the La-Fooles of London, "as ancient a family as any is in Europe." These pretenders to learning and high breeding unite in their empty boasts of success with the ladies, at this point foreshadowing the false wits of Restoration comedy.

Sir Amorous' kinswoman, Mrs. Otter, has married beneath her station and feels much superior to the crass vulgarity of her husband, Captain Otter, who has three drinking cups known as the bull, the bear, and the horse. The marital quarrels of the Otters increase the noisiness of the proceedings in *The Silent Woman* and make poor Tom Otter, who always comes off second best in the arguments with his wife, keenly aware of the seamy side of matrimony. They also help to convince Morose of his folly in having married even a supposedly dumb wife. Otter's habit of interlarding his remarks with Latin and a similar characteristic of Cutbeard, the barber, make them ideal mock representatives of theology and the law, when Morose finally determines upon a divorce. The scene in the fifth act in which they get the old man to admit his impotence and then bring witnesses against his wife's chastity is undoubtedly the most hilarious in the play. It is the culmination of the plot against Morose that is engineered by his nephew, in revenge for having been disinherited. Aided by his friends, the nephew has persuaded his uncle to marry a girl with a reputation for silence, who as soon as the ceremony is performed develops into a noisy creature, with the result that Morose immediately wants to be rid of her.

This hatred of sounds, which is the central theme of *The Silent Woman*, exposes the fundamental triviality of the play. It is farcical not only in execution but in conception. Love of quiet is no such basic human concern as the love of gold treated in *Volpone*. If love of quiet be deepened and enlarged to become a love of solitude and scorn for one's fellow mortals, a philosophical problem more far-reaching than avarice is involved, but Jonson in this play refused to face it. This subject had to wait for Molière to treat it in *The Misanthrope* ("Le Misanthrope"), of which *The Silent Woman* is a boisterous forerunner. Perhaps Jonson himself was not sufficiently detached from life to consider the dilemma of the self-contained man as anything more than a colossal jest.

If *Epicoene* is more superficial than *Volpone* it is also gayer, and it shows a marked advance in Jonson's ability to construct a well-integrated plot. It justly deserves the particular praise on that score for which Dryden singled it out in the *Essay of Dramatic Poesy*; it is a classic example of the artfully contrived surprise ending. The audience is as amazed as the hero's uncle, or as his officious and complacent friends, when the silent woman whom Morose has married turns out to be a boy. As the price of being freed from his unpleasant alliance, Morose agrees to a financial settlement with his nephew, who at the final curtain reveals the imposture that he has arranged. The incident of a boy taking the place of a bride, which appears in Plautus' *Casina* and Aretino's *Marescalco*, fills out the story of the surly man that comes from Libanius. Although there may be some difference of opinion as to whether it is wise for a dramatist to keep an important secret from his audience, there can be no question that the technical skill with which Jonson manages his complicated plot is extraordinary. It gives to *Epicoene* a proportion and balance which one looks for in tragedy but rarely expects to find in a thin and uproarious comedy.

V

In 1610, one year after the performance of *Epicoene*, Jonson produced his comic masterpiece, *The Alchemist*. In this play he improved on the excellent technique of *Epicoene*, he treated foibles of more weight than moroseness, but he avoided the tragic implications of *Volpone*. Most important, he had found a subject closely related to the life of his own day which gave him a superb opportunity to depict his favorite humour, love of wealth. Although the study of alchemy, which had once been of immense importance, still flourished in Jonson's time, it was beginning to forfeit the serious attention which it had held for two hundred and fifty years; its technical vocabulary was already a subject for ridicule. Both in itself and for the state of mind of which it was a symptom, it exactly suited the purpose of the comic dramatist.

The unique suitability of this subject in the early seventeenth century has tended to interfere with the subsequent popularity of the comedy which deals with it. That *The Alchemist*, written, like *Volpone*, in verse, has signally triumphed over the difficulties of its subject and vocabulary is the highest tribute that can be paid to the ability with which it was conceived and executed. Jonson has here caricatured indelibly the absurdities of a mad scramble for money, whether pursued by unscrupulous knaves or greedy simpletons, in connection with alchemy, the South Sea Bubble, or the ticker tape.

The chief characters in *The Alchemist* are, like those in *Sejanus* and *Volpone*, a selfish superior and his confederate assistant. Subtle, the poor alchemist, is no Roman emperor or magnifico of Venice, and Face, his subordinate, is merely a butler, whose master has left town because of the plague. The struggle between these two rogues has broken out before the opening of the play, but throughout its course they are allies in cheating other people. Subtle furnishes the alchemy; Face provides the house and many of the dupes. They are held together by their mutual use to each other in the "venture tripartite," of which Dol Common is also a sharing member. All things are to be held in common by the three rascals, as in a primitive kind of socialism, but from the beginning there is disagreement between the men, whose rapacious individualistic impulses interfere with the cooperation to which they have agreed. When each sees the chance of marrying a rich young widow, open warfare breaks out between them. The younger and more spirited of the two is about to succeed, but Lovewit, the master of the house, returns, and Face has quickly to subside into his old role of butler.

This change of front in the last act of *The Alchemist* has been much better prepared for than the corresponding moment in *Volpone*. Face attempts a few lies, as does Tranio, the clever slave in Plautus'

Mostellaria, under like circumstances, but he soon has to throw himself upon Lovewit's mercy. His master, partially from inherent good nature and partially from a self-centered willingness to marry the widow in question, forgives his erring butler and ends the play in the jovial tone of Justice Clement in *Every Man in His Humour*, which was perhaps revised about this time. Lovewit is not a formal dispenser of rewards and punishments, but his behavior has the effect of letting Face go scot-free, while Dol and Subtle are forced ignominiously to decamp, leaving their plunder behind them. Their fate is not so harsh as Volpone's, but much more severe than that of Morose. *The Alchemist* has not the tragic power of *Volpone*, but it is far superior in quality to the broad humor of *The Silent Woman*. In structural outline it resembles the earlier play, in the details of technical execution it is like the later one, and it combines to excellent advantage the good points of these two preceding comedies.

The young widow, whose love affairs furnish a unifying thread for the last part of the action, is characteristically the most colorless person in the drama, but the man who comes to her assistance is much more sharply defined than the similar character in *Volpone*. Surly, whose anger springs from his well-intentioned dislike of evil but whose bad temper makes him an easy victim for the sharpers, rescues the heroine and then hopes by marrying her to secure the money that he sorely needs. He is not an attractive figure, and we cannot sympathize with him very heartily when Face gathers the other dupes against his enemy, as Mosca did in a similar emergency and with similar success. Surly does not enjoy even a momentary triumph. In this comedy austere virtue like Surly's is not rewarded, whereas Face's clever trickery is pardoned and the joking Lovewit receives a wealthy bride. Face's victory as well as Surly's fate takes off the curse of severe morality in *The Alchemist*. Moderation is the first ethical quality that Ben Jonson demands, but at his most inspired he insists that geniality is of almost equal importance.

The characters who suffer most are those who have neither physical nor spiritual contentment, and the fewer wits they have, the more follies are forgiven them. Dapper, the lawyer's clerk, the stupidest of all the dupes, is very nearly a pathetic figure. Abel Drugger, an ambitious tobacco-man, is punished more severely than Dapper for his desire to increase his business by necromancy and consulting almanacs. The most avaricious person in the play is Sir Epicure Mammon, who dominates the other characters by the range of his sensuous imagination and the glory of the words in which he clothes it. He has a poet's language and a poet's sense of physical beauty, but like his creator he lacks the vision of an inspired seer. The furthest flight of his fancy is a description of the pleasures that will be his after he has secured his wealth. He will have his bed blown up, not stuffed; "down is too hard."

> Then, my glasses
> Cut in more subtle angles, to disperse
> And multiply the figures, as I walk
> Naked between my succubae. My mists
> I'll have of perfume, vapoured 'bout the room,
> To lose our selves in; and my baths, like pits
> To fall into; from whence we will come forth,
> And roll us dry in gossamer and roses.

Sir Epicure Mammon is a poor decayed knight, who is harmless and absurd. His dreams give an element of grandeur to *The Alchemist*, but it is the mock grandeur fitting a realistic comedy.

Sir Epicure has the redeeming trait of taking pleasure in his vain illusions. Except for his avarice, he is the exact opposite of the mean-spirited Puritans, Ananias and Tribulation Wholesome. The Puritans are treated by Jonson more harshly than any of the other dupes, perhaps because they have so little of the joy in living which should pervade true comedy. The two brethren from Amsterdam are nicely differentiated: Tribulation Wholesome is the more practical of the two and concerns himself with the legality of their operations; Ananias, a subtler type, is busy with the details of religious observance, such as saying "Christ-tide" instead of the Popish "Christ-mas." Neither of these Puritans, however, is drawn with so much detail as Rabbi Zeal-of-the-Land Busy in *Bartholomew Fair*, Jonson's next comedy, which was performed four years later, in 1614. Jonson had had time to recover from the failure of *Catiline*, another Roman tragedy, in 1611, and his career as a writer of masques was progressing triumphantly. *Bartholomew Fair*, written, like *Epicoene*, in prose, is the most rollicking comedy that he had yet produced. In it Jonson lavishes the greatest pains upon his portrait of the lugubrious Busy and holds up to unrestrained ridicule this "capital knave of the land."

None of the dishonest tradespeople at Bartholomew Fair are punished at the end of the play, a circumstance which suggests that in this comedy Jonson is not attacking money-making so much as he is enjoying the various picturesque ways by which it may be accomplished. He has not concentrated on one or two thorough rogues, like Subtle and Face, but has scattered his fire over eight or ten lesser cheats, gaining in the breadth of his appeal what he loses in logical and artistic unity. One's attention is distracted from individual details, but the pageant of a varied and active communal life is fully realized. From Ursula, the enormous pig-woman with her dripping-pan, to Ezekiel Edgworth, the efficient young cutpurse, each of the characters has some individualizing trait. Horse-courser and ballad-singer, bawd and whore, tapster and gingerbread-woman, costard-monger and hobby-horse seller, these rascals all succeed in their mercenary designs, and together they give an inimitable picture of the world, the flesh, and the devil, rampant and unashamed.

Lanthorn Leatherhead, the hobby-horse seller, who is also a toy-man (dealer in trinkets) and puppet-manager, may have been intended as a side thrust at Inigo Jones, and John Littlewit, the proctor, possibly bears a similar relation to Samuel Daniel, Jonson's rival in composing masques. The supposedly respectable Littlewit has surreptitiously written a puppet show called *Hero and Leander*, a horrible burlesque on romantic love and friendship, which is performed in the last act. Littlewit is responsible for the visit to the Fair made by Rabbi Busy; he persuades his pregnant wife to express a desire to eat Bartholomew pig, and her Puritanical mother, Dame Purecraft, insists on Busy's accompanying them. Littlewit resembles Jonson's other ridiculously trusting husbands, and Win-the-Fight, his wife, is a slight sketch of the silly woman who cannot resist temptation because she does not recognize it. When she is discovered in disreputable company at the end of the play, her husband's feeble cry, "Oh my wife, my wife, my wife!" summarily closes their ineffective part in the story.

A more vivid, but not much more rounded, figure is Bartholomew Cokes, Esquire, of Harrow-on-the-Hill, the chief gull in this play and one of the most amusing countrymen in town that Jonson created. Cokes goes through a series of unlucky accidents, which show up the Fair for what it is, but which make no impression upon him. At the end of the play he is taking as much pleasure in the puppets as if he had not had his pocket picked twice, lost his sword, cloak, and hat, and had his marriage license stolen. He finally loses his fiancée also, but there is not enough action in these episodes to make a smoothly running plot. The amount of attention given to Cokes is one reason for the lack of proportion that disfigures *Bartholomew Fair*.

Cokes has brought with him to the Fair his tutor, Humphrey Waspe, who disapproves of that institution and of his charge's being there. "Numps" is drawn with a sure and steady hand as a testy fellow who tries to rule his young master with a rod of iron, but who drinks more than is good for him, gets involved in a quarrel, and is put in the stocks for his pains. He suffers this punishment with Busy and Overdo, the other enemies of the Fair, the latter the brother-in-law of Cokes. Justice Adam Overdo is, like Surly in *The Alchemist*, an honest man who gets himself into trouble. His object is to hunt out and exterminate the "enormities" of the Fair, but he suspects all the wrong people of evil-doing and he is moved to especial sympathy for the most notorious cutpurse of the lot. Overdo is falsely accused of a robbery and is put in the stocks, where he overhears some watchmen talking of his legal severity and, moved to repent, decides to abandon his humour of harshness towards malefactors. His change of heart is more genuine than Busy's and more graceful than Waspe's. "I will never speak while I live again, for aught I know," says Numps, to which Overdo wisely objects, "Nay, Humphrey, if I be patient, you must be so too; . . . I invite you home with me to my house for supper: I will have none fear to go along, for my intents are *ad correctionem, non ad destructionem; ad aedificandum, non ad diruendum*."

In this comedy Jonson's ability to observe has triumphed over his natural tendency to reflect. All the earlier plays reveal a strong classical influence at war with a keen sense of reality. In *The Alchemist* these two opposing elements of Jonson's genius were fused together almost perfectly; *Bartholomew Fair* has an equally vital and equally English subject, but behind its closely observed detail there is less evidence of a masterly mind at work. The rogues and the fools in it are cleverly portrayed, but there is a monotony in the constant triumph of the rascals. Two fortune-hunting gentlemen, each of whom succeeds in marrying a rich wife, share in the success of the sharpers. The three critics of the Fair, whether motivated originally by hypocrisy, bad temper, or morality, all give up their humours. Busy, Numps, and Overdo are the most clear-cut figures in this comedy, but they are quite overpowered by the number of photographic personages who swarm across its stage. *Bartholomew Fair* seethes with vigorous movement and it is rightly regarded as a product of Jonson's great creative period, but because its fable is confused, its characters are too numerous, and its material is not selected with painstaking discrimination, it marks a step downward from the height on which *The Alchemist* stands alone.

VI

If *Bartholomew Fair* shows a decline from the lofty achievement of *The Alchemist*, *The Devil Is an Ass*, performed only two years later, in 1616, is a further weakening in Jonson's dramatic art. The humours of the Fair had been powerfully depicted, but feebly organized; the later play was thin as well as confused. Although it purported to be another realistic comedy of London life, it is introduced by Satan and Pug, his subordinate in evil, who enters the service of an English squire. The professed object of this clumsy supernatural machinery is to show that human vices are closely related to the ways of hell, in fact far surpass them; but the stupidity of Pug prevents the play from making this point at all convincing. The lesser devil wanders in and out of the drama, occasionally obscuring the issue but never exerting great influence upon it, until at the very end his being carried back to hell converts his master to honesty.

Fitzdottrel, Pug's master, is more of a dolt than a rogue; his chief wickedness consists in lending himself unresistingly to the villainy of others. He is the victim of so much and such varied trickery that his personality is chiefly of a negative kind. He needs money, and his attempts to procure it bring him into the clutches of the projector, Meercraft, the principal rogue of the play, who is as astonishingly varied in his technique as Fitzdottrel is unbelievably gullible. Meercraft's chief project is to create his dupe the "Duke of Drownedland"; to other victims he offers such attractive possibilities as making fortunes on cosmetics, toothpicks, and forks. These secondary projects might have provided some amusing scenes, but instead of developing them Jonson introduces new schemes to make a fool of Fitzdottrel. He is finally persuaded to pretend that he is mad, and it is from this trickery that he is frightened into repentance by Pug's sudden disappearance from the earth. At the end of the comedy the devil plot and the gullibility plot come together for a moment, but through most of the play they have little connection with each other.

The Devil Is an Ass also contains a variety of minor characters: a lady projectress and her friend, a fine pair of *précieuses ridicules*; a simple-minded lawyer, who believes everything he hears; the lawyer's assistant, a young man contented with his bourgeois birth; and the assistant's father, who is anxious to have his son shine as a gentleman and write the histories of great men like his namesake Plutarch. Each of these persons comes into contact with Fitzdottrel at some point, but as a group they add nothing to the total impression created by the play. Its effect is also impaired by the intrusion of the sentimental story of Fitzdottrel's wife and her lover, who nobly renounce their mutual affection and decide to part. The lack of naturalness in this episode is opposed to the spirit of realistic comedy. The introduction of Pug may be an awkward attempt on Jonson's part to reconcile these diverse elements in his ill-assorted material. He seems at this time to have been losing his grip on the close union between representing folly and recommending virtue which had characterized his best work and to feel the need of divine intervention to make plain his wandering intentions.

He made a more successful effort in the same direction in his next comedy, The Staple of News, which appeared, after a lapse of ten years, in 1626. In this play Jonson continued his treatment of reformation, but he set it against an Aristophanic background which fitted it far better than did the Satanic machinery of The Devil Is an Ass. The core of The Staple of News is the personification of money who acts the role of its heroine. Pecunia is more like Argurion in Cynthia's Revels than like Wealth in the Plutus of Aristophanes. Both moral allegory and whimsical fancy have gone into creating her. In her main function as the symbol of riches her relation to the three Pennyboys is of most importance to the plot. She dwells with the uncle, a miser and a usurer; she is courted, and temporarily won, by the son, a rich young prodigal; finally she is put under the protection of the father, who has a sufficient sum of money and guards it carefully but not avariciously. The father watches over his son in disguise, and when he sees that the boy has learned by experience the folly of extravagance he again turns Pecunia over to him. In the meantime the greedy uncle has gone mad from the loss of Pecunia and indulged in the mock trial of two dogs — a pale imitation of the similar scene in the *Wasps* of Aristophanes. At the end the uncle is won over by his brother's eloquence to accept the wise moderation that Pecunia should enable the spectators to enjoy,

> That she may still be aid unto their uses,
> Not slave unto their pleasures, or a tyrant
> Over their fair desires; but teach them all
> The golden mean; the prodigal how to live;
> The sordid and the covetous how to die:
> That, with sound mind; this, safe frugality.

This moral is too blatantly expressed, but as it is the most important serious implication behind Jonson's comedy it is in place at the end of his last successful drama. *The Staple of News* is the most outspoken of his plays on the subject of money, which more and more came to dominate his thought. In each of his comedies since *The Alchemist* he had been concerned with some money-making scheme of doubtful morality popular at the time. Now a new and not very respectable way of earning one's living had come into vogue with the news-sheets started by Nathaniel Butter and other stationers in 1622. The public's favorable response to these innovations lured the first editors on to unethical excesses, and Ben Jonson's shrewd eye saw here a good subject for critical comedy. It took more courage to write *The Staple of News* than *The Alchemist*, because of the popularity of the subject under attack, but, since newsmongering had no great tradition behind it, it had to be treated in a comparatively superficial and episodic way. The idea of a clearinghouse for rumors, where all gossip should be distributed to the persons most anxious to hear it, was a purely imaginative conception in the Aristophanic spirit of the entire comedy, but it was executed as the picture of a contemporary abuse drawn with keen incisiveness. The ultimate purpose of the News Staple was to put money into the pockets of its managers, and in that sense they are all connected with the main plot of the play by being suitors for the favors of Lady Pecunia.

During a brilliant scene in the third act Pecunia visits the Staple, and its office is shown in action. Various kinds of customers pay for various kinds of news, which is dispensed by two clerks, one called Nathaniel (Butter) and the other qualified for his post by having been recently a barber; Cymbal, the Master of the Staple, directs the entire business in a jesting way that suits the "Prime Jeerer" of a group whose object is to rail and flatter in the most approved fashion. Other jeerers are used to fill out the rather meager satire on newspapers, among them a doctor of physic, a sea-captain, and a poetaster. These shadowy humours are finally routed by Pennyboy, the wise father, who, we are told, was "akin to the poet" and "had the chiefest part in his play." His function is to abash the jeerers and purveyors of news and to reform his son by appealing to the boy's better nature. The principal idea behind this play is that prodigality as well as avariciousness must be checked and turned into a wise liberality. It is carried forward by the sentimental formula which had insidiously entered into *The Devil Is an Ass*, was now frankly accepted in *The Staple of News*, and finally brought about a complete change of Jonson's comic method in the two feeble works that concluded his dramatic career.

The New Inn, or The Light Heart was acted in 1629 only three years after *The Staple of News*, but the decline in its quality is very marked. Apart from the disastrous circumstances attending its first performance, there can be no doubt that here Jonson is out of his usual humour, with a bad artistic result. *The New Inn*, although purporting to be a comedy, has a romantic plot of the kind Jonson had not treated since the days of *The Case Is Altered*. In that play he had added a second lost child to the one taken over from Plautus; in *The New Inn* he involved an entire family in such mistaken relationships. A rather well-contrived first act explains how it happens that Lord Frampul is acting as host of the inn, where his elder daughter is the principal guest, his wife is engaged as a poor charwoman, and his second daughter, disguised in boy's clothes, is supposed to be the host's son. In the last act recognition scenes between all the characters occur, the two girls are provided with husbands, and everything ends happily in the approved romantic tradition, but with very little merriment.

The supposedly comical "militia" scenes in *The New Inn* are one degree lower in quality than the jeering combats in *The Staple of News*. The militia is an organization of the inn servants. It has been formed by the Host's parasite, and it is much approved by Sir Glorious Tipto, who dominates its activities. Sir Glorious, another boasting soldier, is more at home below stairs than in high society. He and his companions do not appear at all in the serious last act, an omission which Jonson explains in the Epilogue by saying that he did not choose to vent "vapours in the place of wit." The author, as well as the audience, must have been bored by the subordinate characters, who were introduced purely to set off the discussions of love and valor that are the chief business of the play. In fact, if *The New Inn* has any literary value it is because of the arguments on these subjects before the "Court of Love," which doubtless pleased the new queen, Henrietta Maria. Her interest in the cult of Platonic love may help to explain these speeches, which are not bad poetry but which make no pretense of making anyone laugh. They are the logical outcome of the dramatic theory established in *The Staple of News*, as at an earlier period *Cynthia's Revels* followed closely upon the heels of *Every Man out of His Humour*.

There might have been no immediate successor to *Cynthia's Revels* if *Poetaster* had not developed the hint of personal satire latent in that allegory, and there might not have been *The Magnetic Lady, or Humours Reconciled* if love matches like those in *The New Inn* had not been susceptible of further ingenious elaboration. Jonson's last play, acted probably in 1632, departed from the poetic tone and romantic plot of *The New Inn*, although it was written in blank verse throughout and contains one case of concealed identity. In spite of these superficial resemblances *The Magnetic Lady* is a humour comedy in which the various characters are brought together by the attractive qualities of Lady Loadstone's niece, whom many of them wish to marry. In the early comedies by Jonson humours had been harshly dealt with; in *The Magnetic Lady* the object is to prove that crookedness in human nature can be straightened out when serious attention is paid to affairs of the heart. It can hardly be said that this aim is convincingly attained, but the attempt provided a novel plan for the old poet's final efforts to depict the eccentricities of contemporary society.

A typically Jonsonian group of characters is presented in *The*

Magnetic Lady. It includes a punctilious courtier, named Sir Diaphanous Silkworm, a soldier, a scholar, a lawyer, a politician, a tailor, a parson, and a doctor, all endowed with the standard traits of their respective professions. The last two are described in epigrams made by "a great clerk as any is of his bulk, Ben Jonson," and elaborate accounts of the other humours given by a Jonsonian moderator remind one of the character sketches prefixed to *Every Man out of His Humour* and inserted into the text of *Cynthia's Revels*. The former play is also recalled by the conversations of three characters who act as an incidental chorus and who repeat for the last time many of Jonson's favorite dicta on comic drama: it must appeal to the judicious; little action is necessary; the unity of time must be observed; general and not particular follies are to be shown; and the last act should "spring some fresh cheat to entertain the spectators with a convenient delight, till some unexpected and new encounter break out to rectify all, and make good the conclusion."

The Magnetic Lady adds little to Jonson's accomplishment in comedy, but it neatly sums up his work in the setting of a love intrigue adapted to his latest period. Most of the characters resemble those in his earlier plays; two of them stand out with particular vividness. The more original of these persons is Mrs. Polish, Lady Loadstone's gossip, who is as loquacious as Sir John Daw and as outwardly pious as Zeal-of-the-Land Busy. She is described as a she-parasite, in other words, a female Mosca. No scruples stand in her way when there is a possibility of making money, and her overthrow at the end is as complete as that of any Jonsonian rogue.

The seeker after gold and the hoarder of it had always obsessed Jonson's imagination; therefore it was natural for him to introduce the male of the species on the stage, once more, in *The Magnetic Lady*. Sir Moth Interest, the usurer, who employs logarithms to help him in his financial calculations, gives a closely reasoned defense of love of money, with subpoints reaching to the "eighthly." Sir Moth's fate is to fall into a well, while looking for the treasure which he has been led to believe is hidden there, a catastrophe which is as artificial as the drawing of Sir Moth's character is rigid. In *The Magnetic Lady* Jonson is nowhere so much at his ease as he was in his earlier comedies, and the remnants of his early vigor, which can occasionally be detected, are in a pathetic state of decadence and disintegration.

When Jonson died in 1637, only five years before the closing of the theaters by the Puritan Parliament, he left behind him a personal and literary influence that was astonishing. He had already inspired Beaumont and Fletcher and other "sons of Ben" to adapt his dramatic practice to new social conditions in a brilliant and superficial way that was to result in the Restoration comedy of manners. More important than the effect he had upon other writers was what he had accomplished in composing and producing the fourteen comedies which make up his substantial contribution to English comic drama. The force of his impressive personality, working with intellectual concentration and dynamic energy upon the weaknesses of contemporary society, had forged a type of comedy which was original enough to be given a new name. The "comedy of humours" is simply an extension of the typical treatment of character essential to social comedy, where in the two or three hours' traffic of the stage exaggerated human weaknesses are to be subjected to the standard of an implied idealism.

Ben Jonson's criterion for judging his characters is as definite as that of the Greek and Roman dramatists, but it is somewhat obscured by the mass of material which surrounds it. Gifted with the creative vitality of the Renaissance as it appeared in Elizabethan England, Jonson could not limit himself to the narrow scope of Plautus and Terence. The society in which he lived was more varied and less formally organized than theirs; a greater number of types lay under his observation. By his time, physical conditions in the theater had become greatly altered and made much more fluid. With this change went a relaxing of the classical unities and the possibility of an increased richness in dramatic texture, which was not without its loss in logical precision and artistic clarity. Jonson's problem was to apply the best of the classical tradition to conditions in his own day. His progress in working out a new technique that would be suitable for his purposes was slow. He did not always take full advantage of his discoveries, but the surpassing excellence of his two or three best comedies is sufficient evidence that he overcame the principal difficulties inherent in his task.

He began his career by imitating Plautus, but even in his earliest plays there are bursts of laughter at the follies of contemporary civilization. Jonson was a classicist in the best sense of the word: "one who

applies the experience of the past to the perplexities of the present."
He had a fund of natural gaiety in his disposition, but at first he let
it be submerged by his critical faculty. He could not refrain from
showing the absurdity of jealousy, of braggadocio, of false pretenses,
and particularly of avarice. His success in picturing these humours
did much to retard his development as a dramatist. It led him into
an excessive use of his theoretical method, which destroyed itself by
dwindling into lifeless allegory and empty satire. He made a fresh
start with tragedy, where he was not so much at home, but the discipline of which greatly improved his moral fiber and his dramatic
technique. It must be remembered that the original version of *Every
Man in His Humour* was much more austere than the one to which
we are accustomed and that Jonson probably did not rewrite it in
its later form until the period of his greatest theatrical successes,
which began with *Volpone* and ended with *Bartholomew Fair*. The
comedies that come at the end of his career mark a decline which is
not without interesting elements, but which has very little glory
attached to it. Its most notable feature is the clear and picturesque
expression, in *The Staple of News*, of Ben Jonson's basic ethical doctrine, the golden mean, as applied to the acquisition of economic
wealth.

Apart from *Every Man in His Humour*, which is perhaps more important historically than aesthetically, Jonson's reputation as a writer
of dramatic comedy rests on the four mature plays, in which he
treated different aspects of material greed. In *Volpone* he made very
clear that the horrible power of inordinate desire had tragic overtones which seriously interfered with spontaneous laughter; in
Bartholomew Fair he showed that one could be highly amused by
the trickery of clever rascals, if one were willing to overlook its lack
of social justification. *Epicoene* is more concerned with noise than
with money, but Morose's disinheriting of his nephew gives the
impetus to the plot, and the settlement of their financial differences
resolves it. In this lively farce love of gold is associated with dislike
of human society, neither subject receiving the careful treatment
that it deserves. *The Alchemist* is a perfect fulfillment of Jonson's dramatic art. In it the discontented fools are punished, the lovers of wit
are vindicated, and the fate of the rogues depends less upon their
skill than upon external circumstances. Jonson has indicated that

things in this world are not all that they should be, but that it is necessary to know what they should be in order to judge them as they are. *The Alchemist* is richly comic because of the contrast between Jonson's personality and his constructive ideals, which are here brought closely enough together to make the slight gap between them appear entertaining without being ridiculous.

In *The Alchemist* Jonson has treated under a multiplicity of forms the eagerness to make money swiftly and painlessly which characterized the life of his day. He associated that defect with pretensions to social graces and to intelligence; without financial backing a person cannot have education or other cultural advantages. To a writer of critical comedy wealth must seem the core of the earthly follies with which he wishes to sport. Aristophanes came to consider it so, when he changed his attack from political to social evils and ended his career by writing the *Plutus*. Plautus and Terence had been conscious of the same fact when they represented lack of money as the most usual obstacle to the marriage of young lovers and possession of it as causing the greatest absurdities among old men. In Ben Jonson's work the laying up for oneself of treasure upon earth is not only the ruling passion of the aged, but it infects youth also. The sordid atmosphere of his plays is lighted here and there by the unhealthy poetry of a Sir Epicure or the deliberate jocosity of a Lovewit, but even these fitful flashes contain a certain grimness, for they are aroused by a yearning after gold or an exultation in possessing it which binds one firmly to the physical universe. Ben Jonson is at his most characteristic when he is depicting those qualities of which he least approved but which he most thoroughly understood. The final impression left by his theory of humours is that it turns the battery of classical comedy upon the evils of an economic civilization. Ben Jonson has often been called one of the most English of authors, and the traditional gibe against the English is to describe them as a nation of shopkeepers.

CHAPTER IV

Spain's Contribution: Lope de Vega and His School

I

IN THE REALM of comedy differences in place are quite as significant as differences in time. During the era in which Ben Jonson was formulating his theory of humours in the face of English practicality, another striking development in comedy was going on in the Spanish peninsula. Lope de Vega Carpio, its outstanding figure, was born about ten years before Jonson and died two years before him. Although strictly he precedes the English dramatist, their dates roughly coincide. The last important writer of Lope's school, Pedro Calderón de la Barca, was thirty-seven years old when Jonson died in 1637. As Calderón lived to be eighty-one, the golden age of Spanish comedy extended well beyond Jonson's lifetime into the period of Etherege and Wycherley. Spanish drama had a distinct influence on English comedy, both before and after the Puritan interregnum, but the leaders of the two movements were completely unlike. Jonson fought against the Spanish in Flanders, and Lope sailed in the Great Armada; there is every reason why the two men, being products of rival civilizations, should have been as opposed in their art as in their lives.

Lope's avowed purpose was merely to entertain, whereas Jonson set before himself the classical ideal of mingling pleasure and instruction, with emphasis on the didactic element. Lope had had some university education, of which he seems to have been rather proud. He knew the comedies of Plautus and Terence, but he preferred to ignore classical example and to appeal to the judgment of his contemporaries. He had a precedent for doing so, in that Spanish drama had already established something of a literary tradition apart from the medieval liturgical drama and brief secular farces which preceded it. Gil Vicente, a Portuguese author, wrote eleven of his plays in Castilian Spanish and with the remaining thirty-two founded a national drama which Spaniards were anxious to rival; Lope de

Rueda began his career under Italian influences but later turned his talents into original and popular channels; Juan de la Cueva experimented with dramatic and metrical technique, and, more important, he insisted upon the need for a Spanish drama which should deal with national subjects in a national spirit. Lope de Vega came at a time when creative dramatic activity was in the air. His immense success with all sorts and conditions of people proved not only that he tried to make the most of his opportunity but that he had an extraordinary aptitude for expressing himself in the dramatic form.

The popularity of Lope was exceeded only by his productivity. He was far too easy a writer to waste time and energy in perfecting a single play when he could dash off a number of comedies in the twinkling of an eye (on one occasion he wrote fifteen acts in as many days). He is said to have composed eighteen hundred regular plays and more than four hundred religious dramas, or *autos sacramentales*, not all of which are extant. According to the catalogue of Rennert revised by Castro,[1] we have 723 titles and 426 accessible comedies, as well as more than forty *autos*, an incredible amount of work for one man, who, while living a full and varied life, did not devote all his literary activity to the drama. Inevitably, the numerous plays that he did write are of a mixed quality. Many of them do not belong in any definite aesthetic category, but considering Lope's prolific nature the literary level of his work is remarkably high. He did not often stop to create characters of great subtlety, but he scarcely ever failed to give a surface of reality to the persons in his plays. His greatest skill consisted in inventing novel situations which would show off to advantage characters that were essentially conventional. The comedy of character was with him generally incidental to the comedy of situation. He is better known for the number of his successful dramas than for having written a few outstanding masterpieces.

A typical Lope play is concerned with ladies and gentlemen of the age of Philip II. Sometimes the characters are of noble birth, and not infrequently peasants are brought on the stage. The principal *labradores* generally turn out to be aristocrats in disguise or children of the nobility lost in infancy, as is the habit in classical comedy.

---

[1] This revision is to be found in Américo Castro's translation into Spanish of Professor H. A. Rennert's *The Life of Lope de Vega (1562–1635)*, published at Madrid in 1919.

There are usually two important men and two important women, at least one pair of whom are lovers crossed by a cruel fate. Sometimes one of the men has killed or wounded a rival in a duel, a chivalric institution very popular with writers of Spanish comedy, and he must take refuge in disguise or in exile. For some such reason the hero is separated from his lady and really or apparently becomes involved with another woman. The heroine is only too prone to believe that her love has been scorned and at the height of the intrigue is ready to commit suicide or to marry someone else. The first act is occupied with the causes of the misunderstanding, the second with a tangle of cross-purposes, and the third (three acts became fixed in Spain as the proper number for a drama) with clearing up the complications and restoring the lovers to each other's arms. If there is a second pair of lovers, they are also reunited, and, if not, some of the other characters are likely to pair off. A general mating is always in order at the end of a Spanish play, as is fitting for the artistic product of a society in which a formal love code was rigidly enforced and in which one's personal honor depended upon living up to it.

The situation rarely ends in tragedy. Hence, however serious the play may be, it is officially classified as a *comedia*. The truly comic element consists partly in the unnecessary fears of the principal characters but even more in the figure of the clown, or *gracioso*, who is always to be looked for in a play by Lope. This person is derived from the clever servant of Latin comedy, with some incidental help from the Italian *commedia dell'arte* and with his function in the plot considerably changed. Occasionally he helps his master in his love affairs; more often he only comments upon them satirically. His usual characteristics are a wagging tongue and a sophisticated view of life. If he becomes involved in the complications of the plot, it is generally because he is in love with the heroine's maid, and his difficulties tend to be of a material sort. His part in the play is chiefly a humorous commentary on the main intrigue, often quite unrelated to it in essence and subordinate to it in importance. The *gracioso* frequently secures his comic effects from such separate incidents as the desire to tell a story in which he is always interrupted or the necessity of filling his stomach, which like that of the parasite in Latin comedy is in a continual state of emptiness. The *gracioso* is, much like Tony Lumpkin, a combination of intellectual cleverness and practical stupidity. He has a theatrical effectiveness which more than compensates for the lack of consistency in his make-up.

Since Lope's turn of mind was not severely rational, he probably did well not to write his plays in prose. He does not save his verse for important moments, as the comic poet can sometimes do with great effect, but habitually composes in the varied forms of Spanish prosody. At these he is a past master, and he passes easily from short lines to long ones or from rhyme to assonance, changing his meter readily to conform to the spirit of his scenes. His skill with language was, like his skill in compounding plots, so facile that he did not pause to consider the philosophical aspect of his subjects. The appeal which he makes is to the senses rather than to the mind. The fertility of his imagination far exceeds the depth of his comprehension. In the sphere of formal comedy, which was only a limited part of his dramatic achievement, he was able to play an endless number of charming variations upon a simple elementary theme.

The Reward of Fair Speech ("El premio del bien hablar") may be regarded as a characteristic play by Lope. In it the intrigue springs entirely from misunderstandings rather than from limitations of character; in fact, all the persons represented on the stage are admirable by nature, the only unpleasant one in the story having been killed in a duel before the play begins. This disagreeable fellow has slandered a woman, and the hero of the drama, who considers himself the self-appointed defender of the fair sex, has taken a suitable revenge. The hero, who must fly for his life, seeks refuge in the house of a lady who agrees to conceal him as the reward of his nobility. Then the heroine's brother falls in love with the hero's sister, who is also brought secretly to the same house. From this situation complications of two sorts result. The external ones are connected with the attempts of the heroine, her brother, and her father to hide from one another the presence of strangers in their house. All their efforts at concealment spring from laudable motives. When the true state of affairs is revealed in the last act, everyone is contented. Even the brother of the dead man, who is also a suitor of the heroine's, becomes reconciled to his enemy and rival at the end of the play.

The internal misunderstandings, which are of more human interest, come from the extreme sensitiveness of the principal characters. Both hero and heroine are consumed by jealousy and suffer agonies from the fear that their lovers may not be constant to them, the heroine not unjustifiably, because she does not know that the hero's sister is his sister and fears that she may be his mistress. Everything is finally straightened out to the satisfaction of all the characters. The general impression left by the play is that life is a tangled skein of individual impulses, in which good intentions may cause temporary unhappiness, but about which it is silly to worry unduly. It is especially foolish to exercise oneself about possible rivals in a love affair, because true love will receive its reward in high society and also in low life. The hero's servant, the *gracioso* of the piece, carries out his love affair on a lower level, both socially and artistically, than his master. After he has suffered a certain amount of physical discomfort in the kitchen, he and the female slave to whom he is attracted decide that marriage is more practically advantageous to them both than single life can be to either of them separately.

Low life is used by Lope not so much for its intrinsic interest as for the brilliant contrast it makes with high society. Sometimes a pair of aristocratic lovers are forced by circumstances to disguise themselves as servants, with results which may be nearly tragic or richly comic, depending on whether the dramatist wishes to emphasize their real or their assumed social condition. In the former case the lovers will be in such straits that they will be glad to kill themselves, like those in *By the Bridge, Juana* ("Por la puente, Juana"); in the latter, they will be used to cast ridicule on their employers, as are those in *The Pruderies of Belisa* ("Los melindres de Belisa"). In this latter case the lovers, already man and wife, are forced to take service as slaves in the house of a widow with a son and a daughter. The son and daughter fall in live with the hero and heroine respectively, the mother and a female servant also start to pursue the hero, and the rivalry of the three women for the supposed slave provides excellent comic effects. It goes contrary to normal relations between the generations, the sexes, and social classes, on which the decorous formality of Spanish life was based.

The most amusing of the three women is the daughter, Belisa, whose reputation for fastidiousness explains the title of the play. Like Portia of Belmont, Belisa makes fun of all her available suitors, and then whimsically fastens her attentions on the slave. At first she is furious at herself and plans to have the slave disfigured by being branded in the face, so that she will stop loving him. Finding that that scheme is ineffective in curing her passion, she has an iron collar and rod put on him to prevent his escape from her mother's house. Her efforts to attract his interest are quite useless, and she then plans to avow her love to him openly; but in the darkness she reveals her feelings by mistake to her mother and rival. At the end she is so infuriated to find out the true state of the hero's position and affections that in a fit of pique she decides to marry a persistent suitor of hers, whom, until that moment, she has scorned. Her natural fastidiousness has received a severe jolt as a result of her irrational impulses, and the audience has been highly entertained at her absurd infatuation for a man she thinks a slave.

Disguise as a madman was even more amusing to Lope and his audience than disguise as a slave. The characters who are thought to be insane in The Mad People of Valencia ("Los locos de Valencia") make a most striking contrast with the real inhabitants of a madhouse. The hero feigns madness to escape detection when pursued on a charge of murder; the heroine has been deserted by her betrayer and in her pathetic condition is detained as an inmate of the madhouse, in spite of her protestations of sanity; the superintendent's niece and her maid pretend to be mad, because they wish to be near the hero, by whose charms they have been overwhelmed. The superintendent is disturbed by his niece's condition and consults a doctor, who says that the only remedy is to have the hero agree to marry the niece. The hero consents to this ruse, and the celebration in the madhouse of the wedding, which is to be no wedding, between two mad people, who are not really mad, is a riotous scene of Rabelaisian mirth. The jealousy of the sentimental heroine intrudes upon this comic atmosphere, and peals of authentic wedding bells soon succeed the jangled discords of lunatic mirth.

Pretended madness is also used for comic effect by Lope in his more serious play, The Fool towards Others, a Wise Woman for Herself ("La boba para los otros y discreta para sí"). In it the principal question at issue is which of two women shall become the Duchess of Urbino. Diana, who is in the weaker position at the beginning of the action, is at last successful with the help of her friends in obtaining the title. While waiting to consolidate her allies, Diana feigns madness and in the process indulges in many amusing whimsicalities. She pretends to know nothing of city life and to be more at home in the kitchen than in the state apartments, she appears to want useless trinkets of all sorts, and she sets her cap at every man she sees. By this method she attaches her rival's suitors to her own party; but the comic mad scenes in this play do not influence the outcome of the political plot so decisively as they are supposed to do.

The Fool towards Others shows very clearly the inconsistency of Lope's position as a writer of comedy. He wants to be diverting at the same time that he tells a story full of romantic adventures, a combination which it is very difficult to achieve. His wisest course is not to try to connect too closely the laughter that he creates with the danger that his principal characters are running. As the heroes and the heroines themselves are never supposed to be made absurd, some of Lope's best comedies are those in which he surrounds his central figures with subordinate characters whose conduct is far from reasonable. In *The Pruderies of Belisa* he achieves a striking comic effect by depicting a whole household of badly behaved people, headed by the temperamental Belisa, who quite throws the conventional pair of unfortunate lovers into the shade. Belisa is ridiculed because she does not succeed in her undertakings, whereas Diana, in *The Fool towards Others*, obtains the object she is pursuing at the expense of dramatic consistency. When the heroine's aim is matrimony, as is Belisa's, and when she accomplishes her purpose successfully, as does Diana, a comedy of a somewhat different stamp is produced, one in which the comic superstructure rises a little less awkwardly from the emotional basis upon which it is imposed.

II

As many of Lope's plays turn upon the laws of the *duelo*, so a large number of them are based upon the conventional code for the treatment of women. Both types of plot hinge upon a point of honor, but since the latter type does not involve death it contains material better adapted to comedy. The extreme care which had to be taken of a Spanish woman's reputation by her father or brother is the expression of a principle which when rigidly applied goes contrary to natural human impulses. The Bergsonian idea that comedy is a spontaneous revolt against an artificial system of conduct lies behind those dramas by Lope in which a pair of lovers outwit the lady's parent or guardian. In *The Greatest Impossibility* ("El mayor impossible"), for instance, the courtiers surrounding the Queen of Naples amuse themselves by discussing what is the greatest impossibility, and the Queen concludes the argument by expressing her opinion: "I, for my part, consider it the greatest impossibility to guard a woman. . . . Roberto, if a woman is in love, I consider it certain that it is impossible to guard her." Roberto objects that he is quite able to guard his sister from all attacks upon her honor. The progress of the story follows the course of his disillusionment.

The Queen supports one of her courtiers in his efforts to win Roberto's sister, in order to prove that the brother is wrong. An intrigue which begins with the object of attacking a theory ends in a violent love affair between the sister and the courtier, neither of whom had been in the least interested in the other before the experiment began. There is considerable subtlety shown in the development of the lovers' feelings for each other, which takes place while the hero's clever servant is engaged in tricking Roberto. Both physically and psychologically the Queen's original theory is completely justified. Human nature will not be restrained by force; the attempt to coerce it results more often than not in creating independence and initiative. A similar proposition is illustrated in the popular farce of *The Madrid Steel* ("El acero de Madrid"). Here the heroine is trying to outwit her father instead of her brother, and the hero's servant poses not as a beggar, as in *The Greatest Impossibility*, but as a doctor, a disguise that was to be used several times more effectively by Molière. *The Madrid Steel* is a confused play, in which one is not quite certain whether Lope's main theme has to do with clever servants deceiving stupid parents, with jealous lovers tormenting each other, or with the determination of young people to marry as they please.

Lope is more successful in handling a plot of this kind when he concentrates his attention upon one central character, particularly if it is a woman strong enough to dominate the situation. The heroine of *If Women Didn't See!* ("¡Si no vieran las mujeres!") is struggling not against the restrictions of a brother or father but against those imposed by an already accepted lover, who is insanely jealous. His strict injunctions, forbidding her to see the Emperor, excite her curiosity to the point where she disobeys him, with results that are nearly disastrous to both of them. The lover is finally provoked into admitting that he cares more for his lady than for the letter of a code which forbids an engaged woman to have anything to do with other men; the heroine rebels against a literal enforcement of this narrow view without yielding a jot in her serious attachment for her lover. The determined woman succeeds in having her own way and at the same time in keeping the man of her choice.

In *The Gallantries of Belisa* ("Las bizarrias de Belisa") the heroine's object is to secure the affections of a man who, at the beginning of the play, is devoted to another woman. She oversteps the code of female propriety in pursuing the man she loves, but she does it so dexterously that she succeeds in winning his heart without compromising her dignity. She saves his life, she helps him financially, and she aids him in his wooing of another woman with such success that, when the other woman capitulates, the hero finds that he is in love with his ally, not with the object of his supposed adoration. Belisa's rival then attempts to turn Belisa against the hero by telling her that he has boasted that Belisa has pursued him. Belisa is not unnaturally angry at such a true interpretation of the facts in the case, but her constancy of purpose overrides even this blow to her pride. She loves the hero so deeply that, although she is angry at his supposed criticism of her, she continues to be of assistance to him, even when he becomes jealous of her relations with another man. Lope has built up an excellent comic situation in *The Gallantries of Belisa* by contrasting a woman's real feelings with the accepted tradition of relations between the sexes. Belisa is an emotional human being, whereas her rival represents the conventional position which woman is expected to hold in the romantic scheme of things. The serious point touched on lightly in this charming comedy is that to succeed in affairs of the heart a woman must herself be moved by human affection; yet she must cleverly conceal her feelings from her lover, or he may take advantage of them. If she cares enough for him and has sufficient self-control, her wits will enable her to snatch him from another woman, however much the cards may seem to be stacked against her.

The heroine of *The Gardener's Dog* ("El perro del hortelano") is in somewhat the same situation as Belisa, except that Diana, Countess of Belflor, has greater difficulties to overcome in obtaining the man of her choice. Teodoro, her secretary, far beneath her in social position, already loves one of Diana's ladies in waiting, who returns his affection. Diana's chief struggle is with herself, to see whether she cares more for Teodoro than for her rank; she is too ruthless a person to regard the lady in waiting as anything more than a pawn in the game. Teodoro's affair with the other woman awakens Diana to a realization of her own feelings. She determines that, whether or not she is to marry the secretary, her lady in waiting is not to have him. The early part of the play consists in a series of variations on this theme. After she has twice suggested to Teodoro that she might marry him and twice refused to do so, the secretary loses his temper and reviles Diana in no uncertain terms, calling her a gardener's dog, that is, a dog in the manger, and refusing any longer to be made a dupe of. This, the central scene of the play, culminates in Diana's striking Teodoro and then characteristically offering him money to assuage his feelings. For a moment it seems as if the comic situation presented in *The Gardener's Dog* was to prove insoluble.

The resolution of Diana's difficulties comes from a conventional intrigue, which takes an unusual turn. Two of Diana's suitors decide to murder Teodoro, whom they recognize as their rival, and Teodoro to save himself asserts that he is the lost son of a count. Diana is delighted to find that her lover is of noble birth and agrees to marry him at once, but the honest Teodoro confesses to her that his supposed parentage is a hoax. Thereupon Diana conceives a daring scheme, which shows how ready she is to grasp at any straw to secure her lover and her honor at the same time. She tells Teodoro that she will keep his secret and that the world need never know the truth. She even goes so far as to suggest the murder of Teodoro's accomplice in the deceit and is only persuaded to stop short of homicide by finding that money can buy her safety from detection. Diana's unscrupulousness, which is clearly indicated throughout the course of the play, is necessary if she is to extricate herself from the almost impossible predicament in which Lope has placed her. His ingenuity in having conceived a plot which depends upon the struggle between a woman's pride and love is equaled by his skill in inventing a plausible and ironical ending.

The vigorous portrait of Diana and the high tension which is set up between the social conventions and this strong woman, who finally gets her way in spite of them, make *The Gardener's Dog* one of Lope's very best comedies. As he tells the story, she would not have been able to succeed if the man whom she loved had not been vacillating and compliant; the hero's lowly birth is balanced by a corresponding weakness in his character. In another of Lope's plays, where the hero and heroine are more nearly matched in rank and ability, they work together against external obstacles in the form of tyrannical guardians and powerful rivals. The heroine of *The Mill* ("El molino") is a duchess loved by a count, but she has two other suitors in the persons of a king and a prince, into one of whose hands she might easily have fallen if her lover had not come to her aid. He disguises himself as a miller's servant and watches over her with great success, as far as she is concerned, but in the process he endangers the state of his own affections. While disguised as a peasant, he encounters the miller's daughter and is temporarily fascinated by her, but when the count returns to court he soon forgets the miller's daughter, who has a suitable lover of her own class, and quickly resumes his devotion to the duchess. A princess appears upon the scene to be a fitting mate for the prince, and at the end of *The Mill* we have three pairs of couples happily married, one royal, one aristocratic, and one plebeian, with due regard to social classifications.

At first a similar social issue appears to be involved in *At the Crossing of the Stream* ("Al pasar del arroyo"), in which the peasant girl for whom the hero deserts his first aristocratic love turns out to be of noble birth also. The peasant girl's rustic suitor is then in an unenviable position, until he is likewise proved to be a nobleman, in fact the brother of the hero. The discovery that all four of the principal characters belong to the same elevated rank makes any marriage between them appropriate and removes the social aspect of the play in favor of a trick played by the hero on his brother. The brother and the hero's first lady are persuaded to marry each other, under the impression that they are marrying the heroine and the hero respectively. The hero's treatment of these two persons cannot be considered very admirable, but it is not less deceitful, only more obvious, than Diana's stratagem in *The Gardener's Dog*. Diana is much cleverer and more single-purposed than the hero of *At the Crossing of the Stream*. He is slow in making up his mind as to which of the ladies he prefers, but as they are both in love with him he has merely to choose one of them in order to decide his own fate.

Don Pedro Giron, the hero of *The Wonders of Scorn* ("Los milagros del desprecio") has not only to overcome a rival or two, but to win a lady who has resolved to shun the company of all men. He accomplishes this difficult task with the help of his servant, who insinuates himself into the heroine's houschold and enlists her maid in his intrigues. The wily servant sets about detaching the heroine's two declared suitors from her by a trick which makes each think that the other has been accepted. He also gets Don Pedro to forswear his love for the heroine in her presence, with the result that she is apparently isolated from all her friends and admirers. The attack of scorn upon scorn is further carried on through the medium of jealousy. The servant tells the heroine that Don Pedro has made fun of her personal appearance, her badly matched eyes, her false hair, and her poor teeth. He also informs her that Don Pedro is in love with another woman. The heroine's natural curiosity is aroused, and she determines to see the paragon that is preferred to her. In an effort to do so she runs into physical danger, from which in desperation she calls on Don Pedro to save her. She needs protection as she has needed admiration, and when her jealousy puts her into a painful position she is ready to succumb to her rescuer's wishes. She agrees to the humiliation of interceding for him with the lady of his choice, who, he then admits, is none other than herself. In this way her final capitulation is managed gracefully but firmly. The emphasis in this comedy is upon the weakness of woman and the natural superiority of man in matters of sex, a thoroughly romantic premise, which is much less provocative than that of *The Gardener's Dog* but quite in accordance with the conventional social ethics of Lope's time.

The same situation, with a slightly more emotional emphasis, is at the core of *The Ugly Beauty* ("La hermosa fea"). In this comedy, in an effort to awaken her interest in him, the hero has it given out that he thinks the scornful heroine ugly and repulsive, while at the same time he woos her in the disguise of his own secretary. Under this form he attracts her attention by praising another lady and then makes love to her for himself. She, in the meantime, thinks that by encouraging the secretary she can revenge herself upon his master, who will be dazzled by her charms when he sets eyes upon her. Her expected triumph is turned to dust and ashes by the appearance of the hero and the discovery that he and the secretary are the same person. She is a trifle placated, at the end of the comedy, by the thought that the hero loved her even when he said that she was ugly, but her attempt to claim a minor victory on that score is too specious to be more than a tacit acknowledgment that the hero's campaign against her arrogance has been completely successful.

The hero also wins the hand of the heroine's cousin for a friend of his, after causing the heroine and her cousin to engage in rivalry over the supposed secretary. The ease with which the men in *The Ugly Beauty* get the better of the women causes the *gracioso* of the comedy to regret that he has no mate when everything goes so smoothly for his masters. He will console himself with money as a reward for his share in the stratagems, but money is a poor substitute for love in the plays of Lope de Vega. The effectiveness of their denouements depends upon the way in which lovers become united after a series of unfortunate adventures, more or less related to the psychology of the persons involved. If the woman is disdainful, the man brings her to accept his terms by playing on her pride and jealousy; if the man is already in love with someone else, the woman secures him by showing her superior devotion and ability. The former is the easier plot for Lope to manage, because he regards the world from the chivalric point of view and considers woman in an inferior position, unless she is aided by money or rank. He was saturated with the spirit of his day and his nation, which gives his comedies warmth, vividness, and passion, but which does not greatly help them towards attaining the impartial detachment needed for intelligent social criticism.

III

What Lope lacked in fusing and directing his comic force, he more than made up for in his range and influence. He did not confine himself to comedy in the narrow sense of the word but wrote *comedias* that are by turns sentimental, moral, and at times even tragic in their tone. *The Slave of Her Lover* ("La esclava de su galán") shows a lady taking service with the father of her lover, in order to gain the old man's permission to wed his son, and suffering untold pangs of jealousy during her slavery. *The Certainty for the Doubt* ("Lo cierto por lo dudoso") has a heroine who gives up the crown offered her by a king because of her love for a nobleman, whose jealousy she fears has overcome his affection for her. In both these cases the noble heroine is rewarded by having a happy end come to her sufferings. Admirable men are also likely to flourish in Lope's plays. *The Flowers of Don Juan, and Rich and Poor Exchanged* ("Las flores de don Juan, y rico y pobre trocados") contrasts a selfish prodigal with his honest poverty-stricken brother, much to the advantage of the latter, who arrives at prosperity in time to save the profligate from utter ruin. *The Frauds of Celauro* ("Los embustes de Celauro") pictures the designing attempts of the villainous Celauro to separate a happily married couple by arousing their jealousy of each other, the failure of his schemes, and his ultimate confession. Celauro is seriously wounded near the end of his exploits, but the audience is given to understand that his life will be saved and he will be reconciled to the virtuous characters amid general rejoicing.

These various dramas give some slight indication of Lope's amazing versatility in the realm of comedy, but they do not include his historical or heroic plays, in which tragedy sometimes predominates and blood flows freely at the command of a king or at the hands of peasants. Neither do they represent every type of Lope's comic writing, which could be suggested only by an extended list of titles. Almost every one of Lope's plays adds something to his literary achievement, which is so widespread that it is difficult to gather it together and secure an integrated impression of it. In fact, it is so widespread that one must look for its effects in the work of other authors also. "The prodigy of nature," *el monstruo de la naturaleza,* as Cervantes called Lope, had an enormous influence upon Spanish dramatic literature both in his life and in his works. In one way or another he touched the careers of Spain's other most notable comic dramatists. Tirso de Molina, Ruiz de Alarcón, and Calderón de la Barca all owed something to him, and he was the direct inspiration of lesser men like Moreto y Cabaña.

Lope and Tirso de Molina each dedicated a play to the other in the most complimentary terms. Tirso, whose real name was Gabriel Téllez, was a priest, but he wrote many gay and ribald comedies. Some of them are very light in texture, like *Don Gil of the Green Breeches* ("Don Gil de las calzas verdes"), in which Don Gil is really the sprightly heroine in one of her disguises, and *The Bashful Man at the Palace* ("El vergonzoso en palacio"), in which a simple shepherd is transplanted to high society, greatly to his chagrin and embarrassment. Tirso was unproductive only by comparison with Lope; he is supposed to have written more than four hundred plays, of which eighty-six are extant. Among them it is possible to find evidences not only of his worldliness but also of his religious feeling. *Martha the Pious* ("Marta la piadosa") is, in its keen satire on hypocrisy, one of the forerunners of Molière's *Tartufe*, and *The Man Damned for Lack of Faith* ("El condenado por desconfiado") is an attack on superficial piety. In this latter play there is a vivid contrast drawn between a bandit who goes to heaven, because before his death he truly repents of his sins, and a hermit who goes to hell, because he has not sincere faith in the goodness of God. The subject of this play is theological, but its manner is distinctly secular, a combination which exhibits Tirso's special gift for letting his sense of humor playfully illumine the gravity of his profoundest thoughts.

It has been asserted that Lope is the author of *The Man Damned for Lack of Faith*, and Tirso's most famous drama, *The Scoffer of Seville, the Guest of Stone* ("El burlador de Sevilla y convidado de piedra"), has sometimes been attributed to Calderón, but there seems to be little doubt that Tirso is entitled to the credit for both these plays. Although *The Scoffer of Seville* is probably based on legendary material and contains the interview between a mortal and a statue, which had already been used by Lope, Tirso was the first person to give the Don Juan story the form in which it has captured the imagination of the world. It is probably the most famous of all comic narratives, but, as Mozart's music suggests, its conclusion lifts it out of the sphere of comedy, where it only partly belongs. The contrast between its author's austere profession and his natural gaiety helps to explain the paradox; and so perhaps does the conflict between sensuous enjoyment and religious fanaticism typical of the Spanish people as a whole. Don Juan, Don Quixote, and Sancho Panza are the most noted characters that Spain has contributed to the literature of western Europe. The story of Don Juan contains both the idealism of the knight of La Mancha and the materialism of Sancho, but it does not blend them together with anything like the art of Miguel de Cervantes. There is a violent opposition between Don Juan's success as a worldly lover and his ultimate destruction that makes his adventures seem to move simultaneously on two separate planes. It is a perception of this incongruity that led Lord Byron to take Don Juan as a fitting subject for his mature philosophy, when he was ready to say with Figaro,

> And if I laugh at any mortal thing,
> 'Tis that I may not weep.

Tirso's version of the story is especially sprawling and unwieldy. There are two noble ladies and two peasant girls to whom Don Juan Tenorio makes love, and two friends of his whom he cheats temporarily of their mistresses. The scene in which Don Juan kills the father of Doña Ana does not occur until nearly the end of the second act, and it is some time later before the libertine encounters the statue of his victim. There follows an exchange of invitations, Don Juan first asking the statue to come to supper with him and the statue then returning the compliment. Don Juan boldly accepts, but his defiance of the supernatural powers brings its own punishment. He falls dead at the feet of the statue, who enunciates the play's judicial dictum, "Who acts so, let him pay so." Juan has been in some amusingly tight places before this catastrophe, as his victims begin to band together against him, but it is not until after his death that they all succeed in bringing their grievances to the King, who rights the wrongs that they have suffered. The last scene establishes the happy mood with which a comedy is supposed to close. Even Don Juan's father admits that his vicious son has deserved to be punished.

If Don Juan had the sympathy of the audience, *The Scoffer of Seville* would be a tragedy, but he is represented as a liar, a thief, and a murderer, who is justly damned. Like Faustus, he wishes to repent at the eleventh hour, but until that last moment he is magnificent in sin. One cannot but have a sneaking admiration for his complete lack of morality and for the courage which he shows in the face of overwhelming odds. His personality is as vigorous as his character is vicious, an antithesis which, if one is conscious of it, gives a highly comic aspect to his adventures. Don Juan is an intensification of the struggles of fallible mankind, as they appear to the Christian Church. His history is a thoroughly religious conception, couched in terms which appeal strongly to erring human beings and which enable the more intelligent among them to laugh loudly at their own weaknesses. Tirso has treated this powerful subject with a certain elementary crudeness, but the essence of the entire matter is latent in his play. It was to be refined upon at a later time by more sensitive and sophisticated artists in Italy, in France, in Germany, and in England. It is a universal story in which is implied all the blindness and perversity of the human animal. It transcends nationality as it transcends comedy; it can be interpreted in a variety of ways. In all its versions Don Juan's escapades are amusing, and his tragic fate never fails to point out the wisdom of a sound morality.

Morality was also the mainstay of Lope's second great contemporary, but not his friend, Juan Ruiz de Alarcón. Alarcón was a Mexican, a hunchback, and a business man. Under none of these forms was he particularly popular with his literary rivals, who seem to have united in vilifying his body and his mind. He was much less productive than Lope or Tirso, writing only about twenty-seven plays, but one or two of them are of such excellence that they give him an important place in the history of Spanish comedy. If Alarcón were a little less rigid and a little more impressive, he might be considered the equal of Lope, or at least of Calderón. His comedies attack a variety of vices, generally related to the subject of love and always properly punished in the sphere of the affections. In *To Change in Order to Improve* ("Mudarse por mejorarse"), the hero attempts to excuse his inconstancy towards an older woman, only to find that her niece, whom he now loves, can offer the same reason to him for an alteration in her feelings. So he loses the niece and must take the aunt, whom he no longer loves. In *The Test of the Promises* ("La prueba de las promesas"), the hero who does not keep his promises is punished by losing his lady and obtaining no mate at all, a fate which is emphasized by the *gracioso*, who, as he pairs off with a maidservant, remarks, "I will be the first lackey to be married in a comedy when his master doesn't marry."

Not marrying at all or marrying the wrong woman seems to be Alarcón's idea of the worst misfortune that can befall a man who deviates from the straight path of upright conduct, and a similar situation is the essence of this author's two best-known comedies, *The Walls Hear* ("Las paredes oyen") and *The Truth Suspected* ("La verdad sospechosa"). *The Walls Hear* has a hero, Don Mendo, who is a philanderer and falls between the two women that at different times he has loved. One of them is proud by temperament, and the other is jealous. The proud lady gives her hand to a timid, poor, and homely suitor; the jealous one accepts a faithful lover who has long been patiently waiting for her. The principal figure, Don Mendo, criticizes one woman to the other and, more important, recounts to his friends the imperfections of the lady to whom he is at the moment devoted. He reviles her to prevent the rivalry which he fears he will encounter if his mistress's good qualities are widely known. According to Alarcón's code, deceit is not justified under any circumstances. The ladies whom Don Mendo slanders eavesdrop on him, and when he again proposes he is refused by them both, because "walls have ears," *las paredes oyen*. The women in this comedy cannot be considered very admirable and Don Mendo certainly had a reasonable motive for his malicious words, but Alarcón does not allow for these extenuating circumstances, so determined is he to emphasize the evil results of bearing false witness.

The Truth Suspected is a more ingenious and more coherent, but no less arbitrary, play. Its hero, Don García, has such a lively imagination that he cannot resist concocting a lie whenever a good opportunity presents itself. He tells such grotesque and fantastic stories that he soon acquires a reputation for falsehood, which makes it impossible for him to tell the truth and be believed. The situation in which he becomes involved on his return to Madrid from the University of Salamanca presents unusual difficulty for a young man of Don García's natural tendencies. He falls in love with a lady named Jacinta, but he is told she is her friend Lucrecia; during most of the comedy he is calling Jacinta "Lucrecia" in the best of faith and formally wooing the young lady who bears that name. His honesty in love contrasts strongly with Don Mendo's inconstancy in *The Walls Hear*, but Don García is not deeply concerned with learning the facts about the young ladies in question. Like many people who live in a world of fancy, he is unwilling to undergo the hard discipline of finding out the truth and of submitting himself to it when he has discovered it. His weakness is of a sort very easy for an artist to forgive, but Alarcón is quite ruthless in condemning his hero. Don García is forced to marry the real Lucrecia, whom he has been wooing in name, and he accepts his fate not because he wants to but because he must. Alarcón's skill in depicting his hero realistically is greater than the breadth of his moral conception. Don García was a liar, certainly, but his wildly absurd inventions could do little harm to anyone else and hardly deserve the severe fate that they receive.

To get no mate, as did Don Mendo, is apparently a worse punishment in Alarcón's eyes than to get the wrong one, as did Don García; at least it would be for a woman, if we can judge by the case of Doña Blanca in *The Examination of Husbands* ("El examen de maridos"). Doña Blanca tells lies in an attempt to secure the man of her choice, but she fails to capture him and instead accepts the hand of another suitor, who has been made to think by her plots that she loves him. Doña Blanca's intrigues, which are more serious than either Don García's or Don Mendo's, are not the principal subject of *The Examination of Husbands*, the final scene of which presents a topic that is an interesting illustration of the theories that lie behind Alarcón's comedies. The two friendly suitors of the heroine are asked whether a woman should marry an imperfect man whom she loves or a perfect man to whom she is indifferent. The suitor who claims that love is more important than perfection wins the debate, and the heroine offers to marry him because of his skill in argument, not because of the truth of his ideas. She really loves her other suitor, whom she thinks a sinner, but she is willing to sacrifice herself on the altar of duty. Her nobility is rewarded, somewhat unnaturally, by having the victor hand her over to his friend, whom she loves and who turns out not to have the defects that she has supposed him to possess. So the heroine obtains love and perfection at the sane time, because she has been willing to subordinate her feelings to her ethical standards.

Don Juan Tenorio put his pleasure before his duty, and in the next world he went to hell. Alarcón's characters are rewarded too plentifully for their virtues and chastised too severely for their failings while on earth. In the one case, comedy verges on tragedy; in the other, its gay sparkle is touched with a lugubrious morality. Neither the impulsive Tirso nor the sedate Alarcón seems as close to the heart of the comic idea as Lope de Vega, who for all his inconsistency and elusiveness perceived that human foibles might be ridiculous as well as reprehensible.

IV

Lope's example stimulated one man greater than either Tirso or Alarcón and at least one who was vastly their inferior. Calderón was as superior to them as Agustín Moreto y Cabaña was beneath them in his capacity for original composition. Nevertheless Moreto has a place in the history of Spanish comedy, rather perhaps for his refinements upon Lope's genius than for his extension of it. In *Fine Don Diego* ("El lindo don Diego"), he uses the device of a wedding under false pretenses employed by Lope in *At the Crossing of the Stream*, but instead of the hero's brother's being deceived into marrying a lady whom he does not love, the foolish fop, Don Diego, is led into matrimony with a servant girl disguised as a countess. This incident became a stereotyped feature of later comedy, especially among English dramatists of the Restoration period, who owed many of their technical practices to Spanish precedents. In *One Cannot . . .* ("No puede ser . . .") Moreto frankly rewrote Lope's *The Greatest Impossibility*, laying the scene in a lower stratum of society, tightening up the structure of the whole piece with an eye to stage presentation, and emphasizing the intellectual point of the play, that one cannot guard a woman when she is in love.

Moreto's most successful effort at adapting Lope is in the comedy for which he is chiefly famous, *Disdain for Disdain* ("El desdén con el desdén"). *Disdain for Disdain* has been said to contain similarities to no less than four of Lope's plays. There can be no doubt that it treats the same subject as both *The Wonders of Scorn* and *The Ugly Beauty*. In Moreto's drama the hero not only pretends to scorn the proud heroine but is even forced to go so far as to declare his love to another woman before the heroine will capitulate. She can endure anything, except to see him marry someone else. He, on his side, must be prepared to resort to the most heroic expedients if he is to be the winner in the game of love. It is easier for the hero to propose marriage to a colorless third person than it is for him to feign indifference when in the presence of his haughty mistress. The psychological interest in *Disdain for Disdain* comes from the contest between the lovers as to which shall first admit an attraction for the other. The woman provocatively puts herself in a defensive position, the man is goaded into attacking her, and after a long, exhausting siege he breaks down her guard. This play presents the duel of sex in an elementary stage. The man is overwhelmingly successful at the end, although in the course of the campaign he has suffered more than the woman. The simplicity of the plot's outline and the mathematical regularity of the intrigue do not prevent *Disdain for Disdain* from being extraordinarily subtle in its detailed observation and analysis of the movements of the human heart.

Moreto's career, although it overlaps those of Tirso and Alarcón, comes a little later than the period of Lope's ascendancy. The span of Moreto's life is bridged at both ends by the eighty-one years during which lived Pedro Calderón de la Barca, the last and greatest of the Spanish dramatists of Lope's school. Calderón, although one of the most confirmed of pilferers in the matter of plots and situations, had a philosophical penetration and a literary delicacy that gave distinction to the substance and texture of his work. A comparison of his masterpiece, *Life Is a Dream* ("La vida es sueño"), with a lesser play of Lope's, *What Must Be* ("Lo que ha de ser"), may not be entirely fair to the greater writer, but it does give an indication of the points in which the disciple surpassed his master.

What Must Be is a story of love between two young people of royal birth, one of them trying to conceal her parentage and the other ignorant of his. The chief obstacle to their union is the passion of Alejandro, an acknowledged prince, for the heroine. Alejandro's death, which removes his rivalry, occurs under most dramatic, if somewhat absurd, circumstances. It has been prophesied that Alejandro will be killed by a lion before his thirtieth birthday, and as a precaution against the prediction's being fulfilled his father has had him kept in confinement. On the day before the expiration of the fatal period Alejandro orders a picture of himself slaying a lion to be painted; in attempting to give an actual blow to the painted animal he cuts himself on a dagger and is killed. Alejandro's insane pride, which leads to his death, is caused by his delight at feeling he can win the heroine's hand, and his unguarded temper is also responsible for the revelation of the hero's lineage, which in turn paves the way for the final union of the lovers. Lope is chiefly interested in his central romance, next in the disposition and character of Alejandro, least of all in the working out of the prophecy as a comment upon the problem of human destiny.

To Lope fate is secondary to dramatic effectiveness; in Calderón it serves to develop character. Like Alejandro in *What Must Be*, Segismundo in *Life Is a Dream* is put under restraint to prevent the fulfillment of a prophecy, in his case that he is a wild beast who will trample on his father. As a result of the treatment inflicted on him, he does develop bestial qualities. When he has an opportunity he shows as ungovernable a temper as Alejandro. On being permitted to assume the rights of a prince, he wishes to hear only martial music, he makes love to all the women in sight, he demands flattery from the courtiers present, and he forcibly attacks anyone who tries to thwart his desires. He drops from a balcony a servant who has cautioned him to be moderate, and he struggles with the nobles who attempt to prevent his rash actions. His violence leads his father to send him back to prison, where, when he awakes, he has a chance to think over the events that have taken place as if they were a dream. It is at this point, at the end of the second act, that Calderón puts into the mouth of Segismundo his famous version of "We are such stuff as dreams are made on": "What is life? A madness. What is life? An illusion, a shadow, a fiction, and the greatest good is small; so all life is a dream and dreams themselves are a dream."

> ¿Qué es la vida? Un frenesí:
> ¿Qué es la vida? Una ilusión,
> Una sombra, una ficción,
> Y el mayor bien es pequeño;
> Que toda la vida es sueño,
> Y los sueños sueño son.

The remainder of the play is taken up with showing how Segismundo begins to practice the philosophy that he has acquired through suffering. When he is rescued from prison by rebel soldiers, he at first shows his natural anger but then checks it with a conscious effort. When he has brought his father to his feet as the prophecy foretold, he raises up the old king and makes peace with him. When he is tempted to seize by force the girl that he loves, he restrains himself and hands her over to his rival, whom she prefers. He himself marries his cousin for political reasons, feeling that the public good must come before his personal pleasure. He even sends to his former prison one of the soldiers that has helped to release him, in order to indicate that hereafter no rebellions against royal authority will be permitted. Calderón here limits his philosophical horizon by showing himself to be a strong upholder of the reigning dynasty and a believer in the sanctity of kingship, providing always that it is in worthy hands; but he has already made it clear that king as well as subject should sacrifice his personal inclinations when they interfere with the well-being of the many other individuals in the social organism of which he is a part.

The difference between *What Must Be* and *Life Is a Dream* is vividly brought out by the fact that, in Lope, the character subjected to fate dies to make possible a happy ending for the conventional pair of lovers; in Calderón, the central figure rises on his dead self to a truer understanding of human problems. It is not surprising to find that most of Lope's best plays are technically comedies, whatever serious elements may be contained in them, and that of Calderón's one hundred and twenty-one extant dramas a large number of the most significant are predominantly tragic. Moreover Calderón wrote about seventy-three *autos sacramentales*, which include some of his best work. He was far more at home than Lope in treating this spectacular variety of morality play, where emphasis is put upon the transitory nature of human life. In it the soul of man must be withdrawn from the seductions of the five senses and brought into a state of grace by an appeal to his better nature. This change is not to take place without divine intervention, generally in the form of Roman Catholic ritual, but at the end the hero's eternal salvation is secured at the expense of the world, the flesh, and the devil. The religious fervor and moral earnestness of Calderón are as notable as is Lope's lack of them; they often lift his poetry to great heights, in spite of its tendencies towards the artificial excesses of Gongorism, but they sometimes interfere with the humanistic spirit necessary for comedy. In *Life Is a Dream* the religious element of the *autos* is eliminated, and their seriousness of purpose is turned into a commentary on the life of one particular character, in an exalted atmosphere where comedy and tragedy do not come into conflict.

Often, however, Calderón's plays can be called comedies only in the sense in which Dante used the word; they may have a happy ending in heaven, but on earth they must be regarded as tales of woe. Such, for instance, is the celebrated version of the Faust story that Calderón called *The Extraordinary Magician* ("El mágico prodigioso"), in which the hero is willing to lose his earthly life for the privilege of being in paradise with the lady whom he loves. The religious idea that death is not of supreme importance interferes with human comedy, and so does the "point of honor" prevalent in the Spain of Calderón's day. The duty of a man to keep his escutcheon clean, by revenging himself on anybody who has tarnished his reputation or that of the women of his family, is always forgiven, and sometimes rewarded, in Calderón's plays. The doctor of his own honor may not be engaged in loving his neighbor as himself, but he is making his peace with God and God's vicegerent, the King. Wives guilty of adultery must be killed, even if their sin has been only of the body, not of the soul, although in the latter case they may look forward to going to heaven, where there is no marrying or giving in marriage. In any event, their murderers are justified and set free by private vengeance as well as by public law.

The King is the embodiment of the Divine Power, and when he punishes a crime with death it may be supposed that his judgment is inspired wisdom; a certain rigidity in this world is necessary to prepare for a fuller freedom in the life to come. There is an interesting example of this attitude and its connection with comedy in *The Three Judgments in One* ("Las tres justicias en una"), in which the King has the principal character garroted to avenge three crimes at once. There is also an underplot concerned with the combination of two clever maids against a servant who is trying to make love to both of them at the same time, with no better success than Falstaff has with Mistress Ford and Mistress Page. The divine vengeance of the King seems to join hands for a moment with the very earthly revenge of two witty women; then Calderón lets the two strands of the plot pursue their ways independently, to their respective conclusions of idle merriment and bloody destruction.

From the point of view of comedy there is a marked similarity between *The Three Judgments in One* and *The Mayor of Zalamea* ("El alcalde de Zalamea"), one of Calderón's most famous and powerful plays. In it Pedro Crespo, an old peasant, becomes the mayor of his town and by virtue of that office executes an aristocratic captain who has ravished his daughter. The conflict is between Crespo's rough nobility of character and the hierarchy of rank which takes advantage of its position for unworthy ends. The play owes its reputation to the figure of Crespo, who combines the sturdy independence of the Spanish peasant with a higher idealism than is ordinarily expected of him. As a servant of the King, Crespo is a loyal subject, but he acknowledges a still more powerful master: "Property and life must be given to the King, but honor is the inheritance of the soul, and the soul is only from God."

> Al Rey la hacienda y la vida
> Se ha de dar; pero el honor
> Es patrimonio del alma,
> Y el alma solo es de Dios.

This sentiment Crespo expresses early in the play to Don Lope de Figueroa, the villainous captain's superior officer, who is puzzled by finding such impeccable yet dangerous views held by a member of the lower classes; theoretically these sentiments are quite correct, but they contain the seeds of revolt against the civil authority that Don Lope represents. The scenes between Crespo and Don Lope, in the first two acts, depend upon the contrast between two characters who hold entirely opposite philosophies of life: Don Lope as a conventional member of organized society is humorously opposed to Crespo, whose worldly position is lower but whose understanding of life is much more deeply rooted.

The comedy contained in this situation is a part of Calderón's idealistic point of view, but because of the sincerity of his feeling he cannot always keep his play on an even intellectual level. When Crespo imitates Polonius in giving advice to his son, there is none of the implied criticism of conventional morality which Shakespeare manages to insinuate into similar words. Crespo's code of action springs from goodness of heart, not from worldly considerations. When an extreme emergency arises he does not waver from practicing what he preaches. According to his duty towards God, as he conceives it, he chooses to revenge his honor as grandly as if he were a great lord. The conflict between Crespo's position as father and as citizen, between his power as mayor and his dependence on royal authority, is resolved by the appearance of King Philip II, who recognizes the justice of Crespo's position and pardons his incidental rashness. Crespo is made perpetual mayor of Zalamea by a King who is able to distinguish between the spirit and the letter of the law. Calderón does not allow this violent story to be fitted artistically with a violent ending, as is a modern version of the same plot, St. John Ervine's *John Ferguson*; to the Spanish writer the world is under the jurisdiction of the Christian God, for whom there is a special providence in the fall of a sparrow.

Calderón's aim, as compared with Lope's, was to ennoble human character rather than merely to display it, and for that reason Calderón introduces a more philosophical note into dramas like *Life Is a Dream* and *The Mayor of Zalamea* than Lope does into corresponding plays like *What Must Be* and *Fuente Ovejuna*. In the latter piece all the inhabitants of Fuente Ovejuna ("The Sheep Well") take vengeance upon a tyrannical nobleman and are pardoned by the King for their violence because of the righteousness of their cause. *Fuente Ovejuna* is a powerful drama, but it does not have the comic touches that are to be found in *The Mayor of Zalamea*, where the antithesis in ideas between Crespo and Don Lope provokes many thoughtful smiles. In both plays we are shown that self-respecting peasants will be supported by the King. Lope emphasizes the stupidity of the natives of Fuente Ovejuna, whereas Calderón shows the innate intelligence of Crespo. In the one case, communal activity is inspiring to one's feelings but depressing to one's mind; in the other, concentration upon two individuals as types of two classes in society suggests the humorous as well as the emotional aspects of civil discord.

V

Calderón wrote more kinds of plays than Lope, but he showed less variety in handling them individually. Lope's works are so diverse as to defy classification, but each of Calderón's fits into a special category. He wrote sentimental comedies and romantic comedies, allegories and chivalric comedies (*comedias caballerescas*), all with the purpose of creating a world different from the actual one and more perfect than it is. He also composed a number of cloak and sword comedies, *comedias de capa y espada*, very similar to the plays of this type that Lope had made popular. Calderón's *comedias de capa y espada* are generally more wooden than Lope's, but they are also more consistently developed. When they are based upon a moral premise, they have an intellectual stamina which redeems them from being merely smooth technical exercises in the art of playwriting.

The Worst Is Not Always Certain ("No siempre lo peor es cierto") is at bottom an attack upon unreasonable jealousy. The hero believes that his lady has been false to him, and he insists that, in order to save her reputation, she must marry her supposed lover, who is no more interested in her than she is in him. The obstinacy of the two victims alone prevents a forced marriage. In the end each of the true lovers is united to the person of his choice. *The Worst Is Not Always Certain* is really a dramatic exposition of the failings of men and the nobility of women. Its strength lies in the fact that its humorous incidents are based upon a jealous disposition, which forms an integral part of the action; its weakness, in the casual way in which the hero is made to abandon his humour, almost as easily as he had become a prey to it.

Jealousy is also a factor in *House with Two Doors Is Difficult to Guard* ("Casa con dos puertas mala es de guardar"). The plot of this play is set in motion by a sister's desire to outwit her brother's watchfulness. In the course of her extravagant willfulness she arouses the jealousy of her lover, her brother, and her brother's lady, who is as innately jealous as the hero of *The Worst Is Not Always Certain*, but whose feelings are not the dominant force in the story. The cross-purposes would never have arisen if the heroine's determination to see a friend of her brother's had not caused her to disguise herself and embark on an affair with him, without disclosing her true identity. Her curiosity is partially at fault and so is her brother's excessive caution, but Calderón does not emphasize either of the moral implications that are inherent in his material. As it stands, *House with Two Doors* is an amusing, ably constructed trifle, based upon a woman's absurd whim.

Feminine psychology also underlies *April and May Mornings* ("Mañanas de abril y mayo"), a comedy which is less concentrated and more easy to follow in its details than is *House with Two Doors*. Its artistic excellence is impaired by its lack of unity, but the variety of its moods gives it an added attractiveness. The main plot depends upon the jealousy of the hero, as does that of *The Worst Is Not Always Certain*; the subordinate one, upon the capriciousness of a woman, as in *House with Two Doors*. The principal heroine endures a great deal of misery from her lover's jealousy. The secondary one inflicts unhappiness on her lover because of her ungovernable coquetry. These two elements are not necessarily antagonistic, but they might have been more closely harmonized. In *April and May Mornings* they have such distinct existences that one is not sure whether the play is preponderantly romantic because of one heroine's nobility or comic because of the other's perverseness.

Calderón brings these two types of heroines into sharp contrast in *Beware of Still Water* ("Guardate del agua mansa"). One of two sisters seems a model of propriety, and the other appears to be an outrageous flirt. The comic idea is to show that each sister is different at bottom from what she seems to be upon the surface. The proper sister is able to manage her own affairs and secures a lover by masquerading as the gay sister, who for all her apparent flippancy is really a weak-willed creature. At first she agrees to marry her boorish cousin, the man of her father's choice, and later, when he refuses to accept her, she succumbs to the lover nearest at hand. The demure sister, on the contrary, shows that a clever woman will get her way by fair means or foul, a point that is touched on lightly in many of Calderón's comedies and handled superbly by Lope in *The Gardener's Dog*. Lope is more interested in his characters than Calderón, who in his *comedias de capa y espada* is chiefly occupied in evolving elaborate complications and creating effective situations with expertness and proficiency.

In *Beware of Still Water* one woman passes for the other by a piece of deliberate artifice. In *Good and Bad Fortune of the Name* ("Dicha y desdicha del nombre"), the position of the heroes is alternated by having Don Felix Colona take the place and name of Don César Farnesio on a diplomatic mission to Milan. Then the true Don César comes to Milan unexpectedly, and he has to take the name of Don Felix, with disastrous consequences as far as the love affairs of the two friends are concerned. One of the lovers becomes jealous of the other, and so does one of the ladies, while the innocent members of each sex suffer almost as much from these unjust suspicions as the persons who are a prey to them. This ingenious intrigue is handled by Calderón with extreme cleverness but in such a mathematical and precise way that the characters do not arouse much human sympathy. There is a slight treatment of jealousy, but even that strong human emotion is used rather to complicate the plot than to illumine character; it is taken for granted as a necessary part of the social system under which Calderón lived and out of which he fashioned his various intricate dramatic patterns. His most common formula was to arrange that one person should be mistaken for another and then to let a narrow code of individual conduct work out its own ludicrous consequences.

Another method of carrying on an intrigue frequently used by Calderón depends on the unwise confiding of a secret. According to the rules of medieval love-making, secrecy is a virtue of the first importance; if a lover tells his feelings to a friend, he is likely to become involved in misery. Calderón carried out this tradition in plays like *Let No One Confide His Secret* ("Nadie fíe su secreto"), in which the hero insists upon telling his emotions and plans to the confidant of his princely rival. These indiscretions repeatedly result in the hero's almost losing the hand of his lady, although he is devoted and courageous. He is aided in his love affair by his imaginative servant, Lázaro. Lázaro's account of the increasingly large number of men from whom he has been fleeing suggests by its sheer impudence and bravado Falstaff's tale of the men in buckram suits. Lázaro explains that his sword is whole because the sparks that it struck welded the pieces of it together. He states that his dagger was driven back by one of his enemies into its own sheath, where it is now safely reposing. This marvelous power of inventiveness saves the situation several times, but the hero would finally have been defeated if he had not thrown himself on the Prince's mercy. The Prince sees that the lady loves the communicative hero and also realizes that it would be undignified if he himself were to marry beneath his royal rank. Prudence and magnanimity combine to motivate his withdrawal from the competition.

The Prince in *Let No One Confide His Secret*, like Diana in Lope's *The Gardener's Dog*, plays the part of a dog in the manger, but the treatment of this situation by the two dramatists is very different. Lope's heroine achieves her ends by means of a dishonest but comic stratagem. Calderón's Prince is removed from the picture by the assertion of his native nobility. There is a difference in the sexes involved and Calderón's character is not the principal one in the play, but the roots of the contrast go deeper than such superficial distinctions. Lope is willing to have Diana resort to an unprincipled stratagem to keep his drama on a comic level that is true to human nature. Calderón insists upon showing the admirable qualities of his imaginary beings, even if as a consequence the laughter that his plays excite is often unsubstantial and illogical.

Neither Calderón nor Lope de Vega can be considered a first-rate writer of intelligent comedy, although both men did more to widen the scope of that genre than Alarcón, whose work more nearly belongs to it. Neither Lope's program of pleasing his audience nor Calderón's of improving it is exactly suited to the production of the highest type of comedy, which requires as its basis an intelligent view of actual life, a philosophy rather than a religion. It is not enough to laugh gaily at human predicaments without paying some attention to the underlying traits of character that give rise to them; it is too much to transcend the physical world in favor of the spiritual elements in man's nature. The comic dramatist must constantly bear in mind the essential incongruity of life, which made the human animal appear to Alexander Pope as "the glory, jest and riddle of the world." Calderón and Lope were both too much bound by the rigid conventions of their environment to accomplish this detachment for more than a moment at a time, but they both made use of contemporary Spanish institutions to secure a variety of incidental comic effects.

Lope was the more free in the use of his material. He did not hesitate to employ any local customs which he thought would add to the humor of his plays. If a man's life was in danger because he had killed his opponent in a duel, Lope was eager to show the absurd incidents that might develop out of this intrinsically serious situation. If the hero had to disguise himself as a slave or a madman, it made no difference to Lope how nearly the plot verged upon tragedy. The hero and heroine would ultimately be joined in holy matrimony, and some other man or woman could be found to pair off with those who were disappointed in their love affairs. Lope seemed particularly disposed not to regard the inclinations of women, unless they were endowed with unusual wealth and position. in a man's world, the hero generally receives first consideration. The heroine shines by the reflected light of her lover. She is the more likely of the two to be a prey to jealousy, because love means more to her than it does to a man of action. Her situation is often critical, but at the end she is sure to be united to the man of her choice — if he returns her love. If he does not, the lovelorn lady is a ridiculous figure in that she has exceeded the position which Spanish feudal society allotted to women.

There is some possibility that a woman may be generous or clever enough to win the affections of a man who does not at first love her. If her rival is stupidly jealous or the man that she loves weakly vacillating, she may be successful in overthrowing the social conventions that prevent a free play of the relationships between men and women. When the hero and heroine combine to get the better of the artificial code of behavior imposed by society, they have to combat tyrannical fathers, as in Latin comedy, or watchful brothers, anxious to take their stand upon a technical "point of honor." The lady must be helpful and the gentleman honorable to make a happy ending possible. If there are several candidates for the heroine's hand, there may be some doubt as to which one will be the successful suitor, but it is more often dubious whom the hero is to marry. When the heroine does not wish to marry anybody, the hero must bend her to his will by flattery or assumed disdain. In that case jealousy plays a large part in the outcome of the intrigue; the man can make use of the woman's susceptibility to this emotion as an assistance to him in his wooing. The emphasis put upon this human weakness in Lope's comedies may be a sign that natural instincts will always assert themselves against conventional formality in relations between the sexes.

Lope was treating an aristocratic society in which women were subordinated to men. They were brought up under strict supervision and rigidly confined to a narrow sphere of activity. When they came to a marriageable age, their honor was of paramount importance to their fathers or their brothers, who were expected to select suitable mates for them. If an enterprising young man secured admittance to the lady's presence, he became an object of suspicion and was immediately challenged to a duel. If the lady herself fell in love with someone whom, in spite of her duenna's carefulness, she had encountered on the street or in the park, her liberty was at once curtailed and she might be sent to a convent as a·punishment. Naturally, then, the comic dramatist seized upon the normal attraction between two young people, at the expense of what was held to be correct etiquette, as a source of humorous complications. Plautus and Terence had followed that formula objectively. The Spanish writers went back to Menander in concentrating their attention upon the feelings of the lovers. The idea of romantic love, which the Middle Ages had glorified, was coming into renewed conflict with social organizations, and comedy was quick to take advantage of the contrast between them. Lope refused to conform unreservedly to the standards of the past, although he was not able to break away entirely from established institutions. He felt the grip of custom strongly, but he was also willing to show the effect of external repression upon the spontaneous impulses of men and women. The difficulty here is that the violence of the human feelings involved often interferes with detached judgment. Then critical comedy has to give way to elevated poetry and a sympathy with the struggles of mankind.

The earnestness which keeps intruding on Lope's comedies was turned into religious sentiment by Tirso de Molina, into ethical dogma by Ruiz de Alarcón, and into mystical philosophy by Calderón de la Barca. *The Scoffer of Seville* combines scurrilous humor and pious sanctity with a naïveté that has made Don Juan the best-known figure in Spanish drama. *The Truth Suspected* chastises an ingenious liar so severely that French comedy sprang from an attempt to imitate its liveliness and rectify its judgment. *Life Is a Dream* has had less fame and less influence than the plays of Tirso and Alarcón, but it is probably the greatest comedy in the Spanish language. It is a unique work and by no means a thoughtlessly amusing one; it treats the incongruities of human life *sub specie aeternitatis*. Segismundo has developed the bestial qualities inherent in all men to the point where they have become a danger to society. His punishment is so severe that he is forced to recognize the unsubstantiality of existence and the necessity of self-restraint, a lesson which is never thoroughly learned in this world. When Segismundo is sent back to his prison, he has died so far as human society is concerned. His second release from captivity is in the nature of a resurrection. Calderón was able to secure comic detachment without profound human understanding. He possessed a unified view of the world a a small portion of God's domain, but he did not possess the buoyancy of spirit which is essential to true comedy and which Lope, with all his limitations of perspective, never lacked. Neither author was able to achieve a well-balanced view of mankind's problems; Lope enjoyed life too thoroughly, and Calderón felt too keenly the brevity of earthly happiness.

One characteristic which these two men had in common and which they shared with the other dramatists of their day was their intense absorption in the subject of jealousy. This emphasis upon misunderstandings between the sexes, which pervades Spanish comedy, may depend partly on national temperament and partly on social conventions in Spain during the sixteenth and seventeenth centuries, but it is also a general human tendency. It is not a congenial subject for the comic muse; plays that are largely concerned with it sometimes turn towards elevated tragedy, like *Othello*, and sometimes towards savage satire, like *The Country Wife*. The Spanish dramatists were so occupied with this distorted aspect of the theme of sex that they did not seem to realize that idealistically jealousy is quite indefensible and that practically it rarely does any good. They sympathized with their jealous characters while they laughed at them, and, after entangling them in absurd situations, neatly straightened out all their love affairs. The principal lovers are finally united, and their disappointed rivals are provided with new mates. Jealousy can best be dispelled when its victims transfer their affections to other objects, a circumstance which may help to explain the many sudden and unmotivated marriages that are likely to take place at the end of a Spanish comedy. Something must be done to terminate the hideous uncertainty of jealousy. In the sphere of comedy the most satisfactory outcome is a happy, if arbitrary, ending. There is sure to be some incongruity between the intensity of the emotion and the comic manner in which it is depicted, between the unnecessary complications to which it gives rise and the abrupt conclusion that brings it to a close. This incongruity permits neither pure comedy nor unadulterated romance, but it is an important element in the formation and growth of romantic comedy, Spain's dramatic glory and its chief contribution to the comic tradition of western Europe.

CHAPTER V

The Height of French Comedy: Molière

I

SPANISH DRAMA did much to enlarge the scope of comedy by introducing into its action romantic adventures and by developing the theme of jealousy latent in all relationships between the sexes, but especially to be observed in the social order of Spain. Such a burst of productivity as that in the golden age of Spanish drama had a far-reaching effect, particularly in France, where the literary soil was already rich enough to be receptive to new influences; in fact the first important French comedy after the Renaissance, *The Liar* ("Le Menteur") by Pierre Corneille, produced in 1643, was based on Alarcón's *The Truth Suspected*. Corneille had at first supposed Lope to be the author of this comedy, which he admittedly took as a model in his divergence from tragic themes and which he followed very literally. "When I decided to change from the heroic to the naïve," he says, "I did not dare descend from such a height without relying on a guide, and I let myself be led by the famous Lope de Vega." Later, when he discovered that Alarcón was the true author, he transferred the acknowledgment of his indebtedness to the proper person. He admired the fertility of invention in the complicated plot of *The Truth Suspected* and objected only to the relentlessness of its denouement.

Alarcón has the ingenious liar forced to marry the lady under whose name his mistress has been masquerading. Corneille softened the outcome of the plot and, it must be confessed, made it far less logical, if considerably more subtle. Dorante, the liar, begins to fall in love with Lucrèce as he sees the possibilities of his winning Clarice diminish. His final triumphant lie is to say that he has loved Lucrèce from the first. In *The Liar* Corneille has not assimilated his material with complete success. The play has the air of a translation until, in the fifth act, the author's sureness of touch wavers with his variation from the original plot. The ending may add to the general gaiety which Corneille was trying to achieve, but it comes unexpectedly and impotently after the mounting complications of the first four acts. Nevertheless, Corneille's play is a landmark in the history of French comedy. It undoubtedly influenced Molière's development.

At the time when *The Liar* was first produced, Jean Baptiste Poquelin, soon to take the name of Molière, was one of a group of struggling actors, called the "Illustre Théâtre," who were attempting to establish themselves in Paris near the Porte de Nesle. The venture was unsuccessful, however, and in 1645 Molière embarked upon his thirteen years of wandering in the provinces. During the first part of this period he attempted nothing so elaborate in the way of authorship as *The Liar*. He was at that time chiefly an actor and the manager of a traveling theatrical company, which was particularly known for its performances of short farces. These farces were often relics of medieval fabliaux told in dramatic form to make them more vivid. From the fifteenth century on, such brief transcriptions of everyday life had held the stage with tenacity, and they were still in high favor when Molière made his debut as an actor. They generally deal with the tricks played on a stupid fellow by a clever rogue, and at their most sophisticated, as in *Maître Pathelin*, the rogue is himself outwitted. Frequently they portray the deceitfulness of women, who struggle with their husbands for mastery in the family circle, and they always depend upon physical fun-making without any philosophy behind it other than the primitive one that craft is justified by its success and that might makes right.

It was to this simple genre that Molière first made an addition, if one may judge from *The Jealousy of the Clown* ("La Jalousie du Barbouillé"), the earliest of his extant works. In it a husband wishes to punish his wife for her capricious behavior, she gets the better of him by a ruse, and, although they are reconciled at the end, it is pretty well understood that for the future the wife will have the situation in her own hands. This sketch has some importance because it contains the germ of one of Molière's mature comedies, *George Dandin*, and because it shows the roots of native tradition from which his best work sprang. It is not entirely a product of French influences, however. In it are to be found traces of the *commedia dell'arte*, which had filtered into France through the frequent visits of touring companies from Italy. This popular type of comedy, which had a definite connection with the informal scenes called "mimes" that flourished under the Roman Empire,[1] was composed of a rough scenario, pantomimed acting, and extemporaneous speeches invented by the actors. The disorganized nature of *The Jealousy of the Clown* may be explained by its combination of these two national traditions. The second half of it resembles a French farce, while the first half is really an Italian pantomime. At the end of the sixth scene there is a long stage direction, the longest in all Molière, which emphasizes the importance of physical action on the stage. It describes how the Doctor is tripped up, falls on his back, and is dragged off by a cord attached to his foot, still talking and counting on his fingers all the reasons why peace is a desirable thing, "until he is no longer seen."

The connection of this horseplay with the French plot of husband versus wife is that the Doctor tries ineffectively to be a peacemaker between the wranglers. When peace is finally restored (not through his efforts), he wishes to read aloud a chapter of Aristotle on harmony, but he is prevented by the supper that has been prepared to celebrate the end of the comedy in an Aristophanic rather than an Aristotelian fashion. The Doctor is not a physician but a learned pedant who delights in elaborate derivations and syllogistic reasoning. He is the *dottore* of the piece, the self-satisfied old man of Latin comedy, adapted to the Renaissance enthusiasm for classical learning. He is "dressed like a physician," as if medicine were the branch of modern science most likely to be confused with pedantry, an assumption which indicates the path that Molière's genius was to follow and furnishes a side light upon his second extant piece, *The Flying Doctor* ("Le Médecin volant").

In *The Flying Doctor* the profession of medicine is held up to ridicule by the ease with which Sganarelle counterfeits being a physician, although he has no knowledge of diseases or remedies. His unintelligible patter completely deceives the heroine's father, and his inability to write a prescription makes it possible for the lovers to meet and effect their marriage. In addition to this attack upon the profession of medicine, Molière introduces an ignorant lawyer, who compliments the false doctor upon his wisdom and skill. The lawyer's remarks, couched in stilted phrases and intermixed with Latin quotations, satirize both the speaker and the physician whom he is

[1] For an excellent discussion of this intricate subject, see Allardyce Nicoll's *Masks, Mimes and Miracles* (New York, 1931).

praising. The other characters in *The Flying Doctor* come from the conventionalized repertoire of Italian popular comedy. There are two young ladies, the father of one of them, her lover, and the two valets, who match their wits against each other. Sganarelle succeeds in duping the heroine's father by pretending to be both the physician and the physician's twin brother in a series of double impersonations, which keeps him flying on and off the stage and speaking as both characters at almost the same time, with the skill of an accomplished ventriloquist. When his plots become too complicated to be practical, the comedy is brought to a close by the father's being persuaded that it is best to approve of true love. *The Flying Doctor* is a short humorous skit, like *The Jealousy of the Clown* and like the other pieces of Molière's provincial repertoire, if we may judge by their titles, which alone have come down to us.

When Molière turned to entertainment of a more pretentious order, he reverted to the example of Corneille, and, using an Italian instead of a Spanish source, he composed a piece that bears a striking resemblance to *The Liar. The Blunderer, or The Mischances* ("L'Étourdi, ou Les Contretemps"), written in verse, in accordance with Molière's practice when he was treating elaborate material of a dignified nature, was performed at Lyons sometime between the beginning of 1653 and the end of 1655. It is an adaptation of *The Indiscreet Man* ("L'inavvertito"), an Italian comedy by Niccolò Barbieri, which, like *The Truth Suspected*, depends upon a single comic theme. In the ·Spanish play a lover lies and lies until his stories become too confusing to be believed; in the Italian drama a stupid lover ruins the clever plans initiated by his servant. In *The Blunderer* the interest is all centered upon Lélie, the blunderer, and Mascarille, his wily assistant. Mascarille, like the slaves in Plautus, concocts numerous stratagems to get the heroine away from the old man who owns her and the rich young man who wants to buy her for himself. Each of his somewhat monotonous plots is foiled by intervention on the part of Lélie, which upsets the scheme Mascarille is planning at the moment and makes it necessary for him to set off on another trail. It is not surprising that, as a result of these accumulated incidents, the servant should get the better of the lover and scold him roundly, and that Lélie in his final discouragement should threaten to kill himself because of his stupidity. It is not even strange that when Dryden came to make over this play in *Sir Martin Mar-all* he allotted the heroine to the man instead of to the master, although in doing so he offended not only against social decorum but against the delicacy of Molière's characterization.

Lélie is made to act like a fool by the exigencies of the plot, but his creator has tried to show that at bottom he is no greater simpleton than the rest of mankind. If one considers the action from Lélie's point of view rather than from Mascarille's, one will see that the apparent blunderer is a consistent and, in fact, an admirable character. His first three mistakes are all caused by ignorance or by courtesy. After it has been established that Lélie is both honest and clever, his honesty is shown to be greater than his cleverness. His later errors are caused by a skillful alternation of unfortunate ability and natural uprightness. Only once does the hero deserve the title of "l'étourdi," and that is when he cannot remember the details of an elaborate deceit in which Mascarille has coached him; but even in this episode and in his later indiscretions we can see that Lélie's stupidity comes from the tremors of a hopeful lover, not from a deep-seated lack of common sense. The one serious charge that can be brought against Lélie is that he never learns from experience. He blunders no less than fourteen times in the five acts of the play, and he would never have won his lady if it were not for a romantic discovery about the heroine's birth, which removes all the obstacles to a happy ending. The conventional device of recognizing a long-lost child is here used so adroitly by Molière that its improbability and artificiality fit perfectly the improbability and artificiality of the main intrigue.

In the second full-length play that Molière composed he employed romantic complications too freely. For that reason *Lovers' Spite* ("Dépit amoureux"), presented first at Béziers in 1656, is not, as a complete work of art, an improvement over *The Blunderer. Lovers' Spite* draws most of its weaknesses from an Italian play, *Self-Interest* ("L'interesse") by Niccolò Secchi. The story of a girl masquerading as a boy unknown to her father is far-fetched, unconvincing, and much too long-drawn-out, but it does have a structural relationship to the lovers' quarrel with which Molière embellished his Italian source. The growth of the gentleman's jealousy and the lady's irritation is delightfully portrayed up to the scene where the lovers try to break with each other. Their mutual affection is stronger than their disdain, however. After they have returned their love tokens and torn up each other's letters, the man feels constrained to ask his lady's pardon, which she grants with apparent reluctance but with real eagerness. The contrast between what the lovers feel and what the situation drives them into saying is emphasized by the repetition of this motif in the case of their servants, who urge their master and mistress on in their quarrel, and then imitate it themselves on a lower and grosser level. The height of the folly is reached when the servant pardons the maid for his jealousy of a rival valet, after he has softened his mistress's anger by making her laugh at his own absurdity. The homely realism of the servants' wooing is further set off by the contrast between the simple kindly lover and his rival, a buffoon in the Italian tradition, loquacious, sure of himself, and determined not to forfeit either his skin or his independence.

Although the lovers' quarrels are the literary gems of *Lovers' Spite*, they are not sufficiently developed to dominate the action. The principal story is largely pathetic in nature, but it gives rise to certain amusing moments like that in which two old men, each actuated by a different kind of self-interest, agree to pardon each other for their faults, without realizing that the trouble between them was based upon a double misunderstanding. A comic scene of still another variety is provided by a tutor, who, when summoned to give information about a pupil of his, replies only in pedantic terms, like the Doctor in *The Jealousy of the Clown*. He talks of Greek and Latin authors with a persistency that prevents his paying any attention to the matter in hand, and although he is a victor in the duel of words he is farcically put to rout by having a bell rung in his ears. This incidental portrait is so foreign to the tone of the rest of the piece that one may consider it mere padding, though it is characteristic of Molière, who always sought an excuse to attack the pretensions of bombastic learning. The material in this case is conventional, and the occasion for it is unwarranted. When Molière decided to isolate figures like the pedant in *Lovers' Spite* and add to them some fresh touches drawn from original observation, he had hit upon the formula that was to make possible his first conspicuous triumph.

The Affected Ladies ("Les Précieuses ridicules") of 1659 is fundamentally not dependent upon any literary tradition. Mascarille, in name and in so far as he is the clever valet, is reminiscent of

Molière's earlier Italianate plays, but there the resemblance ceases. The realistic background of bourgeois family life reminds one of medieval French farces, but the action is not typical of them. It does not concern husband and wife, neither is there any definite matching of wits in the course of it; the object of the imposture practiced by two masquerading valets on a pair of country *précieuses*, newly come up to Paris, is not to win them for the gentlemen whom they have scorned as suitors but to show up the emptiness and absurdity of their pretensions as ladies of culture. The year before *The Affected Ladies* was produced, Molière's company had returned to Paris and had met with great success in playing the lighter pieces of its repertoire. The vogue of Mlle. Madeleine de Scudéry and her bluestocking friends was a marked phenomenon in the Paris of 1659, and it presented a rich field for the comic dramatist. It was natural that the actor-manager should want to try his hand at further original comedies and that the cult of *préciosité* should seem amusing to him. Its affectations had a serious side, a sincere desire to outlaw brutality from society in an age when the amenities of life were making rapid progress, but its exaggerated methods were dangerous for imitators to follow. Molière tried to indicate this distinction by making his *précieuses* "two conceited women from the provinces," who had copied the fine airs of Parisian society, and by stating in his preface that "the true *précieuses* would be wrong to be galled when we act the ridiculous ones who imitate them badly."

The plot of *The Affected Ladies* is very slight. The backbone of this play is an exaggerated picture of absurdities in contemporary manners. The affected ladies do not want to marry because their heads are full of romantic notions which they have culled from *Le Grand Cyrus*; they have taken the names of Polyxène and Aminte as suitable to their belief that courtship and not marriage is an end in life; they call a mirror "the counselor of the graces," and chairs "the conveniences of conversation"; they are thrilled at the mere title of the Marquis de Mascarille, and their heads are so much in the clouds that they are ready to accept any romantic delusion as the indisputable truth. The skill with which Mascarille plays his part in fooling the *précieuses* is carefully prepared for by Molière, but the impostor's psychology is not thoroughly examined. We are told that as a servant he likes to copy the manners of his master and that he has set himself up above other valets, whom it pleases him to call mere brutes. Just why he was willing to masquerade as a nobleman is not made clear, but it may be supposed that he was glad of any opportunity to wear his master's clothes and to counterfeit a man of fashion. He keeps up his part to the last in spite of the unexpected beating he receives from his master, and he leaves the stage with the morality of the piece on his lips: "I see very well that only empty show is liked here and that naked virtue is not valued at all."

These words coming from the mouth of Mascarille have an ironic significance which is not entirely in character but which gives a comic touch to Molière's moralizing. The dramatist has not tried to create human beings in *The Affected Ladies*, but to paint the externals of society in a lively and satiric manner. He has not given the appearance of real life to his material, but he has hit off a certain aspect of artificiality with deadly accuracy. Although *The Affected Ladies* is not a great play, it has in it the stuff of greatness. Under the guise of farce, Molière delivered such a violent attack upon social manners that his comedy gave offense in high quarters and as a result was suspended for two weeks at the insistence of people who felt that they had been satirized. The active opposition excited by *The Affected Ladies* bears witness to that comedy's power and appropriateness, it marks the beginning of Molière's warfare with society, and it may help to explain why in his next plays he steered clear of contemporary problems.

Sganarelle, or The Cuckold in His Own Imagination ("Le Cocu imaginaire"), produced in 1660, is another farce in one act; it contains no local allusions, but it has one carefully studied character, the first of Molière's important Sganarelles. The framework in which he appears is an elaborately concocted series of jealousies treated in the realistic manner of a French fabliau. The pattern of this comedy is ingenious. It attacks both loveless marriages and impractical romance, but its chief interest lies in the character of Sganarelle. His jealousy of his wife is excited by superficial evidence; for a long time he cannot make up his mind to seek revenge at the expense of his physical safety. This conflict between Sganarelle's jealousy and his cowardice is the crucial point of his famous soliloquy in Scene xvii, in which he reasons with himself much as Falstaff does on the battlefield of Shrewsbury. The outcome is different, however, for whereas Falstaff has no personal motives urging him to action, Sganarelle's pride is involved and he finally decides upon revenge — of a certain sort: "Yes, anger overcomes me; it is too much to be a coward: I wish resolutely to avenge myself on the thief. To begin with, in the heat of my anger, I am going to say everywhere that he is living with my wife,"

> Oui, le courroux me prend; c'est trop être poltron:
> Je veux résolûment me venger du larron.
> Déjà pour commencer, dans l'ardeur qui m'enflamme,
> Je vais dire partout qu'il couche avec ma femme.

Sganarelle is not an admirable character, but he is amusing because of the conflict between his two outstanding humours. He is a trifle pathetic, too, in his inability to manage his wife and to avenge his honor. He imagines himself to be a cuckold, from which fact springs his absurdity, but he is also a prey to natural weaknesses. This Sganarelle is the first of Molière's intensely human characters.

Having achieved success in a farce based on jealousy, the next year Molière attempted to treat the same subject in a serious tragicomedy, as he did with slight success in Don Garcie de Navarre, or The Jealous Prince ("Le Prince jaloux"). One reason for this unfortunate attempt may have been Louis XIV's recent marriage to a Spanish princess, Maria Theresa, and the dramatist's desire to pay a compliment to the new queen by treating in a lofty vein a particularly Spanish subject like jealousy. Don Garcie is Sganarelle raised to royal rank and transported into the realm of chivalry. Both parts were acted by Molière himself, and he must have been quite conscious of the similarity between the positions of his two characters. The difference between the ways in which the jealous men act is illuminating: Sganarelle debates with himself on how to avenge his wife's treachery; Don Garcie unpacks his heart in angry words to the lady whom he loves. He is not yet a married man, but a romantic wooer; he can afford to indulge in noble sentiments and high-flown phrases. Molière was not at his ease in the elevated realm of tragicomedy, which he soon deserted to return to more congenial territory, but, like Ben Jonson after the failure of Sejanus, he came back to his chosen field with an increased earnestness of purpose and a deeper understanding of human errors.

II

Don Garcie may be said to mark the end of Molière's period of experimentation, although it was to be some years before his genius arrived at its full flowering. Meanwhile he made rapid strides in his artistic accomplishment, pausing every now and then to gather force by producing some unpretentious trifle, which would please the King, discomfit his personal enemies, or amuse the general public that was beginning to throng to his new theater in the Palais-Royal. *The School for Husbands* ("L'École des maris"), which was produced there on June 24, 1661, four months after *Don Garcie*, has an intellectual fiber that Molière's early dramas had lacked. The source of this play was the *Brothers* of Terence. In turning to Latin comedy Molière found material worthy of his steel. The conflict between two systems of education, the benevolent and the austere, had furnished an excellent subject for Terence, whom Molière imitated by embodying the opposed theories of life in two elderly brothers: Ariste, the elder, is all for conforming to the manners of society and being humane to his fellow man, not realizing apparently that these principles may sometimes prove incompatible with each other; Sganarelle, the younger, is narrow-minded, opinionated, and extremely individualistic. He criticizes Ariste for his dependence on his fellow creatures, makes fun of his conformity in dress, and particularly ridicules the black wig with which his brother covers his white hair. Sganarelle upholds the individual's need to express his personality; Ariste stands for the restraint imposed by society in the interests of the greatest good for the greatest number. The clash of these two imperious demands, both of which exist in any intelligent being, is the main source of social comedy, and Molière's realization of this fact is the secret of his greatness. In the brief scene between the two brothers at the beginning of *The School for Husbands*, the dramatist for the first time put into words the philosophy that was to dominate all his mature work and to produce his most keenly humorous situations.

The background is always that of the happy mean, against which the eccentricities of human nature are to be portrayed. Ariste expresses the reasonable point of view in lucid and vigorous terms: "One should always comply with the largest number, and it is never necessary to make oneself conspicuous. Any excess is offensive, and every really wise man ought, in his clothes and also in his language, not to be too affected but temperately to follow changing custom,"

> Toujours au plus grand nombre on doit s'accommoder,
> Et jamais il ne faut se faire regarder.
> L'un et l'autre excès choque, et tout homme bien sage
> Doit faire des habits ainsi que du langage,
> N'y rien trop affecter, et sans empressement
> Suivre ce que l'usage y fait de changement.

Ariste would rather be a fool than the one wise man in the world; Sganarelle would prefer to be the one wise man in a company of fools. Ariste appeals to the mind, Sganarelle to the feelings. Molière justifies Ariste and excites our sympathy for Sganarelle's failure to triumph over the dictates of organized society. *The School for Husbands* is too neatly organized to be a work of genius, but in it Molière formulated his comic principles with smoothness and clarity.

The specific application of his theory in the case of Ariste and Sganarelle is expounded in the second scene of the play. Each brother has as his ward a young girl whom he is bringing up in accordance with his philosophy of life and whose affection he hopes to win for himself. In changing the sex of Terence's young people and in making them wards rather than children, Molière is able to introduce a romantic element into the situation which was lacking in the *Brothers*, where the point at issue was the relationship of fathers and sons. He also made Sganarelle a more universal type by reducing his age to under forty (Molière himself was thirty-nine at the time when he first played the part) and thus removing him from the special category of old men, in which Terence was particularly interested. Sganarelle believes in shutting his ward up from contamination by the wicked world and keeping her for himself in a state of innocence and perfection. He thinks that no woman can go to balls and receive presents from young men without being completely spoiled. Ariste, on the other hand, is willing to let his ward have all the freedom possible; he believes that a young girl cannot know what love is until she has experienced the delights and disappointments of worldly society. The two girls are introduced into this scene to emphasize the opposing views of their guardians. Then Ariste and his ward disappear until the last act.

The main action of the comedy works out, with almost mathematical precision, the course of Sganarelle's disillusionment. His ward is found to have a young and attractive lover, Sganarelle perseveres in his policy of repression, and the inevitable explosion occurs. The distinctive feature of this somewhat conventional intrigue is that the young lady, and not her lover or his servant, takes the initiative in hoodwinking Sganarelle. In the last act she cleverly contrives to get her guardian to assist at her wedding, leading him to believe that Ariste's ward is to be the bride. Ariste is also told that it is his ward who is to be married, but true to his principles he signs the marriage contract, believing that if the girl wants to marry another man it is wise for him to give up all claims to her hand. When the true facts are revealed, Ariste is able to triumph gently over his brother and Sganarelle has received a further illustration of what he considers the evils of human society. His single redeeming quality, his love for his ward, has been the source of extreme unhappiness to him. His crabbed nature turns this misplaced affection into still another reason for misanthropy. He has been completely deceived by the practical application of his theory of life, but like a consistent comic character he remains unconverted to the last. He stands out from the artificial structure of the play as a living person, the most complex and vivid one that Molière had yet created.

The weakness of *The School for Husbands* is that the other characters in it, especially the young lovers, are conventionally drawn. In his next important piece Molière sought to rectify this fault within a somewhat similar dramatic frame; but before *The School for Wives* ("L'École des femmes") was produced on December 26, 1662, Molière was called upon to furnish a *comédie-ballet* for Fouquet's entertainment to the King in August 1661. *The Bores* ("Les Fâcheux") is a *pièce à tiroir*, that is, a series of separate scenes strung together on a thin connecting thread, in this case the attempts of a young marquis to succeed in meeting the lady he loves. He is prevented from doing so until the end of the play, chiefly by a succession of bores who insist on talking to him of their special interests. This scheme gives Molière an opportunity to draw a number of satirical pictures of contemporary society, like the one in *The Affected Ladies*. His success as a dramatist had by this time introduced him to court circles. The people he pictured in *The Bores* are of the nobility rather than of the bourgeoisie, but there is no great difference in the manner of their presentation. *The Bores* gave him an opportunity to increase his ⌐ range, but it includes too many portraits, none of them overwhelmingly effective. After the first bore, a talkative frequenter of the theater, who is described with much detail but not shown in person, there is no outstanding satirical study. The figure of the hunter was suggested to Molière by Louis XIV and is an evidence of the dramatist's approach to royal favor, but although *The Bores* shows that the dramatist's ability had been recognized in high quarters it adds little to his literary reputation. When printed, it was dedicated to the King and prefaced by the statement that it was conceived, composed, learned, and presented within a fortnight, an accomplishment more remarkable than the quality of the workmanship involved in it.

Between *The School for Husbands* and *The School for Wives* there occurred an event more important in the career of Molière than the production of *The Bores*. On February 20, 1662, the dramatist, at the age of forty, married Armande Béjart, a member of his company, at least twenty years younger than he. Molière had already treated the subject of a marriage between people of unequal ages in *The School for Husbands* and arrived at the conclusion that not age but character was the source of insurmountable difficulties. Ariste had won the affections of his young ward by wise and generous conduct. In *The School for Wives* there are no such reasonable characters to offset the study of unsuitability in years. The play opens, like *The School for Husbands*, with a scene between two men who are disputing a question about which the whole action is to revolve. This time it is not a philosophical problem or a general system of ethics which hangs in the balance but a particular phase of the same universal principles. If one is an individualist, and if he thinks, as Sganarelle did, that children should be brought up in ignorance of the world, he may be willing to agree with Arnolphe in *The School for Wives* that one should marry a fool.

Chrysalde, Arnolphe's friend, has no constructive philosophy like Ariste's ideal view of the world; he supposes skeptically that any husband's plans to escape from being made a cuckold are pure folly. He is an easygoing person who believes in letting well enough alone, whether it be by sticking to one's social position or by accepting what the gods provide in the way of marriage. He goes so far in applying his doctrine of *laissez faire* that at one point in the play he advises overlooking a wife's infidelity, especially if she has a good disposition. According to Chrysalde, the only way to avoid being a cuckold is not to marry at all. Whatever happens, he believes in returning thanks to heaven which has ordered all things for the best. His combination of worldly cynicism and religious complacence makes him more of a human being and less of a mouthpiece for Molière's ideas than Ariste had been. Arnolphe's actions also spring not so much from his philosophy as from his temperament. If he has a philosophy, it is much like Sganarelle's, but we hear very little of his general ideas and a great deal of his high opinion of himself. He believes that he can rise in the world by assuming an exalted title; so he calls himself M. de la Souche, taking the name from the stump of an old tree in his garden. He thinks that he can avoid the usual fate of husbands by marrying a young girl brought up in a convent, and he is so determined to win Agnès' love that he comes to feel real tenderness for her. Sganarelle would have put his hand in the fire for his ward, but he shows none of the intense affection that Arnolphe expresses in his last futile and pathetic attempt to gain Agnès' heart.

The School for Wives everywhere surpasses *The School for Husbands* in characterization, but in no way more notably than in the skill with which the heroine is drawn. Sganarelle's ward is little more than a clever soubrette masquerading under a show of modesty; Agnès is a real innocent, whose intelligence gradually expands under the influence of love. Her softness of heart is touched by her young lover's gentlemanly courtship. She is completely crushed when she learns that she will not be allowed to marry him. The more difficulties he encounters, the more he endears himself to Agnès' sensitive nature, until in the end she admits her love for him to Arnolphe with honesty and straightforwardness. She has not been able to control her feelings. Her heart has gone out spontaneously to the man who has initiated her into the beauties of natural affection, not to Arnolphe, who has unfolded to her, in *Les Maximes du mariage*, the whole duty of a well-behaved wife. Agnès' lover is rather like Lélie in *The Blunderer*, an attractive young man who keeps ruining his own affairs because of his great simplicity. He would have been beaten by Arnolphe in their duel for the possession of Agnès if Molière had not seen fit to resort to a romantic discovery in order to give his play a happy ending. Agnès is found to be someone's long-lost daughter, much as is the heroine of *The Blunderer*, where the conclusion fits better into the artificiality of the whole comedy than it does into the more realistic atmosphere that Molière's skill in characterization has achieved in *The School for Wives*. It is not so well constructed as *The School for Husbands*, but the theme is much more freely handled than in the earlier work. The harshness of the criticisms the later play received is a tribute to the insight and vigor with which it was composed.

Molière was intensely indignant at these criticisms, and in the course of the following year he replied to them in a brilliant dramatic sketch, *The Critique of The School for Wives* ("La Critique de L'École des femmes"). Molière's defense of his art has as its framework a study of aristocratic society not unlike that in *The Bores*. Six persons, gathered in a fashionable *salon*, express different views on the author's recent play. The hostess upholds common sense and the golden mean; her merry cousin satirically agrees with the fools whom at heart she scorns. A prudish *précieuse* attacks *The School for Wives* because it offends her sense of modesty, a vain and snobbish marquis dislikes it because it pleased the pit, or *parterre*, and a pedantic poet criticizes it because it does not conform to the accepted rules of dramatic art. Molière puts his answer to these typical complaints into the mouth of the intelligent Dorante: comedy is a difficult and noble enterprise; the greatest of all rules is to please the public; the interest of a comedy should be not in external action but in the characters' states of mind. He devotes a great deal of attention to defending Arnolphe's psychology, particularly his apparent inconsistencies, on the principle that "a person's being ridiculous in certain things is not incompatible with his being sensible in others" (*il n'est pas incompatible qu'une personne soit ridicule en de certaines choses et honnête homme en d'autres*).

Molière took his critical stand on the high ground of picturing human nature as it is, and his audiences splendidly supported him by filling the theater whenever *The School for Wives* was presented. Jealousy had its share in the attacks leveled against his popular success, and *The Critique of The School for Wives* was answered by Edme

Boursault's *The Portrait of the Painter, or The Counter-Critique of The School for Wives* ("Le Portrait du peintre, ou La Contre-critique de L'École des femmes"). To this Molière replied by *The Versailles Impromptu* ("L'Impromptu de Versailles"), another one-act *jeu d'esprit* in prose, which was produced during October 1663; in it the dramatist burlesqued the rival actors of the Hôtel de Bourgogne, who had inspired *The Portrait of the Painter*, and threw some amusing side lights upon conditions in his own company.

In *The Versailles Impromptu* Molière's actors are represented as gathered together to rehearse a comedy which the King has commanded to be written and performed on a week's notice. They object to the shortness of the time they have had in which to learn their lines, but Molière alternately threatens, ridicules, and cajoles them into doing their best, until the King graciously permits the new comedy to be postponed until a later date. During this slight action the personalities of the various actors and actresses of the troupe are displayed, and Molière even wrote a short quarrel scene to be acted by his wife and himself. The play within the play introduces a variety of affected noblemen and *précieuses*, a pedantic poet, and a man of good sense. Through the mouth of the latter Molière continues to enunciate his aesthetic principles: the function of comedy is to show general types, not particular individuals; real life furnishes such rich material as scandalmongers, false flatterers, fair-weather friends, discontented office-seekers, and impertinent bores; the business of comedy is to attack, and incidentally to offend, all foolish noblemen, *précieuses*, coquettes, and cuckolds; the best revenge that a dramatist can have against his enemies is to write another successful comedy which shall give equal, perhaps greater, offense.

In these words Molière may have been anticipating his next masterpiece, *Tartufe*, but before he was prepared to deliver that severe blow in his warfare with society he amused himself and the King by writing two *comédies-ballets* of very different kinds. *The Compulsory Marriage* ("Le Mariage forcé") and *The Princess of Elis* ("La Princesse d'Élide") were both performed in the early months of 1664. Each was intended to be accompanied by music and dancing, but otherwise they were not in the least alike. *The Compulsory Marriage*, without the additions for a ballet, is a simple "Sganarelle" comedy, somewhat like the early play of that name. Here, instead of being already married, Sganarelle is contemplating matrimony in spite of a friend's efforts to dissuade him from taking that step. Later he becomes disillusioned and wants to escape from his engagement, but it is too late and his fiancée's brother insists, at the point of his sword, that the marriage must take place. The change from Sganarelle's debonair desire to marry to the unwillingness with which he actually has to do so is amusingly sketched. The intermediate scenes contain some animated satire upon two philosophers, an Aristotelian, who babbles of learned subjects, and a doubting Pyrrhonian, who refuses to give definite advice on any topic. *The Compulsory Marriage* is a slight piece, but it is infinitely superior to *The Princess of Elis*, which is more pretentious and also more bombastic. Based on Moreto's *Disdain for Disdain*, it was begun as an elevated tragicomedy in verse like *Don Garcie de Navarre*, but its execution was hurried by the King's command, the end of it was outlined in prose, and the result is not much more than a glorified opera libertto. *The Princess of Elis*, like *The Compulsory Marriage*, is a literary lapse, for which Molière more than compensated in his next phenomenal piece of work.

III

The history of *Tartufe, or The Impostor* ("Le Tartufe, ou L'Imposteur") is a complicated one: the first three acts were presented at Versailles on May 12, 1664; the whole drama was given privately in November of the same year; permission to act it regularly was not granted until February 5, 1669. During the intervening five years it underwent numerous alterations, in one of which Tartufe appeared not as a *dévot*, but as a fashionable gentleman, in an endeavor to placate the opposition excited by this play among men of religion. Molière made every effort to show that Tartufe was not truly pious and that the blasphemies put into his mouth should not be taken at their face value, but he was unable to prevent his contemporaries from being shocked at the truthfulness of the picture he had drawn; it was not, as a nobleman of the day said, that they would have minded an attempt to satirize religion, but that they could not endure ridicule of themselves. More than one individual was supposed to have been the original of Molière's hypocrite and more than one sect felt that it had been pilloried in his work, but Molière claimed that he was launching his attack against conditions which were so widespread that more than one target would be hit by his shafts. Perhaps he had in his mind the secret society of *La Compagnie du Saint-Sacrement*, the avowed purpose of which was to supervise the moral life of the community, but Tartufe stands for any person or organization which attempts to use its spiritual function as a means of self-aggrandizement.

Tartufe is a satiric portrait like that which Molière had already painted of *précieuses*, bores, and impractical philosophers, but it is more incisive than his previous work because its subject is a graver one. Tartufe is comic, when he overreaches himself in his hypocrisy, but he is villainous when he attempts to ruin the tranquil family life of Orgon. The fact that the play is a comedy, not a melodrama, depends upon the importance given to the character of Orgon, a part which was played by Molière and which is a natural sequel to his study of the simple, infatuated Arnolphe in *The School for Wives*. Orgon has the simplicity to suppose that it is the highest wisdom to devote one's attention to a spiritual director and to neglect the ordinary affairs of everyday life. He is so blinded by his infatuation for Tartufe that he opposes the common sense of the other members of his family, the first domestic circle that Molière had used as a dramatic background. The scene of *Tartufe* is laid not in an open street, as had long been the convention of classical comedy, but in Orgon's house, where the various characters are naturally assembled. They include Orgon's children by his first marriage, his second wife, his brother-in-law, and an irrepressible maidservant.

The brother-in-law is the spokesman or *raisonneur* of the piece. Like Chrysalde in *The School for Wives*, he combats the protagonist in exaggerated terms that border on cynicism; like Ariste in *The School for Husbands*, he expresses Molière's ideal philosophy of the golden mean. He oscillates between being a freethinker and a true *dévot*. In both characters he provides the intellectual opposition to Orgon's foolish credulity. The maidservant represents the same point of view in a less consciously critical way but with more healthy vividness. Orgon's wife, like the Queen in *Hamlet*, is of a sluggish disposition, which fits into her contradictory part as the recipient of Tartufe's attentions and the means of his eventual detection. Orgon's son has a fiery nature, which drives Orgon to disinherit his family in favor of Tartufe, and his daughter's docility does nothing to stem the tide of her father's blind obstinacy. Orgon's weakness so far delivers him into Tartufe's hands that, even when his entire family is united against the intruder, he can do nothing to protect his property and his person, until royal intervention pronounces Tartufe a notable traitor. Then the villain is routed and the dupe is cured of his folly in a play which is more substantially dramatic than a comedy of manners usually is and which is perhaps the most effective stage piece that Molière ever wrote.

The strength of its subject and its technical skill unite in the character of Tartufe, the malign presence which broods over the action. After two acts devoted to preparing for the entrance of the hypocrite, we see him executing his wiles with success and then meeting with failure as he overreaches himself. His most skillful casuistry, the argument with Orgon's wife that her carnal sin will be justified in the eyes of heaven, is followed immediately by his overthrow and the disillusionment of Orgon. Upon Orgon's discovery that a man of religion may be fallible, his first impulse is to sever all connections with *dévots* of any kind, but his wise brother-in-law suggests to him the error of his new program: "Your mind never coincides with right reason, and you always jump from one extreme into the other,"

> Dans la droite raison jamais n'entre la vôtre,
> Et toujours d'un excès vous vous jetez dans l'autre.

Orgon is not to suppose that all pious people are as hypocritical as Tartufe has proved himself, but to realize that truly religious men distinguish between the sinner and the sin.

Tartufe is not necessarily irreligious — though so far as we know he has no sincere principles of any kind — and his worldly vice of hypocrisy is not dependent on either belief or disbelief. This distinction between a hypocrite and an atheist being apparently too subtle for Molière's enemies to perceive, the dramatist decided to try to make it clear to them in his next play by presenting a true libertine, who should not, like Tartufe, be given an opportunity to repent of his immorality but should be damned for his complete lack of religious feeling. With uncanny wisdom the dramatist chose for this purpose the legendary figure of Don Juan Tenorio, as it had been established by Tirso de Molina and developed by subsequent French and Italian authors.

Don Juan, or The Banquet of Stone ("Le Festin de pierre") was produced on February 15, 1665. Its form differs from that of *Tartufe* in two important respects: it is written in prose, and it makes no pretense of keeping to the unities. Its sole unifying thread and motivating force is the character of Don Juan, an evidence that Molière was carrying out consistently his comic theory, but developing it more elaborately than he had yet done. *Don Juan* is not so great a play as its immediate predecessor or as its spiritual successor, *The Misanthrope*, but it holds a worthy position as the second part of the magnificent trilogy in which Molière grappled with fundamental human problems. Don Juan himself is a finished portrait of the *grand seigneur* of Louis XIV's court in his most unpleasant aspects. His dress and manners are described as those of a nobleman of the day. The scene with an honest tradesman is introduced solely to show the ways of impecunious courtiers with their bourgeois creditors. Don Juan's expert method of handling women is the central theme, as it had to be in any version of the story. His defense of indiscriminate lovemaking merges into his scorn of marriage, which because of the sacramental nature of that institution brings him into conflict with the Church and with religious issues.

Superficially Don Juan is an unscrupulous member of the French court; underneath his bravado he is an atheist and a disbeliever in divine power. When pressed by his valet for his creed, he replies that he believes two and two make four, and four and four make eight. That is as far as his faith goes, and when he sees the statue miraculously brought to life he discredits the evidence of his own senses. In the original version of the play he offers a poor man a louis d'or if he will blaspheme. In later revisions he less blatantly ridicules the piety which motivates the beggar's unsuccessful appeals for charity. In both cases Don Juan finally gives the poor man a coin "for the love of humanity," thus showing that he does not acknowledge any connection between God and mankind. This humanitarian action is contrasted with his refusal to pay his debts and to acknowledge his deserted wife. In the latter case he is willing to fight a duel to defend his position; bravery is the one positively good quality that Molière's hero possesses. His courage is shown more and more as the play goes on. In the terrifying last scene he is much less frightened than is Tirso's primitive libertine.

Molière's Don Juan, not very consistently, joins hypocrisy with bravery. One who does not fear earthly or spiritual powers need not resort to the coward's last offense of invoking heaven to shield him from punishment, but Don Juan's hypocrisy is not so much a defense as it is an easy means to accomplish further evil. "Hypocrisy is a fashionable vice, and all fashionable vices pass for virtues. The role of an upright man is the best of all roles that one can play today, and the profession of hypocrite has astonishing advantages." Don Juan's crowning hypocrisy is to promise his father that he will reform when he has no intention of doing so, and at this point he adds to his basic infidelity the external deceit of a Tartufe. It is no wonder that Sganarelle, who up to this time has followed his master's evil ways with apprehension, despairingly consigns Don Juan's soul to all the devils.

Sganarelle has always disapproved of his master's conduct, but he is too much of a coward to offer any open resistance to the nobleman's imperious demands. He has the simple wisdom to disapprove of Don Juan's materialistic philosophy because of his wonder at the marvelous way in which the human machine operates, but in attempting to demonstrate what a piece of work is a man Sganarelle tumbles to the ground and his eloquence is dissolved in laughter at his own expense. Like Orgon in *Tartufe*, Sganarelle was acted by Molière, and these two characters are chiefly responsible for the comedy in plays where the principal characters are too ominous to be amusing. Sganarelle's intentions are excellent, but they do not seem to produce more lasting good than Don Juan's evil theories. At the end of the play Don Juan, still unrepentant, is swallowed up by hell-fire, and Sganarelle is left alive to lament his master with the sardonic cry of "My wages!" Don Juan with all his vices is a brave man; Sganarelle sees the right, follows the wrong, and is ignobly comic throughout the action. There can be no doubt that Molière sympathized with the valet's views on life, but he insisted on showing the folly of too great idealism combined with too little wisdom, at the same time that he directed his comedy primarily against religious infidelity.

One of the scenes between Sganarelle and Don Juan expresses

their opposing ideas on a subject which was to interest Molière increasingly in later years and which was to be the theme of his next play. In his early dramatic sketches he had ridiculed the profession of medicine, but it was not until his own health began to fail that his observation of doctors became more acute and exact. When Sganarelle is disguised as a doctor, he tells Don Juan that he believes in medicine because he knows of a case where it has been successful in killing a suffering invalid! Don Juan, on the other hand, states a more critical view when he says that he believes doctors have little to do with curing their patients: "They do nothing but get the glory for lucky successes." Molière realized that medicine was a useful science, but he could not endure the self-importance of doctors. He undertook to ridicule it thoroughly in his next comedy, *Love as a Doctor* ("L'Amour médecin"), which was produced at Versailles in September 1665, as part of a *comédie-ballet*.

Comedy, music, and ballet provide the framework for this entertainment, the simple and conventional plot of which concerns the supposed illness of the heroine, and how it is cured when her lover, masquerading as a doctor, prescribes the remedy of marriage. Meanwhile she has been attended by four real doctors, supposed to have been satirical portraits of four famous court physicians, who are amazing embodiments of medical traits and foibles. They emphasize such tedious technicalities as whether horses or mules are the better means of conveyance in visiting patients and whether bleeding is as useful a remedy as an emetic. A wise doctor delivers a sermon on how physicians should not cheat their patients, classing medical practitioners with flatterers, alchemists, and readers of horoscopes as men who prey on human weaknesses, the greatest of which is the desire to live; *le plus grand foible des hommes c'est l'amour qu'ils ont pour la vie*.

An observation as sweeping as this indicates the increasing depth of Molière's philosophy as it developed from the time of Sganarelle in *The Cuckold in His Own Imagination* through the Sganarelles of *The Compulsory Marriage* and *Don Juan* to the Sganarelle of *Love as a Doctor*. This last Sganarelle opens the play in which he appears by a drolly humorous speech lamenting the difficulties of human life and concluding, "I have had only one wife, and she is dead." Sganarelle consults various people about his daughter's sickness, but he receives such selfish answers from them all that he is justified in deciding their advice is dictated by their own interests. Molière had come to appreciate the tragic aspects of the human dilemma, when he created the sinister characters of Tartufe and Don Juan. He surrounded them both by buffoonery and horseplay, with the result that their painful implications are not too obvious. He was neither willing nor able to surrender himself completely to an utterly gloomy view of life; in his next play he made a supreme effort to combine philosophical truth with worldly incongruity.

IV

The Misanthrope is Molière's greatest work of literary art, but it has always failed to be entirely realized upon the boards of a theater. Produced on June 4, 1666, its markedly pessimistic tone may be due to many things: ill-health, the ban placed upon *Tartufe*, the quarrel with Racine, and perhaps most of all Molière's increasing difficulties with his wife, which were soon to result in their temporary separation. All these circumstances must have impressed the dramatist vividly with the conflict that exists between an individual and the world about him. He had already touched upon this subject in *The School for Husbands*, and now, after having treated the Church in *Tartufe* and religion in *Don Juan*, he returned to a consideration of man's highest moral duty, the obligation that he has to himself. The necessity of expressing one's personality is canvassed pro and con in the first scene of *The Misanthrope*, where a reference is made to the earlier discussion of this same theme in *The School for Husbands*. Alceste is more polished than Sganarelle in his objections to the uses of this world and more profound in grasping that some insincerity must always accompany social conformity. He is seeking to attain the truth in his relations with other men. He refuses to compromise with the eternal verities, even for the sake of momentarily alleviating a difficult situation. His honesty and his rigidity are combined in this brief expression of his faith: "I wish a person to be sincere and, as a man of honor, not to let one word escape him that does not spring from the heart,"

> Je veux qu'on soit sincère, et qu'en homme d'honneur,
> On ne lâche aucun mot qui ne parte du coeur.

The particular reason for Alceste's annoyance at the beginning of the play is that his friend Philinte has been showing great affection for a man whose name he scarcely knows. Philinte attempts to justify himself on the score of natural humanity. He is willing to be polite to all the world, since doing so costs him little and is in accordance with the common sense on which he prides himself. He believes that charity rather than truth should motivate one's actions in this world and that it is sometimes more necessary to tell a lie than it is to be unpleasantly sincere: "Perfect intelligence avoids all excess and counsels that one should be wise with moderation,"

> La parfaite raison fuit toute extrémité
> Et veut que l'on soit sage avec sobriété.

This general statement of Philinte's position echoes the words of Ariste in *The School for Husbands*, "L'un et l'autre excès choque," and deftly sums up the reasonable view of existence which Molière employed as the background of his comic art. Philinte is not an absolute ideal (Molière at his greatest was too consummate a dramatist to attempt to draw perfect human beings), but the friend of Alceste expresses in both his words and his actions the golden mean against which the misanthrope was in revolt. Alceste refuses to praise a mediocre sonnet or to defend a lawsuit in which he is involved; from the first, he threatens to flee to an uninhabited desert, where he may be free from the society of rogues and fools. Philinte attempts to dissuade him from these various acts of rashness and reminds him that, if he does not care to associate with men, there is one woman, Célimène, to whose opinion he is not wholly indifferent. Alceste's idealistic philosophy was, like Molière's, not proof against emotional assaults, especially those concentrated in the person of a young and charming woman.

Célimène is only twenty years old, and she has already been married once; she has surrounded herself with admirers; she is a notorious coquette, and she flirts outrageously with any man in sight. Although she is the essence of the falsehood and artificiality which Alceste abominates, he cannot resist her charms. He is furious at the scandalous gossip which she and her coterie direct against their friends, but he hopes against hope that his love will be able to overcome the worldliness of the coquette's nature and win her affection for himself. It may seem strange that Célimène is sufficiently interested in the misanthrope to permit his attentions, but Alceste is peculiarly attractive to all the women in the play. The attempt of Arsinoé, the prude, to detach him from Célimène's train furnishes the slight plot of *The Misanthrope*. This complication, which is of comparatively minor importance, does not begin until the end of Act III. *The Misanthrope* is a play of contrasting characters, not of external action.

Arsinoé succeeds in arousing Alceste's jealousy of Célimène's relations with other men, although for a time the coquette's skill disarms the misanthrope's anger. Finally Célimène's insincerity becomes transparent to all her acquaintances, and Alceste, who has meanwhile lost his lawsuit, decides to put into execution his early threat of fleeing from the world. He will pay no attention to the practical and moral argument of Philinte: "All these human failings give us opportunities in life to practice our philosophy,"

> Tous ces défauts humains nous donnent, dans la vie,
> Des moyens d'exercer notre philosophie.

He will not live among fallible human beings, but he cannot overcome the irrational attraction which Célimène exerts upon him. The position of the two lovers has become equally isolated for totally opposite reasons. Alceste's misanthropy has exiled him from the society of men; Célimène's love of admiration has alienated her various suitors. Each is fond of the other, and the logical conclusion would be for extremes to meet. Alceste proposes marriage to Célimène, but he lays it down as a condition of their union that she shall go to live with him in his unpeopled desert, which he hopes will prove a veritable Garden of Eden. She is wiser in her realization that the human being is a social animal and must not be cut off from the companionship of other people. "Solitude frightens the spirit of a person twenty years old" (*La solitude effraye une âme de vingt ans*), and, since Célimène is as definite in her position as Alceste is in his, the only solution for them is to separate. Célimène is left to find new lovers, as she assuredly will, and Alceste leaves the stage to seek his happiness alone. His final *tirade* on the glory of freedom for the individual is eloquent and impassioned, but the cautious Philinte is not taken in by it and hopes that Alceste's resolution may still be shaken. On this note the comedy ends, if *The Misanthrope* may be called a comedy. It is, at bottom, a rambling philosophical discourse on the relation between the individual and his environment. There is brilliance of expression in the contrasting lines of Alceste and Philinte, and the creation of Célimène is a marvel of sympathetic understanding, but the abiding interest of the play rests in the universal question that it raises. Since its first performance, there has been disagreement as to what practical solution of the problem Molière meant to offer. From the point of view of his comic method there can be little doubt of his intention. In all his mature plays the central figure is absurd because he deviates from a sensible norm; in most of them he meets with failure because of his refusal, however well-meaning, to conform to the dictates of common sense. His eccentricity is always measured by his divergence from a moral code which is based upon benevolence, not towards one person but towards society at large. The greatest good of the greatest number may not be the highest wisdom, but it is the most effective background for a display of the comic spirit. This utilitarian philosophy is not transcendental in its nature, but comedy has no necessary business with transcendental values. Its serious object is to make people laugh at the momentary foibles of their fellow men, whether these spring from innate or acquired characteristics. Its appeal is to ordinary people, and it has little consideration for genius of any sort. Nothing is more absurd in the eyes of mankind than for one individual to set himself up as superior to the rest of the world, and that is exactly what Alceste has done. He may be a nobler person that Philinte, but he is certainly a more comic one.

Molière makes this point by means of the character of the unselfish Éliante, who loves Alceste but at the end of the play agrees to marry Philinte. She is depicted as seeing clearly that Alceste would be an impossible person to live with, and she accepts Philinte in a marriage which is not a victory for romance but a triumph of common sense. Philinte's future happiness is far more certain than is Alceste's. Alceste, so far as we know, is to spend the rest of his days alone; his occupation will be gone with no one near him whom he can criticize. Molière's sympathies were with Alceste, but his judgment told him that the egoist's attitude towards life was utterly ridiculous, no matter how exalted the strain in which it was expressed. The balance between the comic and the pathetic he nowhere else achieved so perfectly as in *The Misanthrope*, just as he nowhere else depicted a character so theoretically admirable and so practically absurd as Alceste. Rousseau and other romantic advocates of solitude resented the harsh way in which Molière treated the idealistic misanthrope, forgetting that comedy is a social force and that in it human beings are to be judged by social standards. These sentimental critics were notoriously lacking in the sense of humor which was Molière's peculiar gift and which fortified him against the assaults of the world in which his lot was cast. One cannot live according to Alceste's code if he would, and to perceive that it is ridiculous is the surest safeguard against its intellectual attractions. However, one must do justice to the individual's pursuit of truth for its own sake, and this justice is what constitutes the greatness of *The Misanthrope* as philosophical literature. It also prevents it from being an effective play upon the stage, where unmistakable emphasis is necessary for immediate success.

In *The Misanthrope* Molière was more occupied with his ideas than with the story by means of which he was presenting them. The lack of external action and spontaneous laughter in this play was made up for by his next work, *The Doctor in Spite of Himself* ("Le Médecin malgré lui"), which was first produced on August 6 of the same year, 1666, and after September 3 was often performed on the same bill with *The Misanthrope*. The two comedies make a most effective contrast, for whereas *The Misanthrope* has always been considered Molière's masterpiece by literary critics, beginning with Boileau, *The Doctor in Spite of Himself* at once won an immense popular success, which has continued to the present day. It is a continuously amusing piece, but it does not aspire to scale the heights of abstract thought. In it Molière reverts to his satire on doctors, but his tone is less bitter than it was in *Love as a Doctor*, and his hits at medicine are contained in a merrier framework. The plots of the two pieces are very similar. In both cases a heroine who pretends to be ill to escape an unwelcome marriage is cured by the appearance of her lover in disguise. But the character of the Sganarelles in these two plays is quite different. In the earlier play he is the heroine's father, as selfish as are most other human beings; in the later one he is the mock physician, occupied with acting as a doctor when he is really a simple woodcutter. Hs is at first very much embarrassed by the part which has been forced on him by his angry wife, but he soon finds that it is neither so disagreeable nor so difficult as he had supposed. He is able to hoodwink the heroine's father by pretending to be an expert on physiology, and when he is caught in a technical error he can wave aside all criticism with the covering phrase, "We have changed all that" (*Nous avons changé tout cela*). It is no wonder that he likes his ambiguous position and that at the end of the comedy he intends to remain a doctor rather than return to his original occupation.

The final success of Sganarelle's efforts leads him to draw some satirical conclusions on the profession of doctoring, not very different from those of Don Juan. Sganarelle's experience has taught him that clothes suffice to make a doctor, and that people will pay a physician whether he cures them or not: "I find that it is best of all callings, for whether one does well or ill, he is always paid in the same way; here one can ruin a man without its costing anything, and no one ever complains of the doctor that has killed him." These keen thrusts all depend upon the hypothesis that the desire to live is man's strongest instinct, but *The Doctor in Spite of Himself* does not call this instinct a weakness as does *Love as a Doctor*. Between these two medical farces Molière had reached the bedrock of the human problem in *The Misanthrope*. He was now ready to indulge in lighter moods, such as that in which he wrote *The Doctor in Spite of Himself*.

No doubt practical considerations partly entered into Molière's choice of a more popular subject, as they did into his next productions, intended not to draw audiences to the Palais-Royal but to entertain the court. From December 2, 1666, to February 19, 1667, there were elaborate fetes held at Saint-Germain-en-Laye, and for them Molière wrote three *comédies-ballets*: *Mélicerte*, an unfinished heroical pastoral comedy, the scene of which is laid in the Vale of Tempe and the characters in which are shepherds and shepherdesses, real or supposed; the somewhat similar *Comic Pastoral* ("Pastorale comique"), of which only the scenery and the songs have come down to us; and *The Sicilian, or Love as a Painter* ("Le Sicilien, ou L'Amour peintre"), in which the disguise of the lover gives an opportunity to ridicule the flattery of a portrait painter. Into each of these three *comédies-ballets* Molière introduced a role for himself, which should give some scope to his powers of eccentric characterization and which should allow him to play the comically disappointed lover. His experiences in real life were doubtless making him adept at the part. They also were upsetting the steadiness of his artistic impulse, if we may judge from the three comedies by him which were first performed in the year 1668.

V

Amphitryon, George Dandin, and *The Miser* ("L'Avare"), acted on January 13, July 18, and September 9 respectively, are absorbing and tantalizing plays. They are all based on earlier comedies that had once been successful and which Molière has not assimilated so well as he had the Don Juan story. Perhaps his imaginative genius was severely crippled by his personal unhappiness, perhaps he had lost confidence in his creative ability, but, whatever the reason, he could not seem to enter into the spirit of carefree laughter that pervaded the dramas of Plautus or his own apprentice work. Plautus' *Amphitryon* raised a particularly difficult problem, because it presented the deities of an outworn religion; its ostensible object was to excite wanton laughter at the expense of human beings made the playthings of the gods. This program was diametrically opposed to Molière's theory of social comedy, which relied upon showing the absurdities of individual men in conflict with organized society, and therefore the dramatist was wise not to cast his play into realistic form. He adorned it with elaborate scenic contrivances. He wrote the dialogue in the irregular lines and rhymes of *vers libres,* the frees lyrical measure that he ever attempted.

The outline of his story was fixed by Plautus' delight in shee mischief-making, but Molière was not able to direct his laughte wholly against the mortal husband. Jupiter, although omnipoten and divine, was to the eyes of common sense nothing better than a unprincipled interloper in a happy domestic situation. The god quick to recognize his own ambiguous position as a lover mas querading in the guise of a husband. He wants to have Alcmène lov him for himself alone. With unerring logic, he begs her to di tinguish between passion and matrimony. This she has not sufficie detachment to do, and at the end of the play Jupiter is forced to con gratulate Amphitryon on having a wife whose affections are so con stant that they could be won only in the shape of her husbanc

What Amphitryon thought of this compliment we are not told, but the sympathy with which Molière wrote the soliloquies of the deceived husband suggests that his Amphitryon could never have been as acquiescent as was Plautus' on learning he had had the rare good fortune to be made a cuckold by a god. Alcmène herself is not on the stage to hear of the imposture that has been practiced upon her, and her absence does something to relieve the intrinsic unpleasantness of the final situation. The last word is left with Amphitryon's valet, Sosie, who takes Jupiter's protestations with a grain of salt, believing, "On such matters the best thing is always to say nothing."

If Molière had said nothing on this disagreeable subject, we should have lost one of the most effective parts that the dramatist ever wrote for himself. The character of Sosie was as well fitted to Molière's genius as the main plot of *Amphitryon* was antagonistic to it. The valet has as many defects as a man well may have; he is cowardly, gluttonous, and vain, but he has an abounding vitality, which he shares with Sganarelle in *Don Juan* and which makes him always a delightful figure. From the first he is shown as completely disillusioned, particularly with the service of the great in which he finds himself, but he loves to shine by reflected glory and cannot bear to serve a lowly master. When he is forced to decide which is the true Amphitryon, his instinct for prosperity leads him to choose Jupiter, for, as he puts it in a homely and famous phrase, "The true Amphitryon is the Amphitryon where one dines,"

> Le véritable Amphitryon
> Est l'Amphitryon où l'on dîne.

The elements of Sosie are all to be found in Plautus, but Molière has made a definite addition to the story in the person of Cléanthis, Sosie's virtuous and unattractive wife. Mercure, disguised as Sosie, refuses to have anything to do with her. Sosie ludicrously suffers from his substitute's fastidiousness, not from his amorousness.

All that Sosie himself desires from matrimony is the domestic tranquillity that he cannot have. His satiety is contrasted with the impatience of the newly married Amphitryon, and the matter-of-fact Cléanthis makes an admirable foil for her romantic mistress, Alcmène. Disappointed because of her husband's frigidity towards her, Cléanthis struggles with her innate virtue and is in a constant state of trying to summon up courage to take a lover, as Mercure has advised her to do. Whether or not she ever carried out her threats we do not learn, because her part in the play is not fully developed. The servants are last seen indulging in one of their customary quarrels, which results, as usual, in no definite victory for either side.

Molière's next comedy is entirely devoted to picturing an unhappily married couple. In *George Dandin, or The Confused Husband* ("Le Mari confondu") he reverted to prose and to a story of common life. George Dandin, like Sganarelle in *The Compulsory Marriage*, has aspired to a wife who is his social superior, and when the play begins, some time after their marriage, the rich peasant is already repenting his social ambitions. He soon learns that his wife has a lover, and he becomes a prey to insane jealousy, with more reason than Sganarelle in *The Cuckold in His Own Imagination*. George Dandin is the type of deceived husband from the early French fabliaux which Molière had originally sketched in his earliest extant work, *The Jealousy of the Clown*. The core of the plot is the scene common to both plays in which the faithless wife, who has been shut out of the house by her husband, reverses their positions by pretending that she is about to commit suicide. In *George Dandin* this simple situation is elaborated, the dramatist making it the culmination of the husband's numerous unsuccessful attempts to convince his wife's parents of her infidelity. At the close of the play he is still fast yoked to his wife, who would like to secure a divorce on her own terms, but whose father will not hear of his daughter's separation from her rich husband. Dandin and his wife must jog on together in a kind of armed neutrality. She will recommence her meetings with her lover, and her husband will endure his ignominious position as best he can.

The sympathy which Molière always shows with his absurd characters is never more striking than in the case of *George Dandin*, where the introduction of real human beings into a farcical plot is extremely disquieting. Dandin himself is presented as both humorous and pathetic, but also as sensible enough to recognize his own absurdity. His wife is justified in her actions, because she was not consulted in the choice of her husband. The faded gentility of her parents arouses mingled pity and amusement. Each character is laughable, but each has been pushed on to his destiny by perfectly understandable causes. George Dandin wanted to marry into the nobility, his wife's parents wanted to repair their impoverished fortunes, and their daughter is caught between the upper and nether millstones. These characters really belong to a problem play, in which the wife might have been a sorely tried heroine, but the plot is that of an uproarious farce, in which it is not appropriate to pay much attention to the psychology of a betrayed husband.

The contrast between the spirit of Molière's source and that of his own mature social comedy is less striking, but more confusing, in George Dandin than in Amphitryon. The semi-religious material of Amphitryon cannot fittingly be subjected to the test of reasonableness, and the crude horseplay of George Dandin does not stand it well; but harsh realism is more amenable to the intelligence than are flights into the supernatural world. Molière seems to have realized this fact when he again went back to Plautus for the material of his next play and, instead of choosing a primitive story like the Amphitryon, took as his source what is probably Plautus' most subtle comedy, the Aulularia. Molière made a conscious effort to extend the philosophical background which Plautus had suggested, and he lavished great care upon depicting Euclio, or Harpagon, as Molière called the miser.

Euclio is an isolated figure, but Molière surrounds Harpagon with a large family group. He has a son and a daughter, a steward, a housekeeper, and a servant who is an amazing combination of cook and coachman. All these persons are in revolt against Harpagon's narrow stinginess. His son is kept in such poverty that he patronizes a moneylender, who turns out to be Harpagon himself, and father and son are also rivals for the hand of the same young lady. These intrinsically painful domestic situations are at first kept on the level of comedy by each character's ignorance of the other's plans. Later both of them learn the truth, and Harpagon disinherits his son in a fit of uncontrollable anger. Up to this point, near the end of Act IV, everything has been going well for the miser, but the moment of his triumph is followed almost immediately by the theft of the casket, or cassette, containing his buried treasure. His frenzied soliloquy appealing to the audience for help is Molière's most skillful adaptation of Plautus' material. It offered an opportunity for just that combi-

nation of pathos fused with comedy which was the French dramatist's special gift. The thief is the son's valet, whom Harpagon has
dismissed for being too prying, and the miser receives his treasure
back again at the price of giving up all claims to the hand of the
young lady that his son loves. He is only too happy to do so, because he cares far more for his money than for any sort of human
affection.

To make this important point as clear as possible, Molière gave his
miser both a son and a daughter, whereas Plautus' miser had only
one child. This addition to the story provided a brilliant illustration
of the disintegrating effect of avarice on a family circle, but it had to
be eked out by a number of romantic complications which do not
fit very well into the comic atmosphere of the play. The daughter's
lover and the girl whom the son marries are found to be brother and
sister and are provided with a rich benevolent father, who unites
the two pairs of young lovers. The old device of a long-lost father
makes it possible for the play to end happily for everyone, but the
neatness of the construction does not conceal the artificiality of the
story. Even Harpagon is satisfied to have recovered his "chère cassette," instead of receiving the punishment which is due him as a
repulsive comic character. The union of romance and comedy has
here resulted in an amorphous form of art that anticipates modern
drama.

In spite of the intruding romantic interest, there is much genuine
comedy in The Miser. Maître Jacques, who in his double position as
cook and coachman is instructed to give food sparingly to both man
and beast, tries to be an honest man. When he tells the miser the
truth about himself, he is beaten for his pains. Later, when he embarks
on a campaign of deceit, he is threatened with hanging. He is a poor
addlepated fellow who does not know what to make of the contradictory ways of the world. His simplicity of character is cleverly
fitted into the plot, he adds an element of low comedy that the play
sadly needs, and he stands out from his environment because of the
skill with which Molière has drawn him. He is more vivid than any
other character in the story except Harpagon himself, and even Harpagon lacks the clearly defined touches that give life to Molière's
greatest comedy creations. In spite of his petty vanity, his cough, and
his spectacles, he is little more than an intensification of Plautus'

Euclio, a farcical personification of avarice rather than a carefully observed and sympathetically studied human being.

Molière seems to have feared that the character of Harpagon would not prove sufficient to carry his play, because he includes in its plot a large amount of diverse material. In one instance he overreached himself, when he introduced a plan to have a false marquise entrap Harpagon and then let this scheme come to nothing. There was certainly some confusion in the dramatist's mind when he wrote *The Miser*, possibly because it may have been composed in haste; traces of verse discovered in the early scenes of an otherwise prose play point toward either carelessness or a change of plan after the work had been begun. The truth may lie in the fact that, although the *Aulularia* was more fitted for treatment by Molière than was Plautus' *Amphitryon*, it did not present an ideal subject for his genius. Avarice is only a small section of the vast canvas of social eccentricity which Molière was trying to paint, and it is not a section which appealed to him strongly, as it did to Ben Jonson. He could understand the pangs of a selfish lover, he could share in the disappointment of a credulous fool, and he could sympathize with an enemy of society. All these themes are touched on in *The Miser*, but they are subordinated to the central subject of avarice, which Molière did not handle with much greater skill than Plautus had already shown.

VI

After *The Miser* Molière no longer struggled with such complicated aesthetic problems as those he had set himself in the three plays of 1668, but he was content with a return to simpler themes that were more obviously within his province. His next production was *Monsieur de Pourceaugnac*, a *comédie-ballet* first given before the King at Chambord on October 6, 1669. It met with such success that it was transferred on November 15 to the Palais-Royal, where it pleased Parisian audiences as much as it had the court. This musical farce contains the gaiety and the simplicity of outline that had characterized Molière's early triumphs. It is closely related to *The Affected Ladies* in that it is a social satire on country folk in the city. The *précieuses* wish to be considered as Parisians; M. de Pourceaugnac, a Limoges lawyer, is absorbed in the affairs of his own town and rather homesick for his friends and relations. He has come to Paris to make a stylish marriage, from which he is only dissuaded after he has suffered severe physical humiliations. He falls into the hands of unscrupulous physicians, who are paid to subject him to painful remedies. He escapes from them only to become the prey of lawyers, and later he is arrested by an officer, whom he has to bribe to be allowed to go free. At the end of the play he is departing for his beloved Limoges, whence one supposes that he will not soon venture again to expose himself to abuse at the hands of doctors, lawyers, and civil authorities in the great metropolis.

Except for its central figure, who belongs to Molière's gorgeous gallery of badly balanced human beings, *Monsieur de Pourceaugnac* is chiefly important for the success with which it adapts a farcical plot to the needs of *comédie-ballet*. From the time of *The Bores* Molière had apparently thought that such a synthesis was possible, but in all his previous attempts he had tended to put the emphasis upon either the comic story or the operatic libretto, at the expense of the other element in the combination. In the prologue to *Love as a Doctor* the author expresses the hope that a mingling of comedy, music, and ballet may be successfully realized in that play, but at only one point in it, when a quack doctor sings the praise of his favorite remedy, does an element of the fantastic enter into an otherwise satirical and pessimistic work. *Monsieur de Porceaugnac* is much livelier in tone than *Love as a Doctor* and much better adapted to the highly exaggerated view of life that dominates the operatic stage. It seems quite appropriate for the doctors and lawyers to burst into song and dance when pursuing M. de Pourceaugnac, and in fact neither Act I nor Act II would be at all complete without the ballet interlude that follows it. Molière had at last discovered how to weld two different forms of art together into a new pattern, which has characteristics unlike those of its component parts. The dancers and singers must be actors also, and the actors must be performing a play that lends itself to whimsical treatment. The misfortunes that befell M. de Pourceaugnac were of such an impossible nature that it required little imaginative effort for the spectator to quit the sphere of drama and to soar on the wings of Lulli's music to a domain where people do not talk but sing and do not walk but dance. The exigencies of providing court entertainment, together with Molière's sensitiveness to ridiculous effects, were fast leading him into a field which Aristophanes had already adorned and which was to prove a perfect sttting for the combined talents of Gilbert and Sullivan.

Molière's next effort in this genre, *The Magnificent Lovers* ("Les Amants magnifiques"), produced on February 4, 1670, was a step backward, but it prepared the way for *The Middle-Class Gentleman* ("Le Bourgeois Gentilhomme"), the dramatist's most successful union of comedy and ballet. A large part of the triumph of *The Middle-Class Gentleman*, first acted at Chambord on October 14, 1670, comes from the skill with which in it high comedy is made to assist music and dancing. From the first scene, in which the Music Master and Dancing Master are preparing their performances, to the last, in which an elaborate ballet celebrates three marriages, the mood of grotesque exaggeration is consistently maintained. The central idea of the story, the Turkish ceremony at the end of Act IV, was suggested by the King, who had lately received an embassy from the Turkish court and who wished to commemorate that historic occasion. Turkish customs were strange enough in western Europe to appear picturesque and even absurd. They provided Molière with an excellent opportunity to use a gorgeous ballet as part of a comic plot. To focus the comedy, he created a character sufficiently naïve to be deeply impressed by oriental display and sufficiently ambitious to wish to take part in a royal ceremonial. M. Jourdain, retired tradesman, is one of his most brilliant characterizations.

M. Jourdain's anxiety to rise in the social world had been foreshadowed by Arnolphe's desire to be known as M. de la Souche and by M. de Pourceaugnac's eagerness to contract a fashionable marriage. In both these cases the vanity of the principal character had interfered with his own love affair, but M. Jourdain has been married a long time and is now engaged in finding a suitable husband for his daughter. His situation is somewhat like Harpagon's, but whereas Harpagon is a static figure and can only exhibit the result of a lifetime of miserliness, M. Jourdain is in the process of becoming a gentleman. His efforts to fit into a position where he does not belong are hilariously funny. His simplicity makes him an easy prey to the magnificence of Turkish ritual, but before the supreme absurdity of his becoming a Mamamouchi occurs, he has been fooled by musicians, tailors, and cooks. These professional groups take advantage of their patron's ignorance to indulge in ludicrous exhibitions of their wares, which assume the form of dances and make up the interludes, or *intermèdes*, at the end of the first three acts.

Act I, which closes with an entertainment by professional dancers, is occupied with M. Jourdain's training in the arts. He is a novice at dancing, music, and fencing, but he is no less absurd than his instructors, each of whom thinks that his own subject is of supreme importance. The scene between M. Jourdain and the Master of Philosophy most thoroughly exposes the vain pretensions of both the educated man and the man who wishes to become educated. Logic, morality, physics, linguistics, and rhetoric are in turn pilloried in a marvelous dialogue which culminates in M. Jourdain's celebrated discovery that he has been speaking prose for forty years without knowing it. He is vindicated also by learning that his ordinary method of expressing himself is better than any ornate phraseology that can be devised. In short, he exhibits all the virtues of bourgeois common sense, which he so much despises. He never appreciates the absurdities of his ambition, however, and, as his teachers are paid to be flattering sycophants, it is the duty of the critics in his own household to subject him to ridicule. The principal exponents of common sense are a vivacious maid and M. Jourdain's dour wife, who tells her husband some plain truths about the silliness of going to school at his age. Mme. Jourdain naturally frowns upon the would-be gentleman's excursions into high society, which are likely to endanger her domestic happiness, but he pays no attention to his wife's warnings, as he embarks on the policy which is to prove his undoing.

M. Jourdain is strengthened in his delusions by Dorante, an impoverished and unscrupulous count, who tells him that he may soon shine in aristocratic circles and continues to borrow money from him which will never be repaid. Dorante serves a double purpose in the plot: he is M. Jourdain's candidate for his daughter's hand, and he pretends to forward the ex-tradesman's intrigue with a marquise, called Dorimène. Dorimène is a somewhat ambiguous character, necessary to the story but carelessly contrived by Molière. She is evidently not an adventuress, for at the end of the play she agrees to marry Dorante so that he may not have to spend any more money on her. She rather likes the well-meant blunders of M. Jourdain, but she must have been very stupid to have been taken in by the palpable imposture of the banquet scene. Dorante has told Dorimène that he is giving a dinner for her at M. Jourdain's house, but the *bourgeois gentilhomme* is himself paying the bills in the hope of entering upon a fashionable liaison with Dorimène. Dorimène's psychology is not fully explored, and neither is that of Dorante, who, without much consistency, becomes an accomplice in the plot to marry M. Jourdain's daughter to her lover, disguised as the son of the Grand Turk.

The most subtle feature of *The Middle-Class Gentleman* is M. Jourdain's failure to discover that he has been imposed upon during the course of the play's action. At the end of it he is completely happy in a fool's paradise. He is delighted with the wedding of his daughter to the supposed princely Turk, with whom he is proud to be allied. He also believes that the news of Dorimène's approaching marriage to Dorante is a false story intended to blind his wife, so that he may the better continue his affair with the marquise. The underlying pathos of M. Jourdain's position is cleverly minimized by withholding from the audience his disillusionment, which, it seems, is bound shortly to occur. In this way Molière escapes the disagreeable phases of his theme. The plot of *The Middle-Class Gentleman* might easily have been treated with savage disgust, as is shown by Le Sage's handling of similar material in *Turcaret*, but the atmosphere created by music and dancing keeps all unpleasantness temporarily in abeyance. Molière needed just the lightness of mood that the ballet gave to offset the bitterness of his mind in 1668 and to carry him over to the more serene achievements of his later years. *The Middle-Class Gentleman* marks his triumph in one of the slighter fields of drama. Without it one would appreciate less well the variety of his comic genius.

His success with *comédie-ballet* led Molière to try his hand at *tragédie-ballet* also, but fortunately he wasted little effort on *Psyché*, produced on January 17, 1671. He himself wrote only a small share of the work, entrusting the remainder of it to his collaborators, Corneille and Philippe Quinault. The piece pleased audiences, largely because of the spectacle and the acting, but it contains nowhere any evidences of Molière's comic genius. As if to counterbalance his excursion into tragedy, and as it were to pave the way for a return to pure comedy, Molière's next production after *Psyché* was the unmusical farce *The Rogueries of Scapin* ("Les Fourberies de Scapin"), acted for the first time on May 24, 1671. This humorous story of intrigue, founded on the *Phormio*, the most rollicking of all Terence's plots, has in it touches derived from the *commedia dell'arte* and from French medieval drama. It is more in Molière's early manner than anything he had attempted since *The Doctor in Spite of Himself*. Its principal character, a scheming valet, called Scapin, might easily have been named Sganarelle or Mascarille. There are two young lovers, two heroines, two fathers, and two valets, but the entire action centers in the intrigues of Scapin. He extracts money from the two old men, and then, after he has beaten one of them concealed in a sack, he pretends that he is on the point of death. Forgiveness by his dupes speedily restores him to health, and when they have pardoned him for all his deceits the general joy is made complete. This mild but merry comedy is chiefly notable for containing the famous and much-repeated question, "What the devil was he doing in that galley?" (*Que diable alloit-il faire dans cette galère?*).

At the end of the year in which Molière had delighted his uneducated audiences with *The Rogueries of Scapin*, he concocted another *comédie-ballet* for the pleasure-loving court. On December 2, 1671, *La Comtesse d'Escarbagnas* was performed at Saint-Germain-en-Laye as part of the festivities surrounding the marriage of the King's brother. This prose comedy in one act is simply a setting for an elaborate entertainment, which a Vicomte is to give at the home of the Comtesse d'Escarbagnas, ostensibly for the Comtesse but actually in honor of another lady, a situation resembling that in the banquet scene of *The Middle-Class Gentleman*. The Comtesse, like M. Jourdain, makes pretenses to a culture that is beyond her grasp, although of course she is of higher rank than the would-be gentleman. Her folly is that she is a provincial noblewoman, intoxicated by her one brief visit to Paris and now aping the manners of the city on her native heath. She is shown in her original environment, as M. de Pourceaugnac and the *précieuses ridicules* had not been in theirs, but the presence of the cultivated lovers furnishes a background to set off her absurdities. She indulges in many high-flown terms for simple objects, and she would like to contract a brilliant marriage. Lacking more lofty suitors, she encourages a rural councilor and a receiver of taxes, the former of whom she finally agrees to marry "to make everyone angry," as she declares. Apart from its usefulness as the frame for a court *divertissement*, *La Comtesse d'Escarbagnas* is largely a reworking of old material and one more variation upon Molière's recurring theme of social pretentiousness.

VII

From the slightness of *The Rogueries of Scapin* and *La Comtesse d'Escarbagnas* one might have thought that Molière's great period of creative activity was over and that the bitterness of 1668 had dissipated itself into trivial farces and musical entertainments, but the mercurial dramatist still had a surprise in store for his audiences. When, on March 11, 1672, *The Learned Ladies* ("Les Femmes savantes") was performed for the first time, it appeared that for six years Molière's gigantic talent had not been dead but sleeping. *The Learned Ladies* is a return to the high comedy of manners as Molière had practiced it in *Tartufe* and *The Misanthrope*. It is neither so dramatic as the one nor so intelligent as the other, but it combines their qualities and adds to them a sparkling gaiety, suggestive of *The Middle-Class Gentleman*. Its greatest weakness is its subject, or at least the shallow way in which its subject is treated. Hypocrisy and egotism are touched on incidentally, but the main theme is formal education for women. During the course of his career Molière had drawn many *précieuses* and a number of pedants, but he had not before joined an overdisplay of learning to feminine sensibility. The union of these two themes was novel, but Molière seemed to have regarded it as a casual absurdity rather than as a matter of social importance. He worked it out in a plot which is competently handled but by no means remarkable for its originality.

Nevertheless, *The Learned Ladies* is, within its limits, one of the most perfect of Molière's plays, and it may justly be considered a typical example of his art. No other of his comedies contains such a large number of minutely studied characters who express their personalities by interacting upon one another and voicing their various opinions in exquisitely modulated verses. There are ten important persons portrayed, five in favor of learning for women and five opposed to it, not one of whom is hurriedly sketched. Even the hero and heroine, often summarily dismissed by a writer of comedy, are given definite characterizing touches. Henriette is the most distinctly drawn of all Molière's *jeunes filles*. She is too sentimental to be willing to marry her lover when she thinks that her family are financially ruined, but she is human enough to enjoy triumphing over her unsuccessful rival. Clitandre plays the perfect gallant in disregarding his mistress's loss of fortune, but he has a hot temper and attacks pedants, male and female, in forthright words. Into his mouth Molière puts an eloquent defense of the best elements in court life and a bitter denunciation of women who make a wanton display of their intellectual attainments.

Clitandre is attractive to two other women besides the gentle Henriette. Her foolish aunt, Bélise, is not exactly in love with him, but she supposes that he, like many other men, is in love with her and does not dare to woo her directly. Bélise is an exaggerated picture of the unattractive old maid, so vain of her personal charms that she does not dare to look facts in the mirror. She lives in the world of her own imagination, which is more agreeable to her than the hard reality of her daily existence. Her delusions are as harmless as they are ridiculous. Such is not the case with Armande, Henriette's elder but still young and attractive sister, with whom Clitandre had once been in love. She had liked his admiration, but she did not want to marry him, preferring courtship to marriage. Her dream world consists in an eternal round of florid wooing, a prospect which flatters her vanity without ruffling her equanimity or making heavy demands upon her sincere devotion to learning. When she finds that Clitandre is not made of such ethereal stuff and prefers love which connects the body with the spirit, her prudery is at first outraged and then her jealousy is aroused by the rivalry of her more sensible sister. Although Armande does not want Clitandre for her own husband, she cannot endure the thought of his marrying someone else. There is in her soul a real struggle between her love of education and her attraction toward the opposite sex. When she sees Clitandre slipping from her grasp, she says that she has changed her mind and will marry him after all; but it is too late. Clitandre has become thoroughly disgusted with Armande's insidious selfishness. He marries Henriette and leaves Armande, now very nearly a tragic character, alone with "the support of philosophy."

Neither the farcical figure of Bélise nor the emotional one of Armande is as central to the story of *The Learned Ladies* as Bélise's sister and Armande's mother, Philaminte. Philaminte, the leader of the learned ladies, does not allow love, real or imaginary, to interfere with her enthusiastic pursuit of higher education. She has been married for a long time and has passed through that period of life when one's emotions are likely to play havoc with one's philosophy. In her case, the application to books comes into conflict with her duties as wife, mother, and housekeeper. She has decided that Clitandre cannot marry Henriette because he does not appreciate poetry sufficiently, and she proposes as a mate for her beautiful younger daughter the fatuous wit, or *bel-esprit*, Trissotin. In this, as in other matters, she disagrees with her husband, Chrysale, the most flawlessly portrayed character in *The Learned Ladies*.

Chrysale, a "bon bourgeois," is imposed on by his strong-minded wife, who neglects her husband's interests and attempts to dominate him completely, in the cause of what she honestly believes is the higher truth. Poor Chrysale is quite incapable of understanding advanced education, and he is not courageous enough to combat Philaminte's masterful personality. His struggles to assert himself provide many of the most humorous scenes in the play. Again and again he attempts to insist upon having his way, but each time his wife proves to be too resolute to be dislodged from her position. He would probably have remained a nonentity all his life if a ruse of his brother's had not demonstrated the mercenary designs of Trissotin and the unselfishness of Clitandre in their protestations of love for Henriette. Philaminte is convinced of Trissotin's hypocrisy and reconciled to Chrysale's proposal that Clitandre shall be the accepted bridegroom. Whether Philaminte's disillusionment with her adored man of letters will have any permanent effect on her absorption in learning is not discussed, but for the time being her egotistical judgment has been proved wrong, to the great delight of Chrysale. Philaminte is pretty sure to go on managing her husband, and she will probably continue her intellectual pursuits. Whatever the outcome of this particular domestic situation, Molière has made it clear that in his opinion the educational activities of a woman seriously interfere with the happiness of the members of her family.

The Learned Ladies does not explore the full possibilities of its theme, but it does have far-reaching implications as to the social responsibilities of women; its restricted scope makes it better adapted to comic treatment than if it dealt with more fundamental issues. Its slowness in movement throughout the first four acts is counterbalanced by the glory of such incidental scenes as those of the maid's dismissal and of Trissotin's quarrel with a pedantic friend. This comedy is unexcelled by any of Molière's works in the smoothness of its execution, the polish of its verse, and the variety of its characterization. It would have made a fitting close to his dramatic career, but he was not to die until he had delivered one last thrust at his old enemies, the doctors. The serenity of Molière's closing years, during which he had become well established financially and reconciled to his wife, was painfully clouded by his increasing ill-health. At one time the Palais-Royal had to be shut because of his indisposition, but Molière refused to relinquish his career as playwright and actor. He would die in the harness, and he would die fighting. He wrote *The Invalid in His Own Imagination* ("Le Malade imaginaire") and produced it on February 10, 1673, at the Palais-Royal. It had been intended as a court entertainment and was cast in the form of a *comédie-ballet*, but a quarrel between Molière and Giovanni Battista Lulli prevented that eminent composer from writing the music for it, as he had done for all Molière's other work since *The Bores*. The dramatist decided to employ an inferior musician and to give the piece at his regular theater. The artistic loss was not so great as it would have been if the comic material in *The Invalid in His Own Imagination* had not entirely surpassed the music and dancing for which it was intended to be a framework.

Molière was too much in earnest about human frailty to subordinate his subject to the ballet *intermèdes*, which, as modern performances of the play indicate, can be omitted without greatly weakening the force of the comedy. The background of music does, however, help to emphasize the farcical treatment that Molière saw fit to give his comic material in *The Invalid in His Own Imagination*, where an apparently idle jest is used to cloak a breaking heart and a failing body. It was a splendid gesture for a doomed man to ridicule the love of life with his last breath, and by an ironic fatality Molière died a few hours after his fourth performance as Argan on February 17. *The Invalid in His Own Imagination* is Molière's final assault on the absurdities of the world, and it is appropriately directed at those doctors who try to take advantage of the inevitable course of nature. Man is born to die, Molière seems to say, and all the alleviations of the human lot are ridiculously inadequate. The failure of the medical men of the day to relieve Molière's physical suffering explains the vivid pathos of his last high-spirited comedy. *The Invalid in His Own Imagination* is a heroic effort to combine the mingled gaiety and despair that are to be found side by side in all living matter.

To clothe his conception in dramatic form Molière took as his central character a man who employs physicians when he really has no need of them. Argan, the invalid in his own imagination, is a hypochondriac of the first order. He believes that when his doctors' bills decrease in size his health is worse. He is completely under the thumb of his chief medical adviser and quite willing to submit himself to the most drastic remedies, unpleasant as they may be. His obsession is ridiculed by a sprightly maid and meets serious opposition from the heavy arguments of his brother. The brother, as nearly an out-and-out *raisonneur* as is to be found in any of Molière's comedies, expatiates at great length on the folly of Argan in particular and of invalids in general; his view is that nature is the best physician and by itself will ultimately kill or cure. The common sense of this attitude is decidedly dubious, but it has a rational basis in the physical facts of life. It must have especially appealed to Molière, as he saw his own illness becoming too severe to give way before the ministrations of doctors. He had always made fun of man's instinctive desire for continued life, notably in *Love as a Doctor*, and he has Argan's brother suggest to the supposed invalid that a visit to the comedies of Molière would delight as well as instruct him. The reference to his own work gives the dramatist a chance to say that it is not doctors but "the ridiculous side of medicine" (*le ridicule de la médecine*), that he has been attacking all his life. Argan hopes that the doctors will avenge themselves by letting Molière die without the benefit of their advice, and he receives the poignant reply that the sick man will not ask them for remedies; "he has only just strength enough to endure his disease" (*il n'a justment de la force que pour porter son mal*).

The identification of Argan's brother with Molière's point of view makes him a rather colorless and tedious person. He does not intensify the obstinacy of the central figure, as do the critics in the earlier plays; he does not contrive a brilliant scheme to bring about a happy ending, like the similar character in *The Learned Ladies*. He is merely successful in persuading his brother to postpone taking one of his doctor's prescribed treatments, and thus he indirectly causes a quarrel between the physician and his patient, which paves the way for Argan's partial return to sanity. The doctor in his anger refuses to permit the marriage of his nephew to Argan's daughter, which the hypochondriac has ardently desired, in order that he may have a doctor for his son-in-law. The nephew, Thomas Diafoirus, is one of Molière's most exquisite simpletons. He does his wooing in the set terms of a formal speech that he has learned by rote, and he shows his stupidity in medical matters by attacking the new theory of the circulation of the blood; but Thomas will make a conventionally successful physician, because he blindly follows all precedents. The scene in which he appears is one of the most ludicrous in the play. Its effect is to undermine the respect due to medicine by illustrating the stupidity of some of its practitioners.

Argan later finds that his daughter has been receiving attentions from another young man, and he cross-questions his younger daughter, Louison, about the matter. The presence of Louison, the only child in Molière's plays, adds a new note to the dramatist's gamut. Her pretense of being dead to escape a beating and her terror of the omniscience of her father's little finger are delightful excursions into the psychology of children. Although Louison has the best intentions in the world, the naïve testimony she gives her father works against the course of true love.

The heroine's love affair meets more active opposition from another member of Argan's household, his second wife, Béline. Béline is a designing hypocrite, a sort of female Tartufe, whose one aim is to obtain possession of her husband's fortune. She constantly flatters Argan, calling him her "petit fils" and other endearing names, in the hope that on his death he will leave all his property to her. She introduces a notary to make Argan's will, and the scene in which the notary explains various ways of getting around the law contains some amusing hits at the legal profession, not unlike those in Racine's *The Litigants*, which had been produced in 1668. Molière, however, subordinates the satire on lawyers to that on doctors, as if he thought that legal interference in human affairs was less absurd than the intrusion of physicians into matters of life an'd death: lawyers only complicate already involved relationships; doctors meddle with the workings of a higher providence. The difference between the two professions is brought out clearly in *The Invalid in His Own Imagination*, where it is seen that to Molière what happens to a man's material possessions is of small account, and therefore not very amusing, in comparison with what happens to his health. Béline is anxious to secure Argan's money, but she cannot accomplish that object until her husband's death, for which she is impatiently waiting.

Argan's pretense that he is dead reveals Béline's true motives, but the hypochondriac never entirely recovers from his delusion about the sanctity of doctors. He cannot give up his determination to have a medical son-in-law, and when he agrees to his daughter's marriage with the man of her choice he stipulates that her future husband shall become a physician. His brother suggests that it would be better for Argan himself to be made a doctor, because then he would be able to cure his own diseases and not have to rely on any outside aid. This logical extension of Argan's unreasonable position brings the comedy to a delightfully upside-down conclusion and implies that in a world of self-imagined invalids, such as to a certain degree we all are, every man should be his own doctor. In the final *intermède* Argan is admitted into the learned society of physicians, taking the oath to trust in ancient remedies and never to try any new ones except those approved by the Faculty of Medicine. Here again it is *le ridicule de la médecine* which Molière is assailing, its conservatism, its obscurantism, and its self-satisfaction.

The chief enemy of the medical profession in *The Invalid in His Own Imagination* is not Argan's logical brother but his spontaneously merry maid, Toinette. Toinette is the liveliest of all Molière's maid-servants; she combines the intelligence of Dorine in *Tartufe*, the jollity of Nicole in *The Middle-Class Gentleman*, and the common sense of Martine in *The Learned Ladies*. She is the visible essence of the *joie de vivre* which is opposed to long faces and gloomy predictions. Toinette perceives instinctively that length of days brings human beings nearer to becoming *struldbrugs*, and she believes that epicureanism is the wisest philosophy, especially when one is young and healthy. Toinette wants to help Argan enjoy life while he may, although she is wise enough to see that much of his happiness comes from taking pleasure in his bad health. Even so, he may learn to laugh at his absurdities and cultivate a sense of humor at his own expense. Molière had himself achieved this height of comic detachment. He died in the midst of acute suffering, with laughter on his lips.

The tragic overtones of *The Invalid in His Own Imagination* give some indication of how far Molière had traveled since his early days as a writer of light farces, when he had mingled plots common to the fabliaux of his own country with stock figures drawn from the masks of the *commedia dell'arte*. To those undisciplined sources of his inspiration he later joined the example of Italian literary drama, and he then applied his wide knowledge of comic tradition to picturing the life about him in Paris between 1659 and 1673. In the course of these fifteen years Molière composed no less than twenty-two distinguished comedies, of which at least twelve are of major significance. They range all the way from light farce to philosophical drama, from *comédie-ballet* to satire on the latest social foibles. His range is extraordinary, and his personality, like that of every other great dramatist, pervades his most memorable works. His critical attitude towards society is shown in *The Affected Ladies*, his introspective brooding over the subject of jealousy appears in his earliest important Sganarelle, and the trend of his rational philosophy is clearly outlined in the first scene of *The School for Husbands*. In each of his plays from *The School for Wives* on, he welded together these three elements, and in a series of parts written for himself to act he displayed the many sides of his astonishingly varied character. Like Arnolphe, he was inclined to be suspicious of the world; like Orgon, he was now and then fascinated by some clever hypocrite; like Sganarelle in *Don Juan*, he saw the truth but did not always have the moral strength to cleave to it; and, like Alceste, he was acutely conscious of his superiority to the society of which he was a part.

Sosie, George Dandin, and Harpagon, M. Jourdain, Chrysale, and Argan, each has something of his creator's point of view, and they are all both humorous and pathetic. Molière was conscious of his own limitations, and he recognized their absurdity. He was able to divide his individuality into its rational and emotional elements and to set up one side of it against the other without doing harm to either. The most notable example of this method is the skill with which the dramatist drew both Philinte and Alceste in *The Misanthrope*. Philinte pursues his way in accordance with a well-ordered and logical theory of human conduct, which would be the perfect expression of the golden mean if reason could be the guiding principle of existence, as it is a touchstone for great comedy. Alceste is fallible enough to be shaken from such an intellectual attitude by the emotion which the wantonly brilliant Célimène arouses in him and by the idealism which makes him conscious that his duty to himself forbids him to be a mere social conformer.

Molière did not sympathize exclusively with either of these men, but he understood them both. The philosophy of Philinte is the philosophy of his creator, and the conflicting impulses of Alceste are those which swayed the entire life of Molière. Philinte would have reconciled Alceste's dilemma by his mind; without Alceste's conflict between the body and the soul Philinte's mind would have no material upon which to work. This division of the human animal into his component parts gave a clear-sighted dramatist like Molière endless opportunities for comic effects. By playing man's varying foibles off against a constant background of reasonableness he was able to unfold the bewildering panorama of his plays. Gaiety and common sense were rarely lost sight of in the process. If the soubrettes did not provide the one, it became a part of the dramatic texture; if the *raisonneurs* did not express the other, it was implied by the difference between their views and those of the protagonists.

This conflict between practical wisdom and the weaknesses of imperfect mankind is the main source of intelligent comedy. Molière recognized the fact, and time and time again he gave his principal character a logical friend or brother to argue against his eccentricities, to intensify his stubbornness by creating opposition to it, and often to bring about the purging that is requisite for the greatest art. In tragedy this objective is reached by touching the emotions, in comedy by appealing to the sense of humor. A sudden perception of the incongruities in human life is an unfailing source of laughter, and when these incongruities have a basis in systematic thought the highest reaches of the comic experience have been attained. Comedy is essentially analytical in its nature. Laughter is occupied with enjoying the fleeting moment rather than with building up a harmonious connection between apparently irreconcilable phenomena. It throws a searching light upon the inconsistencies of existence. At its most trivial, it takes pleasure in the slightest divergence from the serious business of living. It is not an absolutely vital factor in the human situation, but it helps immeasurably to soften the blows of a hostile world.

On the other hand, laughter need not always be confined to the transitory and the ephemeral; it may deftly and lightheartedly deal with fundamental problems, which may best be discovered by applying the touchstone of reasonableness to the contradictory motives of humanity. This is the paradox of high comedy. It must be spontaneous and cheerful; it must also be carefully considered and dispassionately critical. It must combine an irrational instinct with a rational philosophy, even if in the process it loses a certain vital energy and does not gain complete wisdom as a recompense. The cleansing power of comedy depends not upon pity and terror but upon sympathy and intelligence. The methods pursued by the two chief kinds of drama may be different, but the final results are, at their best, very much alike. *The Misanthrope* skirts the borders of tragedy, and *The Invalid in His Own Imagination* is an uncanny combination of misery and high spirits. Molière solved the intricate problem of ennobling laughter more nearly than any other literary artist, and by virtue of his genius for kindly but uncompromising criticism he must be considered as the greatest writer of thoughtful comedy in the history of the theater.

CHAPTER VI

The Danish National Theater: Ludvig Holberg

I

MOLIÈRE died in 1673, but his plays are still very much alive and they have exerted continued influence upon the comedies written from his day until our own. Molière had gradually formulated a philosophy of reasonableness and learned how to express it in dramatic form. At the top of his bent he had dealt with the basic material of human life, with physical and mental disease, and with pride, both spiritual and temporal. He had also from the time of his first success with *The Affected Ladies* never ignored superficial absurdities, which grow increasingly numerous as the structure of society becomes more organized and more complicated. In spite of *The Learned Ladies* and *The Middle-Class Gentleman*, the education of women and the rise of the middle class continued their rapid advance. Ridicule was not enough to stem the tide of social change that was coming over western Europe at the close of the seventeenth century. The M. Jourdains of that period were beginning to realize that, although they had been born bourgeois, they could by a deliberate effort raise themselves to the status of gentlemen. The leisure class's exclusive monopoly of social cultivation was meeting its first formidable opposition. Commerce was thriving, private fortunes were being accumulated, and the last vestiges of feudal society, which had been based on the possession of land as a reward for military service, were disappearing before the importance of economic wealth derived from barter and trade. The upper class had the tradition of past generations with its heritage of opportunity and experience to rely upon, but the successful merchants were steadily coming to realize the power of their newly acquired money and to insist that they were of more practical value to a nation than was its privileged but decadent aristocracy.

Molière had the perception and the breadth of view to acknowledge that, if there were unscrupulous noblemen ready to profit from the absurd ambitions of a would-be gentleman, there were also serious-minded and intelligent courtiers who would assist a brow-beaten husband to rout the learned ladies of his household. The comic insight of the Frenchman saw the humor in both sides of the issue, and his plays made clear that if the social conservatives were polished and charming they were also often hypocritical and mer-cenary; whereas the naïve bewilderment of those who suddenly found themselves with unaccustomed prestige had a quality of nat-uralness that helped to offset the awkwardness with which they wore their strange new honors. Molière, who had been brought up as a member of the middle class and had risen to a position where he could talk familiarly with the King, was able to see both points of view, and in his literary work he deftly kept an even balance between them.

To do so was a more difficult undertaking than it had ever been before in the history of comedy. During the great dramatic periods in Greece, in Rome, and in Spain, social conditions had been rela-tively static, and elemental human nature had interested the comic playwright more than the external distinctions between a polished gentleman and an honest tradesman. Prior to the time of Molière the middle class had not taken a very influential part in the life of Mediterranean countries, and only in England had the treatment of social upstarts become a vital comic theme. Ben Jonson, with his rigid theory of humours and his insistence upon avarice as the root of all evil, clearly pointed out that the desire to obtain money might lead to downright vice and that the ways in which it was spent might be evidences of incredible folly. Molière's natural tendency was to sympathize with his characters while he laughed at them. Jonson was too severe to pass by even slight moral defects without holding them up to scorn. He considered social manners as trivial, absurd matters, not worthy of serious attention. He expressed himself with force but without urbanity, and he left it to his successors to refine upon his crude but powerful method of attack.

The example of Molière helped the disciples of "Father Ben" to soften the rough technique of their master and to adopt a point of view more favorable to their environment. By the time that the Commonwealth had come and gone and Charles II had returned from his travels, English dramatists were tired of morality and ready to set up a social instead of an ethical standard of comic judgment. Sir George Etherege and John Dryden, William Wycherley and William Congreve insisted that a hero should be first of all a fashionable gentleman and only secondarily an exponent of either the Christian or Platonic virtues. Dorimant must be successful at drinking and playing cards, he must handle his importunate creditors as skillfully as he did his numerous mistresses, but it was not at all necessary that he should pay his debts or settle down in matrimony, until he found a girl who was as clever and wealthy as she was young and handsome. The youthful heiress might be more than a match for him in wit, but he had his sex as an asset and in the war between a beau and a coquette each had as much to gain as to lose by signing an armistice. To fight gracefully with glance and compliment, to mask feeling under an exchange of repartee, to flirt with a fan, and to make love with a snuffbox were arts which were much valued at the Restoration court. The only offender against the social code was the man who attempted to practice these arts without having enough technique to display them effectively. To ape the manners of the French nobility when newly returned from France was an unforgivable offense against good taste, unless one had assimilated the intrinsic virtues as well as the external eccentricities of the Gallic spirit.

Elegance was considered desirable by Stuart courtiers who were trying to domesticate in England what they had learned on the Continent, but the backbone of English respectability was loath to accept foreign ways in religion, in society, and in art. The emergence of sentimental drama showed that English comedy was never entirely able to join the instinctive good sense of Molière with the conscious moral earnestness of Ben Jonson, but something very much like this process went on across the North Sea in Denmark during the early decades of the eighteenth century. At this period the principal Danish dramatist was Ludvig Holberg, who had traveled in France and England as well as in Germany and Italy. He brought home with him the results of his varied dramatic experience and was ready to apply them to the formation of a native school of comedy.

In 1722, when Holberg was thirty-seven years of age, René Montaigu, a Frenchman, assembled a company of Danish actors and opened a national theater in Copenhagen. The royal patent which permitted him to do so was obtained after various difficulties, but the greatest obstacle to Montaigu's success was the lack of available plays written in the vernacular. He began his first season with translations of Molière into Danish, and at about the same time he was lucky enough to stimulate Holberg to the writing of his thoroughly native comedies, almost all of them couched in simple, homely prose. Holberg had already proved himself an able satirist by the mock-heroic poem of *Peder Paars*, in which three years earlier he had held up to ridicule many phases of contemporary Danish life and from which he now drew much material that he recast in dramatic form. During the year 1722 he had five plays acted; during the next two years ten pieces by him were performed on the boards; and when, in 1731, he published a complete edition of his comedies, there was a total of twenty-five titles to his credit, although all these works had not been produced before the closing of Montaigu's theater in 1728. Thus, within ten years, between the ages of thirty-seven and forty-seven, Holberg did his most valuable dramatic writing, at a high rate of speed and presumably at a high pitch of creative excitement. *Don Ranudo de Colibrados*, which he had composed during this same period, did not appear in print until 1745, and the remaining six of his total thirty-two plays were not written until after the reopening of the theater in 1747. Holberg did not actively resume his labors for the stage until 1750. He died in 1754 at the age of sixty-nine. It is not surprising that the comedies of his later years lack the power and distinction of his earlier work.

II

Holberg's five first comedies, which contain much of his best writing for the theater, were acted in 1722, the first year of Montaigu's managership, and printed the next year as the first volume of Hans Mikkelsen's *The Danish Stage* ("Den danske Skueplads"), "Hans Mikkelsen" being the pseudonym under which Holberg had already published *Peder Paars*. These five comedies, which have sufficient variety to give a representative idea of Holberg's comic scope, are: *The Political Pewterer* ("Den politiske Kandstøber"), *The Fickle Woman* ("Den Vaegelsindede"), *Jean de France, or Hans the Son of Frands* ("Hans Frandsen"), *Jeppe of the Hill, or The Transformed Peasant* ("Jeppe paa Bierget, eller Den forvandlede Bonde"), and *Master*

Gert from Westphalia, or The Very Talkative Barber ("Mester Gert Westphaler, eller Den meget talende Barbeer"). In all five of these plays common Danish types of the period are worked into a dramatic pattern which shows the influence of traditional comic practice from the time of Aristophanes to that of Molière. There is in every case a protagonist who expresses the author's views on life, an antagonist who is made ridiculous because of his divergence from these approved standards of conduct, and a number of minor characters divided between those who help to bring punishment on the principal offender and those who share in his fate because of similar deviations from normal behavior. Occasionally there is a character who oscillates between the two camps, who blunders well-meaningly into error and then extricates himself from his evil ways in time to escape a severe penalty. The person against whom the comedy is directed never escapes from suffering for his folly. Generally he repents and will reform his way of life, but sometimes he obstinately continues in his infatuated course after he should have learned from bitter experience the folly of his conduct.

This definite program sounds as if it were dictated by the rigid theory of a pseudoclassicist, not by the creative impulse of an original genius. Nevertheless, Holberg has enough individuality to make his work vivid and unusual. Although it had its roots in the best tradition of the past, its flowering was influenced by conditions in Denmark during the early eighteenth century, when that country was first becoming acutely conscious of the more highly developed civilization of other European communities. *Jean de France*, the most typical of Holberg's first five plays, deals with the social problem raised by an exaggerated form of nationality. The question at issue is debated in the first scene between two old men: should a young man travel abroad to complete his education? One of them, urged on by his ambitious wife, has sent his son Hans to live in Paris for three or four months; the other, the father of Hans's Danish financée, believes that it is a great mistake to allow young men to travel until they have acquired enough maturity and intelligence to profit by the experience. According to him, economic prosperity should be Denmark's primary concern, but now the fatherland stands in danger of being ruined by the intrusion of luxurious foreign habits; tea, coffee, and tobacco ought to be quite unnecessary indulgences, but they are coming to be considered essential in every respectable Danish household. As a result, the cost of living is going up, and, once up, it will never come down. All good patriots should set their faces against the importation of strange commodities and frown on the degenerate Danes who attempt to develop a taste for such things. Here the evil involved in social refinements is emphatically stated from the point of view of a conservative old man, who realizes that wealth makes high society possible but who is not yet far enough removed from the accumulation of money to see that it is valuable only as a means to other ends.

This counsel is required to offset the wild excesses of a foolish fellow like Hans, son of Frands, who goes to Paris and comes back with his Danish name loftily translated as "Jean de France" and with a French vocabulary that is quite incomprehensible to his simple home-keeping countrymen. Because of his vain and capricious nature, his fiancée had never liked him even before his travels; his father had not been wholeheartedly in favor of sending him abroad; and his doting mother, who at first approves of every breath drawn by her darling son, is later dissolved in tears at the thought that she has been partially responsible for her son's extravagant behavior. Hans becomes completely captivated by the heroine's maidservant disguised as a Parisian lady, and he indulges in the most eccentric conduct to gain favor in her eyes. She and her supposed *valet de chambre*, also a Danish servant working in the interests of the true lovers, are not called Pernille and Henrich, but they play the parts generally taken by these characters in Holberg's comedies. As usually happens, the maid conceives the plan which is intended to expose the fool of the piece, and she takes part in its execution, aided by her masculine partner. There is also a certain rivalry and contest of wits between the two servants, who are in basic accord, but neither of whom wishes to admit inferiority to the other. In *Jean de France* the manservant admires the clever maid's skill at intrigue, but he refuses to make love to her, saying, "I like learned girls well enough, but I would object to them as either wives or housekeepers."

The intelligence and ability of these servants help to make up for the casual treatment which Holberg, like many comic dramatists, gives to his conventional heroes and heroines. The clever servants help the lovers to outwit tyrannical fathers and objectionable rivals; like Harlequin and Columbine in the *commedia dell'arte*, they entertain the audience by varied trickery and numerous disguises. Their cleverness is frequently contrasted with the well-meaning stupidity of Pierrot, who appears in Holberg's comedies as Arv, an outdoor servant or *Gaardskarl*. In *Jean de France* Arv's ignorance of French words and manners makes Hans's artificialities all the more apparent; he does not understand Hans's vocabulary, and he gazes openmouthed at the orgy of dancing which the returned traveler forces upon his middle-aged parents. He does not approve of Hans, but he is not clever enough to take part in the plot against him, although he does unconsciously assist in it. He has no more intellectual capacity than Hans, but he has the good sense to be satisfied with his situation in life. He will not follow the absurd French fashions. He is happy in doing day by day the menial tasks that are assigned to him. Arv is a typical feudal peasant, uncontaminated by the new ways of the world which flourish in Paris.

Hans's infatuation with all things French makes him an easy prey to the designs of the masquerading maidservant. She persuades him to button his coat up backwards and to wear around his neck a so-called miniature, which is really a picture cut from a printed book and pasted on a piece of wood. He tries to force the absurd new fashions on people of the town, who are antagonized by his effeminate manners. The final blow is that he gambles and loses, but has no money with which to pay his debts. His fortunes seem to have reached their lowest ebb, but Hans's sense of self-importance is still impervious to outward events. He receives a letter from the supposed Frenchwoman asking him to meet her in Hamburg en route for Paris, and he rushes off to the rendezvous, quite unconscious of the deception that has been practiced upon him. In this way the obnoxious importer of foreign customs is driven from Denmark, which is thereby freed from a dangerous parasite who would have preyed upon the body politic.

A similar but less grave social peril lies in the excessive loquacity of Gert from Westphalia, who in the play named after him believes that it is highly desirable to divert people with lengthy harangues on various momentous subjects, such as his journey from Haderslev to Kiel. In Westphalia people take delight in conversation as a fine art and will sit up the whole night through for the sake of a good talk.

Gert finds the Danes, among whom he now lives, a dull and uncultivated nation, and they consider him a long-winded bore. The question of social intercourse is at stake: shall one say only what needs to
be said, or shall one talk to entertain and instruct other human beings?
Evidently the first person to accept the latter view runs the danger
of overdoing what has formerly been neglected and of becoming as
thoroughly asinine as Gert from Westphalia. Gert is a barber, a member of a profession which from time immemorial has had a reputation for talkativeness. He attempts to display his arts to a man from
Flensborg, but in this case he meets his match and learns to his sorrow that even a Westphalian barber can be outdone in the speed and
diversity of his conversation. He consoles himself, however, with the
thought of how great his posthumous fame will be: "As long as
people live, no one pays any attention to them; but they are scarcely
dead before they are regretted."

Certainly during Gert's lifetime his talents are not appreciated.
The main incidents in the play's loosely constructed plot concern
Gert's driving away the patrons of an alehouse by his lecture on the
constitutional history of Germany, the innkeeper's bringing suit
against Gert for ruining his trade, and the attempt of an unscrupulous
lawyer to get money from both parties in the transaction. The lawyer
is satirized for his casuistry and greed, and he is also used to point the
moral of Gert's bad manners. He arranges to have the barber condemned to three days' silence, during which Gert suffers agonies in
an attempt to express himself. The impression left by the play is that
a confirmed talker's idiosyncrasy is increased, not lessened, by an attempt to repress it. Gert's impulse to amuse and improve his fellow
men has gone so far that it is as essential to him as meat and drink.

Master Gert from Westphalia was originally presented in five acts,
and then, because the rambling story did not please the spectators, it
was compressed into one act. Many of the picturesque incidents, such
as the dispute with the innkeeper, were omitted, and in their place the
conventional love story was considerably expanded. In this version
Gert gives a wonderful new discourse on English politics, in the
course of which he tells how Cromwell had King James beheaded
and how in revenge King James's son later had Cromwell torn to
pieces by four horses. His lecture costs him the hand of the heroine,
and like Jean de France he decides to leave Denmark for more ap-

preciative countries. The excessive talker, like the affected traveler, is entirely discredited. It is an interesting comment on the social situation in Denmark that Gert's adventures were better liked in their refined romantic form than they were when given the cruder and more vigorous treatment that they had first received. The five-act version of the play was an unorganized series of genre pictures, but they were essentially Danish in their subject and spirit.

Holberg would not have been anxious to ridicule the excesses of society if such excesses were not becoming fairly common in the Copenhagen of his day. On the other hand, he would not have written his plays at all if he had not expected them to appeal to an audience which was increasing in intelligence as it came into contact with older civilizations. He was in the peculiar situation of encouraging social development as long as it did not interfere with the national consciousness of the Danish people, but of ridiculing all exaggerations of a tendency with which he was for the most part in hearty sympathy. He approved of refined culture, but he saw its dangers. His position was not quite so anomalous as that of the satirical Wycherley, who was himself a part of the corrupt society he denounced in his plays, but his divided interests forced him into an ambiguity that was often disturbing to his point of view. Holberg resembles very much the character of Lucretia in his comedy of *The Fickle Woman*, who changes her mind so often that it is impossible to tell what her sentiments really are. The dramatist makes Lucretia amusing to his audience, but he does not apply critical standards of any kind to her capricious conduct.

Lucretia emerges from the intrigue unscathed, because Holberg is chiefly engaged in showing by means of her inconstancy the absurdity of the other characters in the play. A lover who is too serious and a lover who is too gay abandon their eccentricities after being exposed to Lucretia's vagaries, and docilely return to their former sweethearts. A narrow and uncompromising pedant falls in love with Lucretia, after a good deal of indecision she finally refuses to marry him, and at the end of the play he is left consoling himself with Seneca's advice to the unfortunate. The pedant does not reform or leave the country; he is a harmless animal who does not actively interfere with the lives of other people. Lucretia compares him to Thomas Diafoirus in Molière's *The Invalid in His Own Imagination*, the perfect type of pedantic imbecility in comic drama, but Holberg is really less severe on him than on his foolish lackey, who bears a strong resemblance to Jean de France. Lucretia escapes even more easily than the pedant, as if Holberg felt that rigidity was more absurd than fickleness. Perhaps he realized that his own outlook on life was not always entirely consistent.

The more certain he was that the subject under consideration was a threat to the growth of social cultivation, the more rigorous was his treatment of it. Imitation of French manners and unnecessary loquacity were more vital and less amusing than political ambitions, especially those in Hamburg, a German city which in Holberg's day took an excessive interest in the machinery of politics. The dramatist's treatment of Jean de France and Gert from Westphalia is correspondingly less good-natured and lighthearted than his attitude toward Herman von Bremen in *The Political Pewterer*. The conception of a pewterer who would like to be a politician is more original than that of a Frenchified fop or a talkative barber, but Holberg probably took the idea for his play from the papers in *The Tatler* describing a political upholsterer. The significance of this choice of subject by both Joseph Addison and Holberg lies in the fact that, in the early eighteenth century, politics were for the first time beginning to engage the attention and energies of middle-class people. The intrusion of successful tradesmen into newly formed political parties resulted in just such incongruities as were portrayed by both the English and the Danish authors. Herman von Bremen's one absorbing interest is politics, much to the dissatisfaction of his customers and the annoyance of his wife. He refuses to accept a son-in-law who is not a politician, and he spends his time with a number of similar fanatics in a club known as the "Collegium Politicum."

Herman is cured of his obsession by a trick played on him by two of his fellow townsmen. He is told that he has been chosen mayor of Hamburg, and his difficulties in filling that office make up the body of the comedy. Herman learns that it is no easy matter to conduct the government of a city and finally prepares to hang himself as the best way out of his misfortunes. He is then told that he has never been a magistrate at all, and his delight is so great that he burns up all his political books and gives his daughter's hand to her unpolitical lover. He is now a reformed character, as he humorously shows by beating his wife for her insubordination, whereas he had previously believed that as a politician he should count twenty before allowing himself to show his anger. His unforgivable sin in the past was his haste in wishing to become a politician before he had learned the internal workings of politics as well as their external mannerisms.

Social deportment is less basic to human needs than aptitudes and training in one's profession. Therefore it may be made a constant source of innocent merriment. The most amusing portion of *The Political Pewterer* is that concerned with Herman's wife, Geske, especially just after she supposes that her husband has become mayor. Up to that time Geske had thoroughly disapproved of Herman's political ambitions, but after she believes that she has become the mayor's lady she readily falls in with her husband's views. She acquires a lap dog, she learns to play fashionable games of cards, and she serves coffee with syrup in it, to the disgust of the fine ladies who come to call upon her. Geske shows the height of bad breeding by scorning her former friends.

Herman's servant, Henrich, is only less ridiculous in the same way because his rise in the social scale is less pronounced than his mistress's. He institutes a system of taking bribes from visitors, he wishes to have his name changed to "von Henrich," and when the hoax is discovered at the close of the play he is far more disappointed than Herman. He is less upset than Geske, however; his final position is, like his first one, halfway between the husband and the wife. He is not so ambitious as Herman was at the beginning and not so discouraged as Geske is at the end. The middle ground which Henrich holds between the extremely violent characterizations of his master and mistress does a great deal to maintain in *The Political Pewterer* the even balance which prevents comedy from drifting into satire.

Holberg's genius lay in his ability to paint such simple honest portraits as that of Henrich, in which real life was handled with a slightly comic edge. When critical ideas were added to this gift but kept subordinate to it, Holberg obtained excellent results, as he did in *Jeppe of the Hill*, which ranks as his masterpiece. It is not by any means his most typical work, but it surpasses *The Political Pewterer* as much as that piece surpasses *Jean de France*. In the latter play the minor figure of Arv helps to humanize a logical comic idea; in *The Political Pewterer* Henrich takes a more important part in an equally effective setting; in *Jeppe of the Hill* Jeppe holds the center of the stage throughout the entire play. We are more interested in him as a worthless and charming person than in the criticism of him implied by his adventures. Jeppe, a Danish peasant, is shown on his home ground, whereas Arv and Henrich, both of whom were apparently born in the country, have been transported to Copenhagen and Hamburg respectively. The artificial atmosphere of a city tends to sharpen the outlines and obscure the basic humanity of comic characters, who when seen in their natural surroundings may be equally absurd but are certainly less harmful to their fellow creatures.

To provide a plot which will reveal the inherent capacity for evil in the heart of a well-intentioned but ignorant peasant, Holberg resorted to the trick played upon Christopher Sly in *The Taming of the Shrew*. *Jeppe of the Hill* carries out the Induction of Shakespeare's play on a large comic scale and makes a striking contrast with the drama in which Giovacchino Forzano, a modern Italian writer, has undertaken to develop the tragic possibilities latent in the same theme. The inciting force in Holberg's play is a nobleman who thinks that the pursuit of pleasure is the general aim of life and who argues that most men are willing to die if only they can first enjoy themselves. He finds his own amusement in laughing at stupid people, but he does not forget the serious consequences which may result if these same stupid people are allowed to exercise unlimited power. He takes pleasure in bringing it about that a drunken loafer, like Jeppe, should suddenly wake up and believe himself to be a lord. At first the humor comes from Jeppe's incredulity, the violent contrast between his two sets of surroundings, and the doctor's attempts to make him believe in the power of his imagination. Later it is Jeppe's presumption in acting the part of a tyrannical nobleman which arouses laughter. He eats and drinks most intemperately and with the worst possible table manners; he shows that he is avaricious and stingy in money matters; he is suspicious of a bailiff's capacities and honesty; and finally, after an orgy of singing and dancing, he prepares to take forcible possession of the bailiff's wife. Jeppe's temporary and unreal power makes his attempts at despotism harmless and amusing, but the traits of his character revealed in the process give point to Holberg's central doctrine that changes in society should not be allowed to take place too swiftly.

The comparative unimportance of social differences is jestingly urged in the scene where Jeppe, believing that he has been poisoned, says farewell to all that he has held dear in life, from his daughter to his piebald horse. The power and glory that he had for a moment enjoyed did not seem to him so desirable in taking their flight as do the familiar pleasures of the hearth and farm now that he is leaving them for the last time. In a very vivid and actual way Holberg makes it clear that life is more precious than social position and that living is made up of a number of apparently trivial details, which acquire significance only when they are about to disappear. He does not suggest that life itself is as much of an illusion as worldly grandeur, merely showing Jeppe's chagrin when he finds that his supposed stay in paradise was the outcome of a practical joke. Jeppe has learned no lesson from his experiences, except not to boast without sufficient corroborative evidence; he has not grasped an inkling of the philosophical truth that may be discovered from a temporary but complete change of one's physical environment.

Jeppe was mentally incapable of assimilating his experience into the realm of abstract thought, like Segismundo, the hero of Calderón's *Life Is a Dream*, which *Jeppe of the Hill* so strikingly resembles. The scenes in which Jeppe and Segismundo awake to find themselves in unaccustomed positions of authority are extraordinarily similar, even to the martial music that both men enjoy, but Holberg's treatment of this theme lacks the poetic implications of Calderón's play. When Jeppe finds himself on his dunghill once more, he simply rolls over and goes to sleep again in an effort to recapture in dreams the grandeur that has been so rudely snatched from him. Holberg's play does not suggest that life is a dream but implies that it is a social pattern which must not be too rudely disarranged. This critical idea is deftly brought to the attention of the audience, but it is not obviously insisted upon. The moral is underemphasized in favor of depicting a vivid character, who transports one into a realm where the suspension of disbelief brings about an aesthetic experience no less valuable than that in Calderón's more frankly philosophical drama.[1]

[1] Gerhart Hauptmann's comedy *Schluck and Jau* is an interesting attempt to treat the Christopher Sly story in an imaginative way without losing the earthy touch that gives Holberg's play its atmosphere of vigorous reality.

III

Holberg never wrote a better play than *Jeppe of the Hill*, but he wrote a great many others which fill out and add to the general impression made by his first five comedies. In 1723, the year in which these five were originally printed, Montaigu's company produced two new, lengthy works by Holberg, *The Eleventh of June* ("Den ellefte Junii") and *The Lying-in Room* ("Barselstuen"). The next year these comedies were published, together with three other slighter pieces, *The Arabian Powder* ("Det arabiske Pulver"), *Christmas Party* ("Jule-Stue"), and *Masquerade* ("Mascarade"), as the second volume of Holberg's dramatic works. Of the plays in this volume *The Lying-in Room* is by all odds the most interesting and important, although it does not rise to the level of the best work in the preceding group. Its defect of sprawling formlessness makes possible the treatment of a vast variety and range of subjects that have to do with childbirth. The central theme is quite clearly the plight of a cuckold in his own imagination, but that is only a thread on which to hang a number of realistic sketches of middle-class people imitating the conventions of high society. Lying-in has become a fashionable social function, and no fewer than eleven women come to offer their congratulations to the new mother in various eccentric ways. She also has to endure the professional rivalry of her medical attendants, and the happy father has to entertain at his own expense the men of the town who come to congratulate him, or to condole with him, on the most recent addition to his family. Altogether the birth of a child was a more than usually trying ordeal for parents in the Copenhagen of Holberg's day. The higher the social class, the more sensible was the way in which the occasion was celebrated; it was only among people who were trying to copy the nobility that gross exaggerations of propriety occurred.

By his discussion of social classes Holberg makes it clear that he regards it as perfectly honorable to be born either a beggar or a nobleman. To him the unforgivable sin is to try to fit into a stratum of society where one is not naturally at home. The sudden increase in one's financial status does not necessarily mean an increase in one's refinement and tastes. The pauper had better remain a pauper and not attempt to become a plutocrat. *The Lying-in Room* shows the results of too much prosperity in one narrow sphere of life; *The Eleventh of June* exposes the unethical means by which newly rich people have often acquired their money. The hero of this comedy is the stupid son of a Jutish farmer who has amassed considerable wealth by a long series of shrewd lawsuits and extortionate loans. The farmer seems to have inculcated in his boy the same prudent, not to say dishonest, principles. He sends his son to Copenhagen to collect the interest on his investments which is due on June 11, and while in the city the youth is determined to save money in every possible way. His stinginess proves to be his undoing, because it leads him to lodge at a cheap and disreputable hotel, where he is compromised by a designing woman and falls into the hands of a gang of blackmailers. The blackmailers extort money from the country fellow in a fashion that is reminiscent of *Monsieur de Pourceaugnac*, but Holberg is much less fantastic and more severely realistic than Molière in treating similar material.

The hero of *The Eleventh of June* has come to collect money from an impoverished aristocrat. To Holberg, at this period in his career, the follies of those who have position and no money are absurd, but less so than the weaknesses of those who have acquired money but have no idea of how to spend it wisely. The gentleman can no longer procure money; the country bumpkin loses what he already has. Social distinction is the dramatist's fundamental standard of judgment. The more truly polished one succeeds in being, the less he will be punished for his minor failings. In *The Eleventh of June* money is simply the touchstone for success in society. At the end of it the hero goes home with his pockets turned inside out and his self-esteem badly damaged. We last see him making the discovery that he has been outwitted by the city knaves and cursing the eleventh of June, which has brought him to such a sorry pass. In *The Eleventh of June* Holberg succeeded in expressing his critical opinions in terms of the characters he had created, but he was not able to merge his characters with the incidents in which they play a part. There is no particular consistency in having a cautious boy, as the hero of this comedy is in many respects represented to be, engage in an intrigue with a strange woman and thus easily become the victim of blackmailers. Perhaps for this reason, Holberg's next two dramatic efforts were of a much simpler sort. They are each in one act, they both depend upon intrigue rather than upon character, and they treat the ways in which credulous people are gulled, whether they are avaricious or amorous.

The Arabian Powder is an extremely conventional piece on the subject of alchemy. It adds practically nothing to Ben Jonson's handling of the same theme, unless it be an extra touch of sarcasm directed at the hypocrisy of timeservers and fair-weather friends. *Christmas Party*, which is more original and vivid, is founded on a local custom, the value of which was much disputed in Holberg's time. It had long been the fashion in Denmark to have a Christmas party to which the neighbors were all invited and at which the whole company played gay and rowdy games together. In cosmopolitan Copenhagen new amusements were being introduced and old traditional entertainments were fast losing their vogue. Ought the ancient way of doing things be preserved? Holberg does not give a very clear answer to this question. He implies that Christmas games are not really vicious, but that there is an element of danger in their disorderliness. It is interesting to note, however, that the middle-aged woman who most loves the games defends them on the ground that they are opposed by people who have such absurd ideas as that the world is round. So Christmas games are associated with the unintelligent and unprogressive classes, although Holberg seems to say that if kept within proper bounds they are a healthy diversion for the old-fashioned peasantry. It would be a pity for simple country folk to imitate the manners of the city without first being educated enough to understand their meaning, but it would be almost equally foolish if the citizens of Copenhagen did not occasionally take advantage of the novel amusements that had been imported from abroad.

Holberg's attitude towards another contemporary social institution is much less ambiguously stated in *Masquerade*, which deals with the fancy-dress balls then much in vogue. In this play there are three points of view expressed by different characters: the conservative disapproval of such newfangled devices, the specious modern defense that they are beneficial because they keep money in circulation, and the middle course which seems to represent Holberg's own convictions: "Let us take the middle course. I do not condemn masquerades because they are masquerades but because a habit is made of them. Masquerades, beside the fact that they furnish recreation for melancholy people, are a very fine invention, for they show men the natural equality on which they were at the beginning, before pride took the upper hand and one human being considered himself too good to associate with another."

This statement is an important passage in gauging Holberg's general point of view. It shows the dramatist recognizing that all men are brothers under the skin and that social distinctions make no very great difference; it also implies that, since man cannot return to a complete state of nature, he had better patronize such artificial institutions as masquerades in an attempt to recapture the natural principles underlying human society. The inconsistency of this position is obvious when one thinks of the results of such calculating make-believe. Holberg applied a social standard to contemporary Danish life and made fun of people who did not come up to his requirements, but he failed to see that his standard was itself ridiculous in the light of the eternal verities. He was nearer to the truth when he made the servant Henrich champion masquerades for his own personal satisfaction. "Our whole life is a chain of miseries," Henrich remarks in tones that prophesy Figaro, and he intends to go to masquerades to snatch what precarious pleasure he can during a servant's painful existence. Beneath the surface the social waters are troubled, but superficially all goes merrily as a fancy-dress party.

IV

The third division of Holberg's plays is made up of five comedies that were acted in 1724 and printed the next year in a single volume. They are: *Jacob von Tyboe, or The Boasting Soldier* ("Den stortalende Soldat"), *Ulysses of Ithaca, or A German Comedy* ("Ulysses von Ithacia, eller En tydsk Comoedie"), *The Journey to the Spring* ("Kilde-Reysen"), *Melampe*, and *Without Head and Tail* ("Uden Hoved og Hale"). Of these five plays *The Journey to the Spring* is the slightest and least interesting. Its plot is the conventional one of a false doctor's helping a pair of lovers, its most original element being the visit to a popular medicinal spring, which is shown on the stage as a pantomime *intermedium* in place of a second act. It seems as if Holberg realized that the source of his literary inspiration was wearing thin and that he needed to rely on picturesque local material, however superficial and lacking in critical implications it might be. In *Melampe* he devoted his attention to ridiculing the fashionable cult for lap dogs, which he had already touched on briefly in *The Political Pewterer*. Here he constructed a pretentious play in five acts on a lost lap dog, and, as if to make clear the difference between the slight value of the dog and the tremendous importance attached to it by its mistress, he threw the story into mock-heroic form. With rhymed verse, with the apparition of spirits, and with the beating of drums for warlike encounters, the tragic fate of Melampe, the lost dog, assumes a purely comic tone. Much of this play is devoted to a satire on war, and there is also implied in it a criticism of decadent aristocracy.

Ulysses of Ithaca is still more of a hodgepodge. Its action begins with the judgment of Paris, covers the period of the Trojan War, and concludes with Ulysses' return home to Ithaca. It is intended as a burlesque of the German comedies that had been performed in Copenhagen with such success that Holberg felt he must do something to offset their prestige. They are particularly ridiculed for their offenses against the doctrines of the three unities; in them, it is said, a man can take a thousand miles at one stride and become forty years older in a single evening. These romantic absurdities are continually exposed by Ulysses' servant, a character something like Sancho Panza, who is always ready to deride the idealistic delusions of his chivalric master. By means of his comments Holberg calls attention to the unnecessarily emotional aspects of love, war, and religion that were commonly expressed in the rodomontade of the German plays. At the very end of the piece he uses a clever device to point out the meretricious display of all insincere art. After Ulysses' servant leaves his master to take a nap, two Jewish merchants appear, wake up Ulysses, and demand the money that he owes them for his costume. As the actors are entirely without resources, the Jews insist upon stripping Ulysses of his fine clothes, and in this way they demonstrate the folly of pretending to act a heroic role in a complicated and realistic world.

However, Holberg was perfectly willing to make use of artificial dramatic technique when justifying his own comic procedure. In the brief, rhymed *New Year's Prologue to a Comedy* ("Nye-Aars Prologus til en Comoedie"), performed in 1723, and also in the Prologue to *Without Head and Tail*, in which the classical gods descend to earth to discuss the drama, the Philistines, Mars and Vulcan respectively, are advised to go to German comedies, where they can get their money's worth of pride, pomp, and circumstance. Each of these pieces also contains an apologia for the critical, national, and social nature of Holberg's art. In the *New Year's Prologue* the task of defending Danish comedy is assigned to Apollo, who submits that every great age of imperial power has had its artistic expression, although he does not strengthen his case by citing John Dryden as the chief glory of Queen Elizabeth's reign. In the Prologue to *Without Head and Tail* it is explained that the play is so called because, in spite of the accepted rules of dramatic composition, it has neither a suitable title at its beginning nor a fifth act at its end. It is absurd to disregard all the limitations of the stage as the writers of German comedy do, but it is equally ridiculous to be confined to ancient precedents which are now outworn. Holberg does not believe that the eccentricities of romantic drama do much to please or instruct, and he will not accept any definite formula for accomplishing these ends. He wishes, not to be feebly dependent upon the tradition of the past, but to interpret its spirit in terms of existing conditions. His theory is an excellent one; unfortunately his practice falls short of it, and he often resorts to hackneyed horseplay and routine intrigues that end in marriage.

The four acts of *Without Head and Tail* give the impression of having been consciously composed to fit the specifications set forth in its Prologue. It deals with the subject of witchcraft and introduces three brothers, the oldest very superstitious, the youngest very skeptical, and the middle one a happy mean in his beliefs. In the course of the comedy the oldest and youngest brothers exchange their positions, but finally they both accept the middle path between agnosticism and blind credulity. Their servants repeat the argument on a lower level. One of them likes to go to masquerades with his pleasure-loving master, and the fact that such harmless amusements are connected with a skeptical attitude seems to indicate that Holberg regards extreme disbelief as less comic than an unintelligent acceptance of the supernatural. An infidel is able to devote himself wholeheartedly to the things of this world, and he will presumably not be so badly balanced in his daily actions as the man whose thoughts are far removed from his actual environment. Besides, as Pernille says in this play, "Disbelief wears off with age, but superstition increases more and more." The first of these errors cures it-self; the other is the insidious enemy of the vital principle upon which the spirit of comedy depends for its existence.

Holberg associated stupidity with superstition and self-satisfaction. He treated the former in *Without Head and Tail*, and he dealt with the latter in *Jacob von Tyboe*. *Jacob von Tyboe* is an elaborate and popular play, the aesthetic value of which is not equal to its scope or its reputation. Holberg has taken the figure of Pyrgopolynices from the *Boasting Soldier* of Plautus, added to it some touches drawn from Thraso in the *Eunuch* of Terence, and given little originality or local color to the composite picture he calls Jacob von Tyboe. Throughout the comedy Tyboe is contrasted with a learned pedant, who, like the boasting soldier, is so overconfident that he has lost all sense of decent humility. Both men prove themselves arrant cowards, but the soldier is the more ridiculous person of the two because he thinks himself the more accomplished. He boasts of his valor and his graceful manners, his ability to dance, to fence, to talk well, and to please the ladies. Holberg emphasizes Tyboe's claim to social distinction rather than to military prowess; the dramatist and his audience were chiefly interested in the refinements of living and not in its basic crudities. The *miles gloriosus* of the classic tradition has practically given way to the upstart in society, who is now treated in the same exaggerated and caricatured fashion as his forerunner. He is not a very credible character upon the printed page, but his simple and monotonous adventures seem to have been extremely effective in the theater and to have exerted a wide appeal among popular audiences.

V

Holberg's fourth group of plays does not reveal any new artistic purpose or technique but exhibits considerable ingenuity in the re-arrangement of old material from a slightly fresh and different point of view. It comprises five dramas, which had been acted before the closing of Montaigu's theater in 1728 but which were not printed until 1731. They are: *Henrich and Pernille*, *Diderich Menschen-Skraek*, *The Pawned Peasant Boy* ("Den pantsatte Bonde-Dreng"), *Pernille's Brief Position as a Lady* ("Pernilles korte Frøiken-Stand"), and *The Bustling Man* ("Den Stundesløse"). To this list must be added *The*

Funeral of Danish Comedy ("Den danske Comoedies Ligbegaen-gelse"), presented on February 25, 1727. It was written by Holberg for a performance which Montaigu feared would mark the permanent closing of his theater, and its general tenor is a lament for Comedy, which has died from lack of patronage. As a matter of fact, Montaigu reopened his theater under royal auspices in the spring of 1728, but the destructive fire that occurred in Copenhagen during October of that year cut short any hope of continued favor from the King; Frederik IV's narrow-minded counselors convinced him that the fire represented the judgment of heaven upon the wickedness of his subjects, and they persuaded him to withdraw the annual subsidy he had recently granted to the comedians. When Montaigu's company finally did close its doors in 1728, it had been in existence for six years, and during that time Holberg had had twenty plays produced. The five that were performed after 1724 were perhaps influenced by the financial difficulties besetting the actors at this period; they tend to emphasize the economic side of life in a way which recalls Ben Jonson's comic treatment of similar characters and situations.

Some of them have specific relations with earlier comedies by other authors. *Diderich Menschen-Skraek* is based upon the *Pseudolus* of Plautus, Menschen-Skraek ("Terror-of-Mankind") being another undistinguished example of the bragging soldier. *Pernille's Brief Position as a Lady* is like Molière's *The Miser* in having a stingy father lose to his own son the girl whom both wish to marry; in this case the old man insists upon marrying a supposed heiress, who turns out to be the heroine's maid, Pernille, masquerading in her mistress's clothes. *The Bustling Man* recalls *The Invalid in His Own Imagination*, with the principal character's absorption in medicine changed to a mania for business. Vielgeschrey, the noisy, bustling man, wants to have his daughter marry a bookkeeper, but he is so careless of practical affairs that he is easily tricked into making it possible for her to marry her true lover. After the marriage has safely taken place, the hero agrees to become an accountant to please his new father-in-law, very much in the vein of Molière's play, to which, however, *The Bustling Man* is decidedly inferior both in execution and conception. Imaginary sickness is a much more vital issue than imaginary business, which never pauses long enough to assume more than passing significance.

Nevertheless, Vielgeschrey is one of Holberg's most memorable comic characters. He is drawn with some variety as well as with extreme consistency. He speedily changes his attention from economic to domestic matters, but always with ceaseless activity. His chief occupations are adding up figures, writing business letters, and supervising the expenditure of money. Occasionally he drops all financial interests and devotes his attention exclusively to his little black hen, who much to his delight has laid him forty eggs since Christmas. In one scene he attempts to save time by being shaved and being measured for a new suit of clothes at the same moment that he is engaged in counting out money. He is as particular about how his plates shall be scoured as about the omission of one shilling from his accounts. He reduces his position to the absurd when he cries out, "I ought to hang myself. But upon my word I have not time even to hang myself." Vielgeschrey is the quintessence of a man who seems busier than he is. As his sensible brother remarks, "You never have leisure, although you never have anything to do." This formula is at least as old as Geoffrey Chaucer's Man-of-Law, but Holberg may be right in proudly claiming that a bustling man has never before been used as the subject of a dramatic comedy. The originality of the material rather than the manner of its development is the chief source of the popularity and excellence of *The Bustling Man*. Although it does not show any marked growth in its author's point of view or method of dramatic composition, it is the most vivid and picturesque play in the fourth group of his dramas.

The least interesting of the five plays acted between 1724 and 1728 is *The Pawned Peasant Boy*, a sort of combination of the plots used in *The Eleventh of June* and *Jeppe of the Hill*. This comedy, which does not hang together very well in spite of one or two amusing situations, makes Holberg's usual points about the connection between money and social position: one without the other is bound to be a source of laughter, but the rich man without suitable manners is funnier than the poor man with them. These doctrines are more neatly developed in *Henrich and Pernille*, a comedy in which the servants take the places of their employers and woo each other under the names of their master and mistress. This is not original material, but it was extremely well adapted to Holberg's personality and art.

He paid little attention to the jealous lovers, who are romantic figures more at home in Spain or France than in Denmark, and concentrated his interest on the roguish servants, whom he draws with the greatest care. They resemble each other in that, although they are not hostile to their superiors, their first thoughts are for their own interests. Pernille is harder than Henrich, as her mistress is softer than his master. In formal society, Holberg seems to say, women of the upper classes are much too protected from the world and women of the lower classes far too exposed to it. Pernille greatly surpasses Henrich in cold-bloodedness; Henrich, although not admirable, is almost pathetic in his foolish self-complacence. He feels that if one appears like a gentleman, he is a gentleman; he believes that, if he can marry a rich girl, he will automatically rise above other men whose incomes are less than his. Neither he nor Pernille discovers until after their marriage that each of them has falsely pretended to have money to entrap the other. Then they are both furious and are on the point of pulling each other's hair out by the roots when they are separated. Their wedding neatly resolves a play which is chiefly a matter of intrigue, but which also contains an element of poetic justice. The final mating of ambitious servants with similar members of their own class is entirely in accordance with Holberg's cautious social philosophy.

VI

The fifth group of Holberg's plays resembles the fourth group in that it is made up of comedies first printed in 1731. It differs from it in that none of its five dramas had been performed by Montaigu's company before it closed its doors in 1728. They are: *Witchcraft, or False Alarm* ("Hexerie, eller Blind Allarm"), *The Fortunate Shipwreck* ("Det lykkelige Skibbrud"), *Erasmus Montanus, or Rasmus Berg, The Unseen Ladies* ("De Usynlige"), and *The Honest Ambition* ("Den honnette Ambition"). A sixth play may be added to this group: *Don Ranudo de Colibrados, or Poverty and Haughtiness* ("Fattigdom og Hoffaerdighed"), which was written before 1731, but which Holberg did not publish with his other dramas at that time. *Don Ranudo* bears all the earmarks of having been conceived when the dramatist was in his prime, before the decided falling off of his creative faculties that later took place. In the fifth group of his plays

Holberg was still at the height of his powers. The variety and significance of his work is here greater than in any group since the
first one.

Witchcraft, as the title suggests, purports to deal with the abuses of
witchcraft and superstition in much the same way as *Without Head
and Tail*. Its principal character states that skepticism causes almost
as much trouble as superstition, but the play itself is entirely concerned with the latter phenomenon as it exists in backward communities. Copenhagen, it appears, is more backward than Paris or
London. When an actor is rehearsing the incantation scene of a
forthcoming play, the inhabitants take him for a conjuror and raise
a "false alarm." The large number of superstitious people introduced
prevents one's taking an interest in them individually but proves unmistakably how prevalent is the evil of which Holberg is here com-
plaining. The group comprises the pious and the aged, foolish girls
and silly fops, in fact anyone whose desires are unfulfilled and uncon-
trolled. From all of them the actor succeeds in getting money under
false pretenses, until he is haled to court on the charge of being a
sorcerer. Then Holberg has an excellent opportunity to join a general satire on lawyers' methods with a specific attack on their prone-
ness to unwarranted suspicion, one of the evils which ordinarily
accompanies belief in witchcraft.

The most striking of the somewhat disconnected scenes in *Witchcraft* are those which deal with the actors' enemies, whom Holberg
identifies with people antagonized by his own comedies. The fickle
Lucretia, the affected Jean de France, and the politically minded
Herman von Bremen, all of whom appear upon the stage in person,
object to the way honest people like themselves have been ridiculed
in the theater. It was an ingenious device on Holberg's part to revive
some of the popular figures from his early plays under the pretense
that they were outraged by his treatment of them, and he evidently
liked the idea so well that he repeated it in *The Fortunate Shipwreck*.
In addition to the three well-known characters who had appeared
in *Witchcraft*, there also come on the stage, in *The Fortunate Shipwreck*, the bragging soldier and conceited pedant from *Jacob von
Tyboe* and the talkative, supercilious women that had appeared in
The Lying-in Room. Holberg insists that there are many models, not
one, for all these types, and that if certain people in the audience feel

insulted by them, he is not to blame: "When one shoots promiscuously, he is sure to hit somebody at last." This sentiment is expressed by the hero of *The Fortunate Shipwreck*, a comic dramatist, who seems to be Holberg's idealized portrait of himself.

The plot of this play is something like that of Molière's *The Learned Ladies*, with the hero's rival giving up all claims to the heroine's hand when he hears that her father has lost his money in a supposed shipwreck. Magister Rosiflengius, who plays the part of Trissotin in this piece, is, as his name implies, an indiscriminate flatterer, combining the worst aspects of pedantry and panegyric. He writes eulogies as a matter of business, one of them being so insincere as to praise a prostitute for her virtue and one so trivial as to glorify a dead lap dog named Melampe. His servant compares notes with the dramatist's servant on the merits of their respective masters. Each asserts that his own is the better, but each admits that there is a decided weakness in being either a flatterer or a satirist; on the one hand, your insincerity may be easily discovered, and, on the other, you are sure to antagonize a large number of people by the frankness of your criticism. The practical rewards of plain-dealing are temporary unpopularity and ostracism from society; those of hypocrisy are prosperity and happiness, until your true convictions are laid bare. This contrast is further developed by the official opinion of the judge in the last act, who, after hearing the complaints brought by the dramatist's victims, decides that Rosiflengius' honey-tongued praise of vice is more dangerous to the body politic than a sincere attempt to render human failings ridiculous. The conflict is a somewhat one-sided one, however. *The Fortunate Shipwreck* is more of a personal apologia than any of Holberg's plays. In it he tends to satirize his enemies rather than to strive for impartial comic detachment towards the failings and accomplishments of other men.

This latter attitude he assumes more successfully in *Erasmus Montanus*, a play which approaches as closely to the ideal of classic comedy as Holberg ever attained. Here a violent but well-proportioned attack is made upon academic education and the follies that come from emphasizing its external forms. Holberg modifies the traditional subject of pedantry by applying it to local Danish customs and making use of the dramatic technique he had developed in the first group of his plays. The absurd protagonist has been away from home and returns infected with the follies he has acquired in his travels. Although pedantry is not a novel theme for Holberg, in *Erasmus Montanus* he makes it convey a fresh impression by arranging his material in a new pattern. The antagonism between wise pedantry and stupid honesty provides a delightful comic contrast. Erasmus, with his ability as a logician and his knowledge that the world is round, is opposed to the village wiseacres, who believe that the world is flat because they have always been told so. Yet Erasmus gets the worst of the situation. His feeling of conscious superiority can be more easily deluded than the sturdy common sense of the country people.

Erasmus is able to prove that it is the duty of a child to beat his parents, according to the arguments of Pheidippides in the *Clouds*, but he does not know enough to refuse to take the king's money from a recruiting officer. He suddenly finds that he has been impressed into the army; in order to extricate himself from that unpleasant situation, he is compelled to betray his intellectual faith by solemnly asserting that the earth is flat. His unorthodox opinions are correct, but Erasmus is so obnoxious in the way he expresses them that people will not believe anything he tells them and in addition want to punish him for his presumption. His parents, who have sent their son to the university and are at first very proud of his display of knowledge, are finally convinced by his senseless conduct that education is a snare and a delusion. His fiancée's parents are from the beginning much less tolerant of learning. They are practical people who cannot see that syllogistic reasoning is of much use when it comes to making one's way in the world. Erasmus is also opposed by a deacon and a bailiff, who recognize in him a possible rival for the prestige they enjoy in the community. The deacon has had some education and sets up to be the most learned man in the village, but he has now forgotten almost all he has ever known and is living on a reputation which he has long ceased to deserve. He is publicly discredited by Erasmus, who proves syllogistically that the deacon is a cock. Later he undertakes to prove that the bailiff is a bull, but that powerful and unlearned man prevents the demonstration by forcibly interrupting it.

Erasmus is told by the recruiting officer that he has learned in the schools just the opposite of what he should have acquired: "A learned man ought chiefly to be distinguished from others by being more temperate, modest, and accommodating in his speech than an unlearned man." An equally sound but more practical view of Erasmus' folly is taken by his uneducated brother, Jacob, who remarks with shrewd common sense: "He who studies the most important things has, I think, the most profound learning. . . . I study farming and the cultivation of the earth." Jacob stayed at home to till the soil and to help his father make money, which has sent Erasmus to the university; he appreciates the dignity of manual labor and its basic importance in the scheme of things. He makes a perfect foil for Erasmus' eccentricities by constantly indicating the absurdity of the scholar's physical movements. Jacob laughs heartily when Erasmus falls off a cart because he was stargazing, or when he gets drenched to the skin because he was too absent-minded to put on a cloak as it began to rain.

The scenes between the two brothers are the most brilliant in the play. Each is drawn with fairness. Erasmus is vain, opinionated, and disagreeable, but he is intelligent and, on the whole, sound in his ideas. Jacob is modest, diligent, and kind, but he has had no opportunities for education, and his mind cannot grapple with abstruse philosophical conceptions. He inclines to believe that the earth is round, but, as he does not see any practical significance in that fact, he would not stick to his opinion against opposition; he is limited by his lack of intellectual development and, pathetically enough, he realizes his weakness. He longs to go to the university, although he despises the education that Erasmus has received there. Erasmus, who scorns his brother's inability to argue, thinks that if Jacob had been sent to school in his earlier years he might have amounted to something after all. In the second scene between them their points of view approach each other rather closely, as if Holberg were trying to bring together the advantages of such cultivation as Erasmus had received and the crude sterling qualities possessed by Jacob. If these two conflicting attitudes had been reconciled, Holberg might have clarified in his own mind not only the problem of whether education was a benefit or a disadvantage, but also the entire question of how far society was a hollow sham and how far its pretenses were actual accomplishments. He raised this issue in the scenes between Erasmus and Jacob and then relinquished it in favor of the broadly humorous situation in which the recruiting officer persuades Erasmus to recant his heretical beliefs.

Comic philosophy and dramatic structure are not perfectly fused in *Erasmus Montanus*, but that play is a work of genius compared to *The Unseen Ladies*, which also deals with an interesting idea and contains some effective situations. The question at issue here is whether a woman should be mysterious and reserved in an effort to lure on her lover or whether natural forwardness is to be recommended in dealing with the less sensitive sex. The hero and heroine carry on a romantic love affair in which the lady tests her lover's constancy by always remaining masked in his presence and by disguising herself as another woman to tempt his virtue. The hero's servant, Harlequin, is much impressed by his master's affection for the unseen lady and correspondingly disgusted at the direct advances made to him by the straightforward Colombine. Colombine is infuriated at being scorned and arranges to have Harlequin entrapped by another masked lady, who turns out to be a horrible old hag. At the end Harlequin and Colombine are to be married, but Harlequin's absurd romanticism has given his wife the upper hand. Even before the ceremony he must face with equanimity the almost certain possibility of becoming a cuckold soon after it. Although some exceedingly amusing scenes occur in the course of this subplot, its mood does not agree very well with the spirit of the main story. The romantic hero and heroine live happily in a world of ideals and illusions; Harlequin and Colombine have to reckon with the physical facts of life. Perhaps this inconsistency may be explained by the difference in the rank of the two pairs of lovers, as if Holberg wanted to suggest that there was one code of conduct for a gentleman and another for a common servant.

Holberg's social philosophy is reduced to its lowest terms in *The Honest Ambition*. The title of this piece is frankly satirical in that "honest ambition" is the central figure's term for what his wife calls "the disease of rank." The contrast between these two phrases provides the comic antithesis upon which the play depends. In subject and characterization, if not in plot, it is strikingly similar to *The Middle-Class Gentleman*. Molière's application of his general philosophy to narrow social conditions was the phase of the Frenchman's art which most appealed to Holberg. The similarities and differences between the two men can be seen very clearly by comparing *The Middle-Class Gentleman* not with *The Honest Ambition* but with *Don Ranudo de Colibrados*, which resembles Molière's play in superficialities of plot but contrasts with it in underlying attitude. This drama, composed at least fourteen years before it appeared in print, seems to have given Holberg a vast amount of trouble in the writing and rewriting. It is distinct from his other comedies in that the scene is laid far from Denmark, in Spain, and its mood of realism is softened by a sympathy for human beings that is seldom found elsewhere in his works.

Don Ranudo is the exact opposite of M. Jourdain. The latter has money but no position; the former is the impoverished descendant of a long line of noblemen. He and his wife, Donna Olympia, who is poorer and prouder than he, have all the airs and graces which come from centuries of accumulated culture, but they do not have the money necessary to keep up their inherited position. Don Ranudo has to use ink to conceal the holes in his black stockings, Donna Olympia is reduced to wearing her maid's castoff dress, and both of them must pretend they are fasting as a penance in order to explain their emaciated appearance to fashionable visitors. A great part of the play is occupied with showing the comic subterfuges of the two decayed aristocrats. Their ideas are ridiculed by contrast with those of their saucy younger daughter, who wants a husband more than she does the reputation of being a lady, and with those of a peasant who believes in cultivating the land and in not living beyond one's income for the sake of hollow glory.

The difficulties confronting the Colibrados family are those which arise at the end of a social epoch, not at its beginning; their inability to solve their problems is as absurd as the would-be gentleman's attempts to satisfy his honest ambition. In the Denmark of the eighteenth century people were largely concerned with the business of becoming civilized, but Holberg was conscious that there were also older and more decadent social groups which were losing their pre-eminence as a result of the march of progress. In both cases it was the question of deportment which interested him. He realized that it was much harder for individuals to forgo the distinction that had once been theirs than it was for them to develop refined habits, to which they were unaccustomed by training and environment.

Don Ranudo and Donna Olympia have a sublime disregard for practical considerations, but their servants, although given Spanish names, are like the sensible Danish characters of Holberg's other comedies. In one way or another they point out the fallacies of empty display. At one point these Spanish versions of Henrich and Pernille pretend that they take Don Ranudo in his long black cape as a ghost, and they parody the litany of ancestor worship in which he and his wife indulge. The maid blames all Don Ranudo's eccentricities upon his being a Spaniard, but Holberg is not quite ready to indict a whole nation for clinging to medievalism in the midst of the modern world. He has the heroine say to her maid: "It is very true that many such people are to be found in Spain; but one must not therefore make that the character of the whole nation." In spite of this caution, Holberg did well to set the scene of *Don Ranudo de Colibrados* in Spain, where aristocratic traditions were more firmly established than they were in Denmark. What he meant was that pride and poverty are likely to go hand in hand at any time and in any place. Don Ranudo and Donna Olympia are universal figures when the bailiff comes to dismantle their fine old house at their creditors' request. They are to have only hunger and poverty in this world, but fortunately their conventional beliefs console them with the thought that in the next world their souls are sure to be saved.

The love which Don Ranudo and Donna Olympia have for titles makes them the victims of a preposterous trick. The daughter's undistinguished suitor passes himself off on them as the Prince of Ethiopia in the same way that the supposed son of the Grand Turk fools M. Jourdain. M. Jourdain will give his money to have a titled son-in-law; Don Ranudo offers his name, which is more precious to him than much fine gold. Don Ranudo's delusion is less well founded than M. Jourdain's, because it is more absurd to consider aristocratic position as the equivalent of wealth than it is to suppose that wealth entitles one to rise in the world. Don Ranudo is less of a social menace than M. Jourdain. The eccentricities of the impoverished grandee can have little effect on anyone outside his own immediate circle, but the wealth of an ambitious tradesman is capable of seriously upsetting the balance of society. In this case Molière is, as usual, more fundamental than Holberg in the object of his comic attack. He is also much gayer in his methods. *The Middle-Class Gentleman* ends in a burst of merriment, with M. Jourdain still unconscious of the trick that has been played upon him; Don Ranudo learns that he has been deceived, and both he and his wife give way to a frenzy of despair. They decide to retire to a cloister, since their worldly goods are gone and they feel overwhelmed by their social disgrace. Holberg usually has his chief comic character repent, at the end, in the interests of morality and general rejoicing, but Don Ranudo courageously sticks to his mistaken principles and by so doing arouses a feeling of sympathy for both his physical and mental sufferings.

In some respects *Don Ranudo de Colibrados* is the most elaborate comedy that Holberg ever composed. It attempts to rise above the plane of empty laughter and to adopt a point of view from which all human activity appears to be pathetic and yet absurd. The undertaking is too ambitious for Holberg to handle with great success. He is more at his ease when treating realistic Danish figures than when dealing with imaginative creations like Don Ranudo. He can quite easily ridicule the unnatural heroics of romantic lovers or paint the struggles of a man trying to rise in the social scale. He is at his best in a play like *Erasmus Montanus*, in which real people are drawn and a social question is raised. Holberg is able to point out the weaknesses and also the advantages of academic education, suggestively but not dogmatically. He creates in such figures as the scholarly Erasmus and, more especially, the uneducated Jacob first-rate examples of comic portraiture, whether compared with the rest of his work or judged by more absolute standards.

VII

After *Erasmus Montanus* and *Don Ranudo de Colibrados* Holberg was never again able to equal his best achievements in comedy. These two plays and the other four in the fifth group were performed on the stage after the national theater at Copenhagen was reopened, in 1747. The theater had been closed since 1728, during which time a fanatically religious king, Christian VI, had sat upon the Danish throne. With the accession of Frederik V, an enthusiastic patron of the arts, a royal patent was again issued to a company of actors. Holberg himself had no definite responsibility in the new enterprise. He was now sixty-two years old, and he had given up writing plays since the publication of his twenty-five comedies in 1731. His old dramas were, however, frequently performed by the new company, and, in 1750, in response to the public's incessant demand for novelty, he once more turned his attention to composing plays. By 1754 he had written six new pieces, three of which had been performed before his death, which occurred on January 28 of that year. His six last plays are: *Plutus, or Lawsuit between Poverty and Riches* ("Proces imellem Fattigdom og Rigdom"), *House-Ghost, or Abracadabra* ("Huus-Spøgelse"), *The Transformed Bridegroom* ("Den forvandlede Brudgom"), *Philosopher in His Own Imagination* ("Philosophus udi egen Indbilding"), *Republic, or The Public Good* ("Republiquen, eller Det gemene Bedste"), and *Sganarel's Journey to the Land of Philosophy* ("Sganarels Reyse til det philosophiske Land"). These six comedies are clearly on a much lower level than the rest of Holberg's work, but they add something to his range and accomplishment. In his old age, at a time when sentimentality was beginning to make itself felt in the theater at Copenhagen, Holberg made a heroic attempt to recapture for the stage the philosophical spirit of Greece and Rome.

According to Holberg's own statement, his *Plutus* was suggested by the play of Aristophanes, not copied from it. The most interesting point of comparison between the two works is that whereas to the Greek dramatist universal wealth was a constructive ideal, which was to be striven for and glorified, to the more disillusioned Dane, living two thousand years later, the omnipotent rule of Plutus was a palpable absurdity to be laughed away with scorn. Aristophanes ends his comedy in a tumult of rejoicing which celebrates the triumph of benevolent Wealth over capricious Zeus. Holberg has Jupiter supreme at the close of his play, when the king of the gods appears to restore the blindness of Plutus and welcome the goddess Poverty back from her banishment. In Aristophanes, Poverty wins the intellectual victory over Wealth's supporters, and yet she is discredited; in Holberg, Plutus outargues Poverty, but after he has ruled for a short time, he is forced to give up his position of authority. Although superficially these two comedies resemble one another, they are built on entirely different intellectual principles. The change in economic conditions produces some good effects and some bad ones in Aristophanes' version of the story, but only disapproval of the new order is expressed by Holberg's characters. The most striking of

Holberg's additions to Aristophanes' material is his introduction of Diogenes, the Cynic philosopher, who constantly points out to greedy people the evils that prosperity will bring even upon righteous men. The importance given to his remarks is an indication of why the imaginative realism of Aristophanes is beyond the reach of Holberg. His plays succeed in magnifying the minute refinements of existence and sometimes of commenting upon them, but they never suggest the wider implications, for which their author sometimes seems to be striving.

Holberg should never have attempted to write a play under the title of the *Republic*. Its literary associations are with Plato's vision of an ideal commonwealth, which Aristophanes had treated superbly from the comic point of view in the *Ecclesiazusae*. Holberg has no such ambitious scope in his *Republic*, where he discusses practical politics under the allegorical form of an ordinary love story. His "Republic" is the invalid mother of an attractive daughter, who has been destined to marry a successful politician and who is courted by a number of projectors. Holberg here outlines more absurd projects than Jonson invented for *The Devil Is an Ass*, one of them being, prophetically, a horseless carriage which moves by clockwork and will prove a great benefit to farmers. Republic's illness is finally cured through the application of a little common sense by her daughter's lover, who in this way wins the heroine's hand. A general air of diffuseness and laborious effort pervades the *Republic*, as if Holberg were working against decided obstacles of temperament and intellectual bias when he attempted to write this play on a political subject instead of a social one.

Holberg could not grapple with the themes of Aristophanes, but in his prime he had skillfully used some of Plautus' plays for popular effect. In his decline he tried to do so once again, and he composed *House-Ghost* upon the model of the *Mostellaria*. This time he followed Plautus even more closely than before, his one desperate attempt at originality being to remove the heroine and her designing maid from the scene. *House-Ghost* is a comedy in which no women appear upon the stage. It turns out to be a lifeless affair compared with Plautus' version of the story, but it seems to have been successful enough to lure Holberg on to writing a companion piece in one act, which should have no men in the cast of characters. Such was the superficial idea behind *The Transformed Bridegroom*, in which a young woman disguises herself as a military officer to drive an amorous old lady out of her humour. The amorous old lady is an addition to Holberg's gallery of comic portraits, but she is not a realistic enough creation to have been drawn by a man with a keen eye for a specific individual's eccentricities.

As Holberg grew older he tended, like many aging people, to philosophize rather than to observe. In his last plays he attempted to rise above petty social standards to issues of a more elevated nature. That he does not altogether succeed in this effort is not extraordinary, but the change in his outlook gives a sardonic significance to his long and pretentious comedy, *Philosopher in His Own Imagination*. Its principal figure is absolutely sincere in his professions of intellectual faith. When his worldliness is unmistakably revealed to him by a trick that has been played upon him, he admits the error of his ways and decides to reform for the good of other people. His career is highly edifying, but it cannot be considered very amusing.

Philosopher in His Own Imagination does not have much of a story on which to hang its serious ideas and its wooden characterizations, and *Sganarel's Journey to the Land of Philosophy* contains almost no thread of narrative. This one-act entertainment is based on a section of Holberg's nondramatic satire dealing with the adventures of Niels Klim in the underground world. In the land of philosophy six supposedly wise men greet Sganarel with an exhibition of their basic foibles: sleeping, howling, and laughing, impracticality, superstition, and skepticism. Sganarel and his master are alarmed lest the doctors of this country should wish to dissect them, and they decide to fly with the help of three women, dressed like the Graces. These women are the wives of philosophers, anxious to escape from their foolish husbands. There seems to be some idea here that art, represented by the Graces, is more noble than philosophy, but the symbolism involved is not very plain. At this time in his career Holberg seems to have cared very little for coherence of action or consistency of detail.

It was undoubtedly an artistic misfortune that the course of contemporary events in Denmark lured Holberg back into writing for the theater between 1750 and 1754. It would have been practically impossible for him to take up his dramatic work just where he had left it; there is some justification for the view that his most characteristic vein had already worn itself thin by 1731. When he again took up his pen, he approached his subjects with the added wisdom and the lessened vitality of increasing years. There is something extremely pathetic about the close of Holberg's career as a dramatist. The feebleness of his last plays throws a sickly light back over his more robust and animated productions. Of his six groups into which his comedies may be divided, the first was by all odds both the most brilliant in conception and the most powerful in execution. When Holberg wrote these early dramas, he was comparatively fresh from two years spent traveling through Europe, during which he must have come into touch with many new ideas that greatly stimulated him. He realized that Denmark had been slower than other nations to develop the social consciousness that the seventeenth century had fostered in France and England. He determined to do his part in directing the new civilization that was on its way.

Holberg thought that the Danes should not slavishly imitate the customs and conventions of other communities, except in so far as they were applicable to their own situation. He himself, by founding a school of national drama, did something to bring an artistic influence into the lives of his fellow countrymen, and he certainly could not have done his work exactly as he did it without the example of Molière. Yet Holberg was never satisfied with merely translating Molière's comedies into Danish or with uncritically following in the Frenchman's footsteps. He changed Molière's characters to make them resemble more closely people as he actually knew them in Denmark; he altered Molière's plots and added to them farcical incidents drawn from the *commedia dell'arte*, from Latin comedy, or from any other source that came to his hand. He realized that his audiences were less intellectually sophisticated than the Parisian public and that they must be appealed to by a much simplified dramatic fare. His use of Parisian styles as an object of ridicule in *Jean de France* is an excellent example of his adapting Molière's attacks on artificiality to the contemporary situation in Denmark. Holberg was also careful to indicate that only a narrow-minded person can see no value at all in a foreign way of doing things.

Then there is the question of whether an individual can rise in the world, no matter what his natural limitations may be. Holberg suggests the possibility of social progress for such persons, and only such

persons, as are qualified for places higher than those they now occupy. He thinks it absurd for middle-class people to attempt to outdo
the nobility in celebrating the birth of a child. He is sure that it is
better to have social position, and the manners that go with it, than
money, without background or culture. He was predominantly a
conservative, not a radical; he admired elegance and charm more
than he did power and energy, possibly because he himself had more
energy than polish in the way he went about his work. In making
it clear that a true comedy should not appeal to stupid audiences,
who must be entertained by scenic effects and interpolated horseplay, he delivered some shrewd hits at the popular taste of the Copenhagen public. Since to him decorum was a matter of the most crucial
importance, he exposed a braggart soldier's false pride in his social
prowess or a superstitious man's tendency to ignore the amenities
of human intercourse with a regularity and ruthlessness worthy of
Ben Jonson. Holberg regarded himself as an honest satirist, but, like
Jonson, he sometimes forgot that it is the business of comedy to make
its home truths palatable to consume and pleasant to digest.

In his last plays Holberg came to realize the truth of the simple
philosophical precept, "Know thyself," but he did not express it in
such a persuasive way that it would carry conviction to the un-
initiated. Perhaps he himself could not appreciate its profundity.
His general imperviousness to the thought of Aristophanes and Plato
hints that, although he understood the practical application of Greek
philosophy to such questions as conscious or unconscious hypocrisy,
he had not grasped its significance in the realm of universals. Great
depth of insight, however, is not necessary for a writer of social
comedy, whose business is less to discover original truths than to
call attention to new and pertinent applications of old and well-
tested platitudes. The conditions of human society are always changing, and as a consequence there is always fresh material with which
the comic dramatist may work in elaborating a familiar design. The
standard of laughter in social comedy must be sanctioned by moral
usage and conventional behavior. Actions beneficial to society are
to be approved, those opposed to the greatest good of the greatest
number are to be severely ridiculed. The arbitrary judgments of old
men, the narrow-mindedness of moneygrubbers, the complete il-
logicality of jealous lovers were fused in Molière's inclusive generali-

zation, "La parfaite raison fuit toute extrémité." His followers could not do more than apply this universal truth to the local conditions which they found surrounding them. Holberg was one of the first writers tacitly to accept the restrictions imposed on him by Molière's supremacy. He treated the superficialities of existence, because in them lay the greatest opportunity for novelty, and because he felt that wise precedents should be established to regulate a rapidly expanding social organism.

Holberg had had sufficient experience in contemporary Denmark and other European nations to make his fellow countrymen laugh with amusement and profit at the Frenchified fop, the would-be German politician, and the impoverished Spanish grandee. The problems represented by these characters were coming to be vital to the Danes in their own lives. Were they to accept foreign fashions, were they to try to rise above the sphere into which they had been born, were they to prize social distinction more than economic gain? Was education an asset or a liability, was busyness a wise or foolish way of life, and could an ignorant peasant ever succeed in subduing his naturally brutal impulses? The answer to this last question was a crucial one for a dramatist interested in the growth of a complicated civilization. *Jeppe of the Hill*, which turns upon that point, contains the distilled essence of Holberg's literary art. In all social categories, whether or not they are artificially constructed, as is Jeppe's superiority during his brief period of power, there is a great deal of pretense. Given a longer opportunity to mature, progress towards real refinement may be accomplished. In the meantime, an infinite number of possible situations arise which provoke laughter and provide entertainment for the ebbing and flowing population of an unsettled community. Holberg seized upon many salient points in the confused life of his day. He depicted with fidelity, if not always with illumination, the humorous contrasts that are brought about by any period of rapid and widespread social change.

CHAPTER VII

The Italian Tradition: Carlo Goldoni

I

THE PERIOD of Holberg's supremacy extended from 1722 to 1731, when the Danish theater was in the process of establishing itself as an artistic medium. There is a certain primitive vigor about this dramatist's approach to the social problems of his time. Although he was not the heir of a great national tradition in the writing of comedy, he was aware of what other countries had accomplished in that genre. He had enough literary background to help in molding his comic material, without being burdened by stereotyped patterns which he was expected to follow. In this respect he was more fortunate than Carlo Goldoni, the Italian playwright, whose career overlapped that of the Danish dramatist by a few years. In 1731, when Holberg published his twenty-five collected plays, Goldoni at the age of twenty-four was beginning his professional life as an advocate, but he was already far more interested in the theater than in the law. By 1736 he had written his first sustained comedy, a minor Don Juan drama entitled *Don Giovanni Tenorio, or The Libertine* ("Il dissoluto"), in which he drew the leading figure from one of his successful rivals in a love affair; by 1748 he was devoting his talents exclusively to composing plays for Medebac's company at the theater of Sant' Angelo in Venice; and by 1750, when Holberg returned to playwriting for the last four years of his life, Goldoni in the heyday of his career was working on the famous sixteen comedies that he had agreed to finish within a single twelvemonth.

The Italian dramatist's rise had not been a meteoric one. His early attempts at writing for the theater had included tragedies, tragicomedies, interludes, operatic librettos, both serious and gay, and scenarios for masked comedies. His greatest successes in the last-named kind were *The Servant of Two Masters* ("Il servitore di due padroni") and *Harlequin's Son Lost and Recovered* ("Il figlio d'Arlecchino perduto e ritrovato"), pieces which are connected with the tradition of the improvised *commedia dell'arte*. It was this tradition which had the strongest influence on Goldoni's writing, and it was from this tradition that he most strenuously attempted to free himself. He seriously objected to the liberties permitted to performers by the general use of masks and by the extemporaneous nature of the texts employed. An author was accustomed simply to outline the plot which he wished the actors to follow; the working out of the dialogue and farcical business was left to the ingenuity of the players who were to impersonate Arlecchino, Brighella, Pantalone, and the Dottore. Goldoni's program was to reform this state of affairs by writing down words suitable to the characters who were to speak them as well as to the plot which they were intended to advance. He began his innovations gradually, by composing at first the part of only one actor and by reducing the importance of the comic masks in favor of the more serious characters.

In this attempt Goldoni showed himself aware of another tradition of Italian comedy, the literary drama as opposed to the popular *commedia dell'arte*. During the seventeenth century there had been no literary Italian comedies worthy of the name, but in the sixteenth century there had occurred an outburst of such creative activity, which drew its inspiration from the work of the Latin dramatists. From about 1486 a revival of interest in the plays of Plautus had taken place, and early in the sixteenth century there appeared two original Italian comedies that were in their different ways imitative of classical precedent. Bernardo Dovizio da Bibbiena produced the *Calandria* ("The Comedy of Calandro"), in which the twin Menaechmuses of Plautus were changed into a brother and sister, engaged in intrigues with a passionate woman and her stupid husband. The *Calandria* is a Roman comedy suffused with the atmosphere of moral freedom permitted in the Italian cinquecento. Lodovico Ariosto wrote the *Cassaria* ("The Comedy of the Chest"), in which two clever servants blackmail a slave merchant and wheedle money out of a father, according to the formula established by Plautine comedy. The elegance of Terence pleased Ariosto quite as much as the ingenuity of Plautus. He admits that in his second play, *The Substitutions* ("I suppositi"), from which by the way of George Gascoigne's *Supposes* comes the subplot of *The Taming of the Shrew*, he combined incidents from the *Eunuch* of the one Latin writer and the *Captives* of the other. He deliberately copied the Roman comedies, because, as he says in the prologue to the early prose *Cassaria*, he hoped by so doing to please an audience to which the established classics already appealed.

Later Ariosto rewrote his first two prose comedies in unrhymed verses called *sdruccioli*, and in his subsequent work he introduced still further innovations. His other two completed plays, *The Bawd* ("La lena") and *The Magician* ("Il negromante"), have conventional plots, but the character drawing, especially of the persons who give their names to the comedies and the foils who set them off, has a certain degree of freshness. In the former the bawd is an unscrupulous woman, determined to make money by all kinds of vice, and her husband is equally unprincipled, although his weakness of fixed purpose leads him to deliver a moral lecture to his wife when her designs are not succeeding. In the latter the magician or astrologer is a quack who tries to cheat a husband, a lover, and a father, all at the same time; he is accompanied by a servant who sees through his master's trickery, makes fun of him while he is successful, and deserts him after his downfall. Both the bawd and the magician are finally disgraced. Ariosto leaves his audience with the pleasant feeling that the vice which he has so vividly depicted is no longer dangerous. In both cases, particularly in *The Magician*, there are numerous incidental allusions to local abuses and corruption in the Italy of that day.

Ariosto's fifth and unfinished play, the *Scolastica* ("Scholasticism"), contains one strikingly original portrait, that of a preaching friar, or *frate predicatore*. It is a brief but telling sketch of a mercenary ecclesiastic willing to dispense the Church's blessing in return for a certain amount of ready cash. In many ways he resembles the dissolute confessors in the plays of Niccolò Machiavelli, Ariosto's chief contemporary in writing comedies, who likewise was much indebted to the classics. Two unnamed comedies supposed to be by Machiavelli, the *Commedia in versi* and the *Commedia in prosa*, are extremely baffling, both as to sources and circumstances of composition; the former, which may not have been written by Machiavelli at all, depends upon a silly misunderstanding caused by a similarity in the names of two of the characters; the latter, a brief farce in three acts, describes how a worldly monk dupes a credulous husband and obtains the love of an all too willing wife. The date and authorship of the *Commedia in prosa* have been much disputed, but it seems probable that it was an early sketch for Machiavelli's comic masterpiece, *The Mandrake* ("La mandragola").

The Mandrake, the finest Italian comedy of the sixteenth century, appeared as early as 1514 and maintained its popularity for well over two hundred years. Goldoni speaks of it in his *Memoirs* as being one of the formative influences in his love for the theater and in his devotion to the art of comedy. Its plot is a simple one of the fabliau type. In it a young gallant becomes the lover of a married woman through the folly of her husband, the cleverness of a parasite, the simplicity of the lady's mother, and the unscrupulousness of her confessor. The ingenious intrigue, which depends upon the supposed efficacy of the herb mandrake in the conception of children, is made to seem credible by the great skill and force of the character drawing. Each of the six principal figures is presented as a person in whose existence one can believe; they all have admirable qualities as well as comic defects. The lover does not embark upon the plot in a disagreeable spirit, and the lady has to be persuaded that it is for the good of her soul; the parasite is motivated by sympathy for the lover as well as by greed, and the lady's mother is pious as well as gullible; the husband's natural eagerness to have children permits him to be easily imposed upon, and the confessor excuses his evil deeds by recalling that "bad companions lead men to the gallows" (*le cattive compagnie conducono gli uomini alle forche*).

The husband, Messer Nicia, and the confessor, Frate Timoteo, are the artistic triumphs of *The Mandrake*. The stupid complacency of the one and the conscious hypocrisy of the other make an effective contrast in a comedy which is as honest as it is amusing. Machiavelli had no illusions about life when he wrote this play; on the other hand, there was no meanness in his disposition and there is a healthy naturalness even in the ironic undercurrents of the final scene. Like all good comedies, *The Mandrake* rises to its greatest heights at the close, with Messer Nicia giving his wife's lover a key to his house and thanking Frate Timoteo for having helped him to procure a child. Each of the characters has got what he wanted out of the action, and no one has been made unhappy in spite of a flagrant violation of conventional morality. There is a clear-sighted detachment pervading *The Mandrake* which one would expect from the author of *The Prince* when he turned his attention from politics to society.

The fearlessness of his attitude towards the Church is shown by his unflattering portrait of Frate Timoteo, but there is always enough humanity in his outlook to acquit him of being wantonly subversive in his ethical doctrines. *The Mandrake* is a sane and courageous protest against tyrannical domination by moral and religious authorities.

In form *The Mandrake* keeps close enough to classical precepts for it to have a firm and substantial structure. A small number of characters express their natures in actions that converge upon a single dramatic situation. The piece has an underlying unity that is not to be found in the work of the comic writers who followed Machiavelli. One of these, Giovanni Maria Cecchi, took great liberties with his material, without a compensating originality of inspiration; another, Pietro Aretino, strung together a number of graphic episodes from contemporary life, without bothering to arrange them logically and neatly. Aretino refused to be bound by classical precedent, believing that "we are living in another manner in Rome than that in which people lived in Athens." He drew, with great vividness, realistic pictures of vain old men, impractical philosophers, and ambitious simpletons, duped by designing courtesans, faithless wives, and hypocritical rogues. His work is brilliantly photographic, but it is not carefully considered and artistically projected.

The only Italian comedy of the sixteenth century beside *The Mandrake* which is of outstanding excellence is *The Candlebearer* ("Il candelaio"), written in 1582, by an author who, like Machiavelli, is more famous in the history of ideas than in the realm of comic drama. Giordano Bruno, eighteen years before he was burned at the stake for heresy, composed this powerful but unwieldy play. In its three loosely connected plots there are satirized the unsatisfied passion of an elderly husband, the dishonest greed of a would-be alchemist, and the pretentious pedantry of a long-winded schoolmaster. These three histories are bound together by the theme of homosexuality, which runs beneath the surface of the entire play, and more obviously by the fact that each of the main characters is tricked and humiliated by a group of rogues masquerading as policemen, or *birri*. The alchemist is the most conventional and least developed figure of the three; Bonifacio, the *candelaio*, or pederast, is a subtle refinement upon the theme of the lecherous old man; Manfurio, the school-master, is so expertly handled and deftly drawn that he is one of the most consummate pedants in comic literature.

Manfurio recalls the pedants of classical drama and the Dottori of the *commedia dell'arte*; he prepares the way for such educated dunces as Molière's Thomas Diafoirus and Holberg's Erasmus Montanus. Like so much else in *The Candlebearer*, he seems to be a summary of the past and by implication a forerunner of the future. By the end of the sixteenth century the Renaissance had virtually completed its course and the modern era was already under way. It is notable that there is no Italian dramatist of the seventeenth century who gives expression to the diverse problems confronting the new world, as Molière does, or any who in the early eighteenth century concerns himself with the resulting social upheaval, as Holberg does. The field was clear for Goldoni in the twenty-eight years between 1748 and 1776 to picture the effect of these changes in the Venice of his day and to treat with urbanity and kindliness the new society that had developed since the times of Machiavelli and Giordano Bruno. Local conditions in the theater compelled him to start doing so under the form of the *commedia dell'arte*, but he gradually emancipated himself from the hard and fast requirements of that rigid dramatic pattern. He achieved a freedom fitted to the genteel character of Venetian life and to his own easygoing disposition. He learned to treat his material, whether derived from Latin, Italian, or French sources, in a manner which was distinctive, if not exalted, and which, if it was rarely impressive, never failed to be consistently agreeable.

II

Goldoni sketched his typical hero in one of his early plays, in which he began his reform of the *commedia dell'arte* by writing out the words of the leading part. *Momolo the Gentleman* ("Momolo cortesan"), as composed in its original form, about 1738, was such a one-character comedy. When it was later revised and called *The Man of the World* ("L'uomo di mondo"), it still revolved about the personality of its principal figure. Girolamo, known as Momolo, is a combination of profligate and saint, a sort of eighteenth-century prodigal son, who sows his wild oats without impairing the nobility of his soul. He has an affair with a mercenary laundress, whose infidelity he discovers and punishes; he flirts harmlessly with a married woman and helps her inexperienced husband out of his gambling difficulties; at last he reforms and settles down in matrimony with a beautiful young girl, who has long loved him faithfully but in vain. His heart is touched because the heroine has sent him her jewels that he may pay his debts of honor. As the curtain falls on the last act Momolo is left in a state of beatific happiness that he cannot truthfully be said to have deserved. His chief accomplishment has been gaily to foil the rogues and cheats by whom he is surrounded.

In *The Man of the World* Goldoni has inverted the ordinary comic emphasis by concentrating attention upon the excellences of the lover rather than upon the follies of his enemies. One is impressed by the rewards of dubious virtues more than by the punishment of minor vices. Momolo would presumably not have reformed if it had not been for the heroine's self-sacrificing generosity. Although she is the motivating force in the story, she is put in a subordinate position by her creator. In this play Goldoni seems to have preferred to let feminine influence be felt indirectly instead of flaunting it openly. He showed his attitude towards women more unmistakably in the character of Bettina, the heroine of *The Honest Girl* ("La putta onorata"), a comedy which was produced in 1749, soon after the dramatist's association with Medebac's company had begun. Bettina, a girl of the people, and the young lady who is the heroine of *The Man of the World* resemble each other in their devotion to rather unworthy lovers. Of the two, Bettina is in the more difficult position: she is subjected to the dishonorable proposals of a licentious marquis; she has to repulse a well-meaning merchant; and even a sturdy Venetian gondolier makes one unwelcome attempt to gain her favor. She disgusts her mercenary sister by withstanding all assaults upon her constancy, until at the end of the play she is joined in lawful wedlock with the man of her choice. The hero turns out to be the son of the merchant, not of the gondolier, Messer Menego Cainello, who has been thought to be his father.

Messer Menego and his friends are realistic portraits of Venetian gondoliers, with hearts of gold beneath their rough exteriors. The scenes in which they appear, although not always germane to the plot, have a vivid truthfulness that is said to have appealed greatly to the real gondoliers in the audience. The use of the Venetian dialect in which Messer Menego and the other plebeian characters speak adds a particular charm to this play, as it does to many of Goldoni's other dramas. Accuracy of observation is one of his outstanding qualities; an ear for colloquial phrasing, one of his greatest gifts. From the realistic point of view the most striking scene of *The Honest Girl* is that representing the exterior of a theater on the Grand Canal with gondolas plying to and fro before it, a boy hawking tickets, and the audience entering to attend a performance. The whole play gives a varied picture of life in Goldoni's Venice and is tinged with a sunniness well fitted to the mood of the story that is being presented.

One of Goldoni's changes in the tradition of the *commedia dell'arte* that helps to create the cheerfulness which dominates his comedies is his treatment of the character of Pantalone. That foolish old man, who had been conventionally duped by lovers and servants, becomes in Goldoni's plays a kindly and benevolent adviser to the young people. Their happiness is now his chief concern. In *The Honest Girl* he is a prosperous merchant who wants to marry Bettina himself but is self-effacing enough to submit to the heroine's wishes. He finally withdraws his attentions in favor of his son and bestows both his paternal blessing and his worldly goods upon the young lovers. *The Honest Girl* was so successful upon the stage that Goldoni was led on to write a sequel, *The Good Woman* ("La buona moglie"), in which new misfortunes befall the long-suffering heroine, now neglected by her selfish husband. Here again Pantalone appears as the good angel and lectures his son in a scene so moving that it is said to have reformed a real rake in the audience.

Otherwise *The Good Woman* is as much of an anticlimax as are most sequels. It makes more obvious than its predecessor Goldoni's preference for picturing virtue instead of ridiculing vice. His method of getting his comic effects is unobtrusively to contrast virtuous people with scoundrels, whom he does not wish to expose straightforwardly and to punish justly. The evildoers generally die or repent; occasionally they are dismissed from honorable society in a harmless, salutary way. Goldoni often makes his offenders against decency too villainous to be good humorous material. He exaggerates the weaknesses of human nature until they appear more dangerous than absurd. Gambling, drunkenness, and illicit love affairs are treated as serious offenses in the two Bettina plays, not as laughable deviations from an ideally perfect code of conduct.

According to these comedies, when goodness exists in the lower classes it is so perfect that it approaches true romance; when it appears in the aristocracy it suggests the more conventional doctrine of *noblesse oblige*. Goldoni inherited the courtly tradition of Renaissance society. He accepted the view of his age that the more exalted the social rank of his characters, the more should be expected of them in the way of decorous deportment. When treating high society, he oscillates between chastising its failings and pointing out the fashion in which a true gentleman should conduct himself. For instance, in *The Nobleman and the Lady* ("Il cavaliere e la dama"), produced soon after *The Good Woman*, he shows a pair of perfect lovers surrounded by a group of decadent individuals. The special subject under discussion here is *cicisbeismo*, the system of gallantry which permitted a lady to have a *cavaliere servente* other than her husband. In fact, one of the wives represented not only receives the attentions of other men but also encourages her husband's devotion to a woman who is her own best friend. This social arrangement, common enough in Goldoni's day, appeared to him as a severe offense against propriety, and he devoted many of his comedies to attacking it. *The Nobleman and the Lady* attempts to show that people engaged in such intrigues cannot understand the noble impulses of true gentility and therefore sometimes interfere with them.

Into the mouth of a benevolent merchant in this play Goldoni puts the words which show his conception of the difference between a superficial and a true nobility. After glorifying the usefulness of honest commerce, the merchant sums up Goldoni's social philosophy by saying that real distinction is a matter of conduct, not of birth: "The vile man is he who does not know how to recognize his obligations, and who, wishing his pride flattered unjustly, makes other people realize that he was accidentally born an aristocrat and deserved to be born a plebeian." True excellence, according to Goldoni, depends upon doing one's duty in that state of life into which one has been born; the merchant must be honest, the peasant must be kind, and the nobleman must be courtly without being supercilious. No gentleman should take advantage of his position to foster vicious institutions like *cicisbeismo*, which will reflect unfavorably upon his class and his country.

Patriotism is the dominant theme in the first extremely successful comedy that Goldoni wrote for Medebac. *The Clever Widow* ("La vedova scaltra"), acted in 1748, shows four suitors, a Spaniard, an Englishman, a Frenchman, and an Italian, laying siege to a clever widow. The Spaniard is represented as absurdly proud of his family tree, the Englishman as silent to the point of speechlessness, the Frenchman as affected in his manners, and the Italian as fiery and jealous by disposition. Each is tested after having been sufficiently ridiculed, and the Italian turns out to be the only constant lover of the four. The Frenchman seems to come next in the author's favor. The Englishman and the Spaniard are completely overwhelmed and discredited. The scheme of this comedy is very simple and somewhat monotonous, as one suitor after another is subjected to a test that will display his true character. It illustrates Goldoni's comic method in an early, embryonic form.

If *The Clever Widow* is the simplest of Goldoni's plays prior to the famous sixteen comedies that were performed in 1750 and 1751, *The Antiquary's Family, or The Mother-in-Law and the Daughter-in-Law* ("La famiglia dell'antiquario, o sia La suocera e la nuora") is the most complex of them. In the first place, it undertakes to satirize a passion for collecting antiques on the part of a person who knows little about them; the antiquary of the title is so thoroughly cheated that at the end of the play he is brought to his senses by chagrin at his losses and by disillusionment at his failure as a connoisseur. In the second place, his fiery wife and his placid daughter-in-law keep the house in a constant uproar by their quarrels over the precedence due to rank or money: the mother-in-law is proud of her social position; the daughter-in-law, conscious that her dowry has kept the family out of debt. Neither of the women has a very good disposition, the father of the family is too occupied with his love of antiques to trouble himself about the domestic discord, and the son has not enough strength of character to stand up against either his mother or his wife.

There is also in *The Antiquary's Family* a designing maid, who is bribed by each of her quarreling mistresses and betrays them both in her own interests; there are two would-be *cicisbei*, who try to make peace because they think it is to their own advantage, but who are so underhanded that they only complicate matters further; there is Pantalone, a rich merchant and the daughter-in-law's father, who acts the part of *deus ex machina*. At the end of the piece Pantalone attempts to reconcile the warring women by dismissing their meddlesome maid and the interfering *cavalieri serventi*, but he finds that it is intolerable for a mother-in-law and daughter-in-law to live together in the same establishment. If circumstances compel them to live under the same roof, it is better for each of them to have a separate ménage. *The Antiquary's Family* concludes with an armed truce, under the conditions of which each woman is to have her own servant and eat her meals apart from the other. Goldoni objected very strongly to a French adaptation of his play, in which the two ladies were completely reconciled, as contrary to human nature. In spite of his kindheartedness, he was not blind to the weaknesses of men and women, which he was sincerely trying to remedy by means of the mingled instruction and amusement that, as he fully realized, is the goal of enduring comedy.

III

In the first of the sixteen comedies which Goldoni completed within a single year he set forth his dramatic program and made clear his objectives. *The Comic Stage* ("Il teatro comico"), which he intended to have placed at the head of his printed works, contains Goldoni's defense of his comic art in a form not very different from that which had already been used for the same purpose by both Molière and Holberg. A company of actors are rehearsing *The Father a Rival of His Son* ("Il padre rivale del figlio"), a farce supposed to have been written by Goldoni himself. The director of the company, here called Orazio, is a thinly disguised portrait of the dramatist. Orazio has many difficulties with the capriciousness of his public and the temperament of his actors, who insist on expressing their respective individualities without any regard for the total aesthetic impression intended by the playwright. At one point he stops the rehearsal because the performer of Brighella adds to his part words which are not in the author's script. Orazio states that he is not at present opposed to all improvisation and wearing of masks, but he demands that the additions to the text should be made in character and that the comic masks should be subordinated to the serious plot. Goldoni is here outlining his plans for the reform of the Italian stage. Like a wise comedian, he intends to make haste slowly.

That Goldoni was no pedant is clear from his ridicule of a poverty-stricken poet who would like to furnish plays for Orazio's company. This poet first offers an old-fashioned comedy, which is ridiculed because of its long title and undignified scenes; then he produces a comedy of character translated from the French, which is rejected because it is sure to contain only one well-drawn character surrounded by a mass of wordiness; finally he attempts to confound Orazio by quoting the *Ars poetica* of Horace, but Orazio explains that his namesake must be interpreted liberally, not literally. Orazio is always attempting to adapt classical principles to existing circumstances. He says that Aristotle himself would not have applied his doctrine of unity of place to a comedy of intrigue, in which it is essential to have movement within one city or at least within one house; moreover, Aristotle wrote before the invention of movable scenery, and he surely would not have been so narrow-minded as to refuse to make use of recent mechanical appliances in the theater. Orazio thoroughly disapproves of unnatural soliloquies that are used for exposition, not for the portrayal of character; he believes that comedies should be unified in action; and he does not object to an unexpected conclusion if proper preparation has been made for it. He knows that no comedy can please everyone in the audience, but he has faith that good comedies will please more people than bad ones will. He is sure that impersonality is needed in a good comedy, which "should aim at the universal and not the particular, at vice and not the vicious man" (*prenda di mira l'universale, e non il particolare, il vizio, e non il vizioso*).

Orazio does not approve of depicting too much vice upon the stage. On this point he expresses quite clearly Goldoni's own modification of classical precepts. He thinks that a play in which a father acts as a pander for his own son would put too much emphasis on evil, even if this evil were punished in the end; it is necessary to have artistic proportion, as well as poetic justice, to instill nobility into the hearts of an audience. "When one wishes to introduce a wicked character into a comedy, one places him sideways and not face on: that is to say as an episode, in comparison with the virtuous character, so that virtue may be the more exalted and vice the more humbled." This is exactly what Goldoni had been doing spontaneously in his early plays and what he was to continue doing consciously for the rest of his life. This important change in the nature of comedy sprang no doubt from an undue caution and a desire to make converts without arousing opposition, not from a strong and self-assertive personality, but Goldoni seems to have been honest in his mild conviction and to have carried it out unwaveringly in the face of many obstacles.

The comic tradition lost something of its vitality and force in this process, but the Italian drama temporarily benefited by Goldoni's attempt to improve existing conditions. He was not content in *The Comic Stage* with expounding his ideas of what a good play should be, but he also criticized the behavior of spectators and laid down rules for his actors to follow. An actress is told that she must turn towards the audience as well as to her fellow actors in order that her words may be audible throughout the house; she is to enunciate clearly and to speak slowly, but not too much so; she is to accompany her words with natural gestures; and, above all, she must work with the other members of the company, not against them. She is also told that, when she is off the stage, industry, tact, and kindliness should motivate all her actions. Goldoni cannot refrain from introducing moral precepts into what purports to be a purely artistic manifesto. He was no doubt anxious to have his plays well performed, and a natural desire for worldly success joins in him with a naïve belief that honesty for the other fellow is the best policy for oneself. *The Comic Stage* is filled with Goldoni's hopes and fears for his own literary accomplishment. It ends on almost a pathetic note. Orazio states that the author of *The Father a Rival of His Son* does not boast of having nearly reached perfection, but that he will be content if he has stimulated more gifted men who will some day make a reputation for the Italian theater.

Near the beginning of *The Comic Stage* the leading lady wonders why such an inferior play as *The Father a Rival of His Son* is being produced, when its author has written sixteen better plays all within the year, and she thereupon proceeds to give the names of the sixteen comedies by Goldoni that were performed in 1750 and 1751. The first is *The Comic Stage*, and the other fifteen are representative of various different phases of the dramatist's work, from the comedy of intrigue through the comedy of character to the comedy of sentiment.

There was a decidedly sentimental streak in Goldoni's nature which led him to write a play on the subject of Samuel Richardson's *Pamela, or Virtue Rewarded* under the title of *Pamela Unmarried* ("Pamela nubile"). The great difference between Richardson's and Goldoni's treatments of the story is that the Englishman was willing to allow a gentleman to marry a servant, whereas to the Italian the union of a nobleman and plebeian would have been an unpardonable breach of etiquette. In Italy the children of such a misalliance would have no legal right to inherit their father's rank and fortune; so Goldoni had Pamela's father turn out to be an exiled Scotch count and in that way smoothed out all the complications. This change in the story would lead one to suppose that Goldoni was extremely conservative in social matters if it were not for one speech of protest delivered by Pamela's friend and confidante, who insists that "a day will come when the small and the great will all be made again into one dough" (*verrà un giorno, che dei piccoli e dei grandi si farà nuovamente tutta una pasta*). This passage sounds like an early declaration of the doctrines of Jean Jacques Rousseau. It is notable as being one of the few places in Goldoni's work where the vague benevolence of the playwright's disposition is formulated into anything like concrete principles.

Pamela Unmarried is not a very amusing play, although it contains one humorous character, a superficial traveler, whose foolish remarks about the pranks he has seen performed by Arlecchino on the Italian stage give Goldoni a chance to criticize the abuses of the *commedia dell'arte*. Goldoni's comedy, like Richardson's novel, is occupied chiefly with praising a conventional morality, without considering deeply the motives from which it springs. Sentimental tendencies have the upper hand in it; the slight attempts at comic characterization are not closely related to the main thread of plot.

In *The True Friend* ("Il vero amico") the dramatist gives more nearly equal attention to the comic figure of a foolish miser and the sentimental one of a self-sacrificing friend. The miser lets it be understood that he has no money, in order that financial demands may not be made upon him. His wealth, like that of Plautus' Euclio and

Molière's Harpagon, is detected and stolen by a servant. His frenzy over the loss of the chest containing his money is described, not shown, and his ultimate reform is prophesied by the hero's noble friend, who finally comes to dominate the action at the expense of its comic possibilities.

The Prudent Lady ("La dama prudente") is another of the sixteen comedies in which sentiment and comedy are unevenly combined. The prudent lady is very nearly a perfect wife, and her husband is an admirable portrait of an absurdly jealous husband. The conflict between jealousy and conventionality taxes the ingenuity of Goldoni, who would like to show that ideal conduct is compatible with existing codes of human behavior. He cannot approve of jealousy, but under a system of cicisbeismo such a passion is natural, not to say inevitable. The only solution seems to be for all the characters to emigrate to Castel buono, a Utopia where wives devote themselves to their husbands and a cicisbeo is unknown, where jealousy is a precaution, not a disease, and a prudent lady can live happily ever afterwards.

Castel buono is an ideal community, to which a husband and wife retire when they find it too difficult to live in the real world; Castell'a Mare in The Punctilious Women ("Le femmine puntigliose") is a slightly more realistic town, to which another husband and wife flee when they find it impossible to get into the society of Palermo. The difference between the two couples is that the first husband is jealous and the second husband is weak, the first wife is a clever woman of the world and the second is an unsuccessful social climber. Both plays are comedies of manners with the women stronger characters than the men, the tone of The Prudent Lady being primarily serious, while that of The Punctilious Women inclines towards satire, until the last act, when the heroine comes to her senses and decides to reform. She exposes the people who have taken money from her for advancing her social ambitions. She determines to enter upon a new course of conduct in Castell'a Mare and delivers a lengthy lecture to the fashionable women who have made a fool of her. This moral conclusion contrasts strongly with the ironical ending of Molière's The Middle-Class Gentleman, in which social ambition is tricked and yet believes that it is still triumphant.

That Goldoni should not be called an Italian Molière is clear from comparing *The Punctilious Women* with *The Middle-Class Gentleman*, and it is even more evident after a consideration of *The Feigned Invalid* ("La finta ammalata") and *Love as a Doctor*, plays which likewise resemble each other in plot. Both comedies display the weaknesses of the medical profession, and Goldoni is not far behind Molière in the number of quacks and charlatans whom he introduces. The measure of the difference between the two dramatists is the difference in the skill and penetration with which the characters of the heroines' fathers in the two plays are developed: Sganarelle is subtly portrayed as a pathetically disillusioned man, who laughs at his own misfortunes and is deceived by the lovers; Pantalone is drawn with fairly obvious strokes as a solicitous parent, who has little sense of humor and is only too happy to have his daughter marry the man of her choice. Molière ends his comedy with an intrigue in which the lovers succeed at the expense of Sganarelle; Goldoni closes his play with a general understanding which satisfies everyone except the ludicrous doctors.

The hero of *The Feigned Invalid* is such a sensitive character that he would be ridiculous if he had not been very deeply in love, and the same thing is true of Florindo, the hero of *The Liar* ("Il bugiardo"), which Goldoni adapted from Corneille's play with the same title. Florindo, a lover so timid that he will not acknowledge his own attempts at serenades or sonneteering, was invented by Goldoni for the sake of contrast with Lelio, the forward liar. Lelio is so skillful in his falsehoods that for a time it looks as if he would win the hand of the heroine — but Goldoni is more rigidly moral than Corneille, or even Alarcón, had been. He insists upon having Lelio return to a Roman girl whom he has promised to marry but whom he has already ceased to love. At the end of the play Lelio's lies are one by one exposed, and he is cast out from respectable Venetian society.

The gradual exposure of a disagreeable character is a frequently recurring element in Goldoni's comic technique. Just as Lelio is exposed at the end of *The Liar*, so Ottavio in *The Fanatical Poet* ("Il poeta fanatico") is left alone amid the ruins of the literary academy that he has attempted to create. He has always been opposed by his practical and shrewish wife; his daughter deserts him when her romance has been satisfactorily arranged; and the members of the academy take their leave as a result of petty intrigues, excessive prudery, or financial advantages. *The Fanatical Poet* is not directed against poetry but against such coteries as "L'Accademia dell'Arcadia," then existing in Rome, and against fanatics like the gentleman of Bologna, described by Goldoni in his *Memoirs*, who died of a broken heart when his literary daughter married against his wishes.

The absent-minded Ottavio in *The Fanatical Poet* is the exact opposite in character of the worldly Don Marzio in *The Coffee Shop* ("La bottega del caffè"), who is likewise finally deserted by all his acquaintances. Don Marzio is the most striking and successful character Goldoni created during the period of his sixteen comedies. He is not such a purely simplified type as the unprincipled liar or the fanatical poet. He is a combination of busybody and slanderer; he delights in repeating gossip and in inventing it on the slightest provocation. He is extremely obstinate and self-confident, he has no consideration for others, and he causes untold trouble for the people in the play. Yet it does not appear, at any time, that Don Marzio is actively malicious or that he has a streak of meanness in his disposition. He is simply thoughtless and self-centered. He loves to hear the sound of his own voice, and he is anxious to have an audience before which he can perform. This desire to take the center of the stage is eventually the cause of his undoing. His lies become exposed, and he is completely discredited by the society in which he moves. He is dumfounded when one door after another is closed in his face and social ostracism forces him to leave Venice.

Don Marzio's verve and vivacity are so great that he is extremely entertaining as well as most annoying. He cannot be called a vicious man, and thus the lines of his part do not fall outside the bounds of comedy. He was drawn with such skill that more than one of Goldoni's contemporaries was offended by the resemblance between Don Marzio and himself. He is not an uncommon type in an urban civilization, in which the culture of a narrow aristocratic circle has recently permeated all classes of society. Don Marzio is the only titled person in *The Coffee Shop*, and he seems a trifle out of his element, particularly in comparison with Ridolfo, the benevolent keeper of the coffee shop. Ridolfo presides like a good angel over the action of the play and, like Pantalone, whom he very much resembles, exerts a benign influence on the other characters. Ridolfo's coffee shop holds the center of the stage, which is set to represent a wide street with the exterior of five houses, between which the action shifts back and forth. There are an inn, a private house, and three shops, above which are to be seen the windows of rooms in a gaming house, where at one point an elaborate meal is served. This realistic development of the convention of classical comedy to suggest the varied life of a community is characteristic of Goldoni's work. He was particularly interested in showing how numerous individuals could arrange their interacting lives so that all of them might live in peace and harmony together; he was really experimenting in social conditions and attempting to learn what was necessary in the way of self-restraint to make man a coöperative, not a competitive, animal. Goldoni himself was sufficiently genial to feel the force of human sympathy, but he was also intelligent enough to appreciate the crudity of man's natural impulses.

The necessity of disciplining oneself in a tendency to repeat everything that one hears and to invent picturesque bits of scandal, if one does not pick them up from other people, is well illustrated in the character of Don Marzio. The social effect of gossip on a large scale is shown in more detail by the last of Goldoni's famous sixteen comedies, *The Women's Small Talk* ("I pettegolezzi delle donne"). Here there are depicted no less than five gossiping women, who, partly from spite and partly from ignorance, almost succeed in separating two young lovers. The situation is finally saved by the kindly old men in the play, who take matters into their own hands and straighten out the mischief caused by the women's idle tongues. The action is set against a background of city life, in which a large number of street Arabs, peddlers, sailors, laundresses, shopkeepers, and dressmakers appear every now and then, amplifying the reverberations of gossip and giving a vivid picture of Venice in the eighteenth century. *The Women's Small Talk* is the earliest of Goldoni's comedies that have come down to us written entirely in the local Venetian dialect. It is focused upon a particular milieu more than upon an individual character like Don Marzio, who seems to have become more prominent in *The Coffee Shop* than Goldoni originally intended him to be. Don Marzio is such a sparkling figure that for a moment he seems to threaten the larger social pattern which Goldoni was beginning to imprint upon his comedies.

IV

After the phenomenally productive season of 1750–51 Goldoni continued to write for Medebac's company at the theater of Sant' Angelo for two years, during which time he composed sixteen more comedies, including two or three of his greatest successes. These are the plays stimulated by the rivalry of Signora Medebac, the leading lady of the company, and the volatile soubrette known as La Corallina. For the latter he wrote dramas like *The Devoted Maidservant* ("La serva amorosa"), which gives less importance to the part of the mistress than to that of the maid. Corallina in this play goes into retirement with her young master when he is driven from his home. She takes care of him in his poverty, makes stockings which she sells to provide money for him, and finally succeeds in restoring him to his rightful inheritance by the comic ruse of a supposed death, employed in Molière's *The Invalid in His Own Imagination*. She is also instrumental in straightening out his love affair. Altogether she serves as *dea ex machina* through a combination of kindliness and craft. It is noticeable that the comic maid, who in Molière and Holberg had begun to share honors with the scheming valet, has here completely driven him from the stage. In comedy, as in life, women were asserting their rights to manage the affairs of other people.

The servingmen in *The Devoted Maidservant* are subordinate to Corallina and do exactly what she tells them to. She finally agrees to marry the less stupid of them, not because she is fond of him but because she wants to efface herself from the path of her master, whom she has really loved during all the time that she has taken care of him. The combination of her suppressed feeling and her lively cleverness produces the charming variety of her character. There is throughout this play a contest in generosity between the master and the maid. At one point he asks her to marry him, but Corallina refuses to consider the proposal because she has too much respect for the social barriers that stand between them. Corallina's tenderness and devotion show that she has an exceptionally sensitive nature, but Goldoni never allows her nobility to be overemphasized at the expense of the shrewder and more practical aspects of her personality.

Even so, Corallina is a far more sentimental figure than Mirandolina in *The Mistress of the Inn* ("La locandiera"), the most famous

part Goldoni ever created. The role of Mirandolina, which was conceived to display the talents of the comic actress Corallina, has served
since Goldoni's time as a vehicle for many skillful performances.
Mirandolina is not handicapped by being in love with a man who
cannot marry her; on the contrary, she is loved by several men
whom she would not think of marrying. She is the keeper of an inn
at Florence, which is frequented by two noblemen, one an impoverished aristocrat and the other a newcomer to wealth. Each of
these men courts Mirandolina, and each shows jealousy of the other,
as they attempt to argue impersonally about the respective merits
of social position and financial independence. The innkeeper has no
serious interest in either of them, although she accepts their presents
willingly enough, and manages to transfer their attentions to two
strolling actresses masquerading as ladies. The newly rich man discovers the truth about the actresses some time before the decayed
nobleman, with the result that rank without money is made to seem
more ridiculous than money without rank. Goldoni may have agreed
with Holberg that the former was harmless and pathetic,[1] but he
did not consider the latter a serious menace to the existing social
order. He had less practical sense than the Danish dramatist and more
innate kindliness of heart.

Goldoni has Mirandolina put both the noblemen in *The Mistress
of the Inn* to rout by deciding to marry someone else. The lucky man
is a servant at the inn, whom Mirandolina's father before his death
advised her to wed, and whom she has always fully intended to make
her husband as soon as she is ready to settle down with anyone at all.
She first has a number of flirtations, the most exciting of which to
her is that with the Cavaliere di Ripafratta, a self-confessed woman-
hater. To captivate his heart is a worthy challenge to Mirandolina's
powers of coquetry. She uses her position as keeper of the inn to
offer him the creature comforts of fine linen and delicious food; she
arouses his sense of rivalry by the attentions of her other lovers; and
finally she pretends to approve of his dislike for the feminine sex.
The Cavaliere gives away his case quite early in the play, when he
admits that, in spite of his indifference to women, he would like to

[1] In *The Swindler* ("Il raggiratore"), written a few years later, the principal dupe,
a decayed nobleman, is treated in much the same manner as Holberg's Don Ranudo
di Colibrados.

have children. When he realizes that in spite of himself he has become attracted to Mirandolina, he attempts to flee from the inn, but Mirandolina takes advantage of her position as innkeeper to present a final bill. She pretends to weep because of his departure, and when he offers to tip her she plays her trump card by pretending to faint. The Cavaliere can no longer resist Mirandoline's fascination; he asks her to marry him, and after she repels his advances he rushes away in a fine fury. He will distrust women all the more in the future, and Mirandolina hopes that his humiliation will prove a salutary lesson to all conceited bachelors.

The Cavaliere-Mirandolina story is a novel union of involuntary sex attraction and intentional trickery, with the trickery gaining the upper hand. This victory of consciously planned deceitfulness prevents *The Mistress of the Inn* from rising to the heights attained by more honest treatments of relations between the sexes. Shakespeare's Beatrice and Congreve's Millamant, as well as their lovers, Benedick and Mirabell, succumb to the power of sex; Molière's Alceste leaves Célimène alone in the realm of society; but Goldoni's Mirandolina neither yields to the force with which she is playing nor triumphs over her own emotions in regard to it. From the structural point of view, the faithful servant whom Mirandolina marries provides an ingenious way out of the situation, but, often as it may happen in life, in a comedy it is not fair for a woman to have her cake and eat it too, to be a remorseless flirt and at the same time a devoted lover. Goldoni's sense of social distinctions made it possible for him to paint sex attraction between people of different ranks as laughable and undignified, but he could not refrain from good-naturedly inserting a happy ending to round off his story. It must be remembered that *The Mistress of the Inn* was written to display the charms of La Corallina, who usually played the role of a maid, so that Mirandolina had to be a glorified soubrette. She must be of low social rank and therefore could not marry into the nobility; she must be clever enough to get the better of a gentleman whom she could meet on equal terms; and she must have enough feeling to be the heroine of a romantic love story. These conflicting demands resulted in a character which is too artificial to be entirely convincing, but which provides an effective acting part, as Mirandolina has always proved to be.

Its practical success was evident from the first. Signora Medebac, who had temporarily left the stage in a fit of pique, came out of her retirement and insisted on reviving *Pamela*, which had given her one of her most popular roles. This rivalry between the two leading women of Medebac's company was finally settled by Goldoni's tact and skill in writing a comedy in which there were two women's parts of equal importance. In *The Inquisitive Ladies* ("Le donne curiose") there are both a romantic heroine, Rosaura, and a mischievous maid, Corallina, who is unencumbered by a love affair of her own. They are joined by two married ladies, and all four of these women become excessively curious about how the men in the play spend their time. The men have a club which is surrounded by such secrecy that it stimulates the women's desire to know what goes on behind its locked doors. When they finally gain access to it, they are amazed to find no signs of vice or black magic there. This slight plot, which in the twentieth century has been made the basis of a delightful comic opera with music by Ermanno Wolf-Ferrari,[1] was suggested to Goldoni because of the excitement that had been caused by the introduction of Freemasonry into Venice. The Pope and the Jesuits had violently opposed what seemed to them an infringement upon the rights of the Roman Catholic Church, but what Goldoni evidently thought to be a harmless social organization. In *The Inquisitive Ladies* he used the incident as an appropriate excuse for a psychological study of the differences between men and women.

The men in this play are given to moralizing and philosophy; the women are inquisitive and unscrupulous. The modest hero is contrasted with the jealous and high-spirited Rosaura, who has more color than the usual pallid heroine of comedy and a touch of unpleasantness in her disposition as well. Perhaps this combination is to be explained by the vehemence of Signora Medebac's nature. Corallina, on the other hand, is gay and inventive, without being enough involved emotionally to take the center of the stage. The hero tries to confide in her the facts about his friends' mysterious meetings, but she refuses to be convinced by mere words and insists that, for her, seeing is believing. Corallina in *The Inquisitive Ladies* is a more conventional figure than in either *The Devoted Maidservant*, in which

---

[1] Wolf-Ferrari has also composed operas with librettos based upon Goldoni's comedies of *The Boors*, *The Clever Widow*, and *The Public Square*.

she assumes the role of the self-sacrificing lover, or *The Mistress of the Inn*, in which under the name of Mirandolina she appears as a triumphant coquette. Mirandolina is neither too sentimental nor too unyielding, but in her mingled brilliance and kindliness she shows an inconsistency that is characteristic of Goldoni's own personality. He could not bring himself to make Mirandolina completely victorious in society because she was one of the common people; he could not make her completely victorious over her own emotions if she was to remain a credible human being. She is as inventive and as unstable as Goldoni himself was. He created many showy parts for Corallina, he antagonized Signora Medebac in the process, and then he compromised with them both by composing *The Inquisitive Ladies*. The whole situation seems to have been distasteful to him, however, and in the spring of 1753 he severed his connection with Medebac's company.

After leaving the theater of Sant' Angelo, where his plays had been produced for five years, Goldoni joined the brothers Vendramin at the theater of San Luca in the autumn of 1753. He maintained his association with this theater until the spring of 1762, when he left Venice forever, with the exception of a brief interlude in 1758–59, during which he wrote two or three comedies to be produced at Rome. Among these Roman comedies is *Pamela Married* ("Pamela maritata"), a sequel to *Pamela Unmarried*, but far inferior to its predecessor, to which it bears much the same relation as does *The Good Woman* to *The Honest Girl*. After its failure on the stage Goldoni admitted that it lacked interest and life, but he also claimed that it showed an extreme care and delicacy, which went unnoticed in the theater. According to his ex post facto statement, this drama was written to be read, not to be acted.

Between *The Inquisitive Ladies* in 1753 and *Pamela Married* in 1759 Goldoni wrote over fifty plays, most of which are more notable for their vivacity and originality than for the finesse of their workmanship. They include dramas in prose and verse, romantic stories of the past and realistic narratives of the present, pictures of people in high and low society, studies of misers and rascals. The plots of these works are taken from books, from actual experience, and from secondhand anecdotes. Considering the amount and variety of this material, it is not surprising that these plays are less remarkable for their literary quality than for their immediate theatrical effectiveness. Goldoni was to write many excellent comedies later in his life, but during the first six years of his association with the brothers Vendramin his creative activity seems to have been at a low ebb.

While writing for Medebac, Goldoni had composed a comedy in verse on the subject of Molière. After he joined the brothers Vendramin he wrote plays about two other literary figures of the past, Terence and Torquato Tasso. No one of the pretentious efforts was a great success, but each of them throws some light on Goldoni's own personality. His Molière is a soft and amiable version of the great French dramatist; his Tasso suffers keenly from the attacks of pedantic critics; his Terence tells the spectators that whereas he used to say to his Roman audiences "approve" (*applaudite*), he now asks that the spectators "sympathize" (*compatite*). Goldoni was even further in spirit from Latin comedy than from the clear-sighted and balanced moderation of Molière.

Goldoni's plays in verse are as a rule on a much lower artistic level than his comedies in prose. When he attempted to combine the familiar Venetian dialect with verse, the result was too forced to be highly effective. He wrote five dramas in this hybrid form, of which *The Public Square* ("Il campiello") is the most attractive. In this comedy the stage represents a public square, around which cluster a number of houses, where the principal characters dwell. The life of the community eddies about these buildings, much as it did in *The Coffee Shop*, but *The Public Square* has no Don Marzio to lend it distinction. Its characters include gossiping old women, attractive young girls, jealous hotheaded youths, and one rather original figure, the churlish, rich uncle of the heroine. He is a boor, or *rustego*, whose fierceness is finally softened by the assaults of youth and beauty. For the most part, *The Public Square* is concerned with a group of people, not with its separate members. It is a series of genre pictures, in which games of chance are played upon the square, feuds break out between rival factions, and a gentleman of high degree finally makes peace by inviting everyone to a fine dinner. The gay, if not profound, spirit of this light piece is well suited to the short tinkling lines of dialect in which it is composed.

The Public Square has some individuality as a work of art, and so does *A Sojourn in the Country* ("La villeggiatura"), Goldoni's first play dealing with a social season in the country, a subject which he was later to treat at further length and in greater detail. His most thoroughly successful production in the years between 1753 and 1759 is an amusing farce called *A Strange Accident* ("Un curioso accidente"), which, like *She Stoops to Conquer*, is supposed to have been founded on a mistake that had once actually occurred. In this case the story was related to Goldoni by the Venetian correspondents of the Dutch merchant involved. It concerns a French lieutenant, interned in the house of a rich Dutch merchant, who is advised by the merchant to elope with the girl whom he loves. The girl happens to be the merchant's own daughter, but the merchant supposes she is the daughter of a neighboring financier. The farcical touches come from the misunderstandings between young people, fathers, and servants; a slightly pathetic element enters with the financier's daughter, who is really in love with the Frenchman; the most subtle part of the play is the conflict between the two old men. Neither merchant nor financier thinks a mere soldier a worthy husband for his daughter, but the merchant thinks that the financier should be delighted with such a match. In the merchant's opinion, unfortunate nobility is a very exact equivalent to accidental riches, and the man who makes his own money in trade is vastly superior to a person who has received either rank or wealth by inheritance. Here the hard-working merchant has not only ceased to be ridiculous but has become definitely an admirable character. His sterling qualities are further emphasized when he is persuaded to accept with a good grace his daughter's choice of a husband, after the marriage has taken place without his knowledge or consent. A substantial plot and a sympathetic understanding of middle-class people make *A Strange Accident* stand out from the general flimsiness of Goldoni's works during his first six years under the managership of the Vendramins. They were to be followed by three years productive of work more restricted in quantity but far more valuable from the literary point of view.

V

While at Rome in 1758–59, Goldoni had lodged at the house of one Pietro Poloni, and soon after his return to Venice he composed a comedy suggested by some of his experiences there. Poloni's daughter had had a violent love affair with a young man, in the course of which both lovers had indulged in ridiculous fits of jealousy. Handkerchiefs were torn, mirrors broken, and knives drawn in the midst of the lovers' quarrels, which seemed amusing enough to Goldoni to be set upon the stage when he urgently needed the subject matter for a new comedy. The result was *The Lovers* ("Gl'innamorati"), like *A Strange Accident* one of Goldoni's minor triumphs, but not a very significant work of art because of the thinness of its material. The lovers are conventionally rigid in their jealousy. All the characters are artificially balanced against one another, except for the heroine's uncle, Fabrizio, who has a certain degree of vitality. He is an old citizen, poor but proud; he does not intend to have his niece marry disadvantageously. He attempts to persuade her to accept a rich suitor. His efforts are unsuccessful, and in the end he is forced to approve of the jealous, but basically generous, hero. Fabrizio is not a fully developed character, but he is the most vivid person in *The Lovers* and prepares the way for Goldoni's more penetrating studies of old men in his next play, *The Boors* ("I rusteghi").

Some critics regard *The Boors* as Goldoni's masterpiece, and it has excellent claims to that title, especially if considered in connection with the two plays that are its logical successors. All three works are written in prose, in the Venetian dialect, and taken together they give a fairly complete impression of contemporary social life in northern Italy. In *The Boors* the society presented is that of the lower bourgeoisie, the four title characters being middle-class merchants, proud of their success in business and conscious of their own importance to the life of the community. Their ability to accumulate property has resulted in their being overimpressed with the power that comes from wealth and decidedly intolerant of other less practical people. They have not had opportunities for self-cultivation equal to the resources at their command. Therefore they appear in an awkward and disagreeable light. They all have gruff outward manners, but each of them is distinguished by details of characterization, particularly in relation to the women of their families. Lunardo, the most boorish of the four, has a pretty daughter and a shrewish second wife, who cannot agree with each other, except in opposing Lunardo and thereby confirming him in his natural obstinacy; Simon, Lunardo's chief friend, has a stupid wife, and so he prudently disregards the opinions of anyone except himself; Maurizio, a widower with an only son, is freed from the annoyance of a wife, and consequently he has hardened into the mold of a crusty old bachelor; Canciano appears to be the most amusing of them all, because his temperamental crabbedness is offset by the charm and intelligence of his wife. Canciano likes to associate with the other austere men and talk over with them the failings of the world in general and of women in particular, but when once Felice, his wife, murmurs, "Isn't that so, Master Cancian?" (*Ne vero, sior Cancian?*) he weakly capitulates to her suggestions, even when she proposes taking a *cavaliere servente*.

The slight plot of *The Boors* concerns the love affair of Lunardo's daughter with Maurizio's son, the intrigues of the women to help the lovers, the men's discovery of their wives' treachery, and the final reconciliation of all parties through the efforts of Felice. She accuses the men of barbarity in trying to marry off a young girl without heeding her personal inclinations, she delivers a powerful sermon on the subject of individual selfishness, and she finally completes her victory by a tactful appeal to the best elements in masculine human nature. "In short," she says, "if you wish to live in quiet, if you wish to be on good terms with your wives, act like men, not like savages; rule, do not tyrannize, and love, if you wish to be loved." This plea is entirely successful, and the surly men give way before it like so many ninepins. Goldoni would probably not have taken the pains to exhibit the incivility of the four *rusteghi* in the first two acts if he had not intended to show in the last one that beneath the roughest of exteriors there is often beating the warmest of hearts.

"Papa Goldoni," as he was often affectionately called, explains in his *Memoirs* that *The Boors* was meant to attack the inconsistency of men who are severe in their family relationships and charming in general society, but he did not entirely succeed in disentangling this subject from an idolatrous admiration for the good old days. The boors believe that young men used to be more cautious and women more docile than they are now; they regret the lavish expenditure of money and the looseness in moral codes that have become the fashion; with proper reactionary fervor, they claim that "the whole reason is liberty" (*tuto xè causa la libertà*). In showing that there is something to be said for their attitude, and also that the boors interpret it in an extremely narrow way, Goldoni again finds himself in an incongruous position. On the one hand, he would like to conserve the best elements in the past; on the other hand, he believes in the ideal of liberty that was to be glorified later in the eighteenth century. *The Boors* attempts to weld together the two sides of this discordant philosophy by depicting families where crucial differences in opinion and temperament are at last reconciled by mutual forbearance and understanding. As a result, a satisfying aesthetic impression is obtained, somewhat at the expense of a lively, diverting story.

Goldoni's next important comedy, after *The Boors*, has a far better developed plot and a much more diversified atmosphere than its predecessor. *The New House* ("La casa nova") contains one *rustego*, who does not appear until the last act and has little time to show his surliness before he is softened by the tears and protestations of the various women in the piece. His niece, who had been temporarily seduced into living a fashionable life, is in love with a poor but honest young man; his nephew has, within two weeks, taken a young bride, who is the cause of all the complications in the plot. The bride comes from a very poor family, but she is an extravagant girl, perfectly willing to plunge her husband into debt if only she can be a success in the world of society. She spends money ruthlessly on clothes, gambling, and idle entertainments; she already has a *cavaliere servente*; and she now insists that her husband should move from the house where he has been living into a costlier apartment. This picturesque incident in *The New House* was suggested to Goldoni by his own recent change of residence and his consequent knowledge of the difficulties involved in transporting an entire household from one establishment to another. The troubles that he had had with the inefficiency of mechanics, who would not complete their work in his new house as they had guaranteed to do, suggested to him the striking early scenes of his comedy, in which the bridegroom remonstrates with a swarm of upholsterers, painters, and carpenters.

The bridegroom's troubles are chiefly caused by the fact that his wife has squandered his money, to the point where he has no cash left to pay his debts. Both his old and his new landlords, as well as the workmen, are pestering him for the money he owes them. He is reduced to a pitiable state of penury, until his wife suddenly reforms and by her penitence persuades the crusty *rustego* to rehabilitate his nephew's shattered finances. This sentimental conclusion is not dictated by logical consistency so much as by dramatic expediency, and it constitutes a blot upon the structure of *The New House*. Before it occurs, there have been a number of amusing situations brought about by the bride's arbitrary and unreasonable demands. She becomes involved in constant altercations with her unmarried sister-in-law over questions of domestic authority and social precedence. The disputes of the two women as to which of them should first receive and return formal calls furnish an excellent opportunity for the display of the mildly satiric elements in Goldoni's art. The nobility which each of them shows at the end of the play is another evidence of the dramatist's good intentions and vague idealism.

The New House treats a more highly developed social group than *The Boors*, and for that reason the unsteadiness of its comic point of view is more noticeable. *The Squabbles at Chioggia* ("Le baruffe chiozzotte") deals with a lower stratum of society and is infused with a gay spontaneity, which captivated Goethe when he saw the play performed at Venice in 1786. The *dramatis personae* of this comedy are, for the most part, not natives of Venice itself but of Chioggia, or Chiozza, a small fishing village on the coast near-by. They speak in such a pronounced dialect of their own that even a Venetian magistrate cannot always understand them. The men are fishermen and sailors, the women are lace-makers and housewives; they are simple, ignorant people, kindhearted but untrained. Their high spirits carry off the comedy with a dash which is quite independent of a consistent philosophy and would not have been compatible with a more thoughtful attitude on its author's part. The people in this play are all well-intentioned. Since decorum is not needed among the peasant folk of Chioggia, they act in a perfectly sincere and unaffected way. Their lack of restraint permits them to give free rein to their feelings. An appeal to their better natures seems a logical solution for the primitive problem presented. No busybody is needed to cause the complications, and no *rustego* has to straighten them out. A Venetian official appears to compel a temporary respect for law and order, as Goldoni must have often done himself, when in his youth he held the position of coadjutor of the criminal chancellor at Chioggia. His recollections of those early days undoubtedly furnished material for the powerful and varied picture of village life that he draws in *The Squabbles at Chioggia*.

This play contains no people of rank or wealth to raise a social problem which Goldoni is unable to answer with conviction. *The Squabbles at Chioggia* lacks intellectual range, but it has an emotional intensity that is rarely found in Goldoni's work. Its characters are voluble and impassioned, unrepressed and naïve. Two husbands, two wives, and two engaged couples are in a constant state of warfare throughout the comedy. The confusion starts because a third young man offers a piece of roast pumpkin, bought from a street vendor, to one of the fiancées in the absence of her betrothed at sea. She accepts the present, and thereafter indiscriminate jealousy starts an immense conflagration. Both pairs of lovers are involved, the married people take sides, and the innocent cause of all the trouble complains to a magistrate that he has been unjustly attacked. In the examination which subsequently occurs, one of the older women amusingly pretends to be deaf so that she will not have to tell her age, and the other one is furious because she has not been questioned at all. A solution of the whole complicated matter is reached when the donor of the roast pumpkin is married off to a third young girl and its recipient placates her jealous lover by her tears. This final episode ends the play on somewhat too sympathetic a note for a vigorous comedy dealing with human weaknesses, but it is not elaborated unnecessarily. It provides just the kindly touch of nature without which no play by Goldoni is complete.

The Squabbles at Chioggia, *The Boors*, and *The New House* may be regarded as a triptych showing life in the northern Italy of Goldoni's day. They represent the common people, the lower middle class, and the upper middle class respectively. Of the three plays, *The New House* has the best integrated plot, and *The Squabbles at Chioggia* gives the clearest picture of life in a social community. In the former, the characters are not very convincing in their sudden reformation; in the latter, they are not very carefully differentiated in their hot-tempered jealousy and honest kindliness. *The Boors* must be admitted to be the most successful of the three plays from the point of view of character drawing. Its plot is tenuous and its social significance is implied rather than expressed, but its general purport is clear: it is

necessary for human beings to restrain their naturally selfish impulses if they are to live together harmoniously on intimate terms;
the increasing congestion of urban life demands that a social code
giving sanction to decent human relationships should be formulated.
The common people of Chioggia are too unsophisticated to be impressed by the value of systematized convention, the lower-middle-
class merchants are just becoming acutely conscious of its power, and
the upper strata of society have grown so accustomed to its pressure
that it no longer exerts any active influence upon their lives.

The last group, or one even a little more aristocratic, is pictured
by Goldoni in the trilogy of plays about *villeggiatura*, in which at this
period he developed ideas that he had already tentatively set forth.
Goldoni tells us in his *Memoirs* that he had observed the luxurious
country estates on the banks of the Brenta and had marveled that the
descendants of people who had amassed their fortunes in that region
should now return there purely for the purpose of spending money.
Cicisbeismo was a logical result of the pleasure-loving life of such a
community, as were gambling, feasting, and dancing, all of them expensive pastimes. The pathos and the humor of the situation come
from the fact that, since it was the fashionable thing to go to the
country for a part of the social season, people with lean pocketbooks
would make a great effort to endure the financial strain of such an
excursion. The preparations to go were difficult, the actual experience was an empty pleasure, and the result often tragic for those who
did not succeed in contracting either the rich alliances or the remu-
nerative friendships on which they had staked their all.

These unpleasant truths Goldoni attempted to set forth agreeably
in *The Craze for a Sojourn in the Country* ("Le smanie della villeggiatura"), *The Adventures of a Sojourn in the Country* ("Le avventure della
villeggiatura"), and *The Return from a Sojourn in the Country* ("Il
ritorno dalla villeggiatura"). The dialogue of these plays is not, for
the most part, carried on in dialect; the characters, although they do
not belong to the aristocracy, are somewhat more cosmopolitan than
those in *The New House*. They include a jolly old citizen and his
daughter, the daughter's two lovers, one of whom is a spendthrift,
the spendthrift's vain and socially ambitious sister, and an unprincipled parasite. These six people go to a fashionable watering place,
where the parasite wins the hand of an elderly old maid, and return

to the city for the pairing off of the four young people. This plot has to be stretched rather thin to do service for three comedies, and the excellence of the trilogy depends not so much upon its story as upon the realistic details in which it abounds: the ladies' efforts to secure new clothes for the excursion, the servants' gossip about their employers, and the firm but polite refusal of Bernardino, a true *rustego*, to pay the debts of his spendthrift nephew.

Bernardino is a rather disagreeable person, but he is amiability itself compared to the leading character in *Master Todero the Grumbler, or The Disagreeable Old Man* ("Sior Todero Brontolon, o sia Il vecchio fastidioso"). Master Todero is avaricious, proud, and obstinate. He makes life miserable for everyone around him, especially for his independent daughter-in-law and his vacillating son. The domestic situation is something like that in *The Antiquary's Family*, with the tyrannical parent a father-in-law instead of a mother-in-law, and with a passion for antiques converted into an uncompromising intention to have one's own way.

Master Todero the Grumbler is the last but one of the comedies that Goldoni wrote for the theater of San Luca before he left Venice in 1762 and journeyed to Paris, in and near which he was to reside for the remaining thirty-one years of his life. The last play that he wrote before his departure is called *One of the Last Evenings of the Carnival* ("Una delle ultime sere di carnovale"). In it Goldoni bade farewell to his native city through the mouth of a designer of silk fabrics, who has received such an attractive offer from another country that he feels he must leave Venice, reluctant as he is to do so. Goldoni had been asked to come to the Comédie Italienne in Paris, and he decided that theatrical conditions in Venice made it wise for him to accept. Carlo Gozzi, his rival since 1759, had recently achieved phenomenal success with *The Love of the Three Oranges* ("L'amore delle tre melarancie"), a fantastic play composed in conscious imitation of the *commedia dell'arte* against which Goldoni had long been struggling. Therefore Goldoni believed that, as a writer of realistic comedy, he had better seek more appreciative audiences, which he expected to find in Paris. That his career in Paris proved a disappointment to him is not so sad a fact as that he felt himself unappreciated in Venice during the very time when he was doing some of his best work in his native city.

VI

By the time Goldoni arrived in Paris the French public had become accustomed to a kind of comedy very different from that of Molière, whose works the Italian dramatist knew and admired. Goldoni had the good taste to value *The Misanthrope* more than any other of Molière's plays, and he was delighted to be able to see that piece performed in Paris. In general, however, newer theatrical fashions had become the order of the day in the French capital. The profound common sense of Molière had given way to the hearty but shallow laughter of Jean François Regnard, Regnard's gaiety had withered before the cynical worldliness of Alain René Le Sage, Le Sage's hardness had been driven out by the delicate subtlety of Pierre de Marivaux, and Marivaux's analysis of the human heart had paved the way for the sentimental comedies of Philippe Destouches and Nivelle de La Chaussée. At the moment, Denis Diderot was the man of the hour in dramatic circles; with him Goldoni had an affinity which for a time threatened to cause serious complications. The resemblance between certain scenes in *The True Friend* and Diderot's *The Natural Son* ("Le Fils naturel") and the similarity of the titles *Il padre di famiglia* and *Le Père de famille* caused Diderot to be accused of plagiarism and as a result to be excessively annoyed with Goldoni. The personal dispute between them was finally settled in an amicable manner, but the important point about the incident is that French and Italian comedy had developed in much the same way during the eighteenth century. Goldoni had been able to retain more of Molière's spirit than had the French successors of that great dramatist, but like them he had been affected by sentimental influences in the direction of an earnest but feeble humanitarianism.

When Goldoni left Venice he had quite emancipated himself from the restrictions imposed by the *commedia dell'arte*. It was therefore a great blow to him to find, on arriving in Paris, that his employers at the Comédie Italienne expected him to provide them with scenarios for masked actors who were unaccustomed to memorizing speeches prepared in advance and who wished to compose their own dialogue extemporaneously. He says that he wrote some twenty-four scenarios during the two years that he was employed at the Comédie Italienne, but that he only set down words for those which he considered good enough to send back to Venice for performance there. Among the most successful of these Italian texts are *The Fan* ("Il ventaglio") and *The Marriage by Competition* ("Il matrimonio per concorso"), of which the former is one of Goldoni's best-known plays. It uses the technique of his social comedies like *The Coffee Shop*, *The Public Square*, and *The Squabbles at Chioggia*, in which the community is of more importance than the individual. Its scene is laid in a public place, upon which open the houses and shops of the fourteen characters, all of whom are discovered on the stage at the rise of the curtain engaged in various occupations connected with business or pleasure. Goldoni seems to have prided himself on this novel opening and on the dumb show at the beginning of the third act, artificial devices which are no doubt traceable to the renewed influence of the *commedia dell'arte* upon his work.

The plot of *The Fan* concerns the complications caused when the heroine unintentionally drops a fan from her balcony and it is broken by its fall. One of her two suitors buys another fan for her and entrusts it to a peasant girl, who also has two lovers. The heroine and the peasant girl's lovers misconstrue the transfer of the fan, and a double series of jealousies is thus set in motion. The fan begins to change hands with astonishing rapidity. It passes from lover to lover, is temporarily in the possession of each of the four men, and at the final curtain is presented to the heroine by the suitor who originally bought it for her. The movements of the fan give a liveliness to the plot which offsets the somewhat saccharine character of the principal lovers, each of whom is ready to faint on the slightest provocation. The peasant girl and her suitors are more realistically amusing, but the most finished comic character in *The Fan* is the Conte di Rocca Marina, a lineal successor of Don Marzio in *The Coffee Shop*. Like Don Marzio, the Conte is a meddler and a gossip, but he is a harmless, not a dangerous, member of society. An impoverished nobleman, he tries to insinuate himself into the good graces of all four suitors, from whose love affairs he is hoping to profit. At one point, the troublesome fan falls into the Conte's hands, and to all intents and purposes he sells it to the highest bidder. His stupidity helps to entangle the plot, and his pliability to unravel it. He is a noisy fly buzzing about the swiftly turning wheel of the play's complicated action.

The Marriage by Competition, which quickly followed *The Fan,* is another ingeniously contrived piece, without much subtlety of characterization. The story concerns two old men lodging in the same inn, one of whom has advertised to find a suitable mate for his daughter. The other fellow also has a daughter, the people who answer the advertisement get one girl mixed up with the other, and much jealousy and confusion ensue. The principal characters are, like Goldoni, Italians living in Paris, and there is a great deal of incidental discussion about the differences between France and Italy, their coinage, their cooking, and their conveyances. It is generally agreed that Paris is a far more luxurious and expensive city than Venice. The unpopularity of Italian comedy is explained, Parisian newspapers are characterized, and there is a detailed description of the new postal system, "la petite poste." Since the Italians in *The Marriage by Competition* encounter the same peculiar customs and manners that must have impressed Goldoni, this play is an important biographical document as well as an entertaining work of art.

Social distinctions are also touched on in *The Marriage by Competition.* The old gentleman who advertises for a son-in-law used to be the servant of the other father, and he is finally proved to be a defaulting merchant. The implication in this case seems to be that to act like an aristocrat or a menial is entirely suitable for a person born in either position, but that an unnatural change in one's status may cause absurdity and unhappiness. Goldoni's social views are further illustrated by the three plays that he wrote in Paris about the loves of Lindoro and Zelinda. In the original scenarios Lindoro and Zelinda, called Arlecchino and Camilla, were represented as servants of a very superior kind, faithful to each other in misfortune and holding up to themselves a high moral standard. The analysis of sentiment in these scenarios pleased the French taste of the day, and apparently they were well performed by sympathetic actors; but Goldoni feared that in Italy neither actors nor audiences could be found to appreciate the nobility of the lower classes. Therefore he gave more elegant names to his characters and explained that, although they were of honorable parentage, misfortunes had compelled them to take the humble positions which they occupy at the beginning of their story. The Lindoro-Zelinda plays are an indication of how thoroughly Goldoni's benevolent nature could fuse with the democratic spirit that was coming to be popular on the Parisian stage, without doing violence to the recognized social classifications that were a part of his Italian background.

An even closer fusion of Italian and French influences was accomplished by Goldoni at the age of sixty-four, seven years after his contract with the Comédie Italienne had terminated. In 1771 his *The Kindly Bear* ("Le Bourru bienfaisant"), a comedy written in French, was performed with great success at the Comédie Française and maintained its place in the repertory of that theater for many years. *The Kindly Bear* is a delightful play, in which underlying tenderness is hidden by a superficial gruffness in a way typical of Goldoni's whimsical inconsistency. He had already drawn various portraits of *rusteghi* in his Italian plays, and the conception of Géronte, a surly but softhearted old bachelor, is not a novel feature of his work. In fact, *The Kindly Bear* furnishes a mild summary of Goldoni's career, a recapitulation of what he had already accomplished, softened by the reminiscent musing of old age. It is a fitting, if gentle, conclusion to a varied and stormy career. Its plot is very slight: an apparently tyrannical uncle wishes his niece to marry the man of his choice and unjustly blames his nephew's wife for her husband's careless way of spending money. Actually Géronte has a very tender disposition and finally agrees to do just what the members of his family want him to.

The minor characters in *The Kindly Bear* turn out to be quite as surprisingly noble as the churlish Géronte. They are all well-intentioned, although sometimes a trifle misguided. Even the servants in this play are on the side of the angels. Géronte's valet endures his master's outbursts of temper with unwavering devotion, knowing that Géronte will soon repent of his violence and heal with kindness the wounds he has inflicted from anger. When the valet stumbles and falls while being chased by Géronte, the apparently infuriated man offers his own cane, and also a considerable sum of money, to the injured servant. Being crossed makes the rich old bachelor fly into a passion, but an appeal to his better impulses is immediately effective in overcoming his unreasonable irritability.

An equally amusing but less basic human contradiction is to be found in the last of Goldoni's plays, *The Ostentatious Miser* ("L'Avare fastueux"). This drama, likewise written in French, was produced at Fontainebleau, without success, in 1776, seventeen years before its author's death during the high tide of the French Revolution. Although *The Ostentatious Miser* does not concern itself with fundamental issues, it presents a neat contrast between reality and appearances, a situation which offers good material for comedy, as, in our own time, Goldoni's fellow countryman, Luigi Pirandello, has made plain. The principal figure in this play is a miser, the Comte de Chateaudor, who conceals his avarice under an appearance of lavish display. He loses the two young ladies whom at different times he hopes to marry, one of them because of his reputed extravagance, the other because he really is a miser. At the end of the comedy he is left without a mate, and the other characters pair off, much to his dismay. He is disowned by all his acquaintances, rather like Don Marzio at the close of *The Coffee Shop*. The comic intention in both these dramas is kept clearly in sight until the final curtain, somewhat at the expense of the human sympathy which Goldoni generally manages to instill into his literary works.

The Comte de Chateaudor is created in such a determinedly unsympathetic way that he resembles a satirical caricature. He has bought his title with money which he now regrets having spent; he plans to order fine clothes for his wedding and then to return them to the tailor after the ceremony; he wants his fiancée to wear jewelry which has been left with him on approval by a tradesman; he refuses money to a playwright who offers to praise his genealogy, even when threatened with blackmail by the desperate author. The Comte's character is a tissue of contradictions that makes him an incredible person. To offset him, Goldoni has inserted into the drama a more humane figure, who is almost equally exaggerated. The Marquis de Courbois has little money and is absurdly impractical in all his financial arrangements, but he is so genial and warmhearted that he gains the hand of a rich widow on the promise that he will allow her to manage his estates after they have been married. Like the blustering bear, Géronte, the Marquis de Courbois wins affection by his innate lovability and generosity. Goldoni seems to believe that human beings always have good intentions in the depths of their souls. It is only when their nature is perverted by unfavorable circumstances that they exhibit the abnormal eccentricities for which they may properly be ridiculed. The Marquis de Courbois is a more fully realized character than the Comte de Chateaudor. In his late years Goldoni could not put his whole heart into creating people that were unattractive in disposition and uncoöperative in dealing with their fellow men.

Throughout his career he found it difficult to reconcile his kindliness with his sense of decorum. Again and again he approached some important human problem with the steady view of the world necessary for sustained and authoritative comedy; then suddenly he sidestepped it with a merry smile and a contagious burst of laughter. His cheerfulness and gaiety carry many of his plays to dramatically effective conclusions, but they do not altogether make up for his lack of philosophical poise. Goldoni seems hardly to have understood the fundamental social incongruities of his day. He accepted certain contemporary conventions, such as that it was unwise to marry outside one's own class, that children should be obedient to parents, and that wives should be subject unto their husbands; but he could not maintain them against an attack from his own inner feelings. He felt convinced that people should be allowed to marry if they loved one another, that parents ought to be long-suffering and sympathetic, and that husbands should be chivalrous enough to carry out the wishes of their wives. In short, he believed in the ideal moral standards of any orthodox Christian sect. The difficulty came when he attempted to fuse the conventional exterior and the idealistic core of his personality into coherent artistic expression.

It was almost impossible for Goldoni to harmonize a belief in pure democracy with the formality existing in Venetian society of the eighteenth century, so he invented the denouement of *Pamela* to overcome that obstacle. It was unnatural for him to allow cynical young men to trick their tyrannical fathers, so he softened his Pantalones until they became kind and understanding observers of youthful folly. It was disagreeable for him to think of undutiful wives, so he attacked the institution of *cicisbeismo* with persistency and vigor. In all these cases there remains a discrepancy between what Goldoni thinks and what he feels that often fails to carry complete conviction to another person's mind or emotions.

The Italian dramatist is most completely at one with himself when he has created a set of diverse characters who can be made to live together intimately in peace and tranquillity. From *The Coffee Shop*, in which Don Marzio was outlawed because of his unfriendly attitude towards society, to *The Fan*, in which all the conflicting interests are reconciled somewhat too artfully, similar issues are presented and similar settlements are proposed. When individual characters merge into the general background and when a community becomes the real hero of a play, Goldoni achieves an artistic and social harmony, which is his chief claim to distinction in the sphere of comedy. It is natural that, as a result, the dramatist's range should be restricted and that some of his most notable comedies should treat narrow phases of Italian life, that these limited canvases should frequently be grouped together into trilogies, and that no one of them should stand out as an undisputed masterpiece. Goldoni had the creative energy to picture the social confusion of the modern world under many different guises, and he had extreme facility in transporting the characters of his imagination to the boards of a theater. He failed to perceive that good intentions are not powerful enough to overcome vital antagonisms in principle. He lacked the constructive wisdom to take a broad view of the hostile elements present in a social organism. Goldoni's genial gaiety is so infectious that his comedies exert a strong temporary fascination, but his conception of human relationships is so shallow that, on continued acquaintance, his plays often seem disappointing. Like Charles Dickens, he lets high spirits and enthusiasm for morality take the place of a constructive intelligence. His comedy is seldom well-balanced, but it is always vivacious and it is always charming.

CHAPTER VIII

Sentimental and Fantastic Comedy: Lessing and Raimund

I

GOLDONI wrote his last play in 1776, but he did not die until seventeen years later, at the advanced age of eighty-six. During the thirty-one years of his residence in Paris the Italian playwright had seen a great change take place in French life and literature. The irresponsible court of Louis XV, to which Goldoni had attached himself, was succeeded by the disastrous reign of Louis XVI and the chaotic period of the Revolution. Goldoni, a cautious conservative, clung to the *ancien régime* as long as he was able to, but never with such enthusiasm that he became an object of suspicion to the popular party. In July 1792 the Italian dramatist lost his royal pension, when many other perquisites granted by the King were suspended; but in the next February the National Convention, at the suggestion of a brother of André Chenier's, voted to restore Goldoni's fixed income in consideration of his old age, his poverty, and his devotion to his adopted country. Ironically enough, Goldoni had died in obscurity the day before this resolution was passed. He must have been too old and feeble to take any active part in the political events of his last days in Paris, but had he been able to do so he would no doubt have found difficulty in defining his intellectual position. There is no reason to believe that he was, like his great French contemporary, Beaumarchais, an unconscious prophet of the new dispensation.

Pierre Augustin Caron, called Beaumarchais, had in his own writing followed rather closely the popular development of French drama during Goldoni's thirty years in Paris. Emphasis upon bourgeois life had tended to diminish both the grandeur of tragedy and the detachment of comedy; the two genres were becoming fused in a new and democratic form of art, to which Beaumarchais gave the name of *drame*. Diderot had initiated this fashion; Michel Jean Sedaine had developed it; the unscrupulous Beaumarchais decided to exploit it. In his earliest *drame*, *Eugénie*, the villainous seducer repents, and his victim forgives him, because of her love for their as yet unborn child; in *The Two Friends* ("Les Deux Amis"), tragedy is averted by the generosity of the friends about financial matters and the noble self-effacement of a rich man, who is an obstacle to the marriage of two young lovers; even in *The Barber of Seville* ("Le Barbier de Séville"), Beaumarchais's first great success, which was performed on February 23, 1775, the sentimental note was not entirely neglected. The heroine thinks for a moment that her lover has betrayed her to his unprincipled master. Then she learns that master and man are, like Snowdoun's knight and Scotland's king, one and the same person.

For the most part, however, *The Barber of Seville* is a dry and detached comedy. Its triumph, Figaro, is a descendant of the clever slave of Latin drama, the *gracioso* of the Spanish stage, and Arlecchino of the *commedia dell'arte*, brought up to date by Beaumarchais, who makes Figaro's past career very similar to his own. In the famous autobiographical passage which ends, "I hasten to laugh at everything for fear of being obliged to weep at it" (*Je me presse de rire de tout, de peur d'être obligé d'en pleurer*) Figaro tells of the difficulties that come to a writer from envy and misunderstanding, to a playwright from the hisses of an organized cabal, and to a subordinate from the tyranny of his superiors. Beaumarchais was thinking of his own sufferings at the hands of the law, the press, and the nobility when he had Figaro denounce in somewhat guarded terms the corruption of contemporary society. Figaro is so concerned with the money he owes for rent, and for his prestige as a barber, that he is not so efficient in helping the lovers as he might have been, but he is one of the gayest and wittiest rogues in all comic drama.

The sequel of *The Barber of Seville*, *The Marriage of Figaro* ("Le Mariage de Figaro"), first performed in 1784, is as different from its predecessor as is the music composed for the two plays by Rossini and Mozart, the former somewhat florid and showy, the latter no less melodious but more exquisite and sparkling. *The Marriage of Figaro* is, in every respect, a maturer piece of work than *The Barber of Seville*. The intrigue is more complicated, the characters are more numerous, and Figaro himself has become a more profound critic of society as a *valet de chambre* than he was as a barber. He fears tha his master will not keep his promise to relinquish *le droit du seigneur* (the right of a feudal lord to the virginity of a female vassal on her wedding night); he suspects that his own fiancée is only too willing to accept the Count's dishonorable proposals. From these two sources comes his distrust of women and noblemen, which culminates in the great monologue of the fifth act. In the early part of the play Figaro has made some palpable incidental hits at the expense of courtiers and politics, the English language, and the little blind god; while he is waiting under the great chestnut trees to observe his fiancée's supposed infidelity, he unlocks his soul in a denunciation of the organized society which has warped and thwarted his life. The nobles, who have taken no trouble except to be born, are vividly contrasted with the ordinary man, who is not allowed to earn an honest living. The bitterness of Figaro's satire helps to explain the excesses of the French Revolution.

How Goldoni, living in Paris at the height of Beaumarchais's popularity as a dramatist, could say that *The Marriage of Figaro* was written merely to amuse and divert the public is incomprehensible, unless one realizes that a revival of Goldoni's *The Kindly Bear* had been projected for the year 1784 and that this revival was three times postponed, perhaps as a result of the success achieved by Beaumarchais's masterpiece. *The Marriage of Figaro* does far more than provoke empty laughter, as Goldoni admitted when he added that the piece contained plenty of satire directed at general classes in society, not at specific individuals. Its various characters represent the elegance of the aristocracy and the vivacity of the common people, the formality and stupidity of the law, the beginning of adolescent passion, and the bitterness of a woman who has been betrayed in her youth. The two latter elements introduce a tinge of sentimentality, which was further developed in the sequel's sequel, *The Guilty Mother* ("La Mère coupable"), a dreary piece almost totally without artistic merit. Beaumarchais's wit took precedence over contemporary sentimental conventions when he produced work of enduring literary quality, as he did twice in his career.

Across the Channel, in England, a somewhat similar literary phenomenon was taking place at almost the same time. Oliver Goldsmith's *She Stoops to Conquer* was acted in 1773, Richard Brinsley Sheridan's *The Rivals* in 1775, and *The School for Scandal* in 1777.

All three of these plays have an incongruous way of mingling mild geniality with a sturdy sense of humor, a combination which was more delicately adjusted in the case of Goldsmith than in that of Sheridan. Tony Lumpkin is the complete expression of Goldsmith's comic philosophy. He is a liar and a drunkard, and he gets into many tight places; but his charm and his ingenuity save him in the end. His lack of formal education does not interfere with his mother wit. He is able to help the lovers and also to get what he wants for himself. When at last he pairs off with Bet Bouncer, the relief of comedy and the satisfaction of morality are achieved in almost equal proportions.

Goldsmith cloaks his sentimental bias in the trappings of farce, except at the conclusion of the play, where Miss Neville refuses to elope without the knowledge of her guardian and is suitably rewarded for her magnanimity. In *The Rivals* Sheridan satirizes the romantic notions which often lead to an elopement and at the same time draws, in the character of Julia Melville, a sentimental heroine of the most tearful sort. In *The School for Scandal* he was even more at odds with his own convictions. As its title implies, this play has a satirical background. Its sparkling display of social foibles had not been equaled in England since the days of Wycherley and Congreve. In the hypocrisy of Joseph Surface it laughs at a parade of insincere morality, but it also contains a spendthrift with a heart of gold in spite of his vices and a young country wife who, after a career of folly and vanity, comfortably settles back into the arms of her devoted old husband. Charles Surface and Lady Teazle must be considered as characters of a sentimental hue; the Sneerwells and the Backbites belong as clearly to a straightforward comedy of manners. Despite this inconsistency, Sheridan's plays have held the stage longer than many more sound and concentrated examples of comic art. The confusion in them caused by the conflicting claims of sentimental and critical comedy is more than offset by the exuberance and variety of such characterizations as those of Bob Acres and Mrs. Malaprop in *The Rivals*, of Puff and Sir Fretful Plagiary in *The Critic*.

Beaumarchais and Goldsmith and Sheridan all attempted to grapple with the dilemma in which a writer of comedy found himself at the close of the eighteenth century. During the course of that hundred years the aristocratic tone of feudal society had almost disappeared. The drawing rooms of the bluestockings were breaking down the intellectual barriers between the sexes, and the rising middle class was gradually demolishing the distinctions between the nobility and ordinary people. Literary categories were also becoming less inflexibly rigid; comedy could scarcely expect to escape the influence of the "goddess of the woeful countenance — the sentimental Muse." The problem was roughly the same in France and in England, but the solution of it in the two countries was strikingly different. Beaumarchais began with a foundation of bourgeois drama and gradually lifted himself above it by means of his keen observation and his incisive wit. His criticism of society was half humorous and half deadly serious. The democratic spirit found in the creator of Figaro a spokesman for its aspirations, if not a participant in its activities. Beaumarchais, at heart an aristocrat, went down to defeat like many another member of the old order, with his colors flying and a jest upon his lips.

In England the political strife was not so bitter, because the bloodless revolution of 1688 had taken off the edge of factional dispute. Restoration comedy suffered as a result, and the eighteenth century saw a continuous decline in dramatic creativeness. Then suddenly Goldsmith and Sheridan appeared, each in his own way trying to offset sentimentality by humor. Goldsmith did it more imaginatively, but also more superficially; Sheridan did it less subtly, but with more penetrating intelligence and with greater brilliance of expression. The English authors seem naïve beside the Frenchman in logical power and in clarity of thought. Beaumarchais was fighting a losing battle, however. His Figaro was the final flicker of the comic spirit in classic drama, making its last stand against the intrusions of the modern scientific world. Goldsmith and Sheridan, too, thought they were espousing the cause of true comedy, but in spite of fans and furbelows they were as much affected by the artistic spirit of the coming age as Beaumarchais was by its social principles. No one of these three dramatists succeeded so well in blending traditional standards and liberal ideas as had already been done before their time in Germany. The dramatic career of Gotthold Ephraim Lessing marks an important stage in the evolution of modern comedy.

II

The period of Lessing's productivity in comedy is confined to the early portion of his life. Born in 1729, he is supposed to have written his first drama during his schooldays at Meissen, where he was a student between the ages of twelve and seventeen. Most of his comic plays and fragments were composed between 1746 and 1750. *Minna von Barnhelm*, his masterpiece in this form, was created between the years 1763 and 1765. Thus Lessing's comedies come well before the time in which Goldsmith, Sheridan, and Beaumarchais were to make their contributions to dramatic literature, and during the period in which Holberg and Goldoni were still actively writing plays. Holberg was nearing the close of his career, and Goldoni was at the peak of his accomplishment, when Lessing began to write comedies. Although Lessing died in 1781, twelve years before the end of Goldoni's long life, he is to all intents and purposes a follower of Holberg and Goldoni. He made use of works by both these dramatists, borrowing situations from a number of Holberg's plays and undertaking a German version of *The Fortunate Heir* ("L'erede fortunata"), one of Goldoni's less well-known and least successful efforts. It is typical of Lessing's treatment of his sources that the German writer consistently attempts to dignify the characters of Goldoni's subplot, giving them more justifiable reasons for displaying their weaknesses, which, at bottom, remain weaknesses still.

The influence of Holberg first made itself felt in Lessing's earliest comedy, *Damon, or True Friendship* ("Die wahre Freundschaft"), which also shows similarities to French and English dramas by La Chaussée and Shadwell, but which, in spite of these resemblances, is an original, juvenile study on the subject of friendship. As in Holberg's *The Fortunate Shipwreck*, contradictory reports about the loss of merchant ships bring out the true nature of the rival suitors for a lady's hand. One lover offers to sacrifice his own interests to those of his rival; the other is willing to be successful at the expense of his friend's happiness. In Lessing the less worthy suitor does not win the heroine, as he does in Shadwell's *Bury Fair*, and the more admirable of the two does not give her up, as in La Chaussée's *The School for Friends* ("L'École des amis"). A straight course is steered between realism and sentimentalism; the hero is a true friend and yet not an insipid lover. Damon is contrasted with an unscrupulous man of business and with his hypocritical friend Leander; for the failings of both of them his virtue furnishes a touchstone. The heroine's sprightly maid contrives to clarify the attitudes of the two lovers and to secure her mistress's hand for the true friend, while the false one is forgiven for his treachery. In the end justice triumphs, without a complete loss of comic impartiality.

From the outset of his career Lessing showed the serious nature of his genius, but he attempted at first to divert it into comic channels. He succeeded in reconciling contrary interests in his first comedy, but he showed that he appreciated the insoluble nature of the problem he had raised, when at the end of the play he had his heroine say: "Damon! Damon! I am afraid, I am afraid, I will be jealous. Not on account of any woman, but on account of Leander."

The difficulty of a perfect reconciliation between love and friendship is no greater than the marked antithesis that exists between higher learning and simple human intercourse. Holberg had indicated the social implications of this theme in *Erasmus Montanus*, and Lessing undertook to treat the same subject in his second completed play, *The Young Scholar* ("Der junge Gelehrte"). He modified his material with deft touches of sentiment, derived from Marivaux, and adorned it with vigorous realistic strokes, drawn from keen observation and painful experience. With Lessing, it is not so much a question of what harm the educated man can do to the structure of society as it is that a pedant is ridiculous in the affairs of love and that an unsuccessful pedant is ridiculous even in the affairs of pedantry. The humor of *The Young Scholar* springs from the fact that Damis has written an essay on "Monads," with which he confidently expects to win the prize offered at the University of Berlin for a paper on that subject. Throughout the play he is constantly sending his servant to get the latest post from Berlin, only to learn at the end that he has not succeeded in the contest on which he has set his heart and risked his reputation.

In the plot of this play Damis figures as the conventionally obnoxious suitor of the heroine. His successful rival provides no standard by which to measure the young scholar's limitations, but in the course of the intrigue various side lights are thrown upon Damis' academic pretensions. He at first refuses to marry the girl of his father's choice, because his only loves are Greek poetesses; then he is captivated by a mischievous maid when she flatters him on his great capacities and wide fame; at last he agrees to marry the heroine, because many famous wise men have had troublesome wives. When he learns that she is kind and good, he sticks to her because her stupidity will increase his glory; he struggles in vain to write a suitable epithalamion for their wedding, and only when he hears of the failure of his prize essay does he decide to give up his fiancée, his servant, and his ungrateful fatherland, to travel alone throughout the world. Damis is a failure in his profession, an indifferent lover, and a useless member of society, which he forswears of his own volition to seek fresh woods and pastures new. He is not ejected by the irate community or forced to reform, as was generally the case in Holberg's comedies under similar circumstances. Lessing was too kind a person to have his characters suffer severely, but he did not hesitate to point out their absurd deviations from normal human conduct.

Damis in *The Young Scholar*, like Damon in Lessing's first play, is contrasted with two different types of men, who serve as foils for the young student's eccentricities. One is his servant, and the other is his father. The servant thinks his master a fool and flatters him for his own ends. He has no scruples about betraying him, for love or for money, and ultimately takes leave of him with the greatest satisfaction. The father, whose worldly interests are politics and money-making, is throughout the comedy at cross-purposes with his son as to whether or not Damis shall marry the heroine. The heroine's maid, Lisette, makes difficulties for them both by working for the romantic lovers in a rather underhanded way. In all of Lessing's early plays Lisette helps the lovers to triumph over deceitful friends and stupid rivals. She embodies the spirit of thoughtless fun so attractively that one does not stop to consider whether her questionable methods are justified by the noble ends she has in view.

Throughout his early comedies Lessing experiments with possible combinations of the comic and the sentimental in an effort to satisfy his own fastidious nature and the varying tastes of his audience. It was quite suitable that, as a schoolboy, he should have been shocked by hypocrisy in friendship and amused by the self-importance of would-be scholars. It was equally natural that, at the ages from seventeen to nineteen, he should have begun to be interested in relations between the sexes. His method of approach was still mainly literary, however. The use of English, French, and Danish drama, which had been evident in his first two plays, was further continued in his next two comedies, *The Woman-Hater* ("Der Misogyn") and *The Old Maid* ("Die alte Jungfer"). Holberg is still much in evidence, reminiscences of Molière and Congreve appear, and several minor authors seem to have been laid under contribution. In both plays Lisette has a part, but she is not such an important character as she had been in Lessing's earlier comedies.

In both these plays Lessing seems to be upholding marriage against the ridicule that it is easy to level against that institution. Wumshäter, the woman-hater, has been married three times, and yet, inconsistently enough, he has decided to disapprove of the fair sex, root and branch. Jungfer Ohldin, the old maid, has had eleven proposals of marriage that have come to nothing. She is now determined to secure her twelfth suitor in spite of all opposition. The misogynist finally has to submit to the marriages of his son and daughter, although he still prophesies disaster for both bridegrooms. The old maid perseveres in her search for a husband and at last succeeds in obtaining one, in spite of the unfair trickery of the envious people who surround her. The widower is made to appear wrong and the old maid right: Wumshäter's children both find worthy mates; Herr von Schlag, the retired captain who marries Jungfer Ohldin, is represented as a model of all the virtues. Herr von Schlag is of high rank, but he is financially embarrassed. Therefore, when he gets the opportunity to make a rich match that will enable him to pay off his debts, he is glad to marry, even though he has no overwhelming inclination for the bride. Nevertheless, Herr von Schlag is not a vulgar fortune-hunter. He is ready to compromise with his fiancée's legal heir over their future financial prospects, and he seems to have only the kindliest feelings toward the old maid whom he is about to make his wife. There is no romantic emotion in *The Old Maid*, only pleasant common sense which straightens out all the difficulties that threaten the peace of mind of the principal characters.

Both *The Woman-Hater* and *The Old Maid* are more successful in detail than as complete works of art. Each has rather lively dialogue, and in each there are incidental scenes that create an agreeable sort of humor. *The Woman-Hater* contains not only the conventional character of an absurdly biased woman-hater but also, incongruously enough, a girl disguised as a man. The comic, not the romantic, aspects of her situation are emphasized by having another girl fall in love with her. The complications are resolved when, at the end of the play, she appears dressed half in men's and half in women's clothes. The ramifications of the plot are diverting, but upon close inspection *The Woman-Hater* is seen to be as unnatural a creation as a girl who assumes two sexes at the same time. It sets out to treat the relations between men and women honestly, but it ends as a hermaphroditical concoction which is neither powerful nor ingratiating.

The Old Maid is undoubtedly a more important play than *The Woman-Hater*, although it, too, is badly constructed. Besides having an anomalous effect, produced by the fact that the noble hero is an impoverished fortune-seeker, this drama causes a recurrent feeling that the story of the old maid's courtship is merely a peg on which to hang a variety of comic portraits. There are a pair of professional matchmakers who close and open the play, themselves married and ready to quarrel on the slightest provocation; there is a talkative and jocose fellow who satirically congratulates the old maid on her physical charms and who slanders Herr von Schlag to her, without any noticeable effect on the action; most striking of all, there is a poet who is hired to write an epithalamium, for which he sadly needs to be paid. He is an impecunious person burdened with a wife whom he does not love and a number of noisy children whom he must support. He rails against marriage, like Wumshäter in the previous play, and he disapproves of freethinking, a subject which Lessing was to treat more thoroughly in a later comedy. His poetry is worthless, and he is scandalously in debt. He is sensitive about his profession and furious when he is mistaken for a tailor. He is pathetic and at the same time ridiculous. Which of the contradictory elements in his character Lessing considered of greater consequence he does not make quite clear, and the same thing may be said of Jungfer Ohldin and Herr von Schlag. Is she ridiculously amorous, and is he consciously heartless? Or are they both middle-aged people who have found out that to live alone is a miserable business and decide that to share each other's weaknesses will be to strengthen their separate isolated positions?

In charitably suggesting that his characters should be given the benefit of this doubt, Lessing goes quite contrary to the practice of the English Restoration dramatists, who almost invariably present their people in an unfavorable light in order to achieve a devastating satiric effect. Jungfer Ohldin, for instance, is hardly recognizable as Lady Wishfort in Congreve's *The Way of the World*, who, from the point of view of plot, is undoubtedly her prototype. When Lessing took a plot from English comedy, as he seems often to have done, he always planned to humanize the characters within the comic framework he had selected. Three of his extant scenarios, intended for comedies which he never executed, illustrate his method. *The Credulous Man* ("Der Leichtgläubige") was to develop the subplot of *The Country Wife*, but Lessing's principal character would presumably have lacked the dash of petty egotism which makes Wycherley's Sparkish a repulsive personality. *The Good Man* ("Der gute Mann") was to have made use of the Plyant plot from Congreve's *The Double-Dealer*, with Lord Plyant changed from a simple fool into a kind and wise man. *The Would-be Wits* ("Die Witzlinge") was to be drawn from Shadwell's *Bury Fair*. In this case Lessing would not have had to alter his source greatly; *Bury Fair* is one of the earliest comedies in English to display genuinely sentimental tendencies. It was natural that Lessing should have been fond of this play, from which he frequently borrows material congenial to his tastes.

In all Lessing's early comedies — and his projected imitations of Restoration drama may be considered under that head — there is an evident struggle between the traditionally comic point of view and what may be called a more imaginative attitude towards human nature. Lessing draws the hypocritical friend, the pedantic scholar, the woman-hater, and the old maid, but besides them there are to be found the true friend, the noble lover, the understanding woman, and the honest old bachelor. Sometimes sentiment prevails, and sometimes comedy; occasionally an almost exact balance between the two moods is achieved, but it is rarely a convincing one. The difficulty in accomplishing this feat may explain why Lessing did not fill out his scenarios based upon Restoration comedy. The problems presented by them may have been too complex to be carried through to a harmonious conclusion. When English incidents do appear in Lessing's work, they are often adapted out of all recognition in an effort to secure an atmosphere of decorum. Unlike Wycherley and Congreve, Lessing tended to emphasize the benevolence of mankind, as if good intentions were a sufficient excuse for all the imperfections of human nature.

III

The direction of Lessing's development was toward serious sentimental drama away from the superficialities of social comedy, but in the process of making this change some unusual modifications of comic technique were evolved. *The Freethinker* ("Der Freigeist"), the most impressive of the works that were written in 1749 and 1750, is an indirect attack upon those people in Lessing's time who regarded freethinking as an unforgivable heresy, but it is more a straightforward apology for free thought than an assault on the narrow-mindedness of religious bigots. This shift in emphasis has a very real bearing upon the tone of the comedy that results. The humor, which had formerly been a matter of primary interest, has now become of secondary importance. The characters are first made basically admirable. Then their noble qualities are expressed in exaggerated forms which seem ridiculous to the outside world. The point of the action is not to reform the characters, who are in no need of conversion, but to bring out the true excellence of their natures, which has been hidden under a deceptive exterior.

The farcical appearance of *The Freethinker* tends at first to conceal its finely tempered point. There are two leading figures in this play: a rich clergyman who proves to be more human than his noble pretensions would suggest, and a poor freethinker, who is not so narrow-minded as he seems to be. The action of the play shows how these exponents of two apparently irreconcilable points of view come to understand and appreciate each other in spite of their great outward differences. The central principle of *The Freethinker* is laid down early in the play by the heroine's old father, when he remarks, "I am only too well convinced that all honorable people believe in the same way" (*Ich bin es nur allzuwohl überzeugt, dass alle ehrliche Leute einerlei glauben*). He is sure that the clergyman and freethinker are not so unlike as at bottom they appear to be. His contention is supported by the way in which the plot is worked out. Theophan, the clergyman, is, from the first, eager to show a Christian spirit towards Adrast, the freethinker, and Adrast is equally resolved to have nothing to do with a man whom he considers a professional philanthropist. The dispute hinges upon whether a man can be friends with one individual and at the same time share in the expansive spirit of true religion.

The misunderstandings between Theophan and Adrast are complicated by their love affairs. The clergyman is engaged to a pious young lady and the freethinker to her gay sister, but each is in love with the other's fiancée. They end by exchanging mates, thereby driving home Lessing's point that coöperation between the spiritual and physical elements in life is advantageous to both of them. The heroine's conservative grandmother hopes that Adrast may be converted to religion by his godly wife and that Theophan may convert his frivolous bride, but Lessing refuses to commit himself on these points.

The main plot of *The Freethinker* is concerned with Theophan's attempts to gain Adrast's friendship. Adrast is poor, as freethinkers in a religious community are apt to be. Theophan tries to reach the agnostic's heart through his pocketbook. Theophan wishes his generosity to be anonymous, but Adrast ultimately learns the identity of his benefactor and imagines that Theophan is motivated by revenge, not kindliness. Theophan is furious at having his actions misinterpreted, completely loses all self-control, and tells Adrast what he honestly thinks of his selfishness. Then, for the first time, Adrast is willing to listen because, for the first time, he is convinced of the clergyman's honesty. Ultimately, as each sees that the other's point of view is not diametrically opposed to his own, the two apparent rivals become friends.

The servants of Theophan and Adrast are made to carry out the opposing attitudes of their masters to absurd lengths, in a scene which is a refined imitation of incidents from Holberg's plays. In comparison with the crude and spontaneous Holberg, Lessing is civilized and sophisticated. Holberg is aware of growing social distinctions but does not know quite what attitude to take toward them. Lessing has become accustomed to the subtleties of formal society but is upset by the lack of moral stamina which underlies the superficial complacence of a cultivated community. This contrast gives comic point to Lessing's treatment of freethinking as a conviction which is honest but unconventional, sincere but disagreeable.

It is clear that, on the whole, Lessing approves of Theophan, the clergyman, but is more interested in Adrast, the freethinker. Adrast is an intricate and baffling character. His personality is never completely realized, although his psychology is minutely examined. In the course of the play Lessing lets fall a number of hints to help explain the peculiar rigidity of the freethinker's temperament. We learn that one of Adrast's reasons for hating men of religion is that his sister married a clergyman who defrauded him of a large sum of money; we hear from Adrast's servant that his master has been a great traveler and so has lacked the stabilizing influence of a permanent home; we realize that Adrast is put in the difficult position of seeing a clergyman betrothed to the girl whom he loves. In drawing him, Lessing has achieved a mood that hovers delicately between intelligent criticism and genuine admiration. The balance between these two antagonistic views is nicely maintained, but beneath the surface a serious emotional undercurrent makes itself felt. Lessing was too intimately associated with practical social problems, raised in his own day by the spread of free thought, to devote his main attention to describing superficial differences of behavior, which spring from contrasting philosophies of life.

The virtues and defects of *The Freethinker* are to be explained by its author's intense absorption in the world of contemporary affairs. *The Jews* ("Die Juden") is a more obvious piece of propaganda, as Lessing evidently meant that it should be; he gave its final title a plural form, although only one Jew takes part in the action. The unnamed Traveler who saves a rich Baron from being robbed cannot accept either the money or the wife offered him as a reward. The Traveler, who has heard the Baron express his generally unfavorable opinion of the Jewish race, is, as he admits at the end of this one-act comedy, himself a Jew. The Baron's expression of his anti-Semitic opinions and the Traveler's defense of his race constitute the intellectual body of *The Jews*, which is otherwise a light comedy of manners, with elements drawn from Sir John Vanbrugh's *The Relapse*. It contrasts the obstinacy and prejudice to be found in the Baron's country household with the benignity and tolerance of the cosmopolitan Traveler.

The Jews contains the kernel of Lessing's poetic masterpiece,

Nathan the Wise ("Nathan der Weise"), written in 1778 and 1779. This dramatic poem can hardly be called a comedy, although it contains plenty of contrasts which would have made good comic material. A hypocrite, a freethinker, and a mystic, Christians, Jews, and Mohammedans are all bound together by Nathan's parable of the rings into an idealistic vision of human unity and coöperation. The childish piety of Daja and the naïve obedience of the Lay Brother appear mildly amusing when contrasted with the divine wisdom of Nathan and the diabolic craftiness of the Patriarch, but in general the tone of Lessing's poem transcends worldly considerations. It is a carefully planned allegorical narrative, in which the brotherhood of mankind is embodied in the relationship that exists between Recha and the Templar. The girl, brought up as a Jew, and the man, who has revolted from conventional Christianity, are both found to be of Mohammedan blood, in fact to be children of the same parents. They cannot, therefore, be joined in marriage, as had been proposed in the play's more romantic moments. They must be content with the less intense satisfaction of having been born into the world under similar circumstances and with a similar inheritance. This lack of a conventional love affair in *Nathan the Wise* heightens the superhuman qualities of the subject, and a similar effect is obtained to a slighter degree in *The Jews*, when the Traveler refuses the hand of the Baron's daughter. The atmosphere of *The Jews* is not in the least rarefied, as is that of *Nathan the Wise*, but the two plays breathe the same spirit of religious tolerance. Both of them were stimulated by Lessing's indignation that his Jewish friends and acquaintances were not given an equal opportunity with their more purely Aryan fellow countrymen.

A subordinate development of this same theme is entrusted to the low-life characters in *The Jews*, who carry out their part in the plot realistically and humorously. The Traveler's servant does not know of his master's racial descent and feels very much cheated on learning that he has been employed by a Jew, but he is quite appeased by money and agrees to continue in the Traveler's service. The Baron's dishonest servants blame the Jews, who are natural scapegoats, for the robbery they have themselves attempted. Later their deceit is detected by the Traveler, whose suspicions of them are aroused by their unnecessarily abusive remarks about his race. By these two minor episodes Lessing suggests that a prejudice against Jews is often based on trivial considerations; also, that if it is indulged without restraint it will lead to greater and greater animosity, which will in time destroy the unscrupulous persons who have exploited it. The generally humane tone of *The Jews* foreshadows Lessing's career as a writer of tragedy and as a dramatic poet, but these developments were not to come until later. Meanwhile, perhaps by way of reaction, he devoted himself to some comparatively lighthearted and unpretentious imitations of Latin comedy.

The only work of this nature which Lessing completed is *The Treasure* ("Der Schatz"), written in 1750, at about the same time as the composition of *The Freethinker* and *The Jews*, or soon thereafter. *The Treasure* is based on the *Trinummus*, one of Plautus' more edifying plays, but one still very far from Lessing's goal of usefulness to contemporary society. It is noticeable that *The Treasure*, although not definitely located in the Roman world, is also not brought up to date by being laid in any recognizable modern city. There is almost no local color to be found in it; Lessing's purpose seems to have been to make the story universal, not particular, in its appeal. He has sought to humanize the characters, and in doing so he has lost the antithesis between a selfish wastrel and an unselfish friend which furnished the backbone of the *Trinummus*. He has the clever servant, who makes an unavoidable mistake in Plautus, tell so many lies that his detection is the result of his own unscrupulousness. By a number of slight touches he suffuses Plautus' complicated plot with an aura of tenderness, without destroying either its external morality or its underlying gaiety.

Lessing used another of Plautus' more moral plays, the *Stichus*, as the basis of his fragment *Women Will Be Women* ("Weiber sind Weiber"), in which he experimented with feminine psychology, drawing two heroines, a sedate and a vivacious one, much as he had done in *The Freethinker*. In his proposed treatment of Plautus' *Pseudolus*, which is included among his fragments under the title of *Justin*, he had greater difficulties than in his other Plautan adaptations, because the *Pseudolus* is one of the Latin dramatist's most ruthless and cynical comedies. He planned some changes in the plot in an effort to fit it to modern times and modern taste, but the proposed alterations did not seem to please him. He relinquished the idea of elaborating *Justin*, as he did that of finishing *Women Will Be Women*, leaving *The Treasure* as his only completed comedy based on classical precedent.

Lessing's experiments with Plautus are very illuminating as to the nature of his dramatic gift. He admired intellectually the form of Latin literature, but he could not imitate the impartial spirit of true classicism, at least in matters of comedy. He did not have much more success with the writers of the comedy of manners. He found himself most at home with those dramatists who were experimenting with the sentimental fringe of human nature. The Lisettes that appear in all his comedies through 1750, with the exception of *The Treasure* (which, like its Roman model, has no feminine characters at all), seem to have stepped out of the plays of Marivaux, and his heroes, who are proved to be more noble at heart than their actions would imply, have much in common with those of George Farquhar and Sir Richard Steele. The dramatic art of Lessing was gradually becoming more serious in matter as well as in manner. Sentimental comedy is not very far from domestic tragedy. A play like *The Jews*, in which the heroine does not succeed in securing the man whom she wishes to marry, prepares the way for Lessing's experiment with *Miss Sara Sampson*, in which a happy ending of the love affair is prevented by the heroine's poisoning her rival.

IV

Miss Sara Sampson was written in 1755. Based on Shadwell's comedy *The Squire of Alsatia* and Charles Johnson's tragedy, *Caelia, or The Perjured Lover*, it illustrates very distinctly the fusion of dramatic genres which took place in the middle of the eighteenth century. George Lillo had experimented with it in England. Diderot and Sedaine were to try their hands at it in France. It is significant that, whereas the French dramatists let their plays end happily after putting their characters through the most excruciating tortures, Lillo and Lessing seemed to feel that a tragic conclusion was demanded by the suffering that had preceded it. If Lessing had allowed Miss Sara Sampson to survive her trials some of the unintentionally ridiculous moments in the action would have been avoided, but the emotional force of the story would also have been considerably weakened. A drab neutrality is often the result of attempting to combine tragedy and comedy.

Lessing seems to have realized the difficulty in mingling the genres. During his last years he devoted less time and attention to the theater. Before he entirely forswore the active stage, however, he made one more attempt at tragedy and one more at comedy, in each case composing his best play of the kind. The tragedy was *Emilia Galotti*, based on the classical story of Virginia, which he completed in 1772, and the comedy was *Minna von Barnhelm, or The Soldier's Fortune* ("Das Soldatenglück"), which was published and performed in 1767. The latter has been called the first modern comedy in any European language. It is certainly Lessing's comic masterpiece, as well as the most substantial comedy to which German literature can lay claim.

Minna von Barnhelm is an extraordinary play which fits into no accepted category and defies rigid classification. It has few literary ancestors, either in plot or spirit. It springs almost entirely from Lessing's own experiences and critical standards. Its action was all but contemporary with the writing, taking place shortly after the Seven Years' War, which came to a close with the Peace of Hubertusburg in 1763. Its story reflects the intense ill feeling between Prussia and Saxony which existed during the aftermath of the war. The principal character, who in spite of the play's title is not Minna von Barnhelm but Major von Tellheim, was almost certainly suggested by Lessing's warm and close friendship with Major von Kleist, who had been mortally wounded at the Battle of Kunnersdorf in 1759. Lessing firmly believed that ethical considerations were more important than artistic ones. He bent all his artistic abilities to a piece of work which he hoped would improve the situation of mankind in his own day and age. In *Minna von Barnhelm* he undertook to depict existing political conditions and to suggest certain reforms which he believed might be brought about through mutual understanding and coöperation. Lessing's maturest comedy is, at bottom, a didactic work, or *Tendenzschrift*, but its serious purpose is cleverly concealed behind a façade of brilliant comic incidents.

One does not at first grasp the full meaning of *Minna von Barnhelm*, or even the main outlines of its plot. This comedy, like its two immediate predecessors, begins indirectly and obliquely. The first act, with its account of Tellheim's poverty and his generous refusal to take money from a poor widow whose husband was in his debt, gives scarcely a hint of the love affair which is to be the main subject of the drama. In the second act the heroine is introduced, at first as a nameless "Fräulein" and later as Minna von Barnhelm, a wealthy young girl, who during the war had plighted her troth to Tellheim and now that peace has been restored is trying to find and marry her lover. The obstacle in Minna's way proves to be Tellheim's pride. Since he has been discharged from the Prussian army and has no other financial resources, he is unwilling to become dependent upon a rich wife. He explains his position to Minna at the end of the second act, during the course of which the events of the past are gradually unrolled. This skillful delayed exposition is accomplished in the leisurely manner that since Lessing's day has become associated with the work of Henrik Ibsen. The dramatic conflict is joined in the first interview between Minna and Tellheim, but further information as to what had already happened to Tellheim during the war years keeps appearing throughout the entire play.

The complicated antecedent action gives a body to the comic misunderstandings between Minna and Tellheim by indicating that political forces underlie the apparent triviality of the situation. Tellheim is meant to represent the Prussian officer at his best, charitable, loyal, and courageous; Minna is the Saxon landowner, emotional and impulsive, but practical and shrewd. Minna oscillates between sentimentally thanking heaven that she has found her constant lover and mischievously planning a trick to make him reveal his true feelings to her. After the long and important scene between them in the fourth act, at the end of which they agree to part, Tellheim is informed that Minna has been disinherited and is therefore no longer rich. The fifth act is taken up with Tellheim's reaction to this news, his decision to seek a fortune for them both, and his pleasure at being able to take care of Minna when he learns that the generous King has taken him back into favor. Minna has the fun of seeing how Tellheim would feel about her poverty, whether he is poor or rich himself, before she admits that her story of being disinherited is all a fiction and that she has invented it to overcome his conscientious scruples about marrying her.

There are three crucial scenes between the lovers near the end of the play. In the first, Minna, the heiress, makes fun of the exaggerated idea of honor held by Tellheim, the retired officer. In the second, Minna, supposedly poor, is told by Tellheim, who really is poor, that his pity for her, now that she is disinherited, is more powerful than was his love for her when she was wealthy. In the third and last, Minna, still supposedly poor, retorts to Tellheim, who has once more become well-to-do, with the same words that he had used to her when he thought that they both were poor: "Equality is the only sure bond of love" (*Gleichheit ist allein das feste Band der Liebe*). These three scenes express very clearly the spirit of *Minna von Barnhelm*: laughter helps to overcome injustice; pity can carry on what laughter has begun; a readjustment of physical conditions is necessary to settle, more or less permanently, the problems which confront human beings. Laughter and pity together must work out the innumerable practical details by which modern society is to progress toward the goal of a unified civilization.

The specific application of this theory in *Minna von Barnhelm* has to do with the reëstablishment of friendly relations between Prussia and Saxony; its general significance lies in the light it throws upon the qualities of which human nature is composed. Minna and Tellheim are contrasting types. If, as he says, she shows "now and then a little mischievousness, here and there a little obstinacy," she is at heart serious and reasonable. Tellheim, on the other hand, is limited and fallible. His conception of honor is so farfetched and exaggerated that it does him more harm than good. He is so illogical and temperamental that he precipitates all the trouble in which he finds himself. His fundamental good nature triumphs in the end, but meanwhile it has been the source of comic embarrassments, which in Lessing's eyes are caused not by the want of a virtue but by the excess of one. This is the sentimental theory of comedy, held by Minna and opposed by her maid, Franziska, who takes the more arbitrary view that white is white and black is black. "I can look," she says, "neither for the good side of a bad man nor for the bad side of a good man." To Franziska, a soldier like Tellheim should be either a ridiculous *miles gloriosus* or a perfect knight, without fear and without reproach.

Against her better judgment, Franziska helps Minna in the plan to punish Tellheim for his reprehensible pride. She acts like the lively, unprincipled maidservant of earlier comedies, but the most high-minded intentions explain her deceitful conduct. The maid has assumed some of her mistress's nobility and the heroine has taken on some of her maid's gaiety, an exchange of qualities which makes it clear that emotional love-making and boisterous horseplay no longer exist on separate artistic planes. Masters and servants will no more receive different literary treatment because of social distinctions. The gradual growth of democracy is mirrored in the disintegration of hard and fast dramatic categories.

Franziska has her own love affair, which is almost as serious as that of her mistress. Franziska's mate is not Tellheim's rough and faithful servant but his old sergeant-major, or *Wachtmeister*, Paul Werner, one of Lessing's most picturesque and vividly drawn characters. "Within ten years you will be either a general's wife or a widow," Werner promises Franziska, when she offers to become "Frau Wachtmeisterin," and the comedy ends on this ambiguous note, which is typical of the whole indeterminate play. On the one hand, there is the possibility of everyone's living happily ever after in a world in which a sergeant-major becomes a general, and a young heiress shares her estate with a poor man some years her senior; on the other hand, there is the chance that the paths of glory lead but to the grave and that inequalities in age, property, and temperament may make it difficult for the course of true love to continue to run smooth. The sudden shifts in fortune that have confronted Minna and Tellheim are not very reassuring omens for their happiness in marriage. The problem presented is not resolved within the action of the play, which creates the impression of constantly evolving life more than of static artistry. Lessing seems to treat his characters as if they were living people: to know them as thoroughly as possible, to sympathize with them as far as he can, and to make fun of their petty limitations.

Naturally, he lets his comic sense have freer rein with his minor characters, although in them too a certain humane strain makes itself felt. The Landlord of the Inn, where the scene of the play is laid, is ridiculed for his caution in money matters, which is explained by his whole-souled devotion to his business. Tellheim's servant carries his admirable loyalty to his master to absurdly impractical lengths. Riccaut de la Marlinière, the French soldier of fortune, who is introduced episodically into the fourth act, is a particularly puzzling character. Whether he was intended to satirize the French nation or merely the German vogue for all things French, he is an objectionable person, a gambler and a cheat. He accepts money from Minna, apparently without any serious intention of repaying it, unless his dishonesty at cards should succeed in refilling his pocketbook. On the other hand, Minna has the optimistic hope that Riccaut's faults are nothing more than vanity, that his lack of moral principles is sheer ostentation, and that he will use some of her money to pay his small debts, settling down on the rest to a quiet and economical life.

Riccaut is an incidental character, but he is also connected with the fate of the principal characters more intimately than at first appears. Although Tellheim insists that the dishonest Riccaut is no friend of his, the Frenchman brings news that the King is taking an interest in Tellheim's case and that the outcome of it is likely to be favorable. From Riccaut's lips we hear the unrestrained praise of Frederick the Great which is an important factor in the political significance of *Minna von Barnhelm*. Enthusiasm for Frederick, as a unifying force in Germany and the reconciler of such antagonisms as that between Prussia and Saxony, comes rather strangely from the dishonest and expatriated Frenchman, but there can be no doubt that Lessing intended Riccaut's remarks to add to the glory of the King, all the more because they are uttered by a discharged mercenary and political sharper, who would not be expected to recognize Frederick's good qualities. Riccaut's Gallic affectations are treated with considerable severity. It is clear that, although Lessing was enough of a humanitarian to advocate the union of German states, he was not sufficiently broad-minded to be a thoroughgoing internationalist. He could apply principles of sympathy and understanding to all those who spoke his own language, but he reacted strongly against making peace with a foreign opponent, especially one whose culture had long dominated Germany. In his literary criticism he openly attacked French standards of art. In drawing Riccaut de la Marlinière he subtly satirized the effect of applying these aesthetic standards to the practical affairs of everyday life.

The compliments paid to Frederick the Great seem fulsome to some people today, and Minna's sentimental raptures on discovering Tellheim's identity are particularly obnoxious to modern taste. These weaknesses in the texture of *Minna von Barnhelm* are the elements that appealed most strongly to contemporary audiences, imbued with patriotism and religious fervor, which expressed itself in a striving for social coöperation within the community. The union of Tellheim and Minna may be taken as a symbol for the possible reconciliation of such extreme opposites as man and woman, age and youth, poverty and riches. It may also imply a certain reciprocity between idealism and common sense, although in this case the issue is not clearly defined. Minna is noble as well as practical; Tellheim is an efficient soldier as well as a high-principled gentleman. The conflict between the virtues and limitations of these two characters comes out most strongly when one investigates the wisdom of Tellheim's strict adherence to an outworn code of honor and the moral justification for Minna's rather heartless trickery. These opposing conceptions are not allowed to meet on a purely comic level, however; patriotism, philanthropy, and romantic love intrude to straighten out arbitrarily the complications that have arisen. That there were complications in existence, Lessing frankly admitted. He laughed at them heartily, but he was too much a man of the eighteenth century not to be affected by the optimistic theories about human perfectibility which were sweeping through the Europe of his day. The miracle is that he was so little troubled by these emotional and intellectual currents that he was able to write a play like *Minna von Barnhelm*, in which comprehension mingles with amusement and which has as its central character the punctilious, impractical, and altogether lovable Tellheim. This complex figure, half seriously, half playfully drawn, is Lessing's masterpiece of dramatic portraiture.

V

After Lessing's time, comic drama in German took on a much more simple and obvious quality. The *Sturm und Drang* period of romantic aspiration had an unfortunate effect upon comedy, which sank to a lower and lower state artistically, although its general popularity was unabated. The most successful comic authors of Germany during the late eighteenth and early nineteenth centuries were August Wilhelm Iffland and August von Kotzebue, the latter more famous for his plays of heart-rending pathos than for his mildly amusing pieces in the realistic vein. In the work of both these men there is a continuous undercurrent of mild social criticism, which generally exalts the lower middle class at the expense of the aristocracy. Iffland and Kotzebue were attempting to appeal to a large and undiscriminating bourgeois audience. Kotzebue is the less forceful of the two. Iffland, at least, seems to be sincerely honest in writing for people whose mentality was not much greater than his own. Kotzebue's unusual facility in dramatic composition suggests that he was deliberately stooping to the level of his constituents. He composed more than two hundred plays in the course of a career that lasted some thirty years, but he never succeeded in equaling his initial triumph of 1789 with the sentimental drama *Misanthropy and Repentance* ("Menschenhass und Reue"). In comedy he wrote a number of competent pieces which are more ingenious than profound and more superficially amusing than intellectually satisfying. One of the best of them, *The German Provincials* ("Die deutschen Kleinstädter"), contrasts the natives of a small town with a cultivated and rather arrogant visitor from a near-by metropolis, to the latter's disadvantage.

The German Provincials was performed in 1803, three years before the composition by another writer of a far greater comedy in a somewhat similar vein. *The Broken Jug* ("Der zerbrochene Krug") is a one-act comedy in verse, written by a poet known chiefly for his tragic dramas, the unfortunate Heinrich von Kleist. Kleist never attempted any other work in the mood of *The Broken Jug*, which shares with *Minna von Barnhelm* the distinction of having been called by some critics the best comedy in the German language. If it lacks the variety and scope of *Minna*, its artistic compression creates a powerful effect within restricted limits. The scale on which it is constructed is uniformly small: its scene is laid in one place, a village courtroom; it has one principal character, Adam, the local judge; its action unravels a simple plot, which discloses Adam's duplicity and guilt. At the beginning of the piece we learn that Adam has recently barked his shins and lost his wig, that an examining magistrate is coming to inspect the administration of justice, and that the case to be tried concerns a broken jug belonging to Frau Marthe Rull. By the end of the play it is discovered that the responsibility for the broken jug rests upon Adam himself, who, in an effort to seduce Frau Marthe's daughter, has caused all his own misfortunes.

Therefore he must lose his position as judge of the village. The suspense in the gradual discovery of Adam's treachery gives to *The Broken Jug* the quality of a detective story in which the criminal is masquerading as a false detective and a real detective succeeds in exposing him.

Sometimes *The Broken Jug* is gaily amusing. At other moments it is almost morosely savage, as Kleist broods over the evil in human society, which can be removed only by an occasional bit of good luck, not by consistently wise management. This fatalistic atmosphere, which pervades much of Kleist's work, no doubt induced him to take for the subject of his other comedy the classical legend of Amphitryon. In his treatment of this story Kleist shifts the center of interest from the husband, whose plight had been emphasized by Plautus and Molière, to the wife, who is made an example of suffering humanity caught in the toils of forces beyond its control. Alkmene's psychology is very carefully studied by Kleist. He is anxious to explain how it could happen that a devoted wife might have a child by a man other than her husband and what the effect of such an occurrence would be upon a sensitive disposition. Alkmene is released from her painful position by Amphitryon's decision to eliminate himself from the picture, a selfless act which would have seemed more noble if there had been any satisfactory alternative for him. After Amphitryon has submitted to the will of the gods, Jupiter reveals himself, and Alkmene's happiness is restored. She has been more frightened than angry at the way in which the gods have dealt with her. This story, which comes from Middle Greek Comedy and shows classical divinities taking a mischievous hand in the affairs of men, is suitable material neither for realistic social comedy nor for serious drama of an elevated and poetic nature.

A hybrid quality, of not being definitely above the human conflict in the clear ether of a tranquil faith and yet of not being quite a part of the actual world, is characteristic of the German comedy that flourished just before and just after the period of Kleist's preeminence. It is adapted to expressing political and literary criticism more by implication than by direct statement. In it supernatural figures, like those of the Greek gods in their more undignified moments, direct the dramatic action in a spirit that is dictated not so much by the imagination as by the fancy. To carry out this delicately adjusted program, the characters and machinery of familiar fairy tales were of great assistance to playwrights who feared that their serious views might prove dangerously unpopular. In 1797 Ludwig Tieck, just then turning towards romanticism, made use of the Puss-in-Boots story in *The Booted Cat* ("Der gestiefelte Kater"), a play which is fundamentally an attack on the rigidity of the law and an exaltation of liberty and equality. Tieck seems to feel, with regret, that the populace as a whole would tend to uphold law against inspiration. In *The Booted Cat* the esoteric magic of Mozart's *The Magic Flute* ("Die Zauberflöte") comes to the aid of idealistic principles, which, it seems, are not sufficiently dominant in simple fairy tales.

Tieck's example was followed more formally and with greater rigidity by Count August von Platen-Hallermünde, who began his career in 1823 with a piece called *The Glass Slipper* ("Der gläserne Pantoffel"), an attractive combination of the stories of Cinderella and the Sleeping Beauty. *The Glass Slipper* contains almost no thoughtful criticism of any kind, but *The Fatal Fork* ("Die verhängnisvolle Gabel") of 1826 is an amusing Aristophanic parody of the tragedy of fate, or *Schicksalsdrama*, which had an immense vogue in Germany during the early part of the nineteenth century. In Platen-Hallermünde's last play, *The Romantic Oedipus* ("Der romantische Ödipus"), the author points out by means of the Chorus that he has moral aims, that he is championing clarity and simplicity at the expense of carelessness and vagueness, and that he approves of classical self-restraint, not romantic enthusiasms. The purpose of *The Romantic Oedipus* is to expose how ridiculous Sophocles' tragedy would seem if it were rewritten in the style of contemporary German romanticism. Platen-Hallermünde particularly detested the work of the dramatist Immermann, whom in *The Romantic Oedipus* he ridiculed as Nimmermann, but he was also opposed to all the grotesque exaggerations that were the literary fashion of his day in Germany. In *The Fatal Fork* he wrote that Vienna has "a folk comedy which is gayer than the whole German theater" (*ein Volkslustspiel, das lustiger ist, als sämtliche deutsche Theater*).

Since both Tieck and Platen-Hallermünde wrote heterogeneous plays that somewhat resemble the partly robust and partly fantastic comedy that had grown up in Austria, it is not surprising to find that these two critical and poetic authors should find much to admire in the popular Viennese theater. The libretto of Mozart's *The Magic Flute*, which Tieck had complimented in *The Booted Cat*, is one of the best-known survivals of the light drama which flourished for many years beside the Danube. With its clownish Hanswurst and its rough horseplay, its supernatural machinery and its incidental music, this kind of comedy achieved relative permanence as well as immediate popularity. Though it had been attacked during the classical period as vulgar and tawdry, it continued to exist, with or without music, but always with Hanswurst or some similar buffoon to give it humor and vivacity. In the nineteenth century this minor genre of comic writing became dignified by an author of uncommon ability, Ferdinand Raimund.

Raimund found the popular Austrian drama divided roughly into realistic farces, or *Lokalpossen*, and farces with magic elements, or *Zauberpossen*, a division which went back some seventy-five years. At that period Philipp Hafner had formalized the crude material of desultory popular entertainment into the outlines of an artistic pattern. The two types of farces into which Hafner separated the chaos of folk drama persisted in Vienna until the age of Metternich. At the Leopoldstädter Theater, where they were chiefly played, Raimund received his training as an actor. His early ambition was to excel at tragedy, but his natural abilities lay in the opposite direction. From acting he progressed to authorship, when, more or less by chance, he was offered the opportunity to complete a text left unfinished by Karl Maisl, an established playwright of the farcical school. This text, *The Barometer-Maker on the Magic Island* ("Der Barometer-macher auf der Zauberinsel"), proved such a great success that Raimund determined to undertake further and more original dramatic writing. He composed altogether eight notable comedies, beginning with *The Barometer-Maker* in 1823 and concluding eleven years later with *The Spendthrift* ("Der Verschwender"), produced two years before its author's tragic suicide in 1836.

VI

The Barometer-Maker on the Magic Island, Raimund's first prentice work, is a primitive sort of musical *Zauberposse* in two acts. It begins with a supernatural scene in which a powerful fairy is told that she must give three magic gifts to some mortal man and is persuaded to bestow them on Bartholomäus Quecksilber, or Quicksilver, a jolly barometer-maker from Vienna, who has been shipwrecked on the Magic Island, where the gifts are preserved. Virtue and vice are opposed in the persons of Quecksilber and the Princess of the Island. Raimund always contrives that the fairy world of the Viennese *Zauberposse* shall extend human sympathy and encourage people to assist one another as best they can.

The greatest excellence of *The Barometer-Maker* as a work of literature is the skillful depiction of Quecksilber's character. The contrast between Vienna and the Magic Island is emphasized throughout the play, a contrast not always in favor of the fairy realm. At first Quecksilber is ready to criticize Vienna, where a rascally printer left off letters from his barometer and as a result discredited his work, but he soon comes to prefer his own homely way of life to the superficial elegance of the Magic Island. His simple taste in food, his ignorance of poetry, and his crude manners are ridiculed by all the islanders, except Linda, the Princess's maid, who, as she languishes in the refined atmosphere of Fairyland, longs for the plebeian delights of the Prater, a famous Viennese park. At the end of the comedy Quecksilber and Linda decide to set off for Vienna, leaving the Magic Island to get along as best it can without them. The Austrian city, dearly loved by its loyal citizens, is a pleasanter place in which to live than a more rarefied community, where, among other sophisticated refinements, the subtleties of evil are likewise sure to thrive.

A general note of healthiness is struck in Raimund's plays from the outset of his career. In *The Diamond of the King of Spirits* ("Der Diamant des Geisterkönigs"), Raimund's second and more original work, virtue triumphs within an elaborate and involved framework. The hero of this piece is subjected to a series of trials in his attempt to reach the diamond statue, which Hope tells him is to be found in the palace of the King of Spirits. He is torn between the claims of loyalty, wealth, and love, but in the end love wins the day and is found to be identical with truth. Although *The Diamond of the King of Spirits* is a vast improvement in structure over *The Barometer-Maker*, its principal character is a much less delightful person. The entertaining element in this story comes from the adventures of the hero's servant, Florian Waschblau, who hates to set out with his master from Vienna, because he is in love with a cook-maid there. For a time Florian is turned into a poodle dog as a punishment for his worldly thoughts, but later his willingness to sacrifice himself for his master is rewarded by reunion with his beloved Mariandl. These adventures are all presided over by the King of Spirits, who is introduced as a lazy and selfish tyrant but turns out to be a benevolent despot with a soul attuned to the music of the spheres. His presence gives a unity of plot and mood to the drama, which is not, however, equal to *The Barometer-Maker* in comic vigor.

Raimund succeeded in combining the excellences of his first two works when in 1826 he composed the first of his three masterly comedies, *The Peasant as Millionaire, or The Maiden from the Fairy World* ("Der Bauer als Millionär, oder Das Mädchen aus der Feenwelt"). At the commencement of this drama, Fortunatus Wurzel, a lucky man sprung from peasant roots, has been endowed by Envy with the money which is to plunge him into misfortunes. He has become the laughingstock of his friends; his servants have learned how to fleece him of his wealth; he has begun to eat and drink to excess; he refuses to allow his foster daughter to marry a poor fisherman and tries to get her to marry a rich jeweler. The antithesis between fish, by which man can live, and jewels, which have no vital function to fulfill, suggests the symbolic nature of the story. Wurzel's foster daughter, who is really a maiden from the fairy world, refuses to marry the jeweler. When she is disinherited she flies from her father's house. After she has gone, Wurzel's hair turns white, and he gradually becomes more and more melancholy. Finally he is ready to acknowledge that wealth without affection is harder for old age to endure than poverty with love. His subsequent reformation makes it possible for him to return to the simple way of life which he had earlier enjoyed.

The peasant who has become a millionaire bitterly laments his past folly. With repentant sobs, he threatens to make himself a horrible example to the world. "I will have my misfortune printed," he exclaims, "and run about with it myself and cry: For a kreuzer, the beautiful description that we have just received of the poor unlucky man who from a young ass became an old one!" Wurzel does not become a peddler of ballads, as he here ironically suggests, but he descends to being an ashman, a menial occupation which he glorifies in a celebrated song with the refrain "Ein Aschen! Ein Aschen!" In depicting the absurd Wurzel's conversion to a belief in the social value of self-restraint, Raimund has arrived at the combination of jollity and sincerity for which he had striven in his early plays.

As if he felt that the weakness of *The Peasant as Millionaire* was its lack of dignity, in his next two pieces Raimund tried too deliberately to make up for that deficiency. The idea behind his fourth comedy, *The Chained Fantasy* ("Die gefesselte Phantasie"), is particularly interesting in this connection. It seems to be a sort of defense for the mildness of its author's artistic inspiration. Fantasy is represented as a creature with iridescent wings, who inspires poets in a literary contest and helps a king's son, disguised as a shepherd, to win the hand of a beautiful young queen. When Fantasy is put in chains, she refuses to inspire Nachtigall, or Nightingale, a harpist from Vienna. Then Nachtigall in despair falls back on a popular Viennese song, which he alters to fit the solemn occasion for which it is required. Raimund seems to have especial sympathy with Nachtigall, who is intended to be the leading comic figure in *The Chained Fantasy*, perhaps because he fully realized how difficult it was to dignify a popular form of art. He had himself taken the crude Viennese *Zauberposse* and attempted to raise it to a higher literary sphere. It is an ironic circumstance that *The Chained Fantasy*, in which he is making a plea for free imagination at the expense of academic training in the arts, should have been one of his least successful dramatic productions.

After the comparative failure of *The Chained Fantasy* Raimund attempted a still more ambitious and less inspired piece of work, *Moisasur's Magic Curse* ("Moisasurs Zauberfluch"). The magic curse of Moisasur, a wicked magician, is that the Queen of the Kingdom of Diamonds is to have an old body with a young spirit and to weep diamond tears, until in the grasp of death she weeps tears of joy. The spell is lifted, because of the nobility of the Queen and her husband in a story which resembles that of Admetus and Alcestis, with the sexes reversed. *Moisasur's Magic Curse* provides plenty of opportunity for elaborate scenic effects, but it has no important comic character such as those that hold the center of the stage in Raimund's most vibrant work.

VII

The background of mountains in *Moisasur's Magic Curse* may have suggested to Raimund the machinery for the sixth of his dramatic pieces and the second of his outstanding successes, *The Mountain King and the Misanthrope* ("Der Alpenkönig und der Menschenfeind"). In it he concentrated his attention upon one fallible person, whose humor of misanthropy is purged, as Wurzel's love of money had been in *The Peasant as Millionaire*. The misanthrope, called Rappelkopf, a rattle-brained fellow, has been disillusioned about mankind: first, by losing money he had invested in his brother-in-law's business; and second, by his three dead wives, one of whom was domineering, one of whom was jealous, and one of whom was moonstruck. He now has an affectionate wife and daughter, but his suspicious nature leads him to believe that they are trying to have him killed. So he destroys the furniture in his house, tears up his old love letters, and, like Timon of Athens, sets out into the woods to enter upon the life of a hermit. Here he meets the strange Mountain King, by whose magic he is so frightened that he agrees to reform. His repentance is completed when he returns home in the guise of his wife's brother and hears other people express their unfavorable opinions about himself. Finally the Mountain King appears in the form of Rappelkopf, and the real misanthrope is obliged to watch how he used to act when he dwelt among men.

The climax of the piece comes when the apparent Rappelkopf strikes the real one, with the result that a duel almost takes place between these two embodiments of the same personality. After peace has been restored, the real Rappelkopf attempts to prevent the apparent Rappelkopf from committing suicide because of financial ruin. When he fails, he is told that his old self has gone out of the world, because a new man is born within him. The psychological change that has taken place in Rappelkopf's attitude towards existence is made clear by the dramatic symbols of a dual personality. The fact that Rappelkopf is far from heroic during the body of the play and that his gradual reformation is accompanied by many temporary backslidings prevents *The Mountain King and the Misanthrope* from being too saccharine a moral treatise. Raimund's best work depends not upon the ends sought but on the means employed.

He seems to have been interested in why men commit their follies, the nature of which he takes pretty much for granted. By applying intelligence to the combined magic and horseplay of the *Zauberposse* he welds romantic idealism and scientific detachment together into a form of analytical psychology.

Raimund was to carry his method still farther than he had done in *The Mountain King and the Misanthrope,* but before he wrote his third important comedy he experienced one more failure. *The Mischief-Making Crown* ("Die unheilbringende Krone") is an over-elaborate drama in four acts, with a tragical main plot and with no first-rate comic figure. This play met with a most unfavorable reception, which so discouraged its author that he did not bring another production to the stage until more than four years had elapsed.

When, in 1834, Raimund again presented a play, his work had taken on a different tone. *The Spendthrift*, his last comedy, is probably his artistic masterpiece. It certainly has an undercurrent of deeper pathos than any of his earlier and more lighthearted entertainments. In this case the hero, Julius von Flottwell, does not reform in time to have before him a long, happy, and useful life. He learns his lesson just soon enough to escape the worst effects of his besetting sin, an unrestrained tendency to spend money foolishly. Flottwell has not been given his money by evil spirits; supernatural agencies of good are not all-powerful in determining his career. *The Spendthrift* is the only one of Raimund's plays that opens without fairy machinery. It starts with what purports to be a realistic situation and then follows Flottwell through the various scenes of a rake's progress. In the first act he is surrounded by sycophantic servants and parasitic friends; three years later, in the second act, he indulges in a duel and elopes with a beautiful girl, on whom he has already squandered a large fortune; in the third act, which takes place twenty years later, Flottwell, having lost his wife, his child, and his property, returns to his ancient estate as a beggar.

Besides being a painfully exact study of harsh economic facts, *The Spendthrift* also contains a transcendental element. Flottwell is loved by the Fairy Cheristane, who originally helped him to accumulate his money but now sees that he is making bad use of it. In the first act she asks Flottwell for the gift of one year of his life, which, from affection and natural goodness of heart, he is only too willing to grant her. The year selected by Cheristane is Flottwell's fiftieth one. She disguises her subordinate spirit as the beggar that Flottwell will be in his fiftieth year. During the second act this supposed beggar appears to the still young and prosperous spendthrift. The money which this beggar can secure from Flottwell by charity or deceit is saved from the prodigal's ruin and returns to him in his real fiftieth year, because, as the spirit tells him, "What you gave to the poor man, you have in the fullest sense given to yourself,"

> Was Du dem Armen gabst, Du hast's
> Im vollen Sinne selber Dir gegeben.

Flottwell reforms, but not until it is too late for him to enjoy on earth the fruits of his changed social philosophy. Cheristane tells him at the end of the play that he has only a short time longer to live. Then he will be reunited with her in the boundless kingdom of love, where all spirits are permitted to meet. *The Spendthrift* will end happily in the next world, but in this one it comes to a pretty dreary conclusion.

It is even more obvious in this play than in Raimund's earlier work that the forces of magic are merely exaggerated representations of human traits. Even if the Fairy Cheristane had never interfered in the affairs of Flottwell, he would still not have been totally ruined by his vicious tendencies. He has a faithful servant, named Valentin, who is fond enough of him to assist him in his impoverished condition. Valentin, perhaps Raimund's most typical and most famous character, embodies his creator's belief that, since there is no happiness to be gained in this world from material possessions, the best recourse is to laugh as merrily as one can at all specimens of mankind, including oneself. In the last act Valentin and Rosa, the sharp-tongued maidservant with whom he was in love, are married and have acquired five children, whom Valentin supports indifferently well by his old profession of carpentry. Valentin's household is delightfully described, with a wealth of minutely observed detail. Rosa has become somewhat shrewish with advancing age, her eldest child and only daughter is the responsible member of the family, her three boys are full of mischievous high spirits, and the baby, who is just beginning to talk, toddles around, demanding constant attention. To this household Flottwell comes in his poverty, and here he is received most kindly by everyone except the embittered Rosa.

Rosa's common sense tells her that they are under no obligations to Flottwell. She does not see any reason why they should support him for the rest of their lives, but Valentin refuses to accept his wife's decision. "Oh, there are things of which our philosophy does not dream" (O *es gibt Sachen, wovon sich unsere Philosophie nichts träumen lasst*), he tells Rosa, in the tones of a peasant Hamlet. While working at his plane, he has learned many fundamental facts and pondered on them. In the popular Song of the Plane, or *Hobellied*, in which he sets forth his philosophy, he sings that the plane of Fate smoothes out life for the rich and poor, the old and young, the merry and sad; so, for his part, he will keep on at his work until death calls him. Valentin's threat to leave Rosa and take the children with him brings his wife to her senses. She agrees to receive Flottwell in his poverty just before the spendthrift regains enough of his money to be able to support his faithful friends in a better style than that to which they have grown accustomed. In this way the fairy world increases the happiness that comes from cheerfully accepting one's destiny and keeping on friendly terms with other imperfect individuals.

This benevolent cheerfulness, which finds its fullest expression in the character of Valentin in the last act of *The Spendthrift*, is the culmination of Raimund's attitude towards human problems and human conduct. He began with the mythology of a standardized fairy realm and kept adding to it elements drawn from his own experience. In *The Peasant as Millionaire* he for the first time brought his vivid sense of real life into touch with his perceptions of another world and created a fanciful sermon on the root of all evil. In *The Mountain King and the Misanthrope* the unsocial nature of avarice appears in the heightened form of misanthropy, a human failing with which Raimund cannot sympathize, but of which he gives a clear-cut picture. He is more at his ease in *The Spendthrift* with the subject of profligacy, which he can condemn with his mind and understand with his feelings. The lack of consistency in his outlook is accompanied by a lack of clarity in his technique, but despite these weaknesses he is a deft and resourceful writer of dramatic comedy. If his place is not among the greatest masters, his deficiencies may be partially explained by the equivocal position in which he found himself. He was a commoner catering to the aristocracy, an idealist living under a reactionary monarchy, and a mature artist burdened with the tradition of an outworn, rather childish cosmology.

VIII

The pleasant but unsatisfying compromise made by Raimund between fairyland and the actual world could hardly have continued for long in the Viennese theater. In the absence of a great genius more able than Raimund had been to synthesize closely these two divergent elements, as Shakespeare did in *A Midsummer Night's Dream*, one of them was bound to get the better of the other. In the realm of comedy it was natural that the materialistic strain should prevail, as it came to do in the work of Raimund's chief contemporary and immediate successor, Johann Nestroy. In 1833, the year *The Spendthrift* appeared, Nestroy made his first marked success with a *Zauberposse* delightfully entitled *The Evil Spirit Lumpazivagabundus, or The Disorderly Trio* ("Der böse Geist Lumpazivagabundus, oder Das liederliche Kleeblatt"), which also deals with profligacy. Instead of treating the subject in a reflective way, Nestroy simply handled with zest a story which showed how widespread the evil of extravagance was and then slyly suggested that only love could hope to cure it.

Nestroy's plays are most amusing, but they are often so local in their references and allusions as to be entirely comprehensible only in Vienna, to the Viennese. They are filled with obscure and intricate puns. They subtly ridicule abuses of authority under Hapsburg rule. They parody contemporary dramatic art and operatic successes, like Friedrich Hebbel's *Judith* and Richard Wagner's *Tannhäuser*. Although their plots are frequently thin and absurd, the situations which occur in them are usually novel and humorous.

Nestroy is at the top of his form when he is writing realistic farces, where his ingenuity at devising clever theatrical effects can have free play. In *Eulenspiegel, or Trick upon Trick* ("Schabernack über Schabernack") he represented Eulenspiegel, the mischievous hero of a popular German folk tale, as a merry vagabond who vies with a jovial landowner in playing roguish pranks to assist a pair of young lovers. In *On the Ground Floor and on the First Floor, or The Caprices of Luck* ("Zu ebener Erde und im ersten Stock, oder Die Launen des Glücks"), of 1825, he showed great inventiveness in working out

complicated relationships between a poor family that lives downstairs and a rich family that lives above them. Both sets of rooms are
shown on the stage at the same time, with the action alternating between them or going on in both places simultaneously. The love
affair between a daughter of one family and a son of the other is
finally adjusted, when the rich man becomes poor and the poor man
rich, with the result that they exchange apartments. This complete
reversal of existing economic conditions contains the essence of
Gilbertian Topsy-turvydom.

Less original but no less amusing is *He Will Go on a Spree* ("Einen
Jux will er sich machen"), in which a grocery clerk, who hears he is
to be made a partner in his employer's business, decides to go to a
near-by metropolis to celebrate his promotion. He becomes involved
in all sorts of extraordinary adventures, at the end of which he
emerges with the hand of a rich widow, whom he has met by accident. The hero of *The Shattered Man* ("Der Zerrissene") proposes
marriage on the spur of the moment to another widow, in order to
get some amusement out of his monotonous life, and immediately
finds himself in the center of more excitement than he had bargained
for. He is thought to have been killed by a rival, and, while still very
much alive, he is able to observe his old friends without being seen
by them. The theme of *The Shattered Man* is something like that of
Raimund's *The Mountain King and the Misanthrope*, with emphasis on
the humorous and satiric aspects of the situation at the expense of its
possible philosophical implications.

If Nestroy's plays show how Raimund's comic method is weakened when deprived of its idealistic background, the work of another
Austrian dramatist of the time reveals the dangers of the opposite
tendency, that of insisting on the seriousness of comic material instead of treating it in a carefree way. Franz Grillparzer was a skillful poet and an able playwright, but he cannot be considered a
writer of comedies, although two of his plays have been so described.
The first of the two, *The Dream, a Life* ("Der Traum ein Leben"),
produced in 1834, the same year as Raimund's *The Spendthrift*, belongs in the category of fantastic dramas with a pleasant ending, like
the magic comedies of Raimund. The general suggestion for *The
Dream, a Life* came from Calderón's *Life Is a Dream*, which Grillparzer had already translated from Spanish into German. In Cal-

derón's play, by ruminating on events which have actually happened as if they had taken place in a dream, the hero learns that the externals of life are a snare and a delusion. In *The Dream, a Life* the hero has a dream which seems to him like an actual experience and teaches him a salutary lesson. A similar doctrine, that resolute self-control is necessary to human happiness, runs through both dramas, but it is treated rather differently in the two cases. Calderón undertook the paradoxical task of making life appear like a dream. Grillparzer adopted the simpler expedient of giving to a dream the significance of an entire lifetime.

At the end of his dream Rustan, the oriental hero of *The Dream, a Life*, jumps from a bridge over a stream and destroys his vicious personality, much as the pretended Rappelkopf, in Raimund's *The Mountain King and the Misanthrope*, throws himself from a cliff into a stream and thus destroys his worse self. Rustan wakes up to forswear pride and ambition, and, like Rappelkopf, rejoices in the disappearance of his former evil shape. The difference between these plays is that, whereas Raimund has brought out the humorous nature of the scene in which Rappelkopf sees himself as others see him, Grillparzer has kept his whole narrative on the high level of serious romantic poetry. Grillparzer is more elevated, Nestroy is more ludicrous, than Raimund. *The Dream, a Life*, *The Mountain King and the Misanthrope*, and *The Shattered Man*, make three interesting variations upon the theme of a man having the miraculous detachment necessary to observe, without prejudice, the life of which he is ordinarily a part. The subject may be treated with dignity, with boisterous laughter, or with an attempt to combine these two contrasting moods. Raimund's work contains a quality of light fantasy that is lacking in Nestroy's lusty ridicule and Grillparzer's ecstatic aspiration.

The Dream, a Life is, on the whole, a labored piece of work, and Grillparzer's *Woe to Him Who Lies!* ("Weh dem, der lügt!"), which does not depend upon supernatural machinery, is even more artificial in its effort to compress the highest morality into a rational and consistent framework. This latter play is called a comedy by its author, and it has generally been so classified. It expresses a philosophical view toward the truth, which would provide the proper setting for a comic treatment of falsehood. At the end of the last act Bishop Gregor states his mature belief that lying is at bottom only a gay cloak of transitoriness which God has hung upon the shoulders of man to preserve him from the blinding light of truth. Unfortunately, the measured consciousness of this definition interferes with Grillparzer's application of it to a specific narrative.

The ingeniously contrived plot of *Woe to Him Who Lies!* is too complicated to be entirely successful in giving concrete expression to abstract ideas. Bishop Gregor, who at the beginning of the play believes that every sort of lying is unforgivable, has by the end of it come to realize that under certain conditions a lie is justifiable. Leon, the hero, a young kitchen boy, starts his adventures with every intention of obeying the Bishop's injunction never to lie. At first he is willing to give an erroneous impression if he utters no falsehood, but later he learns from the heroine that truth is more than a matter of lip service. From then on, he insists upon telling the whole truth, even though he thinks that doing so will ruin the success of his exploits. Meanwhile, Edrita, the heroine, has decided that the single ideal of truth is too difficult for one person to achieve, and she embarks on a policy of lying to accomplish her own ends. The comic contrast between the attitudes of the man and woman is further emphasized when Edrita's lies fail to fulfill their purpose and Leon's truthfulness enables him to triumph more by chance than by good management. Grillparzer gives a final twist to the central theme by making both the lovers lie about their feelings for each other, although neither of them is deceived as to the other's motives and intentions.

There is intellectual subtlety in the various kinds of falsehoods told in *Woe to Him Who Lies!* which far transcends the many simple denials of fact in Alarcón's *The Truth Suspected* and Corneille's *The Liar*, or the elaborate ramifications of a few basic untruths in Goldoni's play also called *The Liar*. Grillparzer is more philosophical in his point of view than Alarcón or Corneille or Goldoni, but much less amusing and vivacious than any one of the three. *Woe to Him Who Lies!* failed dismally upon its first presentation. Although it has since been more successful on the stage, it is so heavy and roundabout that, if it is to be appreciated, it must be approached with the utmost seriousness. It is a striking example of how a great writer can go astray when he attempts to divert his genius into unfamiliar and incongenial channels.

Woe to Him Who Lies! has sometimes been grouped with *Minna von Barnhelm* and *The Broken Jug* as one of the three outstanding comedies in German, but the poetic nature of Grillparzer's play is very different in quality from the calm deliberation of Lessing's drama or Kleist's detailed observation of a provincial society. Kleist was, like Grillparzer, primarily a tragic poet, but in *The Broken Jug* he subordinated his despair to his curiosity and permitted emotion to be felt only in the undercurrents of his story. There is some disparity in *The Broken Jug* between the trivial action and the moral satire implied by it, but Kleist's achievement is superior to anything of its kind in German comedy. Lessing's comic masterpiece is even more remarkable. *Minna von Barnhelm* touches on relations between separate German states, between the sexes, between the generations, and between social classes. It deals with so many subjects at once that it gives an impression of presenting the entire panorama of life, not a limited number of carefully selected incidents. If it is not a comedy at all according to established classical precedents, it points out new developments in art and society. In spirit it anticipates events which did not take place until after Lessing's death in 1781.

The end of the eighteenth and the beginning of the nineteenth century were periods of crucial importance in European civilization: the periods of the French Revolution, the Napoleonic wars, the rapid rise of industrialism, and the growth of German nationalism. It was an age of great writers — of Boswell, Burke, and the Romantic Poets in England, of Chateaubriand in France, of Schiller and Goethe in Germany — but not an age of great humorous writing for the theater. Yet in spite of wars and rumors of wars there flourished in Vienna a popular comedy, which, for a moment, was raised to the status of literature by the work of Ferdinand Raimund. In Breslau and Berlin, Lessing had already composed *Minna von Barnhelm*, a superlative comic drama of an original sort. The conflict between idealism and the physical facts of life was unusually intense at this stage in the world's history. Neither Lessing nor Raimund had the talent, or genius, necessary for a comic playwright to resolve it satisfactorily. Both men sympathized with the downtrodden members of society; both possessed a fund of high-spirited gaiety. By combining these qualities in different proportions, each made a novel and substantial addition to dramatic comedy.

CHAPTER IX

Crosscurrents in Russia: Gogol, Turgenev, and Chekhov

I

DURING the late eighteenth and early nineteenth centuries dramatic comedy in Germany and Austria had diverged widely from the normal standard established by Molière and his immediate successors. Molière had been able to do two seemingly impossible things at the same time: he indicated plainly the intellectual grounds for his dislike of certain human characteristics, and he also made clear his compassion for the unfortunate individuals who displayed these failings. His successors attempted to follow the pattern he had set up. The ablest of them succeeded in making some minor changes in it. Holberg put his emphasis upon the externals of culture, as was not surprising in a country which, during the first half of the eighteenth century, was just beginning to be touched by the Latin civilization of western Europe. Denmark was strongly influenced by travelers going to France and coming from it; Russia also was affected by similar currents in society, which were fostered under royal patronage by Peter the Great and Catherine II.

The first Russian comedies of importance were composed early in the reign of Catherine the Great by Denis Ivanovich Fonvizin, a member of the educated upper class, who had enjoyed the opportunity of traveling extensively in Europe. On his return Fonvizin followed the example of Molière, or rather Holberg, and attempted to adapt the French dramatist's method to conditions in his native land. Like Holberg, Fonvizin believed that the new French culture, which was all very well on its home ground, could easily be carried too far. There was the danger that when it was transplanted to another country it would produce such shallow types as Holberg's Jean de France. In Fonvizin's first comedy, *The Brigadier General*, which appeared in 1766, he introduced unattractive examples of both the unenlightened Russia of earlier days and the modern imitation of foreign customs. A retired brigadier, who talks the jargon of war, and an elderly councilor, who has retired to the country on the gains of an unscrupulous judicial career, are contrasted with the brigadier's son, who looks upon all patriotism as provincial, and with the councilor's wife, who has been in Paris and copies its fashionable ways with disastrous results. It is easy to see that Fonvizin had enough comic detachment to recognize the fallibility of an extreme point of view, whether it was fundamentally conservative or superficially up-to-date.

Fonvizin's second and far better known comedy, *The Minor* (1782), takes a similar attitude towards a more elaborate social group. On the estate of the Prostakovs, a family of simpletons, are to be found a motley crowd of ill-assorted humour characters, representative of the worst characteristics of the old regime. There is a weak husband, a mean and domineering wife, a brutish brother-in-law, and a completely spoiled son, sixteen years of age. The brother-in-law exhibits the weakness of an animal's body; the spoiled son, that of a coxcomb's arrogance. There are also present four noble examples of the established order: the serious-minded heroine, the brave military hero, a government inspector, who ultimately has the high-handed Prostakovs removed from their estate, and the heroine's uncle, who is an epitome of all the virtues. Throughout *The Minor* the scales are heavily weighted in favor of the virtuous characters, as if Fonvizin were more interested in expressing his constructive views on the state of Russia than in entertaining his audience with the antics of absurdly caricatured types. *The Minor* is filled with didactic speeches from all the admirable people, especially from Starodum, the heroine's solemn old uncle.

Starodum has been trained at the court of Peter the Great, where, as he says, a person was sensibly called "thou" in the singular, not "you" in the plural; he has learned of the corruption and chicanery now existing in the civil service and at the imperial court, but he has not lost his belief that the soul is the most important part of mankind. He approves of Fénelon's *Télémaque*, although he distrusts the demoralizing effect of most French literature; he believes that a nobleman should devote his energies to serving his fatherland and its people; he feels sure that marriage should be based on a friendship which resembles love rather than on a love which resembles friendship. He realizes that a wise czar looks out for the welfare of his subjects and avoids the flattery of fawning courtiers. He demands that the present tendency toward education be diverted into proper channels.

An interest in education lies at the heart of *The Minor*, many scenes in which have to do with the three tutors whom Prostakov's wife has engaged to give instruction to her spoiled boy. She says that in her own youth the children of the nobility did not have to bother about an education, but now that Catherine II has decreed some schooling for the sons of noblemen she wishes her son to be given the same opportunities that other boys receive. A stupid representative of the old order, she regards these new ideas about education, which she does not understand, as sheer nonsense. The tutors whom she has selected are either rogues or fools, and she does not attempt to help them in their difficult task of disciplining her pampered boy. When in a later one-act play, *The Choice of a Tutor* (1792), Fonzivin repeats the situation, he suggests that there were many such doting mothers in Russia at the time. In *The Choice of a Tutor* there is a good tutor as well as a bad one, and it is not surprising to find that the good teacher differs very slightly from Starodum in *The Minor*. He believes in the reforms of the Empress, but he does not wish to go over wholeheartedly to newfangled foreign methods; he thinks that Russia should be good enough for the Russians and that his countrymen ought to appreciate the value of their national heritage.

The ten years which had elapsed between *The Minor* and *The Choice of a Tutor* had marked something of an epoch in French history. It is interesting to observe how the outbreak of the Revolution affected Fonvizin's attitude towards France. Although he was never sympathetic to unintelligent imitation of another society, in 1782 he prized the advances in art and science made by the French. By 1792 he showed that the stupid Russian aristocrats who had wanted their children educated in France were becoming frightened at the idea of the leveling down which was taking place in that country. They were beginning to believe that primitive barbarism at home was better than sophisticated barbarism abroad. Even the model young teacher in *The Choice of a Tutor* disapproves of the French experiment. He regards the doctrine of equality as dangerous to the welfare of a community, which requires that one part of the population should make sacrifices for another in the interests of the general good. Fonvizin indicates his belief that there should be a just proportion between those who make the sacrifices and those who profit by them, but he seems to be unwilling to press this controversial issue any farther. In his political ideas he was generally sympathetic to the France of the Bourbons, as in his aesthetic ideas he approached the comedies of Molière through Holberg's vigorous but naïve modifications.

The second important writer of dramatic comedy in Russia was also influenced by the work of Molière. Alexander Sergeyevich Griboyedov's *Woe from Wit* is a variation on the theme of *The Misanthrope*. It is a rather solitary masterpiece, the only important work written by its author, and the one comedy of real significance that appeared in Russia during the period of the romantic revival. Griboyedov finished his play in 1823, after working on it for a number of years, but he was not allowed to have it performed until 1831. The reactionary policy of the last years of Alexander I's reign caused a large amount of secret opposition to the government among liberals, which came to a head in the Decembrist Conspiracy of 1825. Griboyedov seems to have been connected with this conspiracy, although after the plot was discovered he was acquitted of complicity by government investigators. Some of the ideas current among the Decembrists have no doubt found their way to the lips of Chatsky, Griboyedov's hero. Otherwise, Chatsky echoes the conservative views of Fonvizin's Starodum in denouncing social mannerisms and foreign affectations.

The great difference between *The Minor* and *Woe from Wit* is that, in the former, virtue is rewarded and vice is punished; in the latter, the plot is not conducted or resolved in a clear-cut fashion. Chatsky, a mouthpiece for Griboyedov's disapproval of a corrupt court and Francophile society, does not, at the end of the piece, marry the girl with whom he has been in love; Sophya, the fashionable heroine, does not win the sly clerk who fascinates her, but who is caught in a compromising rendezvous with a lady's maid. The intrigue in *Woe from Wit* indirectly shows up the absurdity of all the principal characters, particularly the clever ones. Chatsky, Sophya, and the clerk are all duped by their own intelligence, or pretenses to intelligence.

The ability to stand apart from the actual social conflict and to observe it without taking sides is Griboyedov's particular comic gift. He avoids the blatant morality of Fonvizin, but he does not rise to the philosophical penetration of Molière. Chatsky is not so subtle a study in human psychology as Alceste; he is chiefly used to describe and comment upon the eccentric members of a limited social group. He also criticizes, with disagreeable severity, the upstart clerk, with whom Sophya thinks she is in love. The infatuation of the heroine for the worthless clerk is the central incident of *Woe from Wit*. It is intended to make clear the decadence of the aristocracy and the unprincipled opportunism of the rising lower clasess. Griboyedov is so scrupulously fair to his two principal characters that one does not know which of them is the more at fault. Sophya is selfish and coldhearted, but also ingenious and determined; Chatsky is noble and full of fine sentiments, but vacillating and ineffective. The duel between them is evenly matched, and the battle is undecided at the end. Chatsky angrily shakes the dust of Moscow from his feet, and Sophya is dragged away by her father to the country.

It is interesting to notice that Sophya's father, a corrupt officeholder, refers with approval to certain conditions at the court of Catherine the Great. The same period which was considered the vicious present by the unsympathetic characters in *The Minor* is regarded as the glorious past by the satirized persons in *Woe from Wit*. From the comic point of view, what seems to many people unbearable at a given moment will, in the course of time, shine brightly by the reflected light of other evils, which as yet they know not of. This emphasis on change, social and political, is one of the noticeable factors in the history of Russian comedy. It did not flourish actively until the feudal system was in the process of passing into modern industrialism without having first been carefully reorganized on a stable bourgeois basis. The difficulty that any individual would have in adjusting himself to shifting conditions was not made unmistakably clear in Russian drama until the time of Chekhov, but both Fonvizin and Griboyedov displayed a genuine interest in certain problems of social transition. Fonvizin pointed out the advantages of Catherine's reforms, if they were not carried forward too impetuously; Griboyedov was anxious to moderate the extremist policies of a revolutionary movement which seemed to him an inevitable and justified protest against tyrannical oppression.

II

In *Woe from Wit* Griboyedov made an effort to disclose the corruption in politics and the dissipation in society which he felt characterized Moscow during the first quarter of the nineteenth century. The third important writer of Russian comedy, and by all odds the greatest of the three, undertook to portray a similar state of affairs in a small country town. In 1836 Nikolay Vasilyevich Gogol produced his famous comedy *The Inspector-General* ("Revizor"). In it he did not attempt to show the nobility and the landed gentry, or the peasants and the serfs, but concentrated his attention upon typical middle-class citizens of an undistinguished sort. They are the Chief of Police, the Superintendent of Schools, the Judge, the Postmaster, and the District Physician, men who are responsible for the welfare of their fellow citizens and who pride themselves on their public offices. They are drawn in rough outlines, with the gusto and verve which has caused Gogol to be called the father of Russian realism.

If he is the father of Russian realism, his realism is built upon a romantic basis. Beneath it is the same idealism that underlies Griboyedov's *Woe from Wit*, a hope that social conditions may be improved throughout Russia as a result of clearer insight and sounder culture. Griboyedov put his violent views into the mouth of his protagonist, Chatsky, rather too obviously; Gogol, with what seems like deliberate self-restraint, has no character in *The Inspector-General* formally express the author's own sentiments. He is unwilling to commit himself to a definite attitude towards the problem he has taken up, but he does attempt to present all sides of the subject. His determined effort to be impersonal is shown by the "Notes for the Actors" which he prefixed to his drama. In them he describes the bodies, clothes, and mannerisms of the principal characters, with a minute power of observation that reminds one of Ben Jonson's detailed description of men and their habits. By the time *The Inspector-General* is over we know a great deal about the lives of a number of small Russian officials, where they get their money and how they spend it, their relations with their neighbors and their families, their amusements and their hypocrisies. The fact that they have their transparent hypocrisies introduces the element of judgment from an ideal standpoint, which lies concealed behind the numerous persons and incidents in the foreground of Gogol's work.

The weakness of realism is that the numerous physical facts it presents may distract attention from the underlying meaning of a work of art. Its strength is that the emphasis on these same physical facts may stimulate the spectator to a new awareness of the physical limitations of mankind. The more petty objects there are in the world, the more necessary it is that they should be arranged with delicacy and skill to serve some useful purpose. The appearance of a single integrated personality is an excellent way of displaying the absurdity of people whose houses and minds are cluttered up with too many pieces of useless bric-a-brac. In Kotzebue's *The German Provincials* a man from the city is introduced into the restricted atmosphere of a small German town and succeeds in exposing its narrow-minded superstitions. Kotzebue's hero is a rather unpleasantly smug person. It would have been quite as easy for the dramatist to satirize him as to ridicule his environment. Gogol did not wish to run the risk of having the sympathy in his story lie in the wrong quarters. As the disturbing influence in his comedy he took a young man who is quite as much of a rascal as the townspeople among whom he finds himself. He is more successful, because he has had a wider experience and because circumstances play into his hands more easily, but one feels convinced that his triumphs will be hollow and short-lived.

The plot of *The Inspector-General* is supposed to be based upon a story that Pushkin told Gogol of how he had once been mistaken for a government inspector in a small Russian town. Gogol imagined an impecunious and unprincipled junior clerk in such a position, and the result is the character of Khlestakov. Khlestakov has lost all his money by playing cards with an infantry captain and is about to be put in jail by an indignant innkeeper. He is not a bad sort of fellow. Though easygoing and pleasure-loving, he is appreciative of life's experiences and endowed with a lively imagination. "The more sincerity and simplicity the actor puts into this role," Gogol wrote, "the better he will play it." He is attended by his elderly and taciturn manservant, who likes to lecture his master behind his back, but who takes a part in his disreputable schemes and extricates him from his precarious position before it is too late. These two persons appear in only the three central acts of the play. They are used by the dramatist to point out the weaknesses of his other characters, and yet they themselves have the failings of the average sensual man. The world is made up of people like that, Gogol seems to say, and on the title page of his comedy he prints the significant motto, "Don't blame the looking-glass if your face is crooked."

Khlestakov has a confidant in a friend of his who does not appear upon the stage but to whom he writes a letter describing his experiences as the supposed inspector-general. This letter, which is intercepted by the Postmaster and read in the last act after Khlestakov's departure, contains the essence of the play. Khlestakov describes to his friend how all the inhabitants of the town, thinking him to be an inspector-general, have bribed and flattered him; for the two days he has lived there, he has been treated like a king by a pack of knaves. He comments on the stupidity and amorousness of the townspeople, their drunkenness and bestiality, the foul odors that come from them, and the bad manners that they display. Still he regards them all as hospitable and kindhearted. These are the people of whom Gogol says, "Their prototypes may be found in almost any community." They have been tricked by Khlestakov, but only because of his greater poise; he can criticize the food given him at the inn more volubly than the Chief of Police can apologize for its inadequacy. The first scene between these two important characters is an excellent example of Gogol's plan and method. In it Khlestakov thinks that he is being arrested for debt and the Chief of Police believes that his dishonesty is being investigated by a higher official. Each man is a rogue with certain pardonable weaknesses, each supposes the other to be more respectable than he really is, and each is afraid that his own true character will be detected by his opponent.

Gogol's exposure of personal insincerity and official corruption reaches into every department of governmental activity. Each one of the town's magistrates is eager to offer money secretly to the supposed inspector, on the understanding that he as an individual will not be reported upon unfavorably. The Chief of Police, who is virtually the mayor of the city, is the principal target for satire. He is a self-made man, who has arrived at his present position by taking bribes and by persecuting mercilessly those who cannot or will not pay him for his patronage. Within limits, he is a clever man, or he could not have risen so far in the world. There is little doubt that, after the fiasco of Khlestakov's visit has been forgotten, he will retrieve himself and again solidify his position with the dishonest members of the community.

The members of the family of the Chief of Police, his vain wife and his ignorant daughter, provide the only feminine element in a play which is too occupied with the framework of society to devote much attention to matters of sex. Both mother and daughter are coquettish in their different ways, and each is much interested in clothes and fashions. They are jealous of each other's place in Khlestakov's affections. Their rivalry brings about an amusing scene, when the daughter finds Khlestakov on his knees before her mother. This situation is highly farcical, but, like many other ridiculous incidents in the play, it is also a revelation of character. When the Superintendent of Schools lights his cigar at the wrong end, when the Chief of Police puts a hatbox instead of a hat on his head, when Khlestakov slips and almost falls in his drunkenness, one laughs, but one is made acutely aware of the Superintendent's nervousness, the Chief of Police's excitement, or Khlestakov's carelessness, as the case may be.

The two minor characters in *The Inspector-General* who perhaps best exhibit the peculiar quality of Gogol's art, on a small scale, are the landed proprietors, Dobchinsky and Bobchinsky, a close parallel to Tweedledum and Tweedledee. They are both described as being short and stocky; they both speak very fast and use many gestures. Dobchinsky, the taller and the more serious, wants to legitimatize his eldest son, who was born out of wedlock. Bobchinsky, the more expansive and lively, has the great ambition of wishing to be talked about in St. Petersburg. When Dobchinsky is chosen by the Chief of Police to be present at the first interview with Khlestakov, Bobchinsky follows them, peeps through a crack of the door off and on during the conversation, and finally, when the door falls off its hinges, is catapulted into the room. The result is that his nose is severely scratched, and he appears throughout the rest of the play with a ludicrous plaster on it. Bobchinsky and Dobchinsky vie with each other for the credit of having been the first person to suppose that Khlestakov was the expected inspector-general. At the end each is anxious to disclaim the responsibility for the false identification.

They present a pitiable picture of amazement and futility in the final tableau, when it is announced that the real inspector-general has just arrived to investigate conditions in the town.

Dobchinsky and Bobchinsky are rather like flies on the wheel of the comedy's action. In this respect they are not unlike the more important characters in the plot. There is a suggestion throughout the play that the individual life is not significant compared with the social fabric of which it is a part. Inspectors may come and inspectors may go, it is implied, but the little town with its corrupt magistrates will continue, and the world is made up of thousands of such small communities. By exposing the follies of this particular town Gogol laid himself open to the Chief of Police's gibe that authors are dangerous Liberals. Gogol was more liberal than the Liberals, however, when, on being hailed by them as their spokesman and champion, he insisted that he was not working for any one narrow political party. He hated the dishonest officialdom in the Russia of his day, but he also realized that under every uniform there was a human being as simple and inoffensive as Dobchinsky or Bobchinsky. *The Inspector-General* not only shows the difference between what men seem to be in public and what they are in private life, but in an indirect and tantalizing way it hints vaguely at the mystery of what human beings are really like at bottom.

Gogol makes the Chief of Police declare that all men have their little failings, and it is God himself who has arranged it so, whatever Voltaire and his followers may say to the contrary. This statement expresses Gogol's central position very fairly. He is a satirist up to a certain point, beyond which he is a humanitarian. He has found that farce, which is only an exaggerated kind of realism, is artistically a happy medium between the extremes of ridicule and sympathy. These two opposing attitudes, which had been struggling in the work of eighteenth-century writers like Goldoni and Lessing, came to a sort of comic synthesis in the rough horseplay of *The Inspector-General*. The same uproarious mixture of criticism and understanding suffuses Gogol's great comic narrative, *Dead Souls*, written a few years later. In it the writer's appreciation of humanity has, if anything, increased, and his indignation at social abuses is no less intense; but the projected scope of this novel is too vast to be fully realized, and *The Inspector-General* must be considered Gogol's most finished literary production. It compresses into the five acts of one play its author's sensitive interpretation of his experience on earth.

Gogol's immense reputation as a dramatist rests primarily upon this one remarkable play, although he tried his hand at a number of other comedies and comic sketches. *The Vladimir Order*, begun before *The Inspector-General*, was never finished; probably the censor would not have permitted the performance of such a bitter attack upon the Russian bureaucracy. It was to have shown how an ambitious official failed to maintain his sanity when the intrigues of his enemies proved more successful than his own underhanded schemes to obtain the much-coveted Vladimir Order. *The Inspector-General* is a more normal treatment of the theme of the deceiver outwitted. A later one-act piece, *The Gamblers*, is a lighter version of the same story. It deals with a professional gambler, who takes part in cheating a country bumpkin and then finds that he himself has been cheated by his supposed confederates. There is a good deal of structural ingenuity displayed in *The Gamblers*, which is a straightforward comedy of intrigue with few subtleties of thought or feeling.

Marriage, Gogol's other completed play, is of greater importance. It contains no philosophy, but it paints a realistic picture and shows how an individual's personality may prevent his fitting into an organized social scheme. Its subject is how matrimony can be achieved — or avoided. Podkolyossin, its hero, likes the idea of getting married, but he cannot face the actual ordeal. He resorts to a professional matchmaker, he gets a married friend of his to propose for him, and finally he escapes by a window rather than go through with the wedding ceremony. The audience is left with the impression that, although it is a miserable thing to be a bachelor, for most men marriage is a heavy chain. Reluctance to face the wedding ceremony is no doubt a common masculine characteristic, but it is a reluctance which in the great majority of cases seems to be successfully overcome. For this reason, *Marriage* treats a minor theme. It deals with an ungovernable impulse, not with a general way of life.

Marriage contains some secondary material which was influential in shaping the later realistic drama of Russia. It shows in considerable detail the machinery by which marriages are arranged. The heroine and her aunt debate the wisdom of marrying a nobleman or a merchant, the various suitors explain the qualifications which they demand in a wife, and the professional matchmaker carries on her trade with great relish. The matchmaker is, like Juliet's nurse, a version of the classical go-between or bawd, adapted to the social conditions of the time. Her love of money and her delight in seeing young people mate are her outstanding characteristics. The comedy arises when human feelings become entangled in her practical activities. The matchmaker in *Marriage* is brought into comic relief by being contrasted with the hero's friend, whom she also helped to marry off and who now believes that all the bachelors of his acquaintance should get themselves wives. There is a kind of rivalry between these two agents of procreation, both of whom are checkmated by Podkolyossin's undignified retreat through the window. If love laughs at matchmakers in romantic comedies, in realistic ones they may be rendered ridiculous by a succession of trivial events. One of the most unsatisfactory features of *Marriage* is the casualness of its conclusion. Podkolyossin could perfectly well have resisted his impulse to escape. It might have been even truer to life for the reluctant lover to have succumbed to his fate than it is for him to make his way out of the toils. *Marriage* is aimless in a way in which *The Inspector-General* is not.

The Inspector-General rises superior to the limitations of realism. It stands by itself among the dramatic works of Gogol and all other Russian writers, and it has sometimes been called the best play written in the Russian language. On its own ground it has certainly never been surpassed. Everything about this unique comedy grows upon one with continued acquaintance. One must interpret its profuse material for oneself and not be disconcerted to find that it is by turns a farce, a satire, and a sentimental comedy. Its plot has artistic structure without being rigidly formal. Its texture is a happy combination of individuality and universal truth. Its vitality is extraordinary; its inventiveness seems never to flag; it has the creative quality of life; it lacks only the consistent intellectual meaning which life itself so often seems to lack.

III

Gogol's *Marriage* and *The Gamblers* were published in 1842. The next year marks the beginning of the work of an author more important in the realm of the novel than in that of the theater, Ivan

Sergeyevich Turgenev. Turgenev began his literary career as a writer of plays. For nine years, from 1843 to 1852, he devoted his energies chiefly to that form of art. Toward the end of this period he began writing the short stories which compose *A Sportsman's Sketches*, and these proved so successful that they turned his attention away from the drama. His comedies are by no means negligible, however; in his own way he helped to carry on the tradition that had been formulated by Gogol. His admiration for Gogol was very great, as he showed not only by several references in his plays and novels but by an enthusiastic tribute written at the time of Gogol's death in 1852. This obituary notice was displeasing to Nicholas I, who, fearing that Russia might be infected by the revolutionary spirit of 1848 in western Europe and distrusting authors as dangerous Liberals, had Turgenev imprisoned for a month and then exiled to his country estate for a year and a half. It is true that, like Gogol, Turgenev was acutely conscious of the social abuses of his day, but he treated them more in his stories than in his plays. In the drama he devoted his principal attention to a psychological analysis of human beings, particularly in matters of love.

Turgenev wrote ten plays in all, the greater part of his dramatic work being composed in the three years from 1847 to 1850. One of the ten pieces is *Lack of Caution*, a tragedy of intrigue with a Spanish setting. Two of them are mere sketches which do not pretend to do more than outline a situation. *A Conversation on the Highway* contrasts a decadent young landowner, who has lost all his money, and a simple old coachman, who is devoted to his master from habit rather than from conviction; the difference between the cynicism of the one and the superstition of the other is used to illustrate the chasm separating social classes, in morality as well as in economics. *Lack of Funds* pictures another impecunious young aristocrat, who is living beyond his means in St. Petersburg and whose faithful old servant urges him in vain to return to the country home of his mother.

Lunch with the Marshal of the Nobility portrays the inefficiency of rural magistrates; *A Provincial Lady* hints at venal corruption in higher governmental circles. In this latter piece the wife of a poor official in a small town is trying to get her husband a more important position in St. Petersburg by flirting with a count, who is an influential old admirer of hers. The wife has just got the count to promise that her husband shall secure the coveted post when the husband returns unexpectedly and finds the count on his knees before the wife. The count is chagrined and feels that he has been duped, but he nobly agrees to carry out his promise. How far the wife has been playing with him is the crucial point of this comedy. After the discovery she continues to hint that her affection for him may be real. "A comedy can be played well only where one feels what he is saying," she maintains, and that statement contains the heart of Turgenev's comic theory. *A Provincial Lady* is partly a comedy of social situation, hinging upon the desire of the lady and her husband to live in the metropolis, and partly a comedy of sentiment, with the lady's feelings perhaps more involved than she has been willing to admit, even to herself.

The same sort of ambiguity created by a conflict between sentiment and comedy pervades Turgenev's two-act drama, *The Parasite*. The heartlessness of an aristocratic husband and the sympathetic nature of his well-to-do wife are brought into opposition when the parasite who has been a hanger-on of the family asserts publicly in a moment of drunkenness that he is the wife's father. The husband refuses to believe the story and succeeds, as he thinks, in buying off the parasite's claims, but the wife feels that the poor man has told the truth and arranges to see him again without her husband's knowledge. The comedy ends with the dramatic irony of a misunderstanding between husband and wife which permits both of them to think that they are in the right. The background of *The Parasite* is a picture of life on a large country estate. As in the work of Gogol, the tendency toward realism fuses to a certain extent the satirical and emotional factors which are in conflict beneath the surface of Turgenev's art.

Another of his longer plays, in which the same fundamental contrast occurs, is *The Bachelor*, a detailed analysis of various kinds of love. The main subject of this drama is the struggle in the heart of an old bachelor between paternal and sexual love for his young protégée. To this principal theme several subsidiary ones are closely related. The heroine's young fiancé is torn between ambition and affection for the girl, whom he considers beneath him in social position; she is attracted at the same time to both her lover and her protector. The girl is so much the most interesting character in the piece that Turgenev might well have developed her part at greater length. He is always extremely successful with his portraits of young women uncertain of their own feelings. The heroine of *The Bachelor* is not a comic figure like her fiancé, who gives her up for worldly considerations, nor a sentimental one like her self-sacrificing guardian, but somewhere between the two extremes. Soon after she loses her young lover, she tells the old bachelor that some day later on she may consent to become his wife.

Turgenev handles with exceptional delicacy love affairs to which there is some obstacle, such as social position, age, or temperament. In *An Evening in Sorrento* he shows how a woman of thirty loses a man of twenty-eight, with whom she is in love, to a young girl of eighteen. In *Where It Is Thin, There It Breaks* the heroine agrees to marry a dull, phlegmatic man whom she does not love when the volatile and artistic one to whom she is attracted does not propose to her. *Where It Is Thin, There It Breaks* is the most effective of Turgenev's minor works for the theater. Of them all it most closely resembles his dramatic masterpiece, *A Month in the Country*, particularly in respect to the background against which the principal intrigue develops. The love affair in the slighter play takes place on a country estate, presided over by a flighty but not altogether impractical woman of the upper middle class. Her complicated household is composed of such diverse characters as an elderly female relative, who hates being compelled to accept the bread of charity, a French governess, who is always sewing and sighing for Paris, and a ruined ex-captain, who looks like a bully but is really a servile flatterer. They drift on and off the stage, exchanging random observations which have little to do with the plot and which intensify the air of casualness that envelops the entire proceedings. These characters are depicted, with a candor that seems almost brutal to an Anglo-Saxon, as futile creatures who discuss eating candy and mushrooms, who play at pool or preference, and who, when it begins to rain, have not the faintest idea of how to amuse themselves. With their cultivation and their incompetence, they are striking examples of the leisureliness and aimlessness of one stratum of social life in Russia during the middle of the nineteenth century.

This same atmosphere of apparent tranquillity and concealed uneasiness pervades Turgenev's one superlative comedy, *A Month in the Country*. The owner of the rural estate on which this play takes place is a stupid, well-intentioned man who cannot become reconciled to the fact that, although the Russian peasants are intelligent, they refuse to work consistently. He knows that they have no patience, but he respects them nevertheless. His establishment consists of his wife, his ten-year-old son, his elderly mother, his mother's companion, his son's two tutors, and a young girl dependent on the family. The life of the mother, her companion, and the German tutor is desultory, unmotivated, and only enlivened by games of preference. At the end of the play they are just where they were when it began, except that the coquettish companion is about to leave to marry a country doctor, who has analyzed for her, with extraordinary detachment, his own assets and liabilities as a husband. This doctor serves as a sardonic chorus throughout the comedy. He describes himself as a jolly but satiric person, not a very good doctor but a successful, self-made man. He is a curious mixture of brutality and honesty, shrewdness and naïve complacency.

The doctor comments slyly on the principal characters in the play, but he does not take an active part in the plot beyond acting as an amateur marriage broker for a rich middle-aged neighbor, who wants to marry Vera, the young girl of seventeen, dependent on the family. Vera finally agrees to marry the shy but kind neighbor after she has discovered that she cannot marry Belyayev, one of the tutors, with whom she has fallen in love during the month that he has been on the country estate. The character of Vera, which Turgenev himself did not consider of first importance, is one of the most finely drawn in the whole piece. The gradual unfolding of her love for Belyayev is indicated with great tenderness. She is so much of an unformed girl that she does not admit her love even to herself, until the avowal is drawn from her by the apparent sympathy of Natalya, the landowner's wife. When Vera has come to understand her own feelings, she also suddenly realizes that Natalya is her successful rival with the tutor, and she finds it hard to forgive the older woman's treachery. Vera is a girl with a straightforward emotional nature, which gradually comes to dominate her and which teaches her the harsh realities of Turgenev's comic world.

Belyayev is a much less fused and admirable human being. A

simple young man, neglected by his father, he has managed to get an education and is now supporting himself by being a tutor. Though he is drawn to Vera, who reminds him of his sister, he is much more fascinated by the older and more accomplished Natalya. When he realizes that Natalya loves him, he is flattered and believes for a moment that he loves her, but he soon realizes the absurdity of his position. He falls under the influence of Rakitin, an older man, who is also in love with Natalya and who tells the young tutor with deep sincerity what a painful thing it is to be in love. Rakitin is motivated partly by jealousy and partly by a consideration for Natalya's true welfare. He himself leaves the estate to save her honor, taking the burden of her love affair with Belyayev upon his own shoulders. Rakitin cares for Natalya profoundly, but by disillusioning the young tutor he brings about the temporary unhappiness of the woman to whom both of them are devoted.

Natalya is the central figure of *A Month in the Country*. Turgenev admits that he was most interested in her, and hers is an effective part, although a somewhat theatrical one. Her character is not altogether persuasive, in spite of the fact that her actions can be partially explained by the lack of a sufficient outlet for her average intelligence and her more than average emotional energy. Turgenev tells us a good deal about Natalya's past history, as if he wished to suggest that her psychology may be largely accounted for by her early environment. She had a stern father, to whom she had always been slavishly obedient and whom she feared even after he became old and blind. Her childhood was a constant series of repressions; she had little real youth of her own. Now that she is a married woman and has reached the dangerous age of twenty-nine she is eager to try to recapture at second hand some of the normal sensations which she had never experienced in her girlhood. She is slow to appreciate the state of her feelings for Belyayev, but when she once does so she is ruthless in attempting to gratify them. After the tutor's departure, she is for the moment completely heartbroken, but one suspects that Rakitin's solution of the difficulty was the best one for her ultimate happiness. Natalya will sooner or later recover from her painful experience. She will be fortunate if, later on, she does not meet another attractive young man, with no Rakitin to give him mature counsel.

A Month in the Country ends without having reached a very deci-sive conclusion. Natalya, her husband, her husband's mother, her son, and her son's German tutor will continue living on the estate. Life will go on in much the same way as it has done heretofore, and Natalya will no doubt continue to be restless and dissatisfied. She and Belyayev seem to be badly coördinated people by comparison with Rakitin and Vera, both of whom have secured emotional tran-quillity at the cost of immediate happiness. No one of the four princi-pal characters in this play has an agreeable prospect for the future. Only Natalya's stupid husband thinks that everything has come out in the best possible way for himself and all the others.

Turgenev's constant preoccupation seems to be with the idea that love is a capricious and unpredictable emotion, strong enough to up-set any sensitive human being's equilibrium but not powerful enough to cause him to direct his complete energies into a single concen-trated channel. All of the people in *A Month in the Country* have more or less violent passions, but no one of them is able to satisfy his im-pulses. There is some inhibiting force within them all which makes it impossible for them to express themselves as they would like to do. The practical circumstances of their lives have too much influence over them. They lack the strength of character that they should have if they are to be the masters of their own fates. This weakness pro-vides excellent material for a highly individualized and original type of comedy. A sense of humor becomes identified with a perception of what man would be in contrast to what the innumerable details of life have made him become. A makeshift arrangement is the best outcome that can be hoped for in matters of the heart, which have to be organized according to man-made conventions, of marriage, of property, and of class distinctions. Unless there should be a radical shift of attitude towards these human institutions, there is no possi-bility that a healthy balance can be established in the unsteady society which is pictured in the comedies of Turgenev.

IV

The plays of Turgenev are based fundamentally upon the un-predictable fluctuations of human passion in matters of sex; those of Gogol are chiefly concerned with the chicanery and deceit which flourish in the world of affairs. Of the two writers Gogol was the more immediately influential. Gogol's objective attitude towards society was intensified in the work of Alexander Nikolayevich Ostrovsky, who in the thirty-five years between 1850 and 1885 composed some forty plays of the greatest variety. Ostrovsky was long one of the most popular of Russian playwrights within his own country, but his reputation never extended widely beyond its limits, perhaps because his forte was the depicting of local conditions. He did not have the clear intelligence and undeviating purpose necessary to lend general significance to commonplace events. He was a most successful practical man of the theater; his plays are often moving or amusing. Perhaps he more than anyone else gave body to the realistic tradition which had been unconsciously initiated by Gogol and which had been developed in a specialized direction under the hands of Turgenev.

Ostrovsky's most famous play is *The Thunderstorm*, a pure tragedy, which ends with a suicide. Often his dramas leave neither a definitely tragic nor a definitely comic impression upon the audience. He gives the subtitle "Pictures from Moscow Life" to one of his comedies, and another is described as "Scenes from Village Life in Four Pictures." "Pictures" is a very suitable word to use in describing much of Ostrovsky's dramatic work. His method is to show a situation as nearly as possible as it actually exists, without emphasizing either its pathetic or satirical elements.

The Poor Bride is a play which is a good example of Ostrovsky's uncertainty whether to treat life from a serious or from a humorous point of view. The heroine is forced to marry a coarse, uneducated fellow, a bribe-taker, a drunkard, and a light-o'-love, in order to save her mother from financial ruin. In the last act of the play the wedding is celebrated in a scene which is a brilliant example of realistic technique. Servants and wedding guests move back and forth across the stage commenting on the action, music for dancing is heard from an adjoining room, and the state of mind of the principal characters is indicated by short scenes and scraps of dialogue. The bridegroom parts from his former mistress, a new character who has not even been heard of before, and promises the bride not to drink vodka or take snuff in the future. The bride consoles herself with the dubious hope that she may be able to reform her dissolute husband;

she takes a certain amount of perverse pleasure in the sacrifice that she is making for her mother. How the marriage will ultimately turn out is not a matter that concerns Ostrovsky. The bride's beauty has been exchanged for the bridegroom's wealth; it is a fair bargain on both sides, and no one should complain of having been unjustly treated.

Occasionally Ostrovsky's plays end in a more sentimental fashion. In *Enough Stupidity in Every Wise Man* a designing villain, who has been completely successful for three and a half acts, is shamed and put to rout in the last act and a half of the drama. *Enough Stupidity in Every Wise Man* emphasizes the fact that simple human beings like to be flattered, even when they know the painful truth about themselves, and also points out that some flaw is to be found in the armor of the most hardened hypocrite. *Fairy Gold*, in which an erring wife returns disillusioned to her husband, offers some social criticism in the contrast between the substantial husband, a hard-working railroad engineer, representative of the rising industrial classes, and the impecunious lover, a decayed aristocrat, characteristic of the faded gentility of the past. "Fairy gold," we are told, is money that has not been honestly earned and disappears as soon as one attempts to touch it. From this play alone one might imagine that Ostrovsky was a sincere advocate of the new commercial Russia, but in *Poverty Is No Crime* he gives an entirely different slant to a similar economic problem. Here the wealthy business man is dishonest, and the hero is a poor clerk who finally wins the heroine in spite of the father's objections. The most sympathetic character in this play is Lyubim Tortsov, the spendthrift uncle of the heroine. This kindly drunken rascal, who is largely responsible for the happy outcome of the plot, does not mind being poor so long as he can be irresponsible and gay.

Lyubim Tortsov, in *Poverty Is No Crime*, is an effective acting part, and so is Neschastlivtsev, the wandering actor in *The Forest*, another play in which poverty is considered no crime. Neschastlivtsev is a sort of "servant in the house" or "third floor back," who comes unexpectedly into a confused situation, straightens out all the difficulties inherent in it, and passes on to a mysterious future, leaving peace and tranquillity behind him. In this case Neschastlivtsev has quixotically given up his social position because of his love for art, and although he has been a failure as a tragic actor he does not regret his choice of a profession. After a brief visit to the estate of his aunt, during which he arranges many complicated matters of finance and the heart, he determines to take to the road again and departs with a rousing denunciation of bourgeois life, which seems to him as dark and impenetrable as the forest that stands on his aunt's estate. *The Forest* is a well-made play. Like most of Ostrovsky's dramas after *The Thunderstorm* (1859), it is influenced by the technical dexterity of the French stage. The later work of this dramatist is much less original in nature than that with which he began his career.

From the purely comic point of view Ostrovsky probably never surpassed his first play, *We Shall Settle It between Ourselves*, the scene of which is laid among the merchant class of a large city. Ostrovsky seems to have studied this society with infinite care and to have drawn it with unusual fidelity and comprehension. The plot of *We Shall Settle It between Ourselves* is an adaptation of the deceiver outwitted, which had already been employed to good effect by Gogol. Its principal figure, Podkhalyuzin, a person rather like Uriah Heep, begins life as the clerk in the employ of a merchant whose finances are in an unsound condition. Podkhalyuzin gradually worms his way into his master's confidence and pretends to be willing to help him in a feigned bankruptcy, by which the rascally merchant hopes to retrieve his business affairs at the expense of his creditors. This feigned bankruptcy proves to be Podkhalyuzin's opportunity to get the better of his master. He succeeds in securing for himself most of the merchant's tangible assets and also the hand of his daughter. He makes a cold-blooded agreement with the selfish girl, who is anxious to further her own interests, even at the expense of her parents. In the last act of *We Shall Settle It between Ourselves* he and she are safely married and refuse to fulfill their past obligations or to give financial assistance to her father, who is now in a debtors' prison at the suit of his creditors. The designing husband and wife seem to understand one another quite well, and as yet no rift has appeared to mar their frankly mercenary partnership.

Ostrovsky's pictures of the sordid and disagreeable world into which he introduces us do not provide the relief of either noble suffering or hearty laughter. The flat realism which he presents is more inclusive than that of Gogol or Turgenev and therefore less selectively refined than that of the earlier writers. It is, however, a powerful description of the externals of a mediocre social group. It is, in addition, thoroughly representative of the aesthetic tendencies of the nineteenth century in Russia and elsewhere throughout Europe. The continuous rise of the middle class tended to stimulate a kind of art which does not make excessive demands upon the imagination. Ostrovsky offered his audiences plenty of variety in scenes drawn from observation and experience. In some of his plays the merchants are good; in others they are bad. In some, children get their way; in others, parents or guardians get theirs. Conditions are never the same in any two cases, and therefore, in his view, no general principles can be extracted from the welter of human society. The aim of a realistic artist like Ostrovsky is to present life as he sees it, vividly and accurately, with the utmost photographic exactness.

In contrast to the objectivity of Ostrovsky's work, another eminent Russian writer went to the opposite extreme of personal prejudice in the selection and interpretation of his material for the theater. The danger of too great subjectivity was encountered by Count Lev Nikolayevich Tolstoy, who was primarily a novelist and much less detached in his attitude toward life than a pure dramatist such as Ostrovsky was likely to be. Most of Tolstoy's plays were composed after 1879, when he received the religious illumination which turned all his subsequent writing in the direction of idealistic morality. Of his ten plays only two were written before 1879, and these two, *The Nihilist* and *The Contaminated Family*, are neither of great literary value. The ideas they contain are, oddly enough, opposed to each other. The former ridicules an absurd prejudice against Nihilists; the latter records how a conservative family frees itself from the contamination of liberal ideas. Tolstoy evidently did not value these two plays very highly, since he did not have either of them published before his death.

Toward the end of his life Tolstoy composed for his own satisfaction a number of sermons in dramatic form that breathe the pure faith of simple morality plays but offer few opportunities for a display of comedy. A comparison of one of the plays written not long after his conversion with his last work for the theater makes clear his increasing absorption in transcendental values. In 1886 he published *The First Distiller*, in which a little devil concocts a strong drink and demoralizes the home of a pious peasant; in 1910 he wrote

The Root of All Evil, in which a drunken tramp steals tea and sugar from a peasant family but penitently returns them after he has become sober again. In *The Root of All Evil* drunkenness has become a prelude to moral regeneration; in *The First Distiller* it is amusingly described as an invention of the devil and a hazard to mankind.

The First Distiller was published before Tolstoy's death, as were the two dramas which are his best work for the theater: *The Power of Darkness* is a lurid tragedy of horrible intensity; *The Fruits of Enlightenment* is an elaborate and skillful comedy, which contains the essence of Tolstoy's mature personality, here engaged in directing an oblique attack against his enemies' position. The members of the aristocratic family depicted in *The Fruits of Enlightenment* are entirely absorbed by social diversions and appear ridiculous because of their devotion to trivial affairs. The father believes in spiritualism; the mother is worried about her health; the boisterous son is occupied with dogs and horses; and the daughter, a fashionable young woman, is full of masculine affectations. Tolstoy draws in great detail the unpleasant members of this family, their friends, dependents, acquaintances, and guests. His object is to pillory the externals of fashionable life, its superficiality and its hypocrisy, its attention to petty detail, and its entire lack of contact with reality.

In order to make his attitude clear, Tolstoy introduces into the household three simple peasants, all plain, honest people who know what they want and go steadily ahead to get it. Their straightforwardness of manner and their consistency of purpose contrast strikingly with the casual uncertainty of the entire aristocratic group. They have come to ask the master of the household to sell them some land with a small cash payment down. The master is tricked into making this sale by a clever maidservant, Tanya, who takes advantage of his outstanding weakness, his implicit confidence in spiritualism. She arranges a fraudulent séance, during which he is induced to complete the sale of the land. Even when he discovers that he has been imposed upon, he is still as confirmed as ever in his delusion about the validity of his pet hobby.

The importance of Tanya in the plot of *The Fruits of Enlightenment* gives Tolstoy a plausible excuse to introduce the servants of the household, who interest him more than their masters or even than the rough peasants. The relations between employers and employed was a matter that greatly exercised Tolstoy in the period following his conversion. He disapproved strongly of a system of society in which one class had to be subservient to another. According to his ideas, if every man cultivated the land and owned no property, Russia would come to resemble an earthly paradise. The peasants seemed to him entirely right and the aristocrats entirely wrong, while the servants of the rich were the unfortunate victims of a system for which they were not responsible. That is why, at the end of the play, he has Tanya's lover, the son of a peasant, leave his employment in the city and return to his father's house, taking his bride with him. The beneficent influence of rural life, it is implied, will make all human beings who are touched by it recognize the close bond that connects them with one another.

One scene in *The Fruits of Enlightenment* takes place in the kitchen of the house, where the servants deliver many trenchant criticisms on the useless life led by their employers. The upper classes of society are said to spend their days in eating and drinking (without regard for fast days), in playing cards, in dancing, and in practicing on the piano. The ladies are attacked for their immodest dress and the attention they give to clothes; the men, for ruining their horses by neglect and spoiling their dogs by indulgence. There is a long discussion of how doctors impose upon their patients, and much gentle sarcasm is directed at people who pay too much attention to their health. Tolstoy is here striking at the pathetic attempts of the idle rich to find something with which to occupy their energies when they are not compelled to do any productive work. He delivers some incidental thrusts at fumigation and quarantine, new scientific developments which seem to him highly ridiculous, and he mentions with evident scorn the recent theory of microbes. In general, he is opposed to the discoveries of science, which, he thinks, interfere with man's working out his emotional salvation for himself. He believes in a simple, natural religion, which is not dependent upon the miracles of science or spiritualism to confirm it.

The Fruits of Enlightenment is at bottom a religious tract, like the other plays written by Tolstoy after his conversion, but its message is hidden under a large number of incidental thrusts at an unmotivated way of life. It is a scathing denunciation of the cultivated society that grows up with comparative economic prosperity; it has in it the seeds of an attack upon the established capitalistic system. Written in 1889, it reads somewhat like a prophecy, if not of the Russian Revolution, at least of the World War. Bernard Shaw is justified in calling it the first in the long series of Heartbreak Houses which were to picture the conditions that culminated in 1914. Its artistic weakness is its tendency to be a document in contemporary propaganda, but the partial and one-sided view it presents is a great relief after the indeterminate attitude towards Russian life which permeates the plays of Ostrovsky. Neither Tolstoy nor Ostrovsky are great writers of comedy, but their accomplishments in the theater help to connect the masterpieces of Gogol and Turgenev with those of a still greater dramatist, Anton Pavlovich Chekhov.

V

Besides his many delicate short stories Chekhov wrote four superb plays and ten or more lesser dramatic works. The earliest of these latter appears to have been *On the High Road*, composed in 1884 and forbidden production by the censor in the same year. The liberal tendencies of the reign of Alexander II were largely nullified by his successor, Alexander III, who ascended the throne in 1881, when a reactionary period in Russian history set in. The conservatism of Alexander III intensified the uncompromising idealism of Tolstoy. It must have been somewhat responsible for the air of frustration which pervades Chekhov's work. It is to be found in a subdued form in *On the High Road*, which is called a "dramatic study." Chekhov attempts to be as detached and objective as Ostrovsky, but to Ostrovsky's freedom from prejudice he adds a subtlety and finesse not unlike Turgenev's penetrating analysis of human character. Like some of his predecessors, Chekhov was not sure at first whether his genius lay in depicting life from the tragic or from the comic point of view. In his four great plays he balanced implied tragedy against superficial incongruities, and from the union of these two unharmonious elements he created a novel genre which may best be described as ironic comedy.

On the High Road strikes this note of irony when, at the end, Merik, the tramp, begs the Christian pilgrims to have mercy on his soul because he has not been able to kill the faithless wife of a ruined landowner. Merik is a clear-sighted irreligious fellow, a sort of Blanco Posnet in embryo. He holds the beliefs, common in Chekhov, that happiness is always behind one, but that one must do his best to help other people in this difficult world. He is a robber and a thief when it suits his convenience. He is quite ready to die. He admits that his disillusionment with life has been the work of a woman. He feels that he has been unable to accomplish even the one high-minded action of losing his life in a noble cause. The scene of *On the High Road* is laid at an inn, where a large group of miscellaneous characters are assembled to pass the night. They furnish a varied background, from which the picturesque and complex personality of Merik stands out with startling vividness.

A more ambitious early attempt of Chekhov's to deal with un-usual psychological states was the tragedy called *That Worthless Fellow Platonov*, in which the hero, a philanderer caught in the toils of his own deceit, is finally killed by one of his discarded mistresses. Chekhov treated a simplified version of the situation more success-fully in *Ivanov*, published in 1889. In this latter play there are several minor characters who are early sketches for figures in Chekhov's mature comedies. There is a poverty-stricken gentleman, who can-not bring himself to propose to a rich widow who would accept him in an instant, and there is a friendly doctor, who gives the impres-sion of being cold and conceited, although he is really competent and honest. The characters of these two men, as well as that of Ivanov, the hero, who at last summons up the moral courage required to shoot himself, are developed partially by innuendo and partially by discussion on the part of the other people in the play.

Besides Chekhov's experiments with formal tragedy, he tried his hand, in the years between 1884 and 1890, at a number of lesser pieces of various kinds. *Tatyana Repina*, intended to parody a play by his friend, A. S. Suvorin, is a macabre flight of the poetic imagina-tion. *A Tragedian in Spite of Himself* begins as the comic monologue of a henpecked husband, who has to carry a number of parcels home every night, and ends with the speaker chasing an innocent friend around the room as he calls wildly for blood. Another play for a single speaker is *The Swan Song*, in which the leading character is an old comedian whose career is over. Alone in a provincial theater with his friend the prompter, he reviews the events of his past life and comments in a maudlin tone on his present misfortunes, recovering himself sufficiently near the end to assert that "where there is art and genius, there can never be such things as old age or loneliness or sickness." For a moment, genius can annihilate time; in the long run, time will get its revenge and blot out the individual artist. This basic paradox runs through all Chekhov's work and explains many of its superficial inconsistencies.

Contrasts of this kind are used to secure humorous effects in Chekhov's four one-act farces, written chiefly to amuse audiences, as they have been most successful in doing, both in Russia and elsewhere. *The Proposal* shows two people who disagree on every point becoming engaged, because common sense tells each of them that marriage is a desirable state. In *The Bear* a sentimental widow and a boorish gentleman decide to get married, in spite of their widely different temperaments, because of the strong physical attraction that exists between them. *The Anniversary* relates how the celebration of the fifteenth anniversary of a certain bank has to be postponed because of the intrusion of two women upon the time of one of the bank officials. The romantic shallowness of one woman and the financial necessity of the other interfere equally with business. Together they prove disastrous to a rigid, but weak-willed, man of affairs.

The Wedding, which is the most elaborate of Chekhov's four farces, has one striking comic figure and one whose lot is grotesquely pathetic. At the wedding breakfast a telegraph clerk who is a disappointed suitor of the bride's pretends that he thinks her family so unintelligent as to be beneath his notice. At the same time a retired naval captain's feelings are hurt when a greedy insurance agent tries to pass him off as an aristocratic general to satisfy the snobbish inclinations of the bridegroom. The captain is a deaf old man, who does not at first understand what is happening. When he does realize the situation, he feels outraged and angrily leaves the party. His departure, however, does not detract from the general hilarity of the wedding celebration.

In the years from 1884 to 1890 Chekhov was experimenting in a number of literary mediums. After 1890 his dramatic productivity was suspended for a time, during which he devoted himself to writing stories and, in his professional capacity as a doctor, to taking part in medical relief work attendant upon the cholera epidemic of 1892–93. When he returned to writing for the theater in 1895 he immediately set himself to the composition of what proved to be, from both a practical and an aesthetic point of view, his first outstanding success. In 1896 occurred the first performance of *The Sea Gull*.

The Sea Gull is essentially a treatise on art. It contains four characters who, in their various ways, represent four different attitudes that artists may take toward their work. Madame Arkadin, a vain selfish woman, is a talented actress; her son, Konstantin Treplev, an idealistic young man, at first wants to try new forms of literary expression, but finally comes to feel that in art inspiration is all that matters; Trigorin, a successful realistic novelist, is jaded and dissatisfied with his accomplishment; Nina, an immature young actress, learns from harsh experience that one must not expect worldly rewards in the sphere of art. These four characters, especially the two older and more static ones, are developed with great dexterity. Madame Arkadin, who is forty-three years old, though she would like to pass for thirty-two is kept young by her devotion to her professional career. She is stingy in money matters and puts a great deal of energy into dressing well. She is unbelievably jealous, but she is a good nurse and has some fine feelings, of an attenuated, sentimental sort. Trigorin is intelligent, good-natured, and melancholy. He cannot keep from writing books, although he knows that his work is of an inferior quality. He tries to forget himself in the theater and in fishing. He wants to be free from the restrictions of his own personality. He would like to recapture his lost youth, but from force of habit he continues in the dreary round of taking notes on his experiences and writing them up in a monotonous series of popular novels.

Although in matters of aesthetic theory and practice Trigorin must not be considered a self-portrait, he probably possesses a larger share of Chekhov's temperament than any of the other characters in *The Sea Gull*. The dramatist was writing from his heart in the second act, where Trigorin bares his soul to Nina, telling her of his ambitions and his failures, his good intentions and the irresistible impulse which urges him on to create. "I have scarcely finished one novel," he says, "when, for some reason, I must begin writing another, then a third, after the third a fourth. . . . I have no rest from myself, and I feel that I am eating up my own life, and that for the sake of the honey I give to someone in space I am stripping the pollen from my best flowers, tearing up the flowers themselves and trampling on their roots. Don't you think I am mad? . . . While I am writing I enjoy it. And I like reading my proofs, but — as soon as it is published, I can't endure it, and I see that it is all wrong, a mistake, that it ought not to have been written at all, and I feel vexed and sick about it. — And the public reads it and says: 'Yes, charming, clever. Charming, but very inferior to Tolstoy,' or 'It's a fine thing, but Turgenev's *Fathers and Children* is finer.' And it will be the same to my dying day, only charming and clever, charming and clever — and nothing more. And when I die my friends, passing by my tomb, will say, 'Here lies Trigorin. He was a good writer, but inferior to Turgenev.'"

Trigorin's comparison of himself to Tolstoy and Turgenev is of particular interest to a reader of Russian comedy. In this sphere Chekhov undoubtedly surpassed his two great predecessors. In *The Sea Gull* he for the first time conceived a variety of contrasting people, described them with great understanding and precision, and placed them in situations where the eccentricities of their characters would be naturally revealed. Sex attraction rather than art is the cause of the complications in *The Sea Gull*, but these two themes are so closely fused that there is no discord between the emotions and the ideas involved. There is an interlocking chain of unrequited love affairs: Madame Arkadin clings to Trigorin, who has long been her lover, and Treplev is in love with Nina, who becomes captivated by the casual attentions of Trigorin. At the end of the third act Madame Arkadin takes Trigorin away to Moscow before further mischief can occur. She seems to have triumphed through her determination and worldly wisdom, but there is a suggestion of impending tragedy for the future.

The relation of the last act to the rest of *The Sea Gull* is one of the chief causes for the fascination exerted by this strange play, but it is also a weakness in technical construction. Two years elapse between the third and fourth acts. In the interval a great deal has occurred: Nina has had a child by Trigorin and been deserted by him, Trigorin has again succumbed to the domination of Madame Arkadin, and Treplev has begun to have some success as an author. Such is the state of affairs when Nina returns to say a last farewell to Treplev and to tell him of the great discovery she has made in her suffering about the nature of art: "In our work — in acting or writing — what matters is not fame, not glory, not what I dreamed of, but knowing how to be patient. To bear one's cross and have faith." Treplev, who has already become disgusted with his literary success and feels that his romantic art is growing as stereotyped as Trigorin's realism has long since become, takes Nina's lesson to heart and, considering himself to be without faith, puts a bullet through his head. His suicide may be considered an artistic blot on the comic detachment of *The Sea Gull*, but Chekhov's idea of comedy is such a somber one that death is not wholly out of place in it. Moreover the ironic, not the tragic, aspects of the situation are emphasized on the stage. When the final curtain falls Madame Arkadin and some of the minor characters are just sitting down to continue a game of lotto, unaware as yet that Treplev has killed himself.

The minor characters in *The Sea Gull* are chiefly responsible for conveying the impression that life continues uninterruptedly, no matter what personal disturbances may occur in its course. There are six of them, each one a fully rounded personality. The two most important to the action are Masha, a gloomy girl who always wears black, and a pedestrian schoolmaster, whom Masha marries without making any pretense of loving him. Masha, the daughter of a steward, is keenly aware of her inferior social position. She dislikes her father, whose attention is occupied with horses and dogs, and whose only contributions to artistic subjects are his stolid reminiscences of great actors of the past. Masha's mother is completely uninterested in her husband. Her affection is all lavished upon a self-contained doctor, named Dorn, who has been loved by many women and is impervious to all assaults upon his emotions.

Dorn, because of the firm hold he has upon his own feelings, must be regarded as the most contented character in *The Sea Gull*, and Sorin, Madame Arkadin's brother, as the most pathetic one. These two men, who have little to do with the working out of the plot, represent the two extreme attitudes between which the principal characters oscillate, and together they help to steady the shifting moods of the comedy. Sorin, a man of over sixty in very bad health, is a thoroughly disappointed individual. He has failed in all his ambitions, and in spite of his twenty-eight years in the Department of Justice he feels that he has never really lived. He is an actual civil councilor, but he does not appreciate what he has achieved and is always yearning for something else. Dorn is the exact opposite in that his desires have never exceeded his accomplishments. He tries to convince Sorin of the absurdity of fearing death and the frivolity of an old man's trying to live like a young one. Dorn is constantly referred to as being satisfied with life, and Sorin is the epitome of discontent. Chekhov, with strict impartiality, shows that the older man is lovable in spite of his many absurdities and that the younger one is a little inhuman for all his worldly wisdom.

If Trigorin represents Chekhov's turbulent emotional life, Dorn may be said to express his creator's ideas. The doctor once received a vague intimation that there was such a thing as a world-soul, but he is without an artist's sensitiveness of perception. He is imaginative enough, however, to suppose that, if he had ever known "the spiritual heights which artists reach at the moments of creation," he would have become discontented with his own smugly comfortable existence. He approves of art and thinks it only natural that artists should be treated better than merchants, because of the idealistic strain in human nature. This combination of sympathy and detachment makes Dorn an ideal mouthpiece for an aesthetic creed, similar to Chekhov's, which he enunciates in the first act: a work of art ought to express a great idea, for a thing is only fine when it is serious; it must treat what is important and eternal; and it must be based on a clearly defined conception, or otherwise the lack of a specific goal will vitiate an author's perceptive insight. This last point is of particular importance in understanding the plays of Chekhov. It leads one to realize that, however incoherent and diffuse his dramas may seem on the surface, there is always some underlying theme which binds the apparently unrelated episodes together.

In *The Sea Gull* this underlying theme is the nature of art, around which revolve the contrasting emotions and thoughts of the various characters. The movement of the play is circular, not straightforward. Its predominant atmosphere, in accordance with Chekhov's ironic view of life, is comic. People say one thing and mean another; their ideas are at cross-purposes with their emotions, and their actions do not agree either with what they think or with what they feel. The dialogue in Chekhov's plays moves on two levels at the same time, one the casual interchange of external commonplaces, and the other a deeper, more intense, and less clearly defined realm of inner illumination. At the end of *The Sea Gull* the contrast between these two planes of experience is so violent that one is shocked into admitting the paradoxical nature of the universe as it appeared to Chekhov. The dramatist was to achieve still greater balance and restraint in the presentation of his material, but *The Sea Gull* made clear that its author was already in possession of a new medium for bringing intelligent comedy into the theater.

VI

With the wisdom gained from his experience with *The Sea Gull* Chekhov set himself to revising one of his earlier plays. *Uncle Vanya,* which was first produced in 1899, is inferior in conception to *The Sea Gull* but more skillful in technical craftmanship. The first version of it, known as *The Wood Demon,* which had been composed ten years earlier, contained a suicide, not at the end of the play, but at the close of the third act. There the prototype of Uncle Vanya kills himself because of the sale of the estate and the hopelessness of his love, without any of the jealousy which motivates Vanya's fury in the revised play. *The Wood Demon* has no single thread of interest to keep it unified in spirit, as *Uncle Vanya* has in the strange individuality of Yelena, the young wife of a retired professor.

Yelena is a beautiful and idle woman, twenty-seven years old. She married the professor thinking that she truly loved him. Now she admits that she would have liked a younger husband, but she intends to remain faithful to the invalid whom she has sworn to love and honor. She has a strong conviction that human beings destroy one another from a lack of sympathetic understanding. She believes that she is fated to play a secondary part in the affairs of the world. She is unhappy in her lot but resigned to it. Her only emotional outlet is music, but her husband does not let her play upon the piano as much as she would like to. She is a decorative individual, not herself productive in any way, but sensitively aware of the complicated lives that surround her. She is the character in *Uncle Vanya* about whom the other people revolve. She serves in this play the same function that the idea of art does in *The Sea Gull*. Although she does not at any time cease to be a human being, it is said that she has mermaid blood in her veins. In her effect on the other characters she resembles an embodiment of art rather than a real woman. Like Irene in Galsworthy's *The Forsyte Saga*, she is a representation of beauty impinging on an active world.

The plot of *Uncle Vanya* bears a decided relation to that of Turgenev's *A Month in the Country*, which, in this instance, is one of the literary sources of Chekhov's inspiration. Yelena is a more subtle character than Natalya in the earlier play, but their situations are much alike. Both women are loved by men who do not attract them, and both are fascinated by men adored by younger girls. In the end both of the wives return to their husbands, and neither of the young girls marries the man of her choice. Superficially the plots are quite similar, but in mood the plays are absolutely different. *A Month in the Country* is, first and foremost, a comedy of thwarted love; in *Uncle Vanya* the love story is used merely as a starting point for the treatment of wider aspects of life. It is not the attitude of artists to their work which occupies Chekhov in this play, as it had absorbed him in *The Sea Gull*, but the larger question of the relation of art to more systematized methods of self-expression.

In *Uncle Vanya* the management of the professor's estate is the important practical task under consideration by the various characters. Uncle Vanya, the brother of the professor's first wife, renounced his share in his family inheritance to buy the estate for his dead sister's dowry. He worked for ten years to pay off all the mortgage that was owed upon it, and he has managed it for twenty-five years on a very low salary. When the professor announces his intention of selling the estate to secure money to live in the city, Vanya is so infuriated that he attempts to shoot his brother-in-law. His attitude toward the professor is complicated by his devotion to Yelena. He discovers Yelena in the arms of the doctor, Astrov, and as a result his mental balance is seriously upset. His outburst at the end of the third act, when he fires a revolver twice at the professor and misses him both times, is the culmination of the action. It results in the professor's departure for the city with Yelena, and in Vanya's remaining behind to take care of the estate with the help of Sonya, the professor's daughter by his first wife. At the end of the play a busy, active life is again to proceed in its accustomed way; its temporary interruption by the disturbing forces of love and beauty has been surmounted at the cost of considerable human suffering. Vanya, who has given up his momentary impulse to kill himself, must go on working for others with Sonya until death releases them.

The attitude of the various characters in the play towards work provides the underlying unity of theme in *Uncle Vanya*. Yelena alone has no theories about it, but her devotion to her husband is itself a kind of work. Her husband, the professor, is extremely rigid in his demands on the people who surround him. He has lectured on art for twenty-five years; theoretically he believes in the importance of work, although his own work has always been of an impractical and selfish sort. Vanya, who has worked hard all his life, has become completely demoralized by the appearance of Yelena. At the end of the play, when he realizes that his love for her is doomed to disappointment, he takes up his work again as a help to him in enduring his mental anguish. Sonya is a thorough idealist. She keeps on doggedly at her work, sustained by her hope of a reward after death. She realizes that there is very little happiness in store for her in this world. She is not beautiful or attractive, and there is no hope that her love for Astrov will ever be returned.

The views of Astrov, the doctor loved by Sonya and drawn to Yelena, give *Uncle Vanya* much of its distinctive tonal coloring. He is a curious combination of idealism and disillusionment. He is the antithesis of Uncle Vanya in that Vanya takes to drink during his temporary loss of ideals; Astrov drinks vodka regularly, and only under its influence can he recapture the dreams of his youth. He has become disgusted with human beings, particularly because of the way they let the old forests be destroyed. His mania is for the preservation of the woods, which, he believes, temper the severity of climate and so make the men who dwell near them into happier human beings. He approves of plain, uneducated people, living in a comparatively primitive state. If he is more sardonic and less kindly than his forerunner, the original wood demon, his external cynicism is really the reverse side of his unconquerable optimism. He does not love life in general, but in particular. He works hard at his doctoring and gardening; he is much moved by absolute beauty when he meets it in the person of Yelena. He is impervious to Sonya's simple nobility, but his belief that only in the grave may one have pleasant dreams is not unlike her confident faith that in heaven she and Uncle Vanya will at last find rest from their painful labors.

Astrov combines in one person the discontentedness of Sorin and the complacency of Dorn in *The Sea Gull*. Chekhov has here been more subtle than in his earlier play about weaving his comic standard into the framework of the action. Astrov disapproves of Yelena but is attracted to her. She introduces an element into his life which confuses and upsets him. He is torn between his struggles to reach an ideal which he knows is unattainable and the materialistic philosophy which he has adopted to protect himself against the disappointments that come to all people in the world. Like everyone else in the play, he realizes that the only practical solution of his problem is for him to work at something. He believes that, however useless one's efforts may be, only in work can mankind find happiness.

No one of the characters in *Uncle Vanya* is essentially an artist, but all of them have artistic sensibilities. Chekhov here seems to be grappling with the problem of how average people can best express their imaginative impulses without attempting to create recognized works of beauty. They cannot hope to be happy in their love affairs, and each of them must try to work out his own salvation for himself. The paradoxical effort to relate individual effort to the welfare of humanity presents a dilemma which is at the basis of Chekhov's sense of humorous values.

In *Uncle Vanya* the playwright had mastered the form of dramatic art which he had created in *The Sea Gull*. In some respects *Uncle Vanya* is the most perfect, as it is the briefest, of his four great comedies. The longest and most difficult of the four is *The Three Sisters*, produced in 1901 after he had his new technique well in hand. In it he attempted to apply his method to more elaborate and varied material than he had yet undertaken to treat.

The subject of *The Three Sisters* is not formal art or its related theme of universal beauty but a still wider topic, the conflict between two ways of life, the ancient and the modern, represented here by the army and the teaching profession respectively. In the small provincial town where the action occurs, a battery of artillery is quartered, and four of the ten important characters in the play are attached to it in one capacity or another. The lieutenant-colonel who commands the battery is a man of forty-two, unhappy in his married life and convinced that, in the present stage of civilization, people cannot hope to achieve on earth the happiness for which they long. A shy and nervous captain says more unattractive things than he means and takes refuge in a Byronic pose, which he has adopted from Lermontov. A lieutenant, with the social rank of a baron, thinks that life will always be much the same; there will be external scientific improvements but not much increase in happiness for the individual. The army doctor, a doddering old man of nearly sixty, is convinced that nothing matters in this world, because it is only through a delusion that we seem to exist at all.

All four of these men are profoundly unhappy in spite of their external military grandeur. They have a common philosophy of despair, although each allows some faint rays of hope to penetrate the gloom of his outlook. Colonel Vershinin, the commander of the battery, believes that happiness may somehow come later if people will learn to work together. Baron Tusenbach, the lieutenant, thinks that, although there is no expecting happiness in the future, one can be so completely wrapped up in the present that he will be satisfied for the time being. He expects that when one is dead one will really be a part of life. He himself has been spoiled in his youth and has never been able to accomplish the work that he has always intended to do. Vershinin is more idealistic and noble than Tusenbach, who is realistic in theory but pathetically impractical in action. These two outstanding representatives of a military caste which has outworn its usefulness are compared with two very different people, who are not worried about theories of existence and for that reason are quite settled and contented in their minds. Natasha, a vulgar girl, marries and becomes a conventional wife, mother, and housekeeper, at the same time carrying on an intrigue with another man. Kuligin, a school teacher, works hard at his daily tasks, is content with his obscure position, and does not mind that his wife, Natasha's sister-in-law, is passionately in love with someone else. He and Natasha, each in his own way, have accepted their respective lots. Because they do not complain about what life has brought to them, they are successful in their own eyes and in the eyes of other people.

Natasha is a despicable, if lively, girl, and Kuligin a noble, if boring, man, but they have much the same effect upon the family of Prozorovs, into which they both have married. The Prozorovs are torn between the old aristocracy of the army and the new democracy of education. They are not satisfied with the past they have lost or the future they have not yet attained. They are struggling between two worlds, one dead and the other not yet ready to be born. Their father had been a general. They had been brought up and educated in Moscow, where they had learned English, French, and German, and where they had been accustomed to having many officers about their house. They came from a family that despised work, but they had been rigorously trained as children to get up at seven in the morning to start the routine of the day. Eleven years before the opening of the play, their father had retired and moved to the small town where they now live. A year before, their father had died, leaving his four children to get on as best they could without him. The weak, artistic son, Andrey, hopes to be a professor; Olga, twenty-eight years old, has been a teacher in the local high school for four years; Masha, now about twenty-two, had married the teacher Kuligin when she was eighteen; Irina, aged twenty, is full of high hopes for the future. At the beginning of the action they discuss their great desire to go back to Moscow, and at the end of it, several years later, they are still regretfully wishing that they could have recaptured the glories of their youth. They have not been able to do so, and they do not realize why they have not gone to Moscow, any more than why all mankind must suffer on this earth. The final words, "If we only knew," strike the wistful keynote of the drama.

In the four or five years that elapse between the beginning and the end of *The Three Sisters* each of the Prozorovs has gone through a number of experiences without having his or her character profoundly modified in the process. Andrey has not become a professor, but he is a member of the Rural Board, a post which he owes to the lover of Natasha, now his wife. Olga, who, if she had had the chance, would have married any good man without loving him, has been promoted to the headmistressship of her school, where she now lives. She no longer feels at home in the Prozorov house, which has become completely dominated by Natasha. The gloomy Masha, already bored with her schoolmaster husband, has fallen desperately in love with Colonel Vershinin, who returns her affection but is irrevocably bound to an uncongenial wife. Irina has been employed first in a telegraph office and then with the Town Council; she is finally going to become a teacher like Olga. She has not fallen in love with anyone, although she has accepted Tusenbach's offer of marriage in order to get away to Moscow. She never really expects her dream to come true, and she is not surprised when Tusenbach's death in a duel makes it necessary for her to continue her routine existence in the little town. At the end of the play the battery of artillery is ordered away, and *The Three Sisters* ends with the scene of parting characteristic of all Chekhov's comedies. Tusenbach is dead, Vershinin and the rest of the officers have gone off, and only the forgetful old doctor is temporarily left behind. He will return in a year, when he has been retired, to live permanently with the Prozorovs. He loved their mother, and, although he cannot remember now whether or not she loved him, his only happiness is to be near her children.

The four Prozorovs are all connected, in one way or another, with the theme of education, which runs like a bright thread through the somber woof of *The Three Sisters*. The only hope for the future of the family and of Russia seems to lie in education. Vershinin, who, as much as anyone in the play, expresses a constructive point of view, holds that as a result of the gradual spread of education among the masses "in two or three hundred years life on earth will be unimaginably beautiful." At present, he thinks, education has not yet begun to be really effective, and the army has already finished its work: "In old days men were absorbed in wars, filling all their existence with marches, raids, victories, but now all that is a thing of the past, leaving behind it a great void which there is so far nothing to fill: humanity is searching for it passionately." In *The Three Sisters* Chekhov, like Vershinin, seems to be searching passionately for something to cling to in this world. Art is beautiful and work is necessary, but for what end shall mankind create and work? Not for imperial glory, certainly. For a more intelligent society? "If we only knew."

The Three Sisters is Chekhov's most ambitious play, and if its standard of judgment had been clearly defined, it would perhaps have been his greatest. It is filled with richness of observation, but it contains almost too much material to be handled effectively in a single drama. Besides its ten important characters, there are four minor ones, and, besides the people we see, we are made acutely aware of Natasha's lover and Vershinin's wife, who do not appear upon the stage. The size of the canvas is immense, and so is its variety and its extent in time. The first act is laid at noon on a Sunday in May, when Irina's name-day is being celebrated; the second is in the evening a year from the next January, while a carnival is being held in the streets; the third is at two o'clock in the morning, just after a fire has occurred in the officers' quarters; the fourth and last is at noon again, this time in the autumn of the year. In the first act Andrey and Natasha are not married; by the end of the play they have given birth to three children. This procession of the seasons and the years gives a sort of epic quality to *The Three Sisters*, which unrolls with a wanton prodigality of splendor, as dazzling as it is confusing.

VII

With his last play, *The Cherry Orchard*, first produced in 1904, Chekhov reached the height of his accomplishment. For it he found a subject of more significance than the aesthetic considerations of his first two great comedies, and one which could be concentrated into a more tangible and concrete form than the wide range of *The Three Sisters*. He managed to focus the entire issue, between the old-fashioned manner of life and the new order, upon whether or not Madame Ranevsky should allow her hereditary estate to be cut up into building lots which could be let on lease for summer villas. This proposition, made possible by the advance of the railroad, would entail the cutting down of the beautiful cherry orchard that had long been the pride of the estate. It would mean sacrificing in the interests of practical economic necessity what generations of landowners had regarded with sentimental veneration. Madame Ranevsky's finances are impoverished, her creditors are clamoring for their money, and the sale of the cherry orchard to pay her debts can only be prevented if she will take the initiative in the real estate development which in time is bound to occur. This she cannot bring herself to do, and she prefers to let the cherry orchard be put up for sale. It is purchased by an enterprising merchant, Madame Ranevsky moves away from the estate, and, after she has gone, the strokes of an axe beginning to cut down the cherry orchard are heard in the distance. For one family at least, the old regime in Russia has definitely come to an end.

Madame Ranevsky and the people who surround her are not only individuals, like all Chekhov's characters, but also embodiments of many general characteristics of the Russian landed gentry. Madame Ranevsky is the widow of a man who killed himself by drinking too much champagne. She now has a lover in Paris, who is anxious to have her return to him there. She is good-natured and kindhearted. She loves Russia and her fellow human beings, to whom she is willing to give her last ready cash, but she has not enough force of character to keep from being an essentially immoral person. Her brother, Gayev, is equally attractive and impractical. He considers himself "a man of the eighties," and he believes that the peasants love him. He is full of schemes to raise money, no one of which could possibly be carried out. He is really happier after the cherry orchard has finally been sold, when he is to have a position in a bank. If embarrassed, as he often is, he takes refuge in the jargon of billiards, a game of which he is exceedingly fond. He appreciates natural beauty, and he sheds tears of sentimental joy over an old bookcase. Gayev and Madame Ranevsky stand for the older generation of Russian aristocrats; they are charming and lovable, decorative but useless. They and their family estate are doomed to disappear before the inroads of railways and commerce.

The younger generation of Russian intellectuals appears in the persons of Madame Ranevsky's daughter, Anya, and Trofimov, the "perpetual student." Anya is a simple young girl of seventeen, happy by temperament and susceptible to new ideas. She is persuaded by Trofimov that the sale of the cherry orchard is not a very great calamity; at the end of the play she is courageously planning to study for her examination in a near-by high school. She admires Trofimov, but they both think themselves as much above love as Madame Ranevsky seems to be beneath it. Trofimov is an uncompromising idealist. A young man of nearly thirty, he has never finished his work at the university, to which he is returning when the play is over. He pays no attention to his clothes or personal appearance because he is so taken up with dreams and theories. He explains to Anya that she need not be saddened by the loss of the cherry orchard: "All Russia is our garden." He believes that Russia must expiate her wicked past by suffering, that everyone should be free, and that by unremitting labor universal happiness may yet be attained. His fine theories are in striking contrast with his inability to manage his own life. He has been twice sent down from the university, he has no money, and he is sure to be hungry when winter next sets in. He falls downstairs awkwardly; when leaving the estate, he is not able to find his galoshes. His weakness and strength are clearly brought out in his conversations with Madame Ranevsky, for whom he is a perfect foil. She thinks that he should take a mistress in order to become a normal human being. He advises her not to go on living in a world of pleasant delusions far removed from the realities of life.

Trofimov is a detached observer who can analyze other people's characters without understanding his own. He is fond of Lopakhin who buys the cherry orchard, but he disapproves of Lopakhin's economic schemes. He feels that Lopakhin, for all his businesslike methods, has the fine delicate soul of an artist and should not try to crush it. Lopakhin is of an active temperament, but the range of his knowledge is narrowly restricted. His father and grandfather had been peasants on the estate of Madame Ranevsky, his father kept a shop after the liberation of the serfs, and now he himself has become a successful merchant. His ambition and his initiative are immense, but he still retains some evidences of his humble ancestry. This conflict in his soul is focused on his attitude toward Madame Ranevsky and the fate of the cherry orchard: on the one hand, he is anxious to preserve for the benefit of its traditional owners the estate on which his family had worked; on the other hand, when he sees that Madame Ranevsky cannot be persuaded, or frightened, into undertaking the proposed development herself, he cannot resist the opportunity to advance his own fortunes. The scene immediately after his purchase of the cherry orchard exhibits the whole range of Lopakhin's character. He has been drinking to celebrate his triumph. He alternates between exultant boasting at his prowess and tearful regret that he is partially responsible for Madame Ranevsky's suffering. He has an artist's sensibilities but a peasant's crudeness in his manner of expressing them.

Lopakhin's lack of skill in adjusting himself to changed conditions of society, from which he has profited, is made very clear by his relations with Varya, Madame Ranevsky's adopted daughter.

Varya is the housekeeper of the establishment, a demure and efficient girl, who would like to go into a nunnery if she had enough money. She must work for her subsistence, however, and when Madame Ranevsky's household is broken up she plans to take a similar position with some other family. For two years it has been supposed that she and Lopakhin, who are very fond of each other, would get married. There is no obstacle to their union, except that Lopakhin is so embarrassed when he is in Varya's presence that he is unable to bring himself to make her a definite proposal of marriage. Lopakhin and Varya are both extremely capable in their separate spheres and yet quite helpless when they are brought together. They represent the rising middle class, efficient in practical matters, but unable to adjust their emotions to the changes taking place in society.

Besides the six main characters of *The Cherry Orchard*, each of whom is limited enough to seem ridiculous at certain moments, there are six subordinate figures who help to develop the main subject, the alterations that are taking place in the structure of Russian society. There is an old valet who disapproves of the emancipation of the serfs, an educated but impractical clerk, a maid who dresses herself up like a lady, and a dandified young valet who has recently returned from Paris with the superior airs of a Jean de France. Besides these four servants, there are two other people whose lives are something of a mystery. The more peculiar of the two is the German governess, whose mother and father were mountebanks, and who herself is an adept at sleight of hand tricks. She knows practically nothing about herself, and she feels completely alone in the world. Her physical isolation is a forcible reminder of the spiritual loneliness felt by the other persons in the play. A neighboring landowner is important, not so much for the emotional background of the action as for its social implications. He is an ineffectual fellow, always wanting to borrow money that he has no apparent prospects of repaying, until some Englishmen find a kind of valuable white clay on his land and he sells them the rights to dig it for a number of years. His story suggests that Madame Ranevsky is not the only decadent landowner who will be able to continue existence temporarily, because of the advances of modern science and industrialism.

The bourgeois world of petty officialdom is introduced into *The Cherry Orchard* in the persons of the station master and the post-office clerk who come, somewhat reluctantly, to the dance in the third act. They have been invited in place of the generals, barons, and admirals who formerly attended Madame Ranevsky's parties. The lower classes are represented by the drunken tramp who crosses the stage in the second act and terrifies Varya, when he declaims socialistic doctrines about the brotherhood of man. His brief appearance is one of the swift incidental touches by means of which Chekhov succeeds in painting a concise and comprehensive picture of Russian society in the early twentieth century.

The Cherry Orchard is a social document, but like all Chekhov's plays it is also a poem. During the second act, just before the appearance of the tramp, a strange sound like that of a breaking harp string is heard mournfully dying away in the distance. The practical Lopakhin explains it as a bucket fallen and broken somewhere off in the stone pits; the superstitious old valet says that a similar evil omen occurred before the emancipation of the serfs. At the very end of the play, when the house has been deserted, the same weird sound is again heard far away, this time mingled with the blows of the axe that is cutting down the cherry orchard. The combination of these two sounds closes The Cherry Orchard on a note in which social change and mystical inspiration are united by an artist's creative intelligence.

In all four of Chekhov's comedies sounds help to establish the immense underlying importance of trivial everyday occurrences. Sometimes a watchman is heard tapping during interior scenes when a storm is supposed to be raging outdoors; every now and then mournful strains are played upon a guitar. In the last act of The Sea Gull Treplev plays a melancholy waltz off stage on a piano; at the close of Uncle Vanya the bells of horses punctuate the departure of the various characters. The Three Sisters has, characteristically, more of these atmospheric sounds than any of the other dramas. It ends to the accompaniment of a military march, as the battery with its band marches away into the distance. It also contains Masha's recurrent poetic phrase, "By the sea-shore an oak-tree green . . . upon that oak a chain of gold," and her superstitious belief that, before her father died, there was a howling in the chimney, much like the noise that the stove now makes. These various appeals to the emotions are simplified in The Cherry Orchard, where they are reduced to a shepherd fluting on his pipe, the Jewish orchestra playing dance music for the party, and the magical combination of the axe strokes with the breaking harp string at the final curtain.

In every respect *The Cherry Orchard* is more restrained than *The Three Sisters* and the best integrated of any of the four plays, with the possible exception of *Uncle Vanya*. It is a much more elaborate and extended drama than the latter, however. There can be little doubt that it is Chekhov's most finished piece of work. In it are to be found ideas about love and art, tradition and education, business and science, all fitted together in a carefully articulated pattern that centers in the sale of Madame Ranevsky's cherry orchard. Chekhov's last comedy seems to have every requisite of the greatest literature except steady and unwavering vigor of execution. With its three companion pieces, it undoubtedly entitles Chekhov to be known as the most distinguished author of Russian comedy, but as an individual piece of work it is in some respects inferior to *The Inspector-General* by Gogol.

These two superlative plays, the masterpieces of Gogol and Chekhov, are the high-water marks of Russian comedy. It is significant that, in their different ways, they depend upon a similar attitude towards life and its comic values. In each of them a moving pageant of existence begins with the arrival of some person from outside the environment portrayed upon the stage and ends with the departure of the stranger to take up his former manner of living. Neither person is much affected by his experience, and neither environment is much altered by having been subjected to his influence. In both cases an infinitesimal modification in personality has been brought about by the sequence of events. A conflict between the idea of external change, characteristic of the nineteenth century, and the slowness of human beings to adjust their lives to this new conception of evolutionary development is at the heart of the best Russian comedy. Chekhov understood the far-reaching consequences of the issue and was profoundly discouraged by it. Gogol, approaching the problem at an earlier period, was stimulated by its novelty rather than depressed by its results. His vitality is his most splendid characteristic. If he lacks the wisdom of Chekhov, he also avoids the air of world-weariness which pervades the later dramatist's most finished work.

Taken together, the comedies of these two writers form a paradoxical commentary on the theme of the individual versus society. In them society is still held to be fundamentally right, as it was in the time of Molière, but there has likewise arisen a consciousness that society is made up of individuals, and that, if individuals are wrong, society must be so too. The fusion that has taken place between the whole and its parts has resulted in a compromise in favor of society, with the result that the individual tends to become neglected, as he is subjectively in Chekhov and objectively in Gogol. In both cases society is the touchstone for individual achievement. The size of one man compared to that of the whole mass is ridiculously or pathetically small. Russian comedy implies that if human beings are wise they will attempt to smile, with as much detachment as they can muster, at the lack of dignified stability in their lives and institutions.

CHAPTER X

Modern Times: Bernard Shaw

I

IN RUSSIA dramatic comedy underwent a radical change in nature during the nineteenth century; in Austria it languished after the time of Raimund and Nestroy until Arthur Schnitzler, born in 1862, the year of Nestroy's death, and Hermann Bahr, born one year later, gave it temporarily renewed social brilliance; in France it became entangled with the romantic refinements of Alfred de Musset, from which it was extricated by the realistic tendency that began with Émile Augier about the middle of the century and culminated some thirty years later in the work of Henri Becque; in England, or perhaps one should say in Ireland, it took a more original path and, as the sequel has shown, achieved extraordinary success.

The first sign of a revival of comedy in the English language was entirely British in origin. In the late 1860's, the tradition of absurdly exaggerated farces, translated or adapted from the French, gave way to "cup and saucer" plays by T. W. ("Tom") Robertson. In the six drawing-room comedies that he produced between 1865 and 1870 he let a breath of fresh air sweep through the artificialities of the well-made play. The title of Robertson's best-known work, *Caste*, is symptomatic of the contemporary interest in serious social problems. In this drama the haughty aristocracy and the unprincipled lower classes are pictured in an extreme and incredible fashion; the question of how far these two opposing elements in society can mingle on equal terms is clearly raised. Robertson's answer is not so satisfactory as his statement of the problem. In theory he does not seem to favor the breaking down of the caste system, but he implies that his titled hero will live happily ever afterward with the charming daughter of a disreputable commoner. The sentimental optimism of Tennyson and Dickens flourishes in the plays of Robertson. The comic contrasts involved in his material are resolved not by laughter, but by generous benevolence, well-fortified by a comfortable income. Love of country and pride in family are the forces that operate in *Caste* to bring about a happy ending.

A sentimental atmosphere also envelops the work of Robertson's immediate successors in the comic revival of the nineteenth century, the authors of the Gilbert and Sullivan operas. The sprightly humor of W. S. Gilbert's texts is much milder than the satirical wit of John Gay's lines in the somewhat similar *Beggar's Opera*, written one hundred and fifty years earlier. A rosy haze of kindly feelings suffuses each of the thirteen Savoy operas produced between 1875 and 1896. The first of them, *Trial by Jury*, is typical of Gilbert's method, in its ridicule, pointed but never barbed, of legal proceedings and in the casualness with which the characters pair off unexpectedly at the final curtain. To Gilbert the details of legal procedure seemed fantastically rigid, as they always have to satirists, and he was doubtless hitting at the lawyer's complacency in the extreme statement, "The law is the true embodiment of everything that's excellent." But he himself displayed a fundamental Victorian complacency in his acceptance of the idea that the law was a necessary support for the material prosperity of which he had every reason to be proud.

Gilbert's treatment of England's greatest practical asset, her navy, is another example of the uncertainty in his comic point of view. There are plenty of absurdities revealed in *Pinafore*, but breathes there an Englishman with soul so dead as not to realize that, at bottom, this popular opera is a great patriotic document? In spite of all temptations to belong to other nations, Gilbert's nautical characters insist on remaining Englishmen, except when, on being transplanted to the western shore of the Atlantic, they sometimes become "Am-er-i-cans." National pride, more than love of searching ridicule, also underlies Gilbert's treatment of the army in *The Pirates of Penzance*. At the end of that delightful extravaganza the pirates yield in Queen Victoria's name, because, with all their faults, they love their Queen, a triumph for the most personal kind of Victorianism. Also, with all their faults, Englishmen have loved their House of Lords, as *Iolanthe* bears continual witness. The external pomp and intellectual prowess of the peerage may be made ludicrous, but, although the extravagant line that the House of Lords "is not susceptible of any improvement at all" suggests that there may be room for improvement, there is no indication that the dramatist believed it in need of drastic reform.

In much the same way Gilbert implies that marriage must be upheld, in spite of the fact that it often goes counter to the impulses of love. Morality is, to him, more important than artistic insight, a Philistine attitude which is expounded to some of Sullivan's loveliest music in what now seems one of the feeblest of Gilbert's librettos, *Patience, or Bunthorne's Bride*. Bunthorne, walking down Piccadilly with a poppy or a lily in his medieval hand, presents a satiric picture of Oscar Wilde, who may have deserved to be laughed at for his stained-glass attitudinizing but could not at that time have justifiably been attacked for all the sins in the aesthetic calendar. Gilbert seems to have selected Wilde as a scapegoat for the whole art for art's sake movement, although there are signs in *Patience* that he also had in mind the peculiarities of Morris, Rossetti, Holman-Hunt, and other members of the Pre-Raphaelite Brotherhood.

In 1881, when *Patience* was originally produced, Wilde's first volume of poems was just about to appear, as a result, its author claimed, of his having at last attracted the attention of a publisher by the eccentricity of his dress. In 1892 Wilde himself made an attempt at writing comic plays with *Lady Windermere's Fan*. The immense popular success of this piece lured him on to concoct two other similar plots, before he struck out in a more original vein with *The Importance of Being Earnest* of 1895. For all Wilde's affectations and superficiality, he had a truer understanding of art, comic and otherwise, than did the naturally humorous, but intellectually limited, Victorian who had made fun of him in the text of *Patience*.

Lady Windermere's Fan and its immediate successors are problem plays such as Sir Arthur Pinero and Henry Arthur Jones were beginning to make fashionable in the Nineties, couched in sparkling, epigrammatic, and sometimes monotonous dialogue. Blackmail is usually an element in the plots of these comedies, which simmer down, in the last analysis, to a battle of wits between the virtuous and the vicious, with sentimental goodness finally overcoming the accepted conventions of organized society. Wilde is apparently pleading the case of the underdog, but as one laughs at the firecrackers which constantly explode from the mouths of his characters, one begins to doubt the warmth of their hearts and to care very little about the state of their souls. With *The Importance of Being Earnest*, "A Trivial Comedy for Serious People," the case is quite different. Here the superficial and platitudinous moralizing about social questions fades away and leaves only a skeleton of narrative, on which hang innumerable bits of scintillating conversation. The plot itself is far removed from everyday experiences, but the brittle mood established by Wilde's well-turned repartee prepares one to accept with comparative equanimity the most preposterous situations.

The elaboration of the basic incident in *The Importance of Being Earnest* is diabolically ingenious. The substitution of a baby for a manuscript is highly diverting, but it does not convey any such social implications as those of which Gilbert made use under similar circumstances. Wilde is not interested in the relations existing between naval captain and able seaman, between pilot and pirate, between king and drummer-boy. Such substitutions raise painful questions of aristocracy and democracy, which Wilde does not appear to consider. Art was to him more entertaining than life; the only thing which he cared for more than to receive entertainment was to dispense it gracefully to other persons. He succeeded in doing so with the utmost success in *The Importance of Being Earnest*, which is one of the most perfect farces in the English language. It would be worthy to stand with *The Taming of the Shrew* and *She Stoops to Conquer* if it were not that the brilliance of the dialogue does not harmonize entirely with the boisterousness of the plot. In the jarring discrepancy between these two qualities, one now and then becomes aware of an unsoundness in the dramatic texture. At such moments one discerns beneath the rich luxuriance on the surface of Wilde's play a pathetic sterility of human material on which to base variety and depth of comic perceptions.

Wilde was an Irishman; he would have been the first person to be amused by an anxious search for deep meaning in his comedies. An Irishman, living a cosmopolitan life in the metropolises of the world, he had largely lost touch with the land which might have been the source of his inspiration. In 1874 he had shaken the dust of Ireland from his feet. It was not until twenty-five years later, when his personal tragedy had been almost played out, that Ireland began to produce dramas which were closely connected with the soil. The Irish Literary Theater and its successor, the Irish National Theater, were deeply rooted in patriotic traditions. Their members were overwhelmingly convinced of the importance of their undertaking.

At first they devoted little time or attention to the lighter side of Irish life. They were militant crusaders with a serious political and artistic purpose, which brooked no interference from the gayer and less impressive varieties of human experience.

Gradually, however, a different attitude came to prevail. In 1902 William Butler Yeats, who was then beginning to work with Lady Gregory and the Fays in the Irish National Theater, produced a little realistic comedy, *A Pot of Broth*. It has been supposed that the impetus for this play, and perhaps some of its execution also, came from Lady Gregory. Certainly it has few of the characteristics one associates with Yeats's other work. Its story, of how a clever beggar fools two simple peasants into believing that to boil a certain stone in water will make a pot of rich broth for them, displays vividness, shrewdness, and an intimate knowledge of Irish life. Lady Gregory herself wrote some twenty-odd similar comedies, dealing with plain people unexposed to education but endowed by nature with a homely wit and a sharp tongue.

Lady Gregory's *Spreading the News* is a sketch built upon the absurdities of falsely reported gossip; *Hyacinth Halvey* is the story of a young man who, do what he will, cannot overcome the annoyingly favorable reputation that has become attached to him; *The Jackdaw* is concerned with the laughable adventures that occur when everyone in the village believes an incredible story about how money can easily be procured. The picturesque natives of Cloon, the village chiefly represented, include farmers and shopkeepers, the butcher and the postmistress. Some of them appear in more than one play, with the result that an onlooker comes to feel increasingly at home in the community of which they are a part. The material for first-rate folk comedy is present here. Unfortunately, Lady Gregory does not treat her humorous subjects with the intellectual detachment that might have made them permanently interesting. Her greatest literary assets are the freshness of her characterization and the air of easy buoyancy which she manages to breathe into all her work.

In one of her plays, *The Image*, Lady Gregory attempts to adorn the naturalistic tradition with the devices of art. It cannot be said that she is very successful in carrying out her purpose. The idea behind *The Image*, as Lady Gregory tells us, is that every man carries in his heart some image of the ideal, which crumbles when, in an attempt to give it tangible form, it is subjected to the light of day. The same plot has been amusingly used by George A. Birmingham for a comedy of intrigue in *General John Regan*. Lady Gregory has tried to create a philosophic background for her play, but she has not been able to rise to the height of her admirable intention. There was an "image" for this comedy in the background of the author's own consciousness, but ironically, and yet appropriately enough, she was not able to transfer her "secret to herself" across the footlights through the medium of drama.

The cycle of Lady Gregory's most original plays started with *Spreading the News*, in 1904, and ended with *The Image*, five years later. John Millington Synge's career as a playwright began one year before Lady Gregory's and terminated prematurely with his death in 1909. His work is incontestably the most important that the Celtic Revival produced in the form of drama. It combines the imagination of Yeats and the humorous realism of Lady Gregory. Synge never lets one forget that his characters are close to the earth and part of its mystery, that their lives are beautiful and at the same time painful. He wrote only six plays in all. Of these six, two are definitely trage-dies, but the two tragedies, although poetic in their essence, are, like the comedies, realistic in their externals.

Synge's deep understanding of the life of country people gives a body to his four comedies that is lacking in Lady Gregory's more superficial treatments of peasant life. In *In the Shadow of the Glen* the cowardice of Nora Burke's lover and the bravery of the passing Tramp take on sufficient human meaning to be more than a comic contrast of petty personalities. When Nora goes out with the Tramp to walk the roads in the grand morning air, and her lover sits down to drink a glass of whiskey with her husband, who has turned out not to be dead after all, Synge has opposed the vigor of life to a craven acceptance of comfortable shelter with so much power that one is not sure whether to laugh or cry.

In *The Tinker's Wedding*, the Church's conventional views about religion and marriage, as embodied in the priest who is to perform the wedding ceremony, are contrasted with the freer attitude towards fundamental issues held by the three tinkers, mother, son, and sweet-heart. The tinkers stand for the imaginative side of man's nature. Synge remarks in the preface to this play, "Of the things which nourish the imagination, humour is one of the most needful, and it is dangerous to limit or destroy it." In this case the humor springs from the impact of the rigid representative of the Church upon the free and easy life of the gypsylike people who act according to their impulses, without regard for the laws of men and priests. Synge sympathizes with their hearty naturalness, but he does not fail to portray also their vulgarity, their profanity, and their limited intelligence. The robust earthiness of the comic conflict between respectable formality and careless sincerity is inherent in the structural design of all Synge's plays.

The Well of the Saints, produced in 1905, two years before *The Playboy of the Western World*, presents a similar incongruity. It depicts two weather-beaten beggars who live happily enough in the realm of the imagination until a passing saint restores their eyesight and they begin to see the workaday world as it actually is. They find that they were not so badly off in their blindness as they had supposed. The parable is not unlike that of Lady Gregory's *The Image*, with the difference that Synge offers the imaginative side of man an unexpected means of escape from its predicament. The beggars in *The Well of the Saints* are again stricken with blindness, and this time they refuse to have the miraculous cure performed upon them; they sentimentally prefer to remain in their sensuous darkness, because in it they can see clearly with the eyes of the spirit.

In much the same way Christy Mahon in *The Playboy* does not regret the end of his love affair with Pegeen Mike, for now he can "go romancing through a romping lifetime from this hour to the dawning of the judgment day." Pegeen too has her liberation. Although she has lost the only Playboy of the Western World, she has at least been freed from the humiliation of marrying the moral and physical coward who had been her suitor before Christy's arrival. During the course of *The Playboy* both Christy and Pegeen have passed through the painful ordeal of learning that, according to the practical wisdom of this busy world, "there's a great gap between a gallous story and a dirty deed." From the entire experience Christy has come to believe that one can dominate one's environment by force, but that it takes imagination to win other people to one's way of thinking and that imagination is a costly luxury for a mature, fully developed person. Pegeen has felt the poetic power of Christy's marvelous wooing, but from realistic motives she lets the bodily form of her dream slip from her, although she will never again return to the crude prose of her previous life. Both Christy and Pegeen will ultimately have profited by the loss of their illusions at the expense of considerable momentary unhappiness. On the surface *The Playboy* ends in wild lamentations, but at bottom there is the serene consciousness that a large measure of truth has been attained by the obscure and devious processes of the imagination.

The Playboy of the Western World is undoubtedly Synge's masterpiece. All the best of Synge is in it, his irony, his knowledge of intricate psychology, his sense of human tragedy, his delight in uproarious knockabout comedy, and his extreme felicity in the use of beautiful words, which can make a dirty deed appear a gallous story. His other plays seem like early studies for this one supreme effort, into which is gathered the vital and refined essence of a sensitive personality.

II

Synge's achievement narrows down into one exquisite work of art. The theater of Synge's compatriot, George Bernard Shaw, has widened its range to include nearly everything in heaven above and on the earth beneath. Synge wrote four comedies; Shaw has written more than forty-four. Synge worked over his material until it emerged in a state of the utmost purity; Shaw has coarsened his texture, to the point where it infuriates most of those who are not wearied by its heaviness. Synge wrote one sweeping indictment of mankind's lack of imagination; Shaw has composed numerous assaults on mental obtuseness and human stupidity. Synge is a poet; Shaw, although he sometimes writes inspired and impassioned prose, moves on a lower aesthetic plane. His great gifts do not include an unlimited capacity for detailed observation, for sensitive nuances of human feeling, and for delicate overtones in language. Nevertheless, he has displayed a wanton prodigality of ideas and an excessive amount of intellectual energy which entitle him to stand with the great masters of dramatic comedy. As a satirist, he is not far removed from Swift and Voltaire; as a man of letters he recalls, though he does not resemble, such colossal literary figures as Dr. Johnson and Goethe; as a writer of intelligent comedy, he belongs to the great Anglo-Irish tradition of Farquhar, of Goldsmith, of Sheridan, and of Oscar Wilde.

Shaw's dramatic career began in 1892, the year in which *Lady Windermere's Fan* was first performed. It has continued almost without interruption for more than forty-five years, during which time he has been constantly active in writing plays, in explaining them with prefaces, and in telling actors how to perform them. There is very little order or system about the way his comedies have appeared, but four periods in his career may be roughly distinguished. There was a tentative experimental note in *Plays: Pleasant and Unpleasant*, which diminishes in *Three Plays for Puritans* and disappears altogether with *Man and Superman*, published in 1903; an increased range of subject and mastery of execution developed during the next ten years, up to the outbreak of the Great War; between 1914 and 1925 he composed the trivial "Playlets of the War" and his three most masterly achievements in widely different fields. The plays that have since appeared with his signature are pale shadows of his earlier performances. They have a quality of desperate patience that is lacking in his more vigorous constructive work.

Throughout his career Shaw has amused himself with "trifles and tomfooleries," which have done a good deal to confuse his audiences and to diminish his reputation as a first-rate literary artist. In 1926 he collected six of his ephemeral pieces under this title and published them, together with *Jitta's Atonement*, his translation of Siegfried Trebitsch's drama *Frau Gittas Sühne*. Shaw's procedure in translating Herr Trebitsch's drama is typical of the aims and method of his original work. *Frau Gittas Sühne.* is a romantic drama dealing with an unfaithful wife, who lives miserably ever after with a husband who will never let her forget her moral delinquency. *Jitta's Atonement* has subjected this story to what Shaw describes as "the disillusioning touch of comedy." The husband's infidelities are also established, with the result that both he and his wife plan to make the best of a bad business by enjoying life as thoroughly as possible in the future. At the end of the play the world at large concludes that Jitta is really too good for her husband, as Shaw, with his partiality for the woman's standpoint in matters of sex, wishes to have her considered by the audience. *Jitta's Atonement* is an attempt to provide a salutary corrective to the excesses of sentimental drama. A similar motive underlies Shaw's new last act for Shakespeare's *Cymbeline*, first performed in 1937, in which Imogen does not throw herself eagerly into Posthumus' arms but has to be cajoled into forgiving him for his rashness in ordering her death.

The Admirable Bashville, or Constancy Unrewarded, the first of the "tomfooleries," is a satire on the form rather than upon the spirit of pretentious plays. *Cashel Byron's Profession*, Shaw's early novel from which the material for this piece was drawn, exalts prize fighting, because it is a healthy profession, over the affectations of effete society. The play has the additional objects of parodying Elizabethan drama and, in the title at least, of delivering a sly thrust at Barrie's *The Admirable Crichton*. The major part of the satire, however, consists in the facile insipidity of the blank verse. Shaw's prefatory remark that blank verse is easier to write than prose must be accepted with the important qualification that good blank verse is much harder to write than good prose. Shaw's natural medium is prose, because his ideas are essentially prosaic, although sometimes both his ideas and his language assume a loftiness that brings them close to poetry.

The merging of poetry and prose, of tragedy and comedy, is suggested by the appearance among Shaw's "trifles" of *The Glimpse of Reality*, a serious little piece which its author describes as a "tragedietta." Its outcome is not tragic, although its plot is engaged with matters of life and death, both for the body and the soul. In it an issue is drawn between a rich pleasure-loving count and a poor hard-working girl, who refuses to help him escape from death at the hands of his enemies. She would be sorry if he had to have a tooth pulled, because that would spoil his pretty mouth, but to destroy his wicked soul would be a positive boon to humanity. The relentless logic of the girl's position impresses the young man so strongly that he begins to feel his life has been one long unreal romance. He decides that in the future he must pay attention to actualities like the soul, and by an unexpected twist of fate he saves his body also. He has been convinced that aristocracy has no inviolable privileges, since death comes to all men alike, regardless of their social advantages.

This serious view of the world underlies all Shaw's work, even that which appears most trivial upon the surface. The heroine of *Passion, Poison, and Petrification, or The Fatal Gazogene* learns from the farcical death of her lover that the ideal must spring from the real and, conversely, that the ideal must receive concrete expression if it is to have any vital meaning. *The Fascinating Foundling*, a Gilbertian skit that deals with a ward in chancery and at one point bursts into rhyme, is based upon the idea that it is better to marry a poor foundling than a rich heiress with a family. Shaw here indicates his belief that life should be reduced to its lowest terms, not clogged by inconsequential obstacles like riches and relations. *The Music-Cure* is not quite the "piece of utter nonsense" which Shaw calls it. It is built on the sound, if rather obvious, aesthetic principle that music hath charms to soothe the perturbed spirit. It is chiefly interesting for its satirical comment on politicians, whom Shaw regards as misguided men, motivated not by eternal truths but by petty considerations of immediate expediency. The mention of the profitable "Macaroni Company" is a passing gibe at a famous financial scandal involving government officials and wireless telegraphy. Shaw takes particular pleasure in attacking specific contemporary abuses and making them representative of universal human weaknesses.

He carried out this principle brilliantly in *Press Cuttings*, which he frankly calls a "topical sketch" of 1909, the year in which suffragette activities were at their height. Shaw sees a connection between votes for women and civil rights for the army. In *Press Cuttings* the Head of the War Office learns that he must give up treating soldiers as if they were schoolboys, and at the same time the Prime Minister finds he has to give up treating women as if they were angels. The most real character in this play is the Irish charwoman, Mrs. Farrell, whose shrewd common sense and devastating tongue shatter many illusions about war, woman suffrage, and relations between the sexes. In the end Mrs. Farrell accepts the hand of General Mitchener, when he wants a wife with practical ability and force of character, without frightening him with any such nonsense as telling him she really loves him.

The creation of Mrs. Farrell makes *Press Cuttings* more than an ephemeral production and certainly the most important piece in the volume *Translations and Tomfooleries*. From it may be disentangled the two principal ideas which form the backbone of Shaw's intellectual equipment: one is that justice can be obtained in this world only by an equal distribution of votes, civil rights, and income from property, as definitively laid down in *The Intelligent Woman's Guide to Socialism and Capitalism*, published in 1928; the other is that the improvement of human life lies in the hands of women, who may produce children destined to transcend their parents in wisdom and comprehension of the Life Force. The first of these ideas, Shaw's political creed, is a brand of Fabian Socialism; the second, his religion, he calls Creative Evolution. On these two commandments hang all the law and the prophets of the Shavian gospel, which received its purest expression in the fable of *The Adventures of the Black Girl in Her Search for God*, written in 1932, the year when Shaw celebrated his seventy-sixth birthday.[1]

III

Shaw's basic ideas were not distinctly formulated when he began his dramatic career at the age of thirty-six. He explains in the Preface to *Plays: Pleasant and Unpleasant* that in 1892, when J. T. Grein of the Independent Theater was looking for an English successor to Ibsen and the Ibsen cult, "I . . . raked out from my dustiest pile of discarded and rejected manuscripts, two acts of a play I had begun in 1885, shortly after the close of my novel writing period, in collaboration with my friend, Mr. William Archer." This play was to have been called *Rhinegold*, because it was to open in a hotel garden on the Rhine and to be concerned with tainted riches. It emerged on the stage, in 1892, as *Widowers' Houses*, a phrase freighted with Biblical rather than Wagnerian associations. There was a transition from romance to morality not only in the title but in the body of the play, where only the original setting and situation remained in recognizable form. According to Archer's scenario, the idealistic hero was to spurn the ill-gotten gains of his future father-in-law. It was this gesture which Shaw found fantastically untrue to the nature of modern man.

Widowers' Houses is built upon Shaw's contention that all capitalis-

---

[1] Edmund Wilson in his brilliant essay on Shaw in *The Triple Thinkers* skillfully analyzes the inconsistencies in Shaw's political and economic theories, but he does not choose to do justice to the religious ideals which give body and meaning to the dramatist's comic art.

tic society thrives on injustice and oppression. The dramatic methods by which this idea is driven home are rather clumsy and heavy-handed, especially in the overcrowded last act. In the second act Shaw's revulsion against Archer's sentimental notions is made as clear as is Fielding's disgust with Richardson's Pamela in the early chapters of *Joseph Andrews*. When an idealistic young doctor learns that his fiancée's father has acquired a large fortune by the callous management of slum property, he at first refuses to have anything to do with such infamous wealth. Then he finds that his own income is derived from the same source, and he is compelled to withdraw from his self-righteous position. He comes to realize that business is business, whether in the course of it human beings are incidentally sacrificed or benefited; he will no longer be hoodwinked by noble sentiments about bettering the living conditions of the poor. In his final attitude he is more small-minded than the slum landlord, Sartorius, who at least believes that humanitarian ideas should be taken into account, if they do not interfere with the lawful pursuit of wealth.

Sartorius' daughter is Shaw's first, and perhaps his most exaggerated, portrait of the woman who pursues and finally captures the man she wishes to marry. She is a thoroughly disagreeable girl, endowed with her father's relentless will, as successful in arriving at her sexual goal as Sartorius is in accomplishing his economic aims. The comedy in *Widowers' Houses* is decidedly bitter, because of the selfish nature of all the characters represented on the stage. It must not be overlooked, however, that they play out their destinies against a background of Christian Socialism, embodied in a clergyman, who is not seen but who is referred to by Shaw as being the real opponent of the slum landlord and his policies.

The idealism that lies behind *The Philanderer*, Shaw's second drama, is less sweeping but more apparent. This play deals chiefly with sex relationships and ignores economics, except for its insistence that suitable financial arrangements are necessary to insure happy marriages. The nearest embodiment of an admirable attitude in matters of sex is that of a True Woman, who is not willing to tolerate unreasonable conventions and is mistress enough of her own feelings to have achieved a state of independent self-reliance. She refuses to marry the Philanderer, and he, in turn, refuses to marry another woman, who only pretends to hold advanced ideas. The Philanderer comes to recognize that he himself is a rather pitiable specimen of humanity; in his moment of self-revelation he learns that hereafter he must try to make the best of his own limitations. *The Philanderer* was written to satirize the Ibsen vogue for the New Woman, but it also indulges in many incidental thrusts at doctors and vivisection, club women and dramatic critics. These digressions tend to dissipate the force of what might have been a brilliant comedy of manners if it had been held more steadily to its central theme. At this period in his career Shaw seems to have been himself too much of a philanderer to be able to treat sex with detachment and objectivity.

He succeeded better with more impersonal social subjects. In his third "unpleasant" play, *Mrs. Warren's Profession*, he returned, with a difference, to the territory he had already explored in *Widowers' Houses*. The difference is the character of Vivie Warren, another example of the true New Woman, here removed from the sphere of sex to that of business. Vivie is the determined, aggressive type of modern girl who pays little attention to older people and even less to men of her own age. Her lover is a poor spineless fellow. She is lucky to be rid of him as she plunges into her calculations with figures at the final curtain. Her relations with her mother are much more complicated and interesting. Mrs. Warren has as much vigor of personality as her daughter, but her energy has been turned into other directions. Vivie learns that the money which paid for her education at Cambridge was earned by Mrs. Warren in operating houses of prostitution. Although she does not mind the stigma of conventional immorality attached to that profession, Vivie refuses to continue to live off its proceeds.

Mrs. Warren and Vivie are alike in so far as they both wish to lead active lives of hard work in order to support themselves and maintain their respective brands of self-respect. Mrs. Warren believes that "the only way for a woman to provide for herself decently is for her to be good to some man that can afford to be good to her." Vivie's passionate convictions are more intelligent, if no more noble: "If I had been you, mother, I might have done as you did; but I should not have lived one life and believed in another. You are a conventional woman at heart." Like Nora in *A Doll's House*, Vivie turns from the hypocrisies of family life and will try to make her way in a brave new world, where women can call their souls as well as their bodies their own. Shaw evidently admires his heroine, but he does not hesitate to show the ruthless selfishness of her moral code. He disapproves of Mrs. Warren's veneer of respectability but finds her at heart a rather genial old blackguard. The contrast between these two women is brilliantly developed in two long scenes between them which make *Mrs. Warren's Profession* more than a tract on socialism or sex. In spite of such technical deficiencies as the pallid characterization of Vivie's lover, it is the most skillful play that Shaw had yet written. In it general ideas are used as the background for a dramatic conflict between two powerful personalities.

The censor refused to permit *Mrs. Warren's Profession* to be performed, whereupon Shaw tried his hand at a more genial and, on the surface, a much less pretentious piece of work. *Arms and the Man* was the first popular Shavian success. Its story, which is worked out in an absurdly farcical vein, is based on a serious idea, the emptiness of the traditional conception of military glory. Captain Bluntschli prefers chocolate to cartridges on a battlefield, because an army travels on its stomach and consequently the best provider is the best soldier. The heroine of the play, Raina Petkoff, is torn in her affections between Bluntschli, the son of a cautious Swiss hotelkeeper, and Major Sergius Saranoff, who has quixotically led a dangerous cavalry charge in a recent battle. Raina has been an exaggerated idealist about love and war, but under the calculated shafts of the professional soldier she succumbs to a more sensible view of these matters.

A subtler person than either of the principal lovers is Major Sergius Saranoff, who has within him something of both Raina's vague idealism and Bluntschli's hard common sense, mixed together very unharmoniously. He is introduced as Raina's "hero" and her partner in "the higher love," but he soon shows a coarser and more earthly side of his nature when he is violently attracted by a handsome and clever servant girl. The conflict in Sergius between the charms of the two women is an evenly matched one. He has absorbed a kind of belated Byronism, half noble aspiration and half relentless cynicism. Sergius is a man with a man's limitations more than an effective stage figure. As Shaw admits, the part presents a challenge to the actor. To the playwright it gives an opportunity for drawing a character who learns painfully and expresses succinctly the point of the entire comedy, that war, the romantic dream of patriots and heroes, is a fraud, a hollow sham, like romantic love.

Love is the central theme of Shaw's next play, *Candida*. Here the dramatist is not so destructive as in the "unpleasant" plays that deal with the same subject. Candida's love for her husband is not blind or romantic. She sees his faults clearly, but because he is weak and needs her protection she cares more for him than for anyone else in the world. She is as much a realist in affairs of sex as her father, a middle-class employer of cheap labor, is in business matters. When Candida's husband, a first-rate clergyman of the Church of England, comes to terms with the business ethics of his father-in-law in the first act of the play, it looks for a moment as if there would be no further conflict between the forces of righteousness and evil. Shaw ex lains this truce in his Preface by stating that, since crude conflicts between vice and virtue can only result in obvious propaganda such as he made use of in his "unpleasant" plays, he is now attempting to depict more delicate gradations of character.

In *Candida* Shaw dramatizes the antagonism between two laudable ideals by embodying them in separate persons. Morell, Candida's husband, represents "the clear, bold, sure, sensible, benevolent, salutarily shortsighted Christian Socialist idealism," and "the higher, but vaguer, timider vision" is the secret in the heart of the poet, Eugene Marchbanks. Marchbanks has a range which is beyond the comprehension of Morell and of Candida; that is why he infuriates the husband with jealousy and temporarily arouses the maternal instincts of the wife. During the course of the play Marchbanks, who has idealized Candida as the living manifestation of the woman of his dreams, comes to appreciate that she could never seriously think of leaving her husband for him. This realization is the glimpse of reality which carries Marchbanks from boyhood into full-grown manhood. Marchbanks, whose existence testifies to Shaw's keen, but passing, interest in Pre-Raphaelite art, is the most dynamic person in *Candida*. The heroine, who gives her significant name to the play, merely makes clear the author's honest opinion of his two principal male characters. The famous auction scene, in which Candida herself undergoes no violent emotion, is a clear expression of Shaw's well-considered opinion about the place of art and conventional morality in the world. The impassioned poet and the idealistic clergyman are both absurdly limited in the eyes of a wise and understanding woman.

Such a penetrating analysis of human nature as that in *Candida* prepared the way for Shaw's critical treatment of the great figures of history. He began this phase of his work in 1895, the year after the writing of *Candida*, with his one-act play, *The Man of Destiny*. It was composed in the vain hope that Ellen Terry would some day act in it; the part of the Strange Lady was modeled on the personality of that charming actress, as it appeared to the fascinated Shaw. The Strange Lady has the brains of her Irish grandmother and her English father's capacity to justify by morality the actions that are dictated by expediency. This combination is irresistible. The youthful Napoleon is beaten by it at love now, as he will be at war later in his life. He has shown himself to be, according to Shaw's formula, "imaginative without illusions, and creative without religion, loyalty, patriotism, or any of the common ideals," but he is also an undisciplined tyrant, an inveterate talker, and a mere pawn in the hands of a resourceful woman.

The treatment of the relation between the sexes, which Shaw was finding more provocative of comic contrasts than his extreme social views had been, was deepened and broadened in the last and richest of the "pleasant" plays, *You Never Can Tell*. Its hero, a self-styled Duellist of Sex, falls in love at first sight with an example of the New Woman, educated by her mother on the liberal principles of Darwin, Mill, and Huxley. These principles, which were considered advanced in the 1870's, are in 1896 quite outmoded in favor of Socialism and Creative Evolution. Consequently the hero of *You Never Can Tell* is able to direct a new scientific offensive against the devotee of Women's Rights and the Higher Education of Women. He is a Philanderer settling down at last, and the heroine is a Vivie Warren coming to the end of her tether. Her mother, who has long ago removed her children from the contaminating influence of their father, has brought her daughter up with a determination to remain independent of the opposite sex. The father's efforts to regain the custody of his two younger children, a pair of unrestrained, indecorous, and charming twins, constitute the sprawling plot of this comedy; the course of its action is obscure at first, indeterminate towards the close, and tenuous throughout, but sufficient to serve as a peg on which to hang a large amount of wit and wisdom.

You Never Can Tell is the first of Shaw's plays to be reminiscent of Jonsonian comedy: the plot is insignificant, the numerous characters are dominated by ill-assorted humours, and there is a distribution of rewards and punishments before the final curtain. In *You Never Can Tell* the judicial function is performed by Bohun, an eminent Q.C. (Queen's Counsel), who sums up his cynical philosophy in the despairing words, "It's unwise to be born; it's unwise to be married; it's unwise to live, and it's wise to die," to which arrant pessimism the waiter, William, slyly replies, "Then, if I may respectfully put a word in, sir, so much the worse for wisdom!" William himself is the brightest ornament of *You Never Can Tell*, which takes its title from his favorite phrase. He is the father of Bohun, with whom he makes a striking contrast, although they both wear uniforms, take fees from customers, and are brought by their occupations into contact with all sorts and conditions of men. From this contact Bohun has learned to dissect and judge human beings. William understands them no less well but is of far more assistance to them because he has a naturally kind and sympathetic disposition.

IV

A tolerant recognition that all human beings have their failings and an eagerness to help improve the lot of man are the fundamental doctrines on which rests Shaw's moral indignation at hypocrisy and stupidity, his "Puritanism," as he called it in the title of the volume that comprised his next three plays. Shaw ridicules the narrow Puritanism of Mrs. Dudgeon in *The Devil's Disciple* and at the same time praises the broad-minded Puritanism of her wayward son, Dick. The struggle between these two intellectual conceptions turns what would have been a conventional melodrama into an intelligent comedy. As Shaw himself points out, its plot is composed of the most stereotyped dramatic material; even its apparent inversion of morality goes back to William Blake's famous critical remark that Milton was on the devil's side without knowing it. The elements that make up *The Devil's Disciple* are commonplace enough, but they are put together with a characteristically Shavian alchemy.

Dick Dudgeon, the saint, like Eugene Marchbanks, the poet, cares more for his ideal than for a woman of flesh and blood. Sentimental notions about sex are ridiculed in the heroine's moment of thinking she is in love with Dick. General John Burgoyne's shrewd common sense about war is very like that of the chocolate-cream soldier. The incidental character of Burgoyne is the most brilliant comic invention in *The Devil's Disciple*. He comments wisely on the human scene, with the acidity that befits an aristocratic general and the author-to-be of a successful literary comedy, *The Heiress*. Burgoyne's shafts, directed against the stupidity of soldiers, of politicians, and of historians, come to a climax in his classic explanation of why General Howe did not receive orders to join Burgoyne in time for the battle of Saratoga Springs: "Some gentleman in London forgot to dispatch them: he was leaving town for his holiday, I believe. To avoid upsetting his arrangements, England will lose her American colonies." Like Shaw, "Gentleman Johnny" has a habit of showing up the seamy side of history, with particular attention to the defects of the English. The plan of *The Devil's Disciple* demands that Burgoyne's satirical wit should be subordinated to enthusiasm that Dick's life is saved and satisfaction that the Americans are to win their War of Independence.

The same attitude toward history, the English, and humanity at large pervades *Caesar and Cleopatra*, the second of *Three Plays for Puritans*. Here Caesar is depicted as being something like Napoleon, although an older and wiser world conqueror. In his magnificent address to the Sphinx, Caesar sees the Egyptian statue as the symbol of his own genius, part brute, part woman, and part god, nothing of man at all. Caesar is represented by Shaw as a man of titanic power, seeking an opportunity to express his great natural capacity for commanding men in their own best interests. If not the noblest Roman of them all, he is the most farseeing and energetic. With penetrating accuracy he analyzes Rome's contribution to history: "What! Rome produce no art! Is peace not an art? is war not an art? is government not an art? is civilization not an art?" Shaw's Caesar has a sense of humor, even about himself. He is not the historical figure, of course, but he probably comes nearer to it than Shakespeare's disappointing minor character. Shaw's sympathetic re-creation of a born leader of the past throws some light on his approval, within limits, of one of Caesar's modern imitators, Benito Mussolini.

Since *Caesar and Cleopatra* was written to provide a worthy part for a heroic actor, Sir Johnston Forbes-Robertson, it is natural that Caesar should dominate the play. Even Cleopatra shines largely by reflected light. She is the more adaptable of the two principal characters, changing under Caesar's instruction from a spoiled and frightened child into a queen who can command people to do her will. At first she makes use of her new-found authority in an arbitrary and tyrannical way. Later she is taught by Caesar that in order to be able to govern others wisely one must first learn to govern oneself. By the last act, when Caesar is about to return to Rome, she has almost learned the important lesson of self-control. She is still only a girl of sixteen, with the best part of her life before her. She realizes that she can never be anything more than a prize pupil to the "old gentleman" who has taught her so much, and, for her part, she would never be able to love a god. She cannot help crying at the thought that Caesar is going out of her life never to return, even though he promises to send a beautiful young Roman, named Mark Antony, back to Egypt in his place. Cleopatra knows that the great intellectual experience of her life is behind her, as she expectantly awaits what is to prove a deeper and more intense emotional adventure.

Caesar and Cleopatra does not pretend to deal with love between the sexes romantically, and neither does *Captain Brassbound's Conversion*, which was written immediately after it. The two plays, although completely different in setting and atmosphere, treat intrinsically the same situation, with the sex of the principal characters reversed. Captain Brassbound is, like Cleopatra, a barbarian who comes into conflict with civilization and is educated in the process. He is taught by Lady Cicely Waynflete, a lady as clever and accomplished in her way as Caesar is in his, that the law and wild justice are equally stupid ways of regulating human conduct. By kindness and persistency Lady Cicely persuades Captain Brassbound that he is very silly to try to revenge a mother whom he never really liked. Then she is embarrassed to find that she has destroyed the one ambition of his life. There is now nothing left for him to do, unless she will let him take service under her by consenting to marry him. The

last scene of the play is a spirited duel of words and personalities between the crude smuggler and the cultivated lady. As Brassbound
continues to insist that he has lost confidence in himself and can no
longer give commands, Lady Cicely weakens under the intensity of
his concentrated gaze and begins to feel that she will have to submit
to him against her will. He has almost roused her passion, and at the
same time she has restored to him his confidence in his ability to command. Lady Cicely, freed from her infatuation, will continue her
triumphant progress through the world, deftly managing the affairs
of other people, and Captain Brassbound will return to his ship
"with a man's power and purpose restored and righted."

After some indecision, Shaw made up his mind to call *Captain
Brassbound's Conversion* by its present title because he thought that
"conversion" would be a suitable key word for one of the *Three
Plays for Puritans*. All of them make a serious effort to treat the problem of the individual's relation to his environment. Dick Dudgeon's
quixotic attempt to sacrifice his life for that of another person, Julius
Caesar's self-restrained poise in governing unruly subordinates, and
Lady Cicely Waynflete's uncanny skill in managing men for their
own advantage are only three different ways of securing peace on
earth, good will to men. The saint, the wise administrator, and the
perceptive woman are three of Shaw's chief agents for carrying out
his philanthropic schemes for the improvement of mankind.

In Shaw's next important play, *Man and Superman*, written between 1901 and 1903, the dramatist succeeded in combining the
various points of view that had been scattered through *Three Plays
for Puritans*. It took a preface, a handbook, a compendium of varied
maxims, and a digression almost as long as the entire text to complete
the work. The interlude, "Don Juan in Hell," which takes up the
greater portion of the third act, is Shaw's first piece of dramatic
writing that is too unwieldy for the practical theater. It is his first
example of dialogue written merely for the sake of argumentative
discussion, without external action to support it. It is his first definite
expression of the idealistic philosophy of life which lay beneath his
socialistic theories. This philosophy had already been implied in his
early plays. It was often to be repeated in his later ones.

The Don Juan legend, suggested to Shaw by A. B. Walkley as the
subject for a comedy, enabled the dramatist to use the principal

characters in that story as mouthpieces for his professed intention to write a new Book of Genesis for the Bible of the Evolutionists: the Devil represents the forces of cynicism and destruction, with an added spice of sentimentality; the Statue of the Commander is average human stupidity, attempting to muddle through its difficulties and finding that there is at least one road paved with good intentions; Don Juan stands for the reason and intelligence, of which Shaw himself has a liberal supply; Doña Ana embodies the vigor and will which he greatly admires. The interlude contains lengthy discussions of heaven and hell, art and marriage, death and life, the last of which is arbitrarily defined as "the force that ever strives to attain greater power of contemplating itself." The stern discipline of thought has made the Statue very uncomfortable in heaven. Don Juan, who is indifferent to the sensuous attractions of hell, yearns to experience the joys of pure intelligence. "Heaven is the home of the masters of reality; hell is the home of the unreal and of the seekers for happiness," he says in explaining his determination to leave hell for heaven. In heaven he will be able to enlist in the service of the Life Force, which will in time produce the Superman. The Superman is not yet created, and in that fact Doña Ana finds an opportunity for herself: "Not yet created! Then my work is not yet done. I believe in the Life to Come," and with a splendid gesture she cries to the universe, "A father! a father for the Superman!"

Awkward as this interlude is for dramatic purposes, it is necessary to give the proper intellectual background for the modern story. Ann Whitefield, the lineal descendant of Doña Ana, selects John Tanner, the reincarnation of Don Juan Tenorio, to be the father of her children. She is ruthless in her pursuit of him, but she is not thoroughly selfish, because she is exerting herself for the sake of her future husband, her children, and posterity at large. She feels the power of the Life Force as much as John Tanner is attracted by her personal magnetism. She is exhausted by her struggle to convince him that they were born for one another. She believes that she has failed in her efforts, only to find that her moment of weakness is the one in which he capitulates. She knows that his surrender will not be all happiness for her, perhaps it will even mean her death, but she perseveres until she has won him and then faints from the strain of her exertion. After that she is quite happy. Although Tanner may go on talking endlessly about his radical ideas, Ann realizes that she is the mistress of the situation because she has a stronger will than her reluctant victim.

Ann Whitefield popularized the Shavian heresy that woman is the hunter, man the prey, an idea which is not nearly so radical as it at first appears to be. Woman's business has always been that of the mother and the homemaker; she has always been the practical animal. Shaw shows this aspect of her nature under another light in the subsidiary love affair of *Man and Superman*. Violet Robinson manages her American husband and her Irish father-in-law with the greatest ease. She is not a siren like Ann and she has no humor, but she possesses intelligence and efficiency, qualities more needed in a wife than in a woman who is still trying to find a mate. She is extraordinarily unlike her brother Octavius, Mozart's Don Ottavio, a poet who is in love with Ann. Ann will not marry Octavius, because she believes that the artist-man, being also a productive creature, is the natural enemy of the mother-woman.

A more serious threat to Ann's supremacy is presented by Tanner's chauffeur, Enry Straker, who attempts to put into action the scientific spirit that has recently come into the world. Straker's ability with machinery has easily made a slave of Tanner, but Ann's creative ingenuity succeeds in overwhelming Straker's mechanical skill. Tanner is capable of understanding all about both Straker and Ann, but he is not able to control either of them. The New Man and the Eternal Women are, in their different ways, active workers in the cause of the Life Force, not theorists and parlor radicals like the modern Don Juan.

V

Man and Superman is an intelligent comedy of the first order. With its publication in 1903 Shaw became a figure of major importance in the field of comic drama. During the next ten years he composed thirteen comedies, twelve of which were published, in four volumes, from 1907 to 1916.[1] Each of these volumes contains two impressive comedies and a shorter one-act play of a more trivial nature. Of these

[1] The thirteenth is *Great Catherine*, a farcical and comparatively insignificant work about Catherine II of Russia, written and produced in 1913 but not published until 1919.

four lesser works, the first is *How He Lied to Her Husband*, in which a sensible husband is flattered, not made jealous, like Morell in *Candida*, by a poet's adoration of his wife; the second is *The Shewing-Up of Blanco Posnet*, with the leading character a horse thief in an American mining town, who finds, like Dick Dudgeon, the devil's disciple, that, in spite of himself, he is on the side of righteousness; the third, *The Dark Lady of the Sonnets*, written to help the Shakespeare Memorial National Theater, imagines Shakespeare discussing with Queen Elizabeth the suitability and difficulties of such an enterprise; the fourth, *Overruled*, is "a clinical study of how polygamy occurs among quite ordinary people innocent of all unconventional views about it." In the last-named piece two husbands each make love to the other's wife and then decide to exchange mates, on the theory that honesty is the best policy in matters of sex. The more conventional of the husbands is overruled by the other one and by the two wives after all four of them have thoroughly discussed the embarrassing situation in which they are involved.

The plan of bringing together people with various attitudes on the same subject is employed in a number of forms by Shaw in the eight major plays composed between 1903 and 1913. The first of them, *John Bull's Other Island*, is, as its name suggests, insular in its outlook; since it is largely concerned with the Anglo-Irish relations of 1904, it has inevitably dated with the passing of time and the establishment of the Irish Free State. Fifteen years before the violent occurrences which led to that event, Shaw advised Home Rule for Ireland, because he believed that all sound government must rest on the consent of the governed and that Ireland would never peaceably consent to be ruled over by the English. On the other hand, he wished to indicate to the Irish audience, for whom *John Bull's Other Island* was written, that in some respects the English were vastly their superiors.

To make his points clear on the stage Shaw created the civil-engineering firm of Doyle and Broadbent. Its senior member, Larry Doyle, is an Irishman by birth, who has lived in America and England since the age of eighteen. Now that he is thirty-six, he is cosmopolitan enough to be disillusioned about his dreamy and futile fellow countrymen. Tom Broadbent is an Englishman with such a sentimental view of the world in general and Ireland in particular that he is ready to support the Gladstonian-Liberal tradition of

"Home Rule under English Guidance." Larry is disgusted by the shiftless Irish; Broadbent idealizes them and exploits them. As a result, the realistic Doyle emancipates himself from his old entanglements, and the efficient Broadbent is persuaded to be the candidate for an Irish seat in Parliament. He also wins the hand of an independent Irish girl and plans to develop an Irish country estate for the benefit of both Irish peasants and English capitalists. Broadbent's ingenious combination of practicality and naïveté makes him a more attractive character than the comparatively consistent Irishman. No doubt Shaw shared Doyle's intellectual opinions and respected Broadbent's excellent intentions.

Doyle believes that Englishmen get what they want, and that Irishmen do not because they are too busy quarreling about it. Doyle regards the heroine, who is almost a personification of Ireland, as "useless," whereas Broadbent considers her "ethereal"; they are both extraordinarily susceptible to her fragile charm. The deeper and more mystical vein in Irish nature is expressed through the mouth of Peter Keegan, an unfrocked priest, who learned his reverent spirit from a Hindu and talks with a grasshopper as with a familiar friend. In a memorable speech he describes heaven as a place where the eternal trinities reside: state, Church, and people; work, play, and life; priest, worshipers, and worshiped; life, humanity, and the divine; "it is, in short, the dream of a madman." Keegan is the embodiment of the dreams which Larry Doyle considers the bane of Ireland's existence. The priest can never feel completely at home in this world, but he is more at his ease with the complacent Englishman than with the intelligent and uninspired Anglicized Irishman.

The three types of men in *John Bull's Other Island*, the theorist, the man of affairs, and the seer, appear under different guises in *Major Barbara*, Shaw's next play, which deals with the munitions industry and the Salvation Army. It is a more complicated but better integrated piece of work than *John Bull's Other Island*, in which the ideas of Doyle, Broadbent, and Keegan are not finally merged, as are the points of view of the three chief characters in *Major Barbara*. In the latter play appear a Professor of Greek who would like to be of some use in the affairs of the world, a successful maker of munitions, who considers poverty the worst of crimes, and the munition maker's daughter, a major in the Salvation Army who has dedicated her life to the redemption of other people's souls. Major Barbara is elated at the thought of taking part in a spiritual war, but her father, Andrew Undershaft, is able to prove to her that an army must subsist in a physical way before it can be effective as a military organization. The Salvation Army is supported by tainted money and therefore does not offer its beneficiaries any workable ideal that a strong and honest man can reasonably be expected to follow.

Shaw summarizes his constructive remedies for the situation at the end of the Preface to *Major Barbara*. They are: a just distribution of property, a humane treatment of criminals, and the return of religious creeds to intellectual honesty. These three ideals may perhaps be realized when men in an influential position adopt a platform as broad and firm as Andrew Undershaft's true faith of an armorer. Society cannot be saved until, as Undershaft paraphrases Plato, "The Professors of Greek take to making gunpowder or else the makers of gunpowder become Professors of Greek," and until the Major Barbaras who yearn vaguely after righteousness make up their minds to die with the colors of a faith securely founded on scientific accuracy. The power obtained through fighting may become a cult and sweep away with it the petty insecurity of halfway measures, taking with it all sense of safety and security for the average well-meaning but timid citizen of the upper middle class.

After contemplating wholesale destruction by gunpowder, Shaw next undertook to investigate the loss of an individual life from lack of proper medical attention. *The Doctor's Dilemma* is called a "tragedy" because of Louis Dubedat's death, but it might more accurately be described as a sardonic comedy directed against physicians for inefficiency and carelessness in safeguarding human existence. In spite of the great technical advances made by modern science, disease is still, as it was in Molière's day, nearly always a painful and sometimes unnecessarily a fatal business. One of the peculiar problems of the medical profession is neatly illustrated by the horns of the dilemma on which Shaw has placed his principal doctor, Sir Colenso Ridgeon. Because his treatment of consumption by opsonin is so elaborate that it can be applied to only a limited number of cases, Ridgeon is forced to choose between curing a decent man with no particular ability and a blackguard who is clearly an inspired artist. As a lover of beauty, the doctor feels that it is easier to replace a dead man than a good picture, but he is finally persuaded that life is more important than art and makes up his mind to sacrifice the painter, Louis Dubedat.

So far Shaw's sympathies seem to be with Ridgeon, but he has complicated the dilemma by making the doctor fall in love with the artist's wife, Jennifer. Nevertheless, Ridgeon makes his decision on purely ethical grounds, and then later allows Dubedat to be treated by a plausible but incompetent doctor, with the result that the patient's tuberculosis develops at alarming speed. After Dubedat's death Ridgeon confesses to Jennifer the reasons for his conduct, but she has already married someone else, so that Ridgeon has "committed a purely disinterested murder." The element of sardonic comedy in this situation is painfully intensified by the care that Shaw has lavished upon the character of Dubedat. This distinguished artist, who is not a man of honor, is represented as having the most delicately sensitive perceptions and the most refined feelings. He has been a cad in his human relations, but he has never been entirely selfish. He has believed in Michelangelo, Velasquez, and Rembrandt, an artistic creed which is too noble to be invalidated by any man's petty weaknesses.

The artistic temperament is beautifully balanced against the scientific spirit in *The Doctor's Dilemma*, where, as in *Candida*, a woman is the pivot of the action. Jennifer with her Cornish wildness cleaves to the imaginative, unreliable Dubedat. She can do so because she does not believe in merely utilitarian standards and has her own peculiar brand of mysticism. Yet she is practical enough to be interested in a remark which contains Shaw's positive advice for reforming the medical profession, "Private practice in medicine ought to be put down by law." The socialization of medicine would have made it unnecessary for Ridgeon to arrive at a personal decision in choosing between the life of one man and another, and impossible for Louis Dubedat to have been treated by a miscellaneous group of sincere, but ignorant, physicians as an expensive plaything.

Shaw's specific suggestions about another social institution, marriage, are contained in the Preface of his next play, *Getting Married*. They are that men and women should be economically independent and that divorce should be easily obtainable whenever it is desired by either party to an outworn marriage contract. *Getting Married,* in which nothing occurs except that a wedding takes place and a divorce is reversed, is "a disquisitory play" in one long act without interruption or intermission. The dispute between a prospective bride and groom about the rights and wrongs of marriage brings forth the views of all the bride's family and friends on the subject. The bride's father and his two brothers represent the Church, the state, and the army; the three women with whom they are in love are a wife, a divorcée, and an old maid respectively. Into the mouth of each, Shaw puts an eloquent justification of the position held toward marriage by the group of which he or she is a member.

To complete the comic picture Shaw adds to these six comparatively normal attitudes towards marriage three much more extreme types of opinion, that of the celibate, the shrewd man of common sense, and the rapt mystic. Mrs. George, the mystic, does not appear until about two-thirds of the way through the play, but from then on she dominates the stage. She is a devil, saint, and pythoness in one, that is, a human creature, a woman, as she insists in a hypnotic trance, during which she speaks with the tongues of men and of angels. She asks to be taken for what she is, an individual who has passed through love in the flesh and has come to comprehend the abstraction of "Christian Fellowship." Meanwhile, she fulfills the practical civic duties of her office as Lady Mayoress.

Neither sublimation of sex into the sphere of religion nor the diffusion of it through a wide range of social activity is an unprecedented phenomenon, but neither of these outlets is so normal as the mating of two people for the purposes of a stable physical union. The usual result of marriage, in fact the only logical excuse for its existence after personal desire has worn away, is the propagation of the race. It is not surprising, therefore, that Shaw followed *Getting Married* with *Misalliance*, a similar long one-act comedy on the related theme of parents and children. *Misalliance* is not so successful as its predecessor, partially because it was a repetition in technique, and partially because Shaw seems to know less about parents and children than about the institution of matrimony. In fact, after a longish Preface on the announced topic, he writes a play which has more to do with relations between the sexes than with differences between the generations. Shaw seems to have felt that he should ex-

plain the result of the woman's having found a father for the Superman and then to have decided that, for everyone concerned in it,
the chase itself was usually more profitable than its results.

There are several children in *Misalliance*, each of whom has a
spiritual parent that is not his physical one, an idea that was later to
be used by James Joyce as the basis of his monumental novel, *Ulysses*.
Parents and children do not get on well with one another in *Misalliance*, but neither do members of different social classes nor people
of the opposite sexes. An aristocratic and a plebeian pair of fathers
and sons are all fascinated by a Polish acrobat who revolts at the
conventional atmosphere of love-making which otherwise pervades
the play. The part given by Shaw to her vigorous personality seems
to imply that all alliances are mistakes except those based on danger
and daring, which will produce the best kind of offspring in the
shape of superior human beings.

Misalliance is really much less a comedy about children and parents
than is *Fanny's First Play*, which Shaw dismisses as a potboiler. He
was no doubt stimulated by the unfavorable reception given to
Misalliance, by both press and public, to put a lighter play on the
same subject into a frame which would ridicule the principal London dramatic critics. In the persons of the four critics who have been
asked to give their opinions on the first play written by Miss Fanny
O'Dowda, Shaw pokes gentle fun at the ultraclassical A. B. Walkley
of *The Times*, the serious-minded E. A. Baughan of *The Daily
News*, the intellectually blasé Gilbert Cannan of *The Star*, and the
average British playgoer, who narrow-mindedly judges a play by
the previous reputation of its author. To these critics, Fanny's first
play seems to be a neat combination of the work of Pinero, Granville-
Barker, and Shaw himself.

The essence of the play under discussion is the difference between
the generations, a theme that is here worked out in simple terms,
with almost mathematical exactness. In Act I a respectable mother
and father are shocked to find that their son, Bobby, has been serving
a sentence in prison for disorderly conduct, when drunk; in Act II
an even more respectable mother and father are similarly shocked
to learn that their daughter, Margaret, has been serving a sentence
in prison for disorderly conduct, when intoxicated by music and
champagne; in Act III Bobby and Margaret decide to break off their

engagement by mutual consent. Bobby offers to marry a girl of the streets, and Margaret accepts the hand of the younger son of a duke, who has been employed as a footman. In prison Margaret has received a spiritual revelation so overwhelming that it enlightens her and also appeals to her conventional mother, who proves to be at bottom a profoundly religious woman.

Shaw himself had always been a profoundly religious person, of an unorthodox stamp, from the time he casually mentioned the admirable clergyman in *Widowers' Houses* through *Three Plays for Puritans* to the varied mystical illuminations of Father Keegan, Major Barbara, Louis Dubedat, and Mrs. George. In *Androcles and the Lion*, the fable which followed *Fanny's First Play*, he for the first time straightforwardly discussed the subject of Christianity. His doing so in an uproarious farce, with scenes imitative of a Christmas pantomime, was almost as great a shock to the superficially devout as his finding much to criticize in the faith of the early Christian martyrs. Among them he pictured a coward and debauchee, a soft-hearted humanitarian, and a man of great strength, who tries in vain to overcome his lust for fighting. The sturdy armorer wrestles with himself in spirit, much as a confirmed pacificist does when his country goes to war, and finds, like most ordinary men, that "the Christian god is not yet." His conclusion is approved by the urbane Emperor in *Androcles and the Lion*, who believes that "the prudent course is to be neither bigoted in our attachment to the old nor rash and impractical in keeping an open mind for the new, but to make the best of both dispensations."

Among the Emperor's soldiers is a young patrician Captain skeptical of both the old gods of Rome and the new god of the Christians; among the Christians is Lavinia, an intelligent freethinker, intolerant of the external forms of traditional religion. When the Captain tries to convince Lavinia of her folly in refusing to sacrifice to the gods of Rome, she admits that there is a certain inconsistency in her position. The Christian god is not to her an entirely satisfactory divinity, but she is willing to wait for the knowledge of God that may some day be vouchsafed to her. "What is God?" the handsome Captain asks her, and Lavinia replies in one of Shaw's most superb brief utterances, "When we know that, Captain, we shall be gods ourselves." This prophetic remark has in it the germ of much of Shaw's later work, which expands, sometimes at too great length, the idea of an evolving consciousness.

The efforts of one mortal to act the part of God toward another, with the inevitable loss of dignity that must ensue, is the subject of the eighth and last of Shaw's long plays written between *Man and Superman*, in 1903, and the outbreak of the World War. The title of *Pygmalion* indicates the creative nature of the theme: the attempt of a professor named Higgins, by means of his skill with phonetics, to cultivate aristocratic speech in the mouth of Eliza Doolittle, a cockney flower girl. Higgins is successful in his experiment, but its results are not just what he had anticipated. Eliza has learned that "the difference between a lady and a flower girl is not how she behaves, but how she's treated." She decides to stop taking care of Higgins in order to make an independent life for herself. She may bully Higgins and admire him, but she can never bring herself to like him. "Galatea never does quite like Pygmalion: his relation to her is too godlike to be altogether agreeable."

Pygmalion is a study in the transference of an individual from one social class to another. Shaw argues that, since the capacity of speech is one of the most divine of human attributes, a person who can change the sounds made by another's voice alters at the same time the soul to which the voice gives expression; also that a person who changes the economic status of another individual is responsible for changing his mentality. Shaw makes the latter point by introducing into *Pygmalion* the picturesque subsidiary character of Eliza's father, one of the "undeserving poor." In his unregenerate state, he prefers not to have too much money, for fear he might acquire the damning virtue of prudence. Later, when Higgins has been accidentally instrumental in procuring £3000 a year for him, Doolittle has to adopt middle-class morality and marry the "Missus," who would not tie herself up to him for life when he was poor. Doolittle appears only twice in the play, once in each of his economic incarnations. The violent contrast between them is meant to emphasize Eliza's gradual growth from a flower girl into a lady, a social phenomenon which is almost too subtly managed to be convincing on the stage.

During the years between *Man and Superman* and the World War Shaw had been developing into a more refined and devious playwright than he had been in the lusty days of the "pleasant and unpleasant" plays. The eight important dramas written between 1903 and 1914 all deal, in one shape or another, with politics, sex, art, and religion. *John Bull's Other Island* has a narrow political subject, the issues in *Misalliance* are confused, *Fanny's First Play* is frankly occasional in its nature, and the idea behind *Pygmalion* is, as its expository postscript shows, not completely realized upon the stage. Yet there are vivid characterization and sincere idealism in all four of these comedies. In aesthetic excellence they must yield, however, to the imaginative treatment of war in *Major Barbara*, the keen analysis of modern science, destructive and beneficent, in *The Doctor's Dilemma*, the daring exploration of possible relationships between men and women in *Getting Married*, and the clear-eyed view of inspired fanaticism which is the real subject of *Androcles and the Lion*. In all eight of these plays Shaw's social doctrines may be detected under various forms, and throughout them there can also be felt an increasing emphasis upon religion at the expense of economics. What the results of this tendency might have been if its peaceful development had not been interrupted, it is impossible to say. The events of 1914 arrived to disturb the equilibrium of Europe and to threaten seriously the Liberal tradition under which Shaw had been living and working. His work, which involved a savage criticism of existing conditions, was not superficially adapted to arousing patriotism. Nevertheless, in his own peculiar way, the dramatist made a conscious and determined effort to support the civilization of which he was a part.

VI

Shaw's efforts to devote his literary energies to the service of his country were of a most paradoxical kind. He first wrote the notorious pamphlet, *Common Sense about the War*, in which the justice he did to Germany's position led him to be considered a traitor to England's cause. Partly to correct this impression, Shaw set himself to writing a little Irish play, which he described as a "recruiting poster in disguise." The disguise was so complete that it concealed Shaw's purpose, and the play remained unperformed, until after it might have had any practical effect. Private Dennis O'Flaherty of *O'Flaherty, V.C.* prefers the unpleasantness of life at the front to the quarrels of his mother and sweetheart at home. He agrees with his

superior officer that conscription would probably have been necessary "if domestic life had been as happy as people say it is." To
criticize conditions existing in time of peace may seem a roundabout
way to justify war, but Shaw's purpose is to expound the truth that
war has its virtues no less than peace has its defects.

Shaw's three other "playlets of the war" are less amusing than
O'Flaherty, V.C., and less effective in their criticism. *The Inca of
Perusalem* implies that Kaiser Wilhelm II, although absurd in his
personal affectations, was not such an imbecile as he was often represented by his enemies to be. Lord Augustus Highcastle in *Augustus
Does His Bit* is an example of English officialdom accomplishing
more harm than good in its effort to help win the War. The heroine
of *Annajanska, the Bolshevik Empress* belonged to what was once an
imperial family, but she has now turned Bolshevik, because she believes that "some energetic and capable minority must always be in
power." She does not suppose that the new regime is perfect, but
she is sure that the old one is too decayed and feeble to be restored
to its former responsible position. Shaw saw more clearly than most
of his contemporaries that radical changes in social organization
were bound to follow in the wake of the War. In *Heartbreak House*,
"A Fantasia in the Russian Manner on English Themes," he summed
up most poignantly his conclusions on the unstable state of European
society just before the outbreak of hostilities.

Heartbreak House was begun in 1913, under the influence of the
English production of three of Chekhov's plays, and completed
three years later during the air raids which furnished the material
for its final incident. It was not published or performed until after
1918, because, as Shaw explains, "War cannot bear the terrible
castigation of comedy." This play, probably the most obscure and
stimulating of all Shaw's dramas, is filled with allegorical implications. The air raid with which it ends is intended to symbolize the
World War, the survivors of which are glad to be safe but feel,
"How damnably dull the world has become again suddenly!" In
fact, some of them even regret that the glorious experience is over
and hope that another of a similar sort will soon occur.

The immediate result of the air raid is the death of two practical
men, a burglar who acts like a man of affairs, and a man of affairs
who acts like a burglar. These two men have interchanged functions

and between them exhibit all the characteristics of predatory capitalistic finance. The relations between Boss Mangan, the employer,
and Mazzini Dunn, his employee, an earnest, incompetent "soldier of
freedom," are like those existing between organized industry and the
spirit of noble optimism, which had at first hoped to be the master,
not the slave, in its partnership with big business. This analogy is
further carried out by Mangan's desire to marry Dunn's daughter,
Ellie, brought up by her father in financial poverty, but endowed
with rich spiritual possessions in the knowledge of Shakespeare.
Ellie is prevented from marrying Boss Mangan by Captain Shotover,
the eccentric old man in whose house the play takes place. She is more
and more drawn to Captain Shotover by a mysterious attraction
which the aspiring idealism of youth feels for the speculative wisdom
of age, until she is finally united to her "spiritual husband and second
father" in a mystical marriage performed in the sight of heaven.

Ellie Dunn's description of "heartbreak" may be taken as the keynote of this play: "When your heart is broken, your boats are
burned: nothing matters any more. It is the end of happiness and
the beginning of peace." Ellie's heart was broken by her first unfortunate love affair, Boss Mangan's by the discovery that other
people had been using him for their own selfish ends, Captain
Shotover's by the way he has been treated by his two daughters.
His elder daughter, an undisciplined woman, has ruined the life of
the weak idealist to whom she is married. His second daughter left
her heart in her father's house when, disgusted by its lack of order,
she quitted it to marry a businesslike, stupid, and ruthless colonial
governor. He and she, in so far as she has been able to forget her
heart, are the representatives of Shaw's Horseback Hall, the unthink-
ing barbarian part of modern society. Her husband never appears
upon the stage and remains an impenetrably hostile force in the
background, but the husband's brother follows his sister-in-law to
her old home and plays on the flute in a melancholy strain. He is an
example of a life broken by the merciless activities of Horseback
Hall, as the husband of Captain Shotover's elder daughter is an example of good material wantonly destroyed by Heartbreak House.
The two granddaughters of the devil go relentlessly on their ways,
sacrificing all who come in their paths and not even respecting the
crazy whims of their half insane father.

Captain Shotover, the central figure of the play, is a scientific inventor, trying to attain the seventh degree of concentration, in order to find means of destroying materialistic, nonproductive fellows who only clutter up the globe. He drinks rum in order to keep away the dreams that tend to steal him from his work, but he believes that stronger than rum is the genius of people who are so sufficient unto themselves that they are only happy when they are stripped of everything, even hope. To commemorate the ship which he commanded and which made a man of him, he has had a room in his house fitted up to resemble the after part of an old-fashioned high-pooped vessel. It does not take a wide flight of the imagination to recognize in this setting the Ship of State, which under the command of a drunken skipper may be run on the rocks by Providence. When the dangerous airplane has passed by and the ship is once more safe, Captain Shotover wearily sits down and immediately falls asleep. Like King Lear, he has achieved a wise serenity, after having been driven half mad by his two cold-blooded daughters and having found peace by the side of a radiant younger woman, with whose enthusiasm his serenity is in perfect accord.

One of the incidental results of the air raid reported in *Heartbreak House* is that the rectory is demolished and "the poor clergyman will have to get a new house." Shaw's attempt to help the clergyman in his search for a new dwelling is his voluminous, plain-spoken, and entirely fantastic "metabiological Pentateuch," *Back to Methuselah*. In the Preface to it, strikingly called "The Infidel Half Century," it is explained that the years between 1870 and 1920 have been dominated by Darwinian Materialism and that it is now a fitting time to begin a crude Bible of Creative Evolution, based on the teachings of the Neo-Lamarckians. Shaw admits quite frankly that he had already made such an attempt in the Don Juan episode of *Man and Superman*; since that effort did not meet with the popular recognition he thought it deserved, he will try once again at the age of nearly sixty-five, with garrulity instead of exuberance. Garrulous *Back to Methuselah* certainly is, but it also has a philosophical clarity that Shaw had never before attained and that should leave no reader in doubt as to the comic standard which, throughout his career, the dramatist had been applying to human frailties and foibles.

Shaw's fable goes back to the beginning of things and predicates a time when there was no death except by accident. In the Garden of Eden, Adam and Eve are instructed by the Serpent that the process of Creation takes place through the stages of Desire, Imagination, and Will. With children assured to him, Adam is willing to limit his span of life to one thousand years, but Abel invents killing animals for food, Cain commits murder, and through violence the term of human survival will shrink until man has to die before he acquires sense enough to know how to live. These prehistoric events are shown in the first of the five parts of *Back to Methuselah* and explained in the second part by one of the Brothers Barnabas.

The Brothers Barnabas, a professor of biology and an ex-minister, have evolved a new gospel, that the duration of human life must be extended to at least three centuries, so that men may come to take it seriously. Hence they adopt, "Back to Methuselah," as the rallying cry of their faith and offer it to two rival politicians as a possible electioneering slogan. Shaw has a delightful time satirizing the limited aims of the two politicians, who bear unmistakable resemblances to the energetic, uncultivated Lloyd George and the smooth, overcivilized Asquith. He has greater difficulty in depicting the way in which Creative Evolution will occur. He resorts to the unsatisfactory method of jumping over the actual events and shifting his scene to a time two hundred and fifty years later, when, in two isolated cases, the miracle has already taken place.

By 3000 A.D., according to the fourth part of *Back to Methuselah*, the British Isles are inhabited exclusively by long-lived people, who are debating whether they shall remain where they are or take possession of the rest of the world, after having exterminated all the short-livers. They do kill one short-lived Elderly Gentleman, who is intelligent enough to believe that the soul is more important than the body, but who would die of discouragement if he were allowed to stay permanently in the British Isles. They do not succeed in killing a Napoleonic dictator, who must live out his miserably incongruous life to its appointed end: either he must abdicate his power and become a common man, or he must endure the defeat that comes to both conquerors and conquered in the game of modern war. He and the Elderly Gentleman represent respectively the strong man with narrow interests and the weak man with good intentions.

The will power of the one and the insight of the other must be combined to arrive at the Shavian ideal.

Shaw's Utopia is presented in the fifth and last part of *Back to Methusaleh* under the title "As Far as Thought Can Reach." His attempt to combine religion and science on equal terms results in a hybrid philosophy which is neither steadfastly religious nor ruthlessly scientific, but which provides an admirable touchstone for modern comedy. After a typically Shavian discussion of the problems involved in artistic and scientific creation, two statues which typify mankind in the crude stage of development we have reached in the twentieth century are destroyed by the annihilating gaze of the wise Ancients. The Ancients have arrived at Captain Shotover's seventh degree of concentration, with the result that they are able to create parts of their own bodies. They finally put away such follies, as children put away toys, and only regret that they are tied at all to the bondage of the flesh. They are still susceptible to accidents, as Adam and Eve were in the beginning. Their desire is to become immortal in a vortex of pure thought. After the Ancients there may come deathless creatures, as before Adam and Eve there was Lilith.

Lilith appears in the Epilogue to *Back to Methusaleh* and so connects its end with its beginning. Whether her rhapsodic soliloquy, which is one of Shaw's most famous and beautiful pieces of writing, is inspired prophecy or empty nonsense, it is interesting to notice that the Ancients' "vortex" and Lilith's "whirlpool of force" are both images used by Aristophanes to describe the mysterious power which is in league with the Clouds. The comic artist is always driven on by his genius to hint at an ideal more sublime than can be comprehended by the human mind. He is justified in laughing at everything within the scope of man's intellectual processes. To visualize what lies beyond one's mental horizon is too difficult a task for anyone but a genuine mystic, and Shaw is not a mystic, as the last part of *Back to Methusaleh* conclusively shows; but it also shows that he genuinely approves of mysticism. Therefore it was a stroke of genius for him to take one of the world's greatest mystics as the subject of his next play, after it was generally supposed that, in *Back to Methusaleh*, he had composed his literary last will and testament.

In the shadow cast by "As Far as Thought Can Reach" Shaw

wrote *Saint Joan*, the play that, all things considered, must be regarded as his dramatic masterpiece. It is not so subtle as *Heartbreak
House* or so vast in its scope as *Back to Methuselah*, but it has neither
the obscurity of the one nor the unsubstantiality of the other. In
spite of its length it is eminently adapted to the stage. It has already
become a testing ground in many lands for the arts of acting and
theatrical production. Shaw was well advised to write in *Saint Joan*,
not of the confused present, as in *Heartbreak House*, or of the unseen
future, as in *Back to Methuselah*, but of the past, upon which time had
enabled him to get perspective and which he had often before
treated with sympathy and originality. It has been said that Shaw
fell in love with Joan of Arc, who accomplished a posthumous
miracle in turning a cynic into a devotee, but it would perhaps be
nearer the truth to insist that the modern dramatist recognized in
the medieval saint a forerunner of his own vain attempt to open the
eyes of deluded humanity. Shaw himself does not hear voices that
carry him beyond the limits of human endurance to martyrdom and
canonization, but he can appreciate those who do, and he can see
with clarity the effect that they have upon other people.

Shaw is by no means a blind worshiper of Saint Joan. He says
that, on the one hand, she was immature and ignorant and that, on
the other hand, she was presumptuous and insufferable. He sums up
her personality by calling her "a born boss." In general he is on her
side, the side of the saints and the angels, but he is somewhat puzzled
by saintliness. He understands more easily the precise attitude that
was taken toward Joan by her critics, both the friendly and the hostile
ones. None of the people whom Joan encounters quite like her, and
no one of them would gladly see her return to earth after her execution; but Shaw has told us explicitly that there are no villains in this
play, as there are none in life. All the persons in it have good intentions. "The angels may weep at the murder, but the gods laugh
at the murderer." Shaw is able to take an unbiased view of a human
tragedy, turning it by his understanding and broad-mindedness into
a superhuman comedy. From this point of view the Epilogue is
undoubtedly, as Shaw has himself stated, the heart of the piece. No
true Shavian can entertain for a moment the idea that the play would
be better without it, and the author has cleverly seen to it that no
leading actress would be willing to dispense with it. Joan's last words

express wistful nobility and spiritual exaltation, but it would be grossly misconceiving their purpose to suppose that they are intended to be divorced from real experience. Joan is for Shaw the embodiment of what he calls "the evolutionary appetite," which finds as many obstacles in its path today as it did during the fifteenth century.

The present obstacles in its path are the bitterly debated issues of what social checks must be brought to bear on rugged individualism; Joan's era was the beginning of a cycle in which individualism opposed itself to concentrated authority. The Middle Ages had been a time of comparative order, during which the Catholic Church ruled supreme in the sphere of religion, the feudal system imposed its discipline in affairs of state, and man reduced woman to the position of a servant, when he did not idealize her unattainable virginity. Joan opposed all these forms of repression. According to Shaw, she was the first Protestant, the first nationalist, and the first feminist, that is, the originator of three important Renaissance movements. Of the three, feminism is the most modern and least significant; therefore Shaw wisely refrained from emphasizing it unduly. However, Joan's wearing of men's clothes gives the dramatist an excellent opportunity to call attention to the human similarities rather than the sexual differences between men and women.

The lack of novelty in Joan's espousal of nationalism is recognized in *Saint Joan*. De Stogumber, the fanatical English chaplain, champions the cause of England almost as vehemently as Joan does that of France, and the cosmopolitan Earl of Warwick admits that he cannot hope to have de Stogumber's approval in burning Joan as a nationalist. De Stogumber and Joan are brother and sister under the skin; the literal-minded de Stogumber becomes instantly converted to Joan's sainthood when he sees her martyrdom with his own eyes. The Earl of Warwick, on the other hand, is thoroughly opposed to Joan. He realizes that her plan to have the kings give their realms to God, and then reign as God's bailiffs, strikes at the root of the power of the aristocracy, which he represents. As a matter of historical fact, by Joan's time the power of the great nobles was already much diminished throughout Europe, but she assisted in its decline by developing the modern method of warfare. In Shaw's play even Joan's allies disapprove of her tactics in the field, because they do not realize that the increasing use of gunpowder is bound in the long run to supersede "the chaffering for ransoms," on which, according to Shaw, the whole system of courtly fighting was based. The destruction of the chivalric code of conduct was bound to be accompanied by radical changes in the organization of society. Feudalism was giving way to a conception of the state as a nation.

The Church as well as the state was bitterly opposed to Joan's innovations. In dealing with the Church's relations to Joan, Shaw is scrupulously fair. His portrayal of Bishop Cauchon is one of his most masterly achievements. Cauchon is entirely conscious of what he is doing and defends himself with the most elaborate scholastic arguments. He insists that Joan ought to be burned, because unbridled individualism is dangerous to the welfare of the whole community, which it is the special duty of the Church to preserve. Joan is an instrument of the devil. Her heresy will result in the destruction of the sanity of Christendom. This theme is further elaborated by the Inquisitor, who in the trial scene defends the position of the Church Litigant as ably as Cauchon with his logical theology had expressed the authoritative view of the Church Militant. Joan's allegiance to God rather than to Catholicism can only be justified before the Church Triumphant, which exists apart from ecclesiastical edifices and clerical vestments.

The ambiguity of Joan's theological position is exposed by a churchman who sympathizes with her ideals and accomplishments, although he cannot sanction the methods by which she goes about her work. The Archbishop of Rheims approves of Joan's deeds until after she has had him crown the Dauphin at Rheims. Then he disapproves of the stubborn pride with which she has set herself above the princes of the Church. In the same way he rationalizes the miracles which Joan has performed, explaining that, although they proceed from natural causes, they are productive of desirable results. To the Archbishop, a miracle is pragmatically "an event which creates faith," and both Church and state have to feed men on the miracle that is called poetry for the good of their souls and the good of their bodies; but a new spirit is rising in the world, a wider epoch is dawning, and in it an intelligent man, like the Archbishop, may seek peace for his spirit with Aristotle and Pythagoras rather than with the saints and their miracles.

Joan has little influence upon the representatives of Church and state, except for the most extraordinary of her converts, the Dauphin Charles. With keen irony, Shaw has presented Charles as more simple than any of his subjects, more deeply impressed by the Maid, and more genuinely fond of her. Charles, a lovable example of the average man, adds an unexpected degree of warmth to Shaw's play. Joan drops all formality with him and accosts him almost at once as "Charlie." The use of familiar nicknames is a step in the direction of leveling all social and economic ranks toward an equality which Shaw believes to be the first condition of bettering the human lot. Certainly, in this case, "Charlie" is vastly improved by his association with Joan, as any weak-willed, well-intentioned individual, even though he is a king, must be by contact with a representative of the Life Force.

It is as a representative of the Life Force that Joan has her greatest meaning to Shaw. He uses his version of her personality as a yardstick for measuring the deflections of ordinary people from the ideal which he constantly holds up to them. Shaw's play is not so much about Joan herself as it is about the effect of her saintliness upon the world. The impulse to write it doubtless came from Joan's canonization, which took place officially in 1920. This apparently inconsistent reversal of ecclesiastical policy must have stirred the dramatist to formulate some disturbing questions and to objectify them for others, if he could not answer them for himself. How is it that the Catholic Church can burn and then canonize its martyrs? How can the rest of us mortals inflict pain and misery on the people whom we most admire? When will this beautiful earth be ready to receive the saints of God?

VII

Shaw closes *Saint Joan* on a note of interrogation, which is also an exclamation of awe and wonder. It is the highest reach of which the comic muse is capable. Anything which comes after it is bound to seem something of an anticlimax. Since *Saint Joan*, through 1938, Shaw has published seven more plays of varying value, none of which belongs in the first flight of his writing. Two of the seven are brief sketches. *Village Wooing*, "A Comediettina for Two Voices," ends with a delightful recipe for making the word "banns" understood over the telephone: "b for beauty, a for audacity, two enns for nonsense, and s for singing," an odd mixture of abstract qualities which may be considered an impressionistic summing-up of the personality of Bernard Shaw. *Village Wooing* is a revival of the sex dialogue from Shaw's early plays, and *The Six of Calais* is one more of his historical *jeux d'esprit*, in which he does not make any momentous change in the story of the burghers as written down by Jean Froissart and illustrated by Auguste Rodin. Neither of these little pieces will increase Shaw's reputation. Even in the five longer plays written since *Saint Joan* his vein of inspiration is not so spontaneous as it once had been. His later works would probably be more buoyant if their author were not pretty well discouraged about the general state of the world, and more attractive if he did not feel that the public was no longer amused by his antics. They are a curious combination of hopelessness over the practical issue of events and peaceful resignation to the fact that what happens on this earth is, after all, of comparatively slight importance in the sight of eternity.

The best of these discussions of recent problems is the first, *The Apple Cart*, which was produced in 1929, more than five years after the first performance of its immediate predecessor, *Saint Joan*. As in the case of Shakespeare, a gap in time as well as a difference in mood separates the plays of Shaw's last period from those written at the height of his powers. *The Apple Cart* is an uneven piece of work. King Magnus' interlude with his Platonic mistress is extremely heavy-handed, and his relations with his motherly wife are most delicately portrayed. Torn between the hurly-burly of the one and the tender ministrations of the other, Magnus is left for the greater part of his dramatic life to wrestle with affairs of state, as a wise and able constitutional monarch ought to do. Shaw's contention is that, in a period when democracy has proved insufficient to support the intense strain placed upon it, one strong administrator is more valuable than an elaborate and feeble system of representative government. Since the confusion of European diplomacy seems to prove that government cannot be administered in an effective way by the people themselves, a powerful dictator, like Mussolini, is an inevitable and desirable sequel to a period of chaotic demoralization. Shaw does not think of Mussolini, any more than of Andrew Undershaft in *Major Barbara*, as a perfect member of the community, but he considers such strong men necessary to a certain stage in civilization, which will reach a still higher plane when it adopts principles more like those of Lenin than those of Mussolini.

Shaw does not idealize Mussolini or King Magnus in *The Apple Cart*, who is "great" only by comparison with the people that oppose him: an irascible and shifty Prime Minister, the venal members of the cabinet, and, behind them all, Breakages, Limited, the largest industrial corporation of the country, which exemplifies the power and destructiveness of capitalism. Magnus has on his side the women of his cabinet. By his charm and common sense he ingratiates himself with the newly appointed President of the Board of Trade, a self-made man who has risen from the gutter and who respects a natural leader, even an aristocratic one. Magnus is a hereditary king, but he is also a dictator who establishes his supremacy by ability and personal magnetism. He finally gets the better of his cabinet by threatening to resign his throne and seek a seat in Parliament, but, as Shaw points out in the Preface, his tactical victory leaves him in a more undesirable situation than if he had carried out his threat. From now on, he must take the full responsibility for his country's welfare and govern it under the almost insuperable obstacles imposed by the economic principles of capitalism.

The Apple Cart is a subtle analysis of the opportunities and pitfalls surrounding dictatorship. It begins with an introductory scene describing the death of a Die-Hard Ritualist from exposure to solitude, which implies that old political forms have become virtually extinct because people will no longer support them with enthusiasm. In the last act the American Ambassador is introduced to show the perils run by poorly governed countries from those organized on a materialistic plane with the most approved commercial efficiency. The Ambassador proposes that the United States should rejoin the British Empire, which Magnus at once realizes means England's being "reduced to a mere appendage of a big American concern." At the epoch when *The Apple Cart* takes place, which is supposed to be sometime after 1962, "what they call an American is only a wop pretending to be a Pilgrim Father," and Germany is "a chain of more or less Soviet Republics between the Ural Mountains and the North Sea."

The Apple Cart denounces the corroding effect of capitalistic wealth in its pursuit of international trade abroad and special privileges at home. *Too True To Be Good*, performed three years later, in 1932, had for its main theme, "not, as usual, that our social system is unjust to the poor, but that it is cruel to the rich." It is, according to the Preface, "a story of three reckless young people who come into the possession of, for the moment, unlimited riches, and set out to have a thoroughly good time with all the modern machinery of pleasure to aid them. The result is that they get nothing for their money but a multitude of worries and a maddening dissatisfaction." During the course of this slight story a general discussion of modern problems is engaged in by all the characters, one of whom resembles Dean Inge and another Lawrence of Arabia. At its conclusion a clergyman, who is also a burglar and the son of an atheist — that is, a professional preacher without morals and without beliefs — is left alone on the stage to deliver the extended monologue which is the literary climax of the play.

"I must preach and preach and preach," the clergyman says, "no matter how late the hour and how short the day, no matter whether I have nothing to say —." Since the final curtain descends on these words, it is not surprising that many critics imagined Shaw to be here admitting his own failure as a moral lecturer. It was hardly fair for him to continue the printed play with the statement that if we could distinctly hear the close of the speech it would probably run, "— or whether in some pentecostal flame of revelation the Spirit will descend on me and inspire me with a message the sound whereof shall go out unto all lands and realize for us at last the Kingdom and the Power and the Glory for ever and ever. Amen." Shaw still seems to be convinced intellectually that the political, economic, and religious views which he has always held are valid for modern times, but emotionally he is not so sure of his position. Shaw's attitude towards the clergyman is like that with which he has regarded all his long-winded heroes. They are too much like himself not to stand in need of salvation from some ministering angel in female form.

The woman who saves Sir Arthur Chavender, the hero of Shaw's next play *On the Rocks*, is a mysterious Lady Doctor who helps to convince him of the soundness of Marxian theories. *On the Rocks*, written in 1933, two years after Shaw's visit to Russia, was as Bolshevik in its political implications as *The Apple Cart* had been Fascist. Because Bolshevism is the form of modern government most nearly based on Shaw's theories, *On the Rocks* is one of his most straightforward plays. Sir Arthur, as a result of his conversion, decides to resign the premiership and spend the rest of his life with his wife in a cottage near a good golf links. He has become a Platonic Communist, with his head but not his heart in the revolution. He will "hate the man who will carry it through for his cruelty and the desolation he will bring on us and our like."

The humor in this play depends upon the contrasting attitudes taken towards Sir Arthur's conversion by the people more or less intimately connected with it. They are mostly divided between the Conservative and Liberal parties, but a few of the less stereotyped characters belong to no specific group. A Cingalese capitalist combines skill in making money with a devastating clarity of intellect, and the elderly Duke of Domesday holds the position of a cultivated onlooker, seeing all sides of every question so clearly that he cannot wholeheartedly espouse any of them. From the comic point of view, the Duke is the balance wheel of *On the Rocks* and gives the play its chief intelligent opposition to the admirable but theoretical ideals which Sir Arthur enunciates and is not willing to try to enforce. The Prime Minister achieves by his withdrawal from politics a personal satisfaction, which he calls the beginning of hope and the end of hypocrisy, but he realizes that something more than pious aspiration is necessary if England is to arise and be saved.

It may be that "all great Art and Literature is propaganda," as Shaw claims in the Preface to *On the Rocks*, but no writing that is deficient in imagination should be considered as a work of art at all. *On the Rocks* is too purely a piece of propaganda to be a first-rate drama, but the Preface to it is, quite consistently, one of Shaw's most brilliant pieces of exposition. It not only contains an attempt to dramatize the trial of Jesus, putting into Jesus' mouth an impassioned defense of the principles of toleration, but, in discussing the limits to which toleration can go, it makes clear "the essential justification for extermination, which is always incorrigible social incompatibility and nothing else." The fact that Shaw disbelieves in the right of private extermination and deplores cruelty under all circumstances does not alter his contention that some people should be killed for the good of the community. His essay on "Extermination" prefixed to *On the Rocks* is perhaps to be explained by his desire to justify, to the British public, Soviet Russia's self-admitted "liquidation of the bourgeoisie." A similar motive may underlie his making the destruction of socially obstructive people the outstanding incident in his next play, called by the unwieldy but provocative title, *The Simpleton of the Unexpected Isles.*

The Preface to *The Simpleton,* on "Days of Judgment," carries out Shaw's ideas on extermination to their logical conclusion: when nonconformity becomes a social danger to the community, an Inquisition or a Cheka must be quickly instituted as an emergency measure to root out heresy; in the course of time the work of an Inquisition becomes formalized into a code of law, and thereafter the power of the Inquisition disappears; but every now and then in the world's history there has been needed a summary decision on the individual's fitness for citizenship; and the apotheosis of all such tribunals has been concentrated into Biblical imagery as the Day of Judgment. "In a living society every day is a day of judgment," at which the question is asked, "whether you are a social asset or a social nuisance. And the penalty is liquidation." On this basis Shaw has reared the somewhat unsatisfactory play of *The Simpleton,* which would have been more impressive if he could have found relevant dramatic material to support his vivid journalistic account of a modern Judgment Day. The appearance of an Angel to herald the end of the world's childhood and the beginning of its responsible maturity prepares for the announcement by means of wireless telegrams and wireless telephone messages that all useless persons, from members of the Stock Exchange through doctors to readers of novels, have disappeared from the surface of the earth.

On the Day of Judgment it also becomes apparent that "four lovely phantasms who embody all the artistic, romantic, and military ideals of our cultured suburbs" never existed at all. Their parents, four Occidentals and two Orientals living together in a eugenic experiment, forget the names of their offspring and how many of them there were; no clue would remain as to what they had been if the Simpleton did not identify them by saying that their names were Love, Pride, Heroism, and Empire. The Simpleton is a clergyman of the Christian religion, weak-minded but not mad. He can survive the Judgment Day because he still has a useful function to perform in the world. After it, however, he must leave the Unexpected Isles and return to England to take up his clerical duties. He looks forward rhapsodically to the future that lies ahead of him: "A village and a cottage: a garden and a church: these things will not turn to nothing. I shall be content with my little black coat and my little white collar and my little treasure of words spoken by my Lord Jesus. Blessed be the name of the Lord." Shaw evidently believes that there is still a place for true Christianity, even after the ruthless extermination that is demanded by a communistic creed.

In Shaw's more recent play, *The Millionairess*, he turns back from the subject of socialism, about which he had been writing in *On the Rocks* and *The Simpleton*, to the subject of dictatorship, which he had treated in *The Apple Cart*. *The Millionairess* also has some affinities with *Saint Joan*. Joan was "a born boss" and so is the millionairess; moreover, the Preface to this play is on "Bosses" and explains Shaw's views on the latest political developments in Europe. As before, he finds much to admire in Mussolini, but he cannot forgive Hitler for his persecution of Einstein and the entire Jewish race. There is the usual good word said for Communism, "the fairy godmother who can transform Bosses into 'servants to all the rest,'" and England is advised to begin its next, long overdue Reformation, "well to the left of Russia, which is still encumbered with nineteenth century superstitions." The constant application of the Shavian gospel to contemporary events in all of the last full-length plays is evidence enough of how seriously their author has taken to heart the perilous confusion of post-War Europe.[1] His continual preoccupation with problems of the immediate present may help to account for the sense of strain that is felt in these comedies. It may also explain the excellence of the prefaces, which in this last period are, for the first time, often superior as works of art to the plays that follow them.

The Millionairess is a suitable fable for enforcing the ideas that lie behind it. Its heroine, Epifania Ognisanti di Parerga, is so successful

---

[1] Shaw's *Geneva*, produced in 1938, deals with the incapacity of the League of Nations, mocks the pretensions of dictators, and concludes that "man is a failure as a political animal." In contrast, it proposes a new sort of ideal supernationalism. The more recent *In Good King Charles's Golden Days* deals with the times of Charles II, one of its chief characters being the scientist Isaac Newton.

in earning her own living that she proves herself ethically entitled to the vast sums of money that she has inherited. Her methods are illustrated by the way in which she enables the poor proprietor of an illegal sweatshop to get the better of Mr. Superflew, a capitalistic sweater of mammoth proportions. Epifania cannot be held down by circumstances. It is the law of her nature to get what she wants, partly because she is practical enough to want only what she knows she can get. Her objective in this case is the hand of an Egyptian doctor, whose mother had made it a condition of his marriage that his future wife should be able to support herself for six months. The plot of *The Millionairess* gives Shaw numerous opportunities to ridicule with ingenuity modern methods of high finance, by which, on paper, something can be made out of nothing.

The story of Epifania's sex relations is much less amusing than their economic background, probably because, like her creator, she is not a hot-blooded person in such matters. Her first husband is a boxing champion, whose lack of vital energy she has found incompatible with her own more active disposition. She selects as a Platonic Sunday husband a decorative fellow whose only distinction is that no man in London knows better how to order a dinner. When she grows angry at his superciliousness, she knocks him out with a savage punch that she has learned from her pugilistic husband. The Egyptian doctor finally fascinates Epifania by his rational imperturbability, with the result that she at once gives up her athlete and her aesthete to pursue the scientific philosopher. She subdues the reluctant doctor by the strength of her pulse, which is like a slow sledge hammer and reminds the Oriental of the heartbeat of Allah. Finding its attraction irresistible, he decides, like a sensible man, to join Epifania in what that dynamic woman challengingly describes as "this infinitely dangerous heart tearing everchanging life of adventure that we call marriage." As is usual with Shaw, the phrasing of the ideas in *The Millionairess* is more impressive than the emotional energy that animates them.

VIII

Shaw has frequently said that he is a thinker by profession. It is true that he is primarily an apostle of ideas, and that the action and characterization in his plays often seem mere pegs upon which to hang them. Unlike Shakespeare, the master of what may be called humane as distinguished from social comedy, he has created no immortal individual figures and no situations that epitomize once and for all universal experience. Although in his finest work the action and characterization have some value of their own, it is the social criticism and the bold proposals for social betterment that vitalize his comedies. The critical ideas seem more likely to assure Shaw of a permanent place in the history of comedy than the constructive proposals, which, however impractical, are needed to give logic and cogency to his argument. The unexpected turns and twists of his thought are sometimes difficult to follow, but his thinking has always a fiery intensity. It is this quality which, joined to his boisterous sense of fun, places him in the ranks of the greatest authors of dramatic comedy.

Shaw is inferior to Molière in his lack of sympathy for human passions, but he is at least the equal of Ben Jonson, with whom in the introduction to *The Millionairess* he compares himself; he says that this play "does not pretend to be anything more than a comedy of humorous and curious contemporary characters such as Ben Jonson might write were he alive now." Jonson and Shaw have the same dry satiric detachment from human foibles, which at times kindles both of them into an ecstasy that is very close to poetic inspiration. They both have a relentless critical sense about their own conduct which prevents them from completely surrendering themselves to the pursuit of their intellectual ideals. They also have in common the fact that each outlived the period of his most distinguished work and continued after his prime to compose plays, which, in the case of Jonson, Dryden pointedly called his "dotages." If the dramas written by Shaw since *Saint Joan* ought also to be so described, they are at least superior to the best work of any other contemporary writer of comedy.

To find an author with whom Shaw can properly be compared, one must go back to Aristophanes. Professor Gilbert Murray has suggested this comparison by dedicating to Shaw his book on the Greek writer of comedy. There are obvious points of resemblance between the two men. They were both born with a remarkably inventive sense of fun and a lively interest in the welfare of their fellow human beings; they have both given expression to their standard of humorous values in a fanciful, yet rational form. Aristophanes, the poet, imagined a perfect world governed by Clouds or Birds, and Shaw, the social theorist, has conceived of an ideal community in which the Life Force will assert itself to produce the Superman. Aristophanes created a fantastic Utopia because he did not believe that conditions on earth could ever again equal those that had existed in the golden age of the past. Shaw hopes against hope that, in the future, the affairs of men may improve and that we stupid beings may become in time less stupid. Aristophanes is a conservative and Shaw is a radical, but the difference between them is not so great as this antithesis might suggest. Aristophanes wrote his plays partly to improve conditions in the Athens of his day, and Shaw cannot suppose that people will ever conform exactly to his pattern for their development. Aristophanes has a practical side; Shaw, an imaginative one. Both men are distinguished for the fine quality of their comic intelligence, a gift which makes it possible for those who possess it to work hard without expecting to achieve success, to think hard without expecting to arrive at the truth, and to laugh hard in the desperate hope of maintaining sanity on this distracted globe.

A SELECTED BIBLIOGRAPHY OF WORKS IN ENGLISH RELATING TO THE SUBJECT OF THIS BOOK

INTRODUCTION

Bellinger, Martha Fletcher. *A Short History of the Drama*. New York: Henry Holt and Company, 1927.

Bergson, Henri. *Laughter; an Essay on the Meaning of the Comic*. Translated by Cloudesley Brereton and Fred Rothwell. New York: The Macmillan Company, 1911.

Charlton, H. B. *Shakespearian Comedy*. New York: The Macmillan Company, 1938.

Clark, Barrett H. *European Theories of the Drama*. Cincinnati: Stewart and Kidd Company, 1918.

Cooper, Lane. *An Aristotelian Theory of Comedy, with an Adaptation of the Poetics and a Translation of the 'Tractatus Coislinianus.'* New York: Harcourt, Brace and Company, 1922.

Crile, George W. *Man — an Adaptive Mechanism*. Edited by Annette Austin. New York: The Macmillan Company, 1916.

Eastman, Max. *The Sense of Humor*. New York: Charles Scribner's Sons, 1921.

Freud, Sigmund. *Wit and Its Relation to the Unconscious*. Authorized English edition, with introduction by A. A. Brill. New York: Moffat, Yard and Company, 1916.

Gregory, J. C. *The Nature of Laughter*. New York: Harcourt, Brace and Company, 1924.

Greig, J. Y. T. *The Psychology of Laughter and Comedy*. London: George Allen and Unwin, 1923.

Jourdain, Eleanor F. *The Drama in Europe in Theory and Practice*. New York: Henry Holt and Company, 1924.

Lawson, John Howard. *Theory and Technique of Playwriting*. New York: G. P. Putnam's Sons, 1936.

Ludovici, Anthony M. *The Secret of Laughter*. New York: The Viking Press, 1933.

Meredith, George. *An Essay on Comedy and the Uses of the Comic Spirit*. New York: Charles Scribner's Sons, 1918.

Nicoll, Allardyce. *The Theory of Drama*. New York: Thomas Y. Crowell Company, 1931.

Sully, James. *An Essay on Laughter, Its Forms, Its Causes, Its Development and Its Value*. New York: Longmans, Green and Company, 1902.

CHAPTER I

Aristophanes. Plays. With the English translation of Benjamin Bickley Rogers. Loeb Classical Library. 3 vols. London: W. Heinemann, 1924.

Cornford, Francis Macdonald. The Origin of Attic Comedy. London: Edward Arnold, 1914.

Croiset, Maurice. Aristophanes and the Political Parties at Athens. Translated by James Loeb. London: Macmillan and Company, 1909.

Dickinson, G. Lowes. The Greek View of Life. New York: Doubleday, Page and Company, 1916.

Hamilton, Edith. The Greek Way. New York: W. W. Norton and Company, 1930.

LeGrand, Ph. E. The New Greek Comedy. Translated by James Loeb, with an introduction by John Williams White. London: W. Heinemann, 1917.

Lord, Louis E. Aristophanes; His Plays and His Influence. Boston: Marshall Jones Company, 1925.

Menander. The Principal Fragments. With an English translation by Francis G. Allinson. Loeb Classical Library. London: W. Heinemann, 1921.

——. Three Plays. Translated and interpreted by L. A. Post. London: G. Routledge and Sons, Ltd., 1929.

Moulton, Richard G. The Ancient Classical Drama; a Study in Literary Evolution. Oxford: The Clarendon Press, 1898.

Murray, Gilbert. Aristophanes; a Study. New York: Oxford University Press, 1933. (The most important work in English on Aristophanes.)

Norwood, Gilbert. Greek Comedy. London: Methuen and Company, 1931.

CHAPTER II

Duff, J. Wight. A Literary History of Rome from the Origins to the Close of the Golden Age. London: T. Fisher Unwin, 1923.

Hamilton, Edith. The Roman Way. New York: W. W. Norton and Company, 1932.

Norwood, Gilbert. Plautus and Terence. New York: Longmans, Green and Company, 1932.

——. The Art of Terence. Oxford: B. Blackwell, 1923.

Plautus. Three Plays. Translated by F. A. Wright and H. Lionel Rogers, with an introduction. London: G. Routledge and Sons, 1925.

——. Plays. With an English translation by Paul Nixon. Loeb Classical Library. 5 vols. London: W. Heinemann, 1916–38.

Terence. Plays. With an English translation by John Sargeaunt. Loeb Classical Library. 2 vols. London: W. Heinemann, 1912.

Wieand, Helen E. *Deception in Plautus; a Study in the Technique of Roman Comedy.* Boston: R. C. Badger, 1920.

CHAPTER III

Baskervill, C. R. *English Elements in Jonson's Early Comedy.* Austin: University of Texas, 1911.

Campbell, Oscar James. *Comicall Satyre and Shakespeare's Troilus and Cressida.* San Marino, Cal.: Huntington Library, 1938.

Dryden, John. "Of Dramatic Poesy, an Essay," *Essays of John Dryden,* vol. I. Selected and edited by W. P. Ker. 2 vols. Oxford: The Clarendon Press, 1926.

Dunn, Esther Cloudman. *Ben Jonson's Art; Elizabethan Life and Literature as Reflected Therein.* Northampton, Mass.: Smith College, 1925.

Eliot, T. S. *Elizabethan Essays.* London: Faber and Faber, 1934.

Jonson, Ben. Works. Edited by C. H. Herford and Percy Simpson. Oxford: The Clarendon Press, 1925–   . (Vols. I and II contain superb introductions to Jonson's plays.)

Kerr, Mina. *Influence of Ben Jonson on English Comedy, 1598–1642.* Philadelphia: University of Pennsylvania, 1912.

Knights, L. C. *Drama and Society in the Age of Jonson.* London: Chatto and Windus, 1937.

Noyes, Robert Gale. *Ben Jonson on the English Stage, 1660–1776.* Cambridge, Mass.: Harvard University Press, 1935.

Palmer, John. *Ben Jonson.* New York: The Viking Press, 1934.

Smith, George Gregory. *Ben Jonson.* London: The Macmillan Company, 1919.

Stoll, Elmer Edgar. *Poets and Playwrights: Shakespeare, Jonson, Spenser, Milton.* Minneapolis: University of Minnesota Press, 1930.

Thorndike, Ashley H. *English Comedy.* New York: The Macmillan Company, 1929.

Woodbridge, Elisabeth. *Studies in Jonson's Comedy.* Boston: Lamson, Wolffe and Company, 1898.

CHAPTER IV

Calderón. *Eight Dramas.* Freely translated by Edward Fitzgerald. London: Macmillan and Company, 1906.

Fitzmaurice-Kelly, James. *A History of Spanish Literature.* New York: D. Appleton and Company, 1898.

Flores, Angel. *Lope de Vega; Monster of Nature.* New York: Brentano's, 1930.

Ford, J. D. M. *Main Currents of Spanish Literature.* New York: Henry Holt and Company, 1919.

Lope de Vega. *Four Plays*. English versions, with an introduction by John Garrett Underhill and a critical essay by Jacinto Benavente. New York: Charles Scribner's Sons, 1936.

——. *The New Art of Writing Plays*. Translated by William T. Brewster, with an introduction by Brander Matthews. New York: Dramatic Museum of Columbia University, 1914.

"Lope de Vega — 300 Years After." *Theatre Arts Monthly*, Vol. XIX, No. 9, September 1935.

Northrup, George Tyler. *An Introduction to Spanish Literature*. Chicago: University of Chicago Press, 1925.

Rennert, Hugo Albert. *The Life of Lope de Vega (1562–1635)*. Glasgow: Gowans and Gray, 1904.

——. *The Spanish Stage in the Time of Lope de Vega*. New York: The Hispanic Society of America, 1909.

CHAPTER V

Ashton, H. *A Preface to Molière*. New York: Longmans, Green and Company, 1927.

——. *Molière*. New York: E. P. Dutton and Company, 1930.

Besant, Walter. *The French Humorists, from the Twelfth to the Nineteenth Century*. Boston: Roberts Brothers, 1874.

Brunetière, Ferdinand. *Brunetière's Essays in French Literature*. Translated by D. Nichol Smith, with a preface by the author. New York: Charles Scribner's Sons, 1898.

Chatfield-Taylor, H. C. *Molière; a Biography*. With an introduction by Thomas Frederick Crane. New York: Duffield and Company, 1906.

Jourdain, Eleanor F. *An Introduction to the French Classical Drama*. Oxford: The Clarendon Press, 1912.

Matthews, Brander. *Molière; His Life and His Works*. New York: Charles Scribner's Sons, 1910.

Molière. *Comedies*. "This text of Molière's plays is taken from the first complete English translation of his works carried out in 1739 by the two playwrights, H. Baker and J. Miller." Introduction by Frederick C. Green. 2 vols. Everyman's Library, nos. 830–831. New York: E. P. Dutton and Company, 1929.

Nicoll, Allardyce. *Masks, Mimes and Miracles*. New York: Harcourt, Brace and Company, 1931.

Palmer, John. *Molière*. New York: Brewer and Warren, Inc., 1930.

Strachey, G. Lytton. *Landmarks in French Literature*. New York: Henry Holt and Company, 1912.

Tilley, Arthur. *Molière*. Cambridge: The University Press, 1921. (A particularly helpful study.)

CHAPTER VI

Campbell, Oscar James, Jr. *The Comedies of Holberg*. Cambridge, Mass.: Harvard University Press, 1914. (The principal work in English on Holberg.)

Dobrée, Bonamy. *Restoration Comedy, 1660–1720*. Oxford: The Clarendon Press, 1924.

Gosse, Edmund W. *Studies in the Literature of Northern Europe*. London: C. Kegan Paul and Company, 1879.

Holberg, Ludvig. *Comedies by Holberg*. Translated from the Danish, with an introduction, by Oscar James Campbell, Jr. and Frederick Schenck. New York: The American-Scandinavian Foundation, 1914.

——. *Three Comedies*. Translated from the Danish by Lieutenant-Colonel H. W. L. Hime. London: Longmans, Green and Company, 1912.

Howitt, William and Mary. *The Literature and Romance of Northern Europe*. 2 vols. London: Colburn and Company, 1852.

Jorgenson, Theodore. *History of Norwegian Literature*. New York: The Macmillan Company, 1933.

Palmer, John. *The Comedy of Manners*. London: G. Bell and Sons, 1913.

CHAPTER VII

Aldington, Richard, trans. *French Comedies of the Eighteenth Century*. London: G. Routledge and Sons, 1923.

Aretino, Pietro. *The Works of Aretino*. Translated into English from the original Italian, with a critical and biographical essay, by Samuel Putnam. 2 vols. New York: Covici-Friede, 1933.

Chatfield-Taylor, H. C. *Goldoni; a Biography*. New York: Duffield and Company, 1913.

Dole, Nathan Haskell. *A Teacher of Dante, and Other Studies in Italian Literature*. New York: Moffat, Yard and Company, 1908.

Duchartre, Pierre Louis. *The Italian Comedy*. Translated from the French by Randolph T. Weaver. New York: The John Day Company, 1929.

Garnett, Richard. *A History of Italian Literature*. New York: D. Appleton and Company, 1898.

Goldoni, Carlo. *Comedies*. Edited, with introduction, by Helen Zimmern. Chicago: A. C. M'Clurg and Company, 1892.

——. *Four Comedies*. Edited by Clifford Bax. London: The Curwen Press, 1922.

——. *Memoirs of Carlo Goldoni, Written by Himself*. Translated from the original French by John Black. Edited, with an introduction, by William A. Drake. New York: Alfred A. Knopf, 1926.

Jourdain, Eleanor F. *Dramatic Theory and Practice in France*. London: Longmans, Green and Company, 1921.

Kennard, Joseph Spencer. *Goldoni and the Venice of His Time*. New York: The Macmillan Company, 1920.

——. *Masks and Marionettes*. New York: The Macmillan Company, 1935.

——. *The Italian Theatre*. New York: W. E. Rudge, 1932.

Lee, Vernon. *Studies of the Eighteenth Century in Italy*. London: W. Satchell and Company, 1880.

Machiavelli, Niccolò. *Mandragola*. Translated by Stark Young. New York: The Macaulay Company, 1927.

Monnier, Philippe. *Venice in the Eighteenth Century*. From the French. London: Chatto and Windus, 1910.

Sanctis, Francesco de. *History of Italian Literature*. Translated by Joan Redfern. 2 vols. New York: Harcourt, Brace and Company, 1931.

Smith, Winifred. *The Commedia dell'Arte; a Study in Italian Popular Comedy*. New York: Columbia University Press, 1912.

CHAPTER VIII

Aikin-Sneath, Betsy. *Comedy in Germany in the First Half of the Eighteenth Century*. Oxford: The Clarendon Press, 1936.

Bateson, F. W. *English Comic Drama, 1700–1750*. Oxford: The Clarendon Press, 1929.

Campbell, Thomas Moody, ed. *German Plays of the Nineteenth Century*. New York: F. S. Crofts and Company, 1930.

Dalsème, René. *Beaumarchais, 1732–1799*. Translated by Hannaford Bennett. New York: G. P. Putnam's Sons, 1929.

Francke, Kuno. *A History of German Literature, as Determined by Social Forces*. New York: Henry Holt and Company, 1907.

Japp, Alexander Hay. *German Life and Literature in a Series of Biographical Studies*. London: Marshall Japp and Company, 1880.

Lessing, G. E. *Dramatic Works*. Translated from the German. Edited by Ernest Bell, with a short memoir by Helen Zimmern. 2 vols. (Volume 2, Comedies.) London: George Bell and Sons, 1878.

Pollak, Gustav. *Franz Grillparzer and the Austrian Drama*. New York: Dodd, Mead and Company, 1907. (Chapter I deals largely with the work of Ferdinand Raimund.)

Rivers, John. *Figaro; the Life of Beaumarchais*. London: Hutchinson and Company, 1922.

Robertson, John G. *A History of German Literature*. Edinburgh: William Blackwood and Sons, 1902.

Sheridan, Richard Brinsley. *The Plays and Poems of Richard Brinsley Sheridan*. Edited with introductions, appendices and bibliographies, by R. Crompton Rhodes. 3 vols. New York: The Macmillan Company, 1929.

Silz, Walter. *Early German Romanticism; Its Founders and Heinrich von Kleist*. Cambridge, Mass.: Harvard University Press, 1929.

Sime, James. *Lessing*. 2 vols. London: Trübner and Company, 1877.

Stahr, Adolf. *The Life and Works of Gotthold Ephraim Lessing*. Translated by E. P. Evans. 2 vols. Boston: William V. Spencer, 1866.

Vail, Curtis C. D. *Lessing's Relation to the English Language and Literature*. New York: Columbia University Press, 1936.

Willoughby, L. A. *The Romantic Movement in Germany*. Oxford: Oxford University Press, 1930.

Witkowski, Georg. *The German Drama of the Nineteenth Century*. Authorized translation from the second German edition, by L. E. Horning. New York: Henry Holt and Company, 1909.

Zeydel, Edwin H. *Ludwig Tieck, the German Romanticist*. Princeton: Princeton University Press, 1935.

CHAPTER IX

Baring, Maurice. *An Outline of Russian Literature*. New York: Henry Holt and Company, 1915.

——. *Landmarks in Russian Literature*. London: Methuen and Company, 1910.

Coleman, Arthur P. *Humor in the Russian Comedy from Catherine to Gogol*. New York: Columbia University Press, 1925.

Dupuy, Ernest. *The Great Masters of Russian Literature in the Nineteenth Century*. Translated by Nathan Haskell Dole. London: John and Robert Maxwell, 1886.

Gerhardi, William. *Anton Chehov; a Critical Study*. London: Richard Cobden-Sanderson, 1923.

Gogol, Nicolai V. *"The Gamblers," and "Marriage."* Translated by Alexander Berkman. New York: The Macaulay Company, 1927.

Kropotkin, Prince. *Ideals and Realities in Russian Literature*. New York: Alfred A. Knopf, 1915.

Lavrin, Janko. *Gogol*. London: G. Routledge and Sons, 1926.

Mirsky, D. S. *A History of Russian Literature from the Earliest Times to the Death of Dostoyevsky (1881)*. New York: Alfred A. Knopf, 1927.

——. *Contemporary Russian Literature, 1881–1925*. New York: Alfred A. Knopf, 1926.

Noyes, George Rapall, ed. *Masterpieces of the Russian Drama*. New York: D. Appleton and Company, 1933. (The most representative anthology of Russian drama in English.)

Ostrovsky, Alexander. *Plays*. A translation from the Russian. Edited by George Rapall Noyes. New York: Charles Scribner's Sons, 1917.

Panin, Ivan. *Lectures on Russian Literature; Pushkin, Gogol, Turgenef, Tolstoy*. New York: G. P. Putnam's Sons, 1889.

Tchekhov, Anton. *Anton Tchekhov; Literary and Theatrical Reminiscences*. Translated and edited by S. S. Koteliansky. New York: George H. Doran Company, 1927.

——. *The Plays of Tchekov*. Translated by Constance Garnett. Preface by Eva Le Gallienne. New York: The Modern Library, 1930.

Tolstoï, Lyof N. *Dramatic Works*. Translated by Nathan Haskell Dole. New York: Thomas Y. Crowell Company, 1923.

Toumanova, Nina Andronikova. *Anton Chekhov; the Voice of Twilight Russia*. New York: Columbia University Press, 1937.

Turgenev, Ivan S. *The Plays of Ivan S. Turgenev*. Translated from the Russian by M. S. Mandell. With an introduction by William Lyon Phelps. 2 vols. New York: The Macmillan Company, 1924.

Wiener, Leo. *The Contemporary Drama of Russia*. Boston: Little, Brown and Company, 1924.

Yarmolinsky, Avrahm. *Turgenev, the Man — His Art — and His Age*. New York: The Century Company, 1926.

CHAPTER X

Armstrong, Cecil Ferard. *Shakespeare to Shaw; Studies in the Life's Work of Six Dramatists of the English Stage*. London: Mills and Boon, 1913. (Shakespeare, Congreve, Sheridan, Robertson, Pinero, Shaw.)

Boyd, Ernest A. *The Contemporary Drama of Ireland*. Boston: Little, Brown and Company, 1917.

Bourgeois, Maurice. *John Millington Synge and the Irish Theatre*. London: Constable and Company, 1913.

Braybrooke, Patrick. *The Subtlety of George Bernard Shaw*. London: Cecil Palmer, 1930.

Broad, C. Lewis, and Broad, Violet M. *Dictionary to the Plays and Novels of Bernard Shaw, with Bibliography of His Works and of the Literature concerning Him, with a Record of the Principal Shavian Play Productions*. New York: The Macmillan Company, 1929.

Burton, Richard. *Bernard Shaw; the Man and the Mask*. New York: Henry Holt and Company, 1916.

Chesterton, Gilbert K. *George Bernard Shaw*. New York: John Lane Company, 1909.

Collis, J. S. *Shaw*. New York: Alfred A. Knopf, 1925. (One of the most brilliant of the numerous books on Shaw.)

Dark, Sidney, and Grey, Rowland. *W. S. Gilbert; His Life and Letters*. London: Methuen and Company, 1923.

Deacon, Renée M. *Bernard Shaw as Artist-Philosopher; an Exposition of Shavianism*. London: A. C. Fifield, 1910.

Duffin, Henry Charles. *The Quintessence of Bernard Shaw*. London: George Allen and Unwin, 1939.

Godwin, A. H. *Gilbert and Sullivan; a Critical Appreciation of the Savoy Operas*. With an introduction by G. K. Chesterton. London: J. M. Dent and Sons, 1926.

Goldberg, Isaac. *The Story of Gilbert and Sullivan, or The "Compleat" Savoyard*. New York: Simon and Schuster, 1928.

Hamon, Augustin. *The Twentieth Century Molière: Bernard Shaw*. Translated from the French by Eden and Cedar Paul. New York: Frederick A. Stokes Company, 1916.

Henderson, Archibald. *Bernard Shaw, Playboy and Prophet*. Authorized. New York: D. Appleton and Company, 1932.

Howe, P. P. *Bernard Shaw; a Critical Study*. London: Martin Secker, 1915.

——. *J. M. Synge; a Critical Study*. London: Martin Secker, 1912.

McCabe, Joseph. *George Bernard Shaw; a Critical Study*. New York: Mitchell Kennerley, 1914.

Palmer, John. *George Bernard Shaw; Harlequin or Patriot?* New York: The Century Company, 1915.

Pearson, Hesketh. *Gilbert and Sullivan; a Biography*. New York: Harper and Brothers, 1935.

Sawyer, Newell W. *The Comedy of Manners from Sheridan to Maugham*. Philadelphia: University of Pennsylvania Press, 1931.

Sen Gupta, S. C. *The Art of Bernard Shaw*. London: Oxford University Press, 1936.

Weygandt, Cornelius. *Irish Plays and Playwrights*. Boston: Houghton Mifflin Company, 1913.

Wilson, Edmund. *The Triple Thinkers; Ten Essays on Literature*. New York: Harcourt, Brace and Company, 1938.

INDEX OF PERSONS AND TITLES

ERRATUM

Page 368, l. 38, for *Petrification* read *Petrifaction*.

INDEX OF PERSONS AND TITLES